CLASSIC
AMERICAN
SPEECHES

★ From the Founding Fathers to the Present ★

CLASSIC AMERICAN SPEECHES

★ From the Founding Fathers to the Present ★

FALL RIVER PRESS

New York

FALL RIVER PRESS

New York

An Imprint of Sterling Publishing Co., Inc.
1166 Avenue of the Americas
New York, NY 10036

Compilation © 2018 Sterling Publishing Co., Inc.
Jacket illustration © tintin75/iStock
Endpaper illustration © dino4/iStock

ISBN 978-1-4351-6846-6

For information about custom editions, special sales, and premium and corporate purchases,
please contact Sterling Special Sales at 800-805-5489 or specialsales@sterlingpublishing.com.

Manufactured in the United States of America

2 4 6 8 10 9 7 5 3 1

sterlingpublishing.com

Jacket design by David Ter-Avanesyan

Contents

Note on the Text

The speeches selected for this volume span more than two centuries and are often inconsistent in their alternating use of British and American spelling, capitalization of proper nouns, and the styles of their transcription. In the interest of preserving their authenticity as historical documents, the publisher has retained these inconsistencies, and silently corrected only noticeable errors.

John Hancock

On the Boston Massacre

(Delivered at Boston, Massachusetts, March 5, 1774,
on the anniversary of the Boston Massacre)

The attentive gravity, the venerable appearance of this crowded audience; the dignity which I behold in the countenances of so many in this great assembly; the solemnity of the occasion upon which we have met together, joined to a consideration of the part I am to take in the important business of this day, fill me with an awe hitherto unknown, and heighten the sense which I have ever had, of my unworthiness to fill this sacred desk. But, allured by the call of some of my respected fellow-citizens, with whose request it is always my greatest pleasure to comply, I almost forgot my want of ability to perform what they required. In this situation I find my only support, in assuring myself that a generous people will not severely censure what they know was well intended, though its want of merit should prevent their being able to applaud it. And I pray that my sincere attachment to the interest of my country, and hearty detestation of every design formed against her liberties, may be admitted as some apology for my appearance in this place.

I have always, from my earliest youth, rejoiced in the felicity of my fellow-men; and have ever considered it as the indispensable duty of every member of society to promote, as far as in him lies, the prosperity of every individual, but more especially of the community to which he belongs; and also, as a faithful subject of the state, to use his utmost endeavors to detect, and having detected, strenuously to oppose every traitorous plot which its enemies may devise for its destruction. Security to the persons and properties of the governed, is so obviously the design and end of civil government, that to attempt a logical proof of it, would be like burning tapers at noonday, to assist the sun in enlightening the world; and it cannot be either virtuous or honorable, to attempt to support a government, of which this is not the great and principal basis; and it is to the last degree vicious and infamous to attempt to support a government which manifestly tends to render the persons and properties of the governed insecure. Some boast of being friends to government; I am a friend to righteous government, to a government founded upon the principles of reason and justice; but I glory in publicly avowing my eternal enmity to tyranny. Is the present system, which the British administration have adopted for the government of the colonies, a righteous government—or is it tyranny? Here suffer me to ask, (and would to heaven there could be an answer,) what tenderness, what regard, respect or consideration has Great Britain shown, in their late transactions, for the security of the persons or properties of the inhabitants of the colonies? Or rather what have they omitted doing to destroy that security? They have declared, that they have ever had, and of right ought ever to have, full power to make laws of sufficient validity to bind the colonies in all cases whatever. They have exercised this pretended right by imposing a tax upon us without our consent; and lest we should show some reluctance at parting with our property, her fleets and armies are sent to enforce their mad pretensions. The town of Boston, ever faithful to the British crown, has been invested by a British fleet: the troops of George the III have crossed the wide Atlantic, not to engage an enemy, but to assist a band of traitors in trampling on the rights and liberties of his most loyal subjects in America—those rights and liberties which, as a father, he ought ever to regard, and as a king, he is bound, in honor, to defend from violation, even at the risk of his own life.

Let not the history of the illustrious house of Brunswick inform posterity, that a king, descended from that glorious monarch, George the II, once sent his British subjects to conquer and enslave his subjects in America. But be perpetual infamy entailed upon that villain who dared to advise his master to such execrable measures; for it was easy to foresee the consequences which so naturally followed upon sending troops into America, to enforce obedience to acts of the British parliament, which neither God nor man ever empowered them to make. It was reasonable to expect, that troops, who knew the errand they were sent upon, would treat the people whom they were to subjugate, with a cruelty and haughtiness, which too often buries the honorable character of a soldier, in the disgraceful name of an unfeeling ruffian. The troops, upon their first arrival, took possession of our senate-house, and pointed their cannon against the judgment-hall, and even continued them there whilst the supreme court of judicature for this province was actually sitting to decide upon the lives and fortunes of the king's subjects. Our streets nightly resounded with the noise of riot and debauchery; our peaceful citizens were hourly exposed to shameful insults, and often felt the effects of their violence and outrage. But this was not all: as though they thought it not enough to violate our civil rights, they endeavored to deprive us of the enjoyment of our religious privileges; to viciate our morals, and thereby render us deserving of destruction. Hence the rude din of arms which broke in upon your solemn devotions in your temples, on that day hallowed by heaven, and set apart by God himself for his peculiar worship. Hence, impious oaths and blasphemies so often tortured your unaccustomed ear. Hence, all the arts which idleness and luxury could invent, were used to betray our youth of one sex into extravagance and effeminacy, and of the other, to infamy and ruin; and did they not succeed but too well? Did not a reverence for religion sensibly decay? Did not our infants almost learn to lisp out curses before they knew their horrid import? Did not our youth forget they were Americans, and regardless of the admonitions of the wise and aged, servilely copy from their tyrants those vices which finally must overthrow the empire of Great Britain? And must I be compelled to acknowledge, that even the noblest, fairest part of all the lower creation, did not entirely escape the cursed snare? When virtue has once erected her throne within the female breast, it is upon so solid a basis that nothing is able to expel the heavenly inhabitant. But have there not been some, few indeed, I hope, whose youth and inexperience have rendered them a prey to wretches, whom, upon the least reflection, they would have despised and hated as foes to God and their country? I fear there have been some such unhappy instances, or why have I seen an honest father clothed with shame; or- why a virtuous mother drowned in tears?

But I forbear, and come reluctantly to the transactions of that dismal night, when in such quick succession we felt the extremes of grief, astonishment and rage; when heaven in anger, for a dreadful moment, suffered hell to take the reins; when satan with his chosen band opened the sluices of New England's blood, and sacrilegiously polluted our land with the dead bodies of her guiltless sons! Let this sad tale of death never be told without a tear: let not the heaving bosom cease to burn with a manly indignation at the barbarous story, through the long tracts of future time: let every parent tell the shameful story to his listening children until tears of pity glisten in their eyes and boiling passions shake their tender frames; and whilst the anniversary of that ill-fated night is kept a jubilee in the grim court of pandæmonium, let all America join in one common prayer to heaven, that the inhuman, unprovoked murders of the fifth of March, 1770, planned by Hillsborough, and a knot of treacherous knaves in Boston, and executed by the cruel hand of Preston and his sanguinary coadjutors, may ever stand on history without a parallel. But what, my countrymen, withheld the ready arm of vengeance from executing instant justice on the vile assassins? Perhaps you feared promiscuous carnage might ensue, and that the innocent might share the fate of those who had performed the infernal deed. But were not all guilty? Were you not too tender of the lives of those who came to fix a yoke on your necks? But I must not too severely blame a fault, which great souls only can commit. May that magnificence of spirit which scorns the low pursuits of malice, may that generous compassion which often preserves from ruin, even a guilty villain, forever actuate the noble bosoms of Americans! But let not the miscreant host vainly imagine that we feared their arms. No; them we despised; we dread nothing but slavery. Death is the creature of a poltroon's brains; 'tis immortality to sacrifice ourselves for the salvation of our country. We fear not death. That gloomy night, the palefaced moon, and the affrighted stars that hurried through the sky, can witness that we fear not death. Our hearts which, at the recollection, glow with rage that four revolving years have scarcely taught us to restrain, can witness that we fear not death; and happy it is for those who dared to insult us, that their naked bones are not now piled up an everlasting monument of Massachusetts' bravery. But they retired, they fled, and in that flight they found their only safety. We then expected that the hand of public justice would soon inflict that punishment upon the murderers, which, by the laws of God and man, they had incurred. But let the unbiassed pen of a Robertson, or perhaps of some equally famed American, conduct this trial before the great tribunal of succeeding generations. And though the murderers may escape the just resentment of an enraged people; though drowsy justice, intoxicated by the poisonous draught prepared for her cup, still nods upon her rotten seat, yet be assured, such complicated crimes will meet their due reward. Tell me, ye bloody butchers! ye villains high and low! ye wretches who contrived, as well as you who executed the inhuman deed! do you not feel the goads and stings of conscious guilt pierce through your savage bosoms? Though some of you may think yourselves exalted to a height that bids defiance to human justice; and others shroud yourselves beneath the mask of hypocrasy, and build your hopes of safety on the low arts of cunning, chicanery and falsehood; yet do you not sometimes feel the gnawings of that worm which never dies? Do not the injured shades of Maverick, Gray, Caldwell, Attucks and Carr, attend you in your solitary walks; arrest you even in the midst of your debaucheries, and fill even your dreams with terror? But if the unappeased manes of the dead should not disturb their murderers, yet surely even your obdurate hearts must shrink, and your guilty blood must chill within your rigid veins, when you behold the miserable Monk, the wretched victim of your savage cruelty. Observe his tottering knees, which scarce sustain his wasted body; look on his haggard eyes; mark well the death-like paleness on his fallen cheek, and tell me, does not the sight plant daggers in your souls? Unhappy Monk! cut off, in the gay morn of manhood, from all the joys which sweeten life, doomed to drag on a pitiful existence, without even a hope to taste the pleasures of returning health! Yet Monk, thou livest not in vain; thou livest a warning to thy country, which sympathizes with thee in thy sufferings; thou livest an affecting, an alarming instance of the unbounded violence which lust of power, assisted by a standing army, can lead a traitor to commit.

For us he bled, and now languishes. The wounds, by which he is tortured to a fingering death, were aimed at our country! Surely the meek-eyed charity can never behold such sufferings with indifference. Nor can her lenient hand forbear to pour oil and wine into these wounds, and to assuage, at least, what it cannot heal.

Patriotism is ever united with humanity and compassion. This noble affection, which impels us to sacrifice every thing dear, even life itself, to our country, involves in it a common sympathy and tenderness for every citizen, and must ever have a particular feeling for one who suffers in a public cause. Thoroughly persuaded of this, I need not add a word to engage your compassion and bounty towards a fellow-citizen, who, with long protracted anguish, falls a victim to the relentless rage of our common enemies.

Ye dark designing knaves, ye murderers, parricides! how dare you tread upon the earth, which has drank in the blood of slaughtered innocents, shed by your wicked hands? How dare you breathe that air which wafted to the ear of heaven the groans of those who fell a sacrifice to your accursed ambition? But if the laboring earth doth not expand her jaws; if the air you breathe is not commissioned to be the minister of death; yet, hear it and tremble! The eye of heaven penetrates the darkest chambers of the soul, traces the leading due through all the labyrinths which your industrious folly has devised; and you, however you may have screened yourselves from human eyes, must be arraigned, must lift your hands, red with the blood of those whose death you have procured, at the tremendous bar of God!

But I gladly quit the gloomy theme of death, and leave you to improve the thought of that important day, when our naked souls must stand before that Being, from whom nothing can be hid. I would not dwell too long upon the horrid effects which have already followed from quartering regular troops in this town. Let our misfortunes teach posterity to guard against such evils for the future. Standing armies are sometimes, (I would by no means say generally, much less universally,) composed of persons who have rendered themselves unfit to live in civil society; who have no other motives of conduct than those which a desire of the present gratification of their passions suggests; who have no property in any country; men who have given up their own liberties, and envy those who enjoy liberty; who are equally indifferent to the glory of a George or a Louis; who, for the addition of one penny a day to their wages, would desert from the Christian cross, and fight under the crescent of the Turkish sultan. From such men as these, what has not a state to fear? With such as these, usurping Caesar passed the Rubicon; with such as these, he humbled mighty Rome, and forced the mistress of the world to own a master in a traitor. These are the men whom sceptered robbers now employ to frustrate the designs of God, and render vain the bounties which his gracious hand pours indiscriminately upon his creatures. By these, the miserable slaves in Turkey, Persia, and many other extensive countries, are rendered truly wretched, though their air is salubrious, and their soil luxuriously fertile. By these, France and Spain, though blessed by nature with all that administers to the convenience of life, have been reduced to that contemptible state in which they now appear; and by these, Britain—but if I was possessed of the gift of prophecy, I dare not, except by divine command, unfold the leaves on which the destiny of that once powerful kingdom is inscribed.

But since standing armies are so hurtful to a state, perhaps my countrymen may demand some substitute, some other means of rendering us secure against the incursions of a foreign enemy. But can you be one moment at a loss? Will not a well disciplined militia afford you ample security against foreign foes? We want not courage; it is discipline alone in which we are exceeded by the most formidable troops that ever trod the earth. Surely our hearts flutter no more at the sound of war, than did those of the immortal band of Persia, the Macedonian phalanx, the invincible Roman legions, the Turkish janissaries, the gens d'armes of France, or the well known grenadiers of Britain. A well disciplined militia is a safe, an honorable guard to a community like this, whose inhabitants are by nature brave, and are laudably tenacious of that freedom in which they were born. From a well regulated militia, we have nothing to fear; their interest is the same with that of the state. When a country is invaded, the militia are ready to appear in its defence; they march into a field with that fortitude which a consciousness of the justice of their cause inspires; they do not jeopardy their lives for a master who considers them only as the instruments of his ambition, and whom they regard only as the daily dispenser of the scanty pittance of bread and water. No, they fight for their houses, their lands, for their wives, their children; for all who claim the tenderest names, and are held dearest in their hearts; they fight pro aris focis, for their liberty, and for themselves and for their God. And let it not offend, if I say, that no militia ever appeared in more flourishing condition, than that of this province now doth; and pardon me if I say, of this town in particular. I mean not to boast; I would not excite envy but manly emulation. We have all one common cause; let it, therefore, be our only contest, who shall most contribute to the security of the liberties of America. And may the same kind Providence which has watched over this country from her infant state, still enable us to defeat our enemies. I cannot here forebear noticing the signal manner in which the designs of those, who wish not well to us, have been discovered. The dark deeds of a treacherous cabal, have been brought to public view. You now know the serpents who, whilst cherished in your bosoms, were darting their envenomed stings into the vitals of the constitution. But the representatives of the people have fixed a mark on these ungrateful monsters, which, though it may not make them so secure as Cain of old, yet renders them at least as infamous. Indeed, it would be affrontive to the tutelar deity of this country, even to despair of saving it from all the snares which human policy can lay.

True it is, that the British ministry have annexed a salary to the office of the governor of this province, to be paid out of a revenue, raised in America, without our consent. They have attempted to render our courts of justice the instruments of extending the authority of acts of the British parliament over this colony, by making the judges dependent on the British administration for their support. But this people will never be enslaved with their eyes open. The moment they knew that the governor was not such a governor as the charter of the province points out, he lost his power of hurting them. They were alarmed; they suspected him, have guarded against him, and he has found that a wise and a brave people, when they know their danger, are fruitful in expedients to escape it.

The courts of judicature, also, so far lost their dignity, by being supposed to be under an undue influence, that our representatives thought it absolutely necessary to resolve that they were bound to declare, that they would not receive any other salary besides that which the general court should grant them; and if they did not make this declaration, that it would be the duty of the house to impeach them.

Great expectations were also formed from the artful scheme of allowing the East India company to export tea to America, upon their own account. This certainly, had it succeeded, would have effected the purpose of the contrivers, and gratified the most sanguine wishes of our adversaries. We soon should have found our trade in the hands of foreigners, and taxes imposed on every thing which we consumed; nor would it have been strange, if, in a few years, a company in London should have purchased an exclusive right of trading to America. But their plot was soon discovered. The people soon were aware of the poison which, with so much craft and subtilty, had been concealed. Loss and disgrace ensued: and, perhaps this long concerted master-piece of policy, may issue in the total disuse of tea in this country, which will eventually be the saving of the lives and the estates of thousands. Yet while we rejoice that the adversary has not hitherto prevailed against us, let us by no means put off the harness. Restless malice, and disappointed ambition will still suggest new measures to our inveterate enemies. Therefore, let us also be ready to take the field whenever danger calls; let us be united and strengthen the hands of each other by promoting a general union among us. Much has been done by the committees of correspondence for this and the other towns of this province, towards uniting the inhabitants; let them still go on and prosper. Much has been done by the committees of correspondence, for the houses of assembly, in this and our sister colonies, for uniting the inhabitants of the whole continent, for the security of their common interest. May success ever attend their generous endeavors. But permit me here to suggest a general congress of deputies, from the several houses of assembly, on the continent, as the most effectual method of establishing such an union, as the present posture of our affairs require. At such a congress, a firm foundation may be laid for the security of our rights and liberties; a system may be formed for our common safety, by a strict adherence to which, we shall be able to frustrate any attempts to overthrow our constitution; restore peace and harmony to America, and secure honor and wealth to Great Britain, even against the inclinations of her ministers, whose duty it is to study her welfare; and we shall also free ourselves from those unmannerly pillagers who impudently tell us, that they are licensed by an act of the British parliament, to thrust their dirty hands into the pockets of every American. But, I trust, the happy time will come, when, with the besom of destruction, those noxious vermin will be swept forever from the streets of Boston.

Surely you never will tamely suffer this country to be a den of thieves. Remember, my friends, from whom you sprang. Let not a meanness of spirit, unknown to those whom you boast of as your fathers, excite a thought to the dishonor of your mothers. I conjure you, by all that is dear, by all that is honorable, by all that is sacred, not only that ye pray, but that ye act; that, if necessary, ye fight, and even die, for the prosperity of our Jerusalem. Break in sunder, with noble disdain, the bonds with which the Philistines have bound you. Suffer not yourselves to be betrayed, by the soft arts of luxury and effeminacy, into the pit digged for your destruction. Despise the glare of wealth. That people, who pay greater respect to a wealthy villain, than to an honest, upright man in poverty, almost deserve to be enslaved; they plainly show, that wealth, however it may be acquired, is, in their esteem, to be preferred to virtue.

But I thank God, that America abounds in men who are superior to all temptation, whom nothing can divert from a steady pursuit of the interest of their country; who are at once its ornament and safeguard. And sure I am, I should not incur your displeasure, if I paid a respect, so justly due to their much honored characters, in this place. But when I name an Adams, such a numerous host of fellow-patriots rush upon my mind, that I fear it would take up too much of your time, should I attempt .to call over the illustrious roll. But your grateful hearts will point you to the men; and their revered names, in all succeeding times, shall grace the annals of America. From them, let us, my friends, take example; from them, let us catch the divine enthusiasm; and feel, each for himself, the godlike pleasure of diffusing happiness on all around us; of delivering the oppressed from the iron grasp of tyranny; of changing the hoarse complaints and bitter moans of wretched slaves into those cheerful songs, which freedom and contentment must inspire. There is a heartfelt satisfaction in reflecting on our exertions for the public weal, which all the sufferings an enraged tyrant can inflict, will never take away; which the ingratitude and reproaches of those whom we have saved from ruin, cannot rob us of. The virtuous asserter of the rights of mankind merits a reward, which even a want of success in his endeavors to save his country, the heaviest misfortune which can befall a genuine patriot, cannot entirely prevent him from receiving.

I have the most animating confidence, that the present noble struggle for liberty; will terminate gloriously for America. And let us play the man for our God, and for the cities of our God; while we are using the means in our power, let us humbly commit our righteous cause to the great Lord of the universe, who loveth righteousness and hateth iniquity. And having secured the approbation of our hearts, by a faithful and unwearied discharge of our duty to our country, let us joyfully leave our concerns in the hands of Him who raiseth up and putteth down the empires and kingdoms of the world as He pleases; and with cheerful submission to His sovereign will, devoutly say, "Although the fig-tree shall not blossom, neither shall fruit be in the vines; the labor of the olive shall fail, and the field shall yield no meat; the flock shall be cut off from the fold, and there shall he no herd in the stalls; yet we will rejoice in the Lord, we will joy in the God of our salvation."

PATRICK HENRY

"Give Me Liberty, or Give Me Death!"

*(Delivered in the Convention of Delegates of Virginia,
March 23, 1775)*

No man thinks more highly than I do of the patriotism, as well as abilities, of the very worthy gentlemen who have just addressed the House. But different men often see the same subject in different lights; and, therefore, I hope it will not be thought disrespectful to those gentlemen, if, entertaining as I do, opinions of a character very opposite to theirs, I shall speak forth my sentiments freely and without reserve. This is no time for ceremony. The question, before the House, is one of awful moment to this country. For my own part, I consider it as nothing less than a question of freedom or slavery: and in proportion to the magnitude of the subject ought to be the freedom of the debate. It is only in this way that we can hope to arrive at truth, and fulfil the great responsibility which we hold to God and our country. Should I keep back my opinions at such a time, through fear of giving offence, I should-consider myself as guilty of treason towards my country, and of an act of disloyalty toward the majesty of heaven, which I revere above all earthly kings.

Mr. President, it is natural to man to indulge in the illusions of hope. We are apt to shut our eyes against a painful truth, and listen to the song of that syren, till she transforms us into beasts. Is this the part of wise men, engaged in a great and arduous struggle for liberty? Are we disposed to be of the number of those, who having eyes, see not, and having ears, hear not, the things which so nearly concern their temporal salvation? For my part, whatever anguish of spirit it cost, I am willing to know the whole truth; to know the worst, and to provide for it.

I have but one lamp by which my feet are guided; and that is the lamp of experience. I know of no way of judging of the future but by the past. And judging by the past, I wish to know what there has been in the conduct of the British ministry for the last ten years, to justify those hopes with which gentlemen have been pleased to solace themselves and the House? Is it that insidious smile with which our petition has been lately received? Trust it not, sir; it will prove a snare to your feet. Suffer not yourselves to be betrayed with a kiss. Ask yourselves how this gracious reception of our petition comports with those warlike preparations which cover our waters and darken our land. Are fleets and armies necessary to a work of love and reconciliation? Have we shown ourselves so unwilling to be reconciled, that force must be called in to win back our love? Let us not deceive ourselves, sir. These are the implements of war and subjugation; the last arguments to which kings resort. I ask gentlemen, sir, what means this martial array, if its purpose be not to force us to submission? Can gentlemen assign any other possible motive for it? Has Great Britain any enemy, in this quarter of the world, to call for all this accumulation of navies and armies? No, sir, she has none. They are meant for us: they can be meant for no other. They are sent over to bind and rivet upon us those chains, which the British ministry ha re been so long forging. And what have we to oppose to them? Shall we try argument? Sir, we have been trying that for the last ten years. Have we any thing new to offer upon the subject? Nothing. We have held the subject up in every light of which it is capable; but it has been all in vain. Shall we resort to entreaty and humble supplication? What terms shall we find, which have not been already exhausted? Let us not, I beseech you, sir, deceive our-selves longer. Sir, we have done every thing that could be done, to avert the storm which is now corning on. We have petitioned; we have remonstrated; we have supplicated; we have prostrated ourselves before the throne, and have implored its interposition to arrest the tyrannical hands of the ministry and parliament. Our petitions have been slighted; our remonstrances have produced additional violence and insult; our supplications have been disregarded; and we have been spurned, with contempt, from the foot of the throne! In vain, after these things, may we indulge the fond hope of peace and reconciliation. There is no longer any room for hope. If we wish to be free—if we mean to preserve inviolate those inestimable privileges for which we have been so long contending—if we mean not basely to abandon the noble struggle in which we have been so long engaged, and which we have pledged ourselves never to abandon, until the glorious object of our contest shall be obtained—we must fight! I repeat it, sir, we must fight! An appeal to arms and to the God of Hosts is all that is left us!

They tell us, sir, that we are weak; unable to cope with so formidable an adversary. But when shall we be stronger? Will it be the next week, or the next year? Will it be when we are totally disarmed, and when a British guard shall be stationed in very house? Shall we gather strength by irresolution and inaction? Shall we acquire the means of effectual resistance, by lying supinely on our backs, and hugging the delusive phantom of hope, until our enemies shall have bound us hand and foot? Sir, we are not weak, if we make a proper use of those means which the God of nature hath placed in our power. Three millions of people armed in the holy cause of liberty, and in such a country as that we possess, are invincible by any force which our enemy can send against us. Besides, sir, we shall not fight our battles alone. There is a just God who presides over the destinies of nations; and who will raise up friends fight our battles for us. The battle, sir, is not to the strong alone; it is to the vigilant, the active, the brave. Besides, sir, we have no election. If we were base enough to desire it, it is now too late to retire from the contest. There is no retreat, but in submission and slavery! Our chains are forged! Their clanking may be heard on the plains of Boston! The war is inevitable—and let it come! I repeat it, sir, let it come!

It is in vain, sir, to extenuate the matter. Gentlemen may cry, peace, peace—but there is no peace. The war is actually begun! The next gale, that sweeps from the north, will bring to our ears the clash of resounding arms! Our brethren are already in the field! Why stand we here idle? What is it that gentlemen wish? What would they have? Is life so dear, or peace so sweet, as to be purchased at the price of chains or slavery? Forbid it, Almighty God. I know not what course others may take; but as for me, give me liberty, or give me death!

American Independence

(Delivered at the State House, in Philadelphia, Pennsylvania,
August 1, 1776)

I would gladly have declined an honor, to which I find myself unequal. I have not the calmness and impartiality which the infinite importance of this occasion demands. I will not deny the charge of my enemies, that resentment for the accumulated injuries of our country, and an ardor for her glory, rising to enthusiasm, may deprive me of that accuracy of judgment and expression which men of cooler passions may possess. Let me beseech you, then, to hear me with caution, to examine without prejudice, and to correct the mistakes into which I may be hurried by my zeal.

Truth loves an appeal to the common-sense of mankind. Your unperverted understandings can best determine on subjects of a practical nature. The positions and plans which are said to be above the comprehension of the multitude may be always suspected to be visionary and fruitless. He who made all men hath made the truths necessary to human happiness obvious to all.

Our forefathers threw off the yoke of popery in religion; for you is reserved the honor of levelling the popery of politics. They opened the Bible to all, and maintained the capacity of every man to judge for himself in religion. Are we sufficient for the comprehension of the sublimest spiritual truths, and unequal to material and temporal ones? Heaven hath trusted us with the management of things for eternity, and man denies us ability to judge of the present, or to know from our feelings the experience that will make us happy. "You can discern," say they, "objects distant and remote, but cannot perceive those within your grasp. Let us have the distribution of present goods, and cut out and manage as you please the interests of futurity." This day, I trust the reign of political protestantism will commence. We have explored the temple of royalty, and found that the idol we have bowed down to, has eyes which see not, ears that hear not our prayers, and a heart like the nether millstone. We have this day restored the Sovereign, to whom alone men ought to be obedient. He reigns in Heaven, and with a propitious eye beholds his subjects assuming that freedom of thought, and dignity of self-direction which He bestowed on them. From the rising to the setting sun, may His kingdom come.

Having been a slave to the influence of opinions early acquired, and distinctions generally received, I am ever inclined not to despise but pity those who are yet in darkness. But to the eye of reason what can be more clear, than that all men have an equal right to happiness? Nature made no other distinction than that of higher or lower degrees of power of mind and body. But what mysterious distribution of character has the craft of statesmen, more fatal than priestcraft, introduced?

According to their doctrine, the offspring of perhaps the lewd embraces of a successful invader, shall, from generation to generation, arrogate the right of lavishing on their pleasures a proportion of the fruits of the earth, more than sufficient to supply the wants of thousands of their fellow-creatures; claim authority to manage them like beasts of burden, and without superior industry, capacity, or virtue, nay, though disgraceful to humanity by their ignorance, intemperance, and brutality, shall be deemed best calculated to frame laws, and to consult for the welfare of society.

Were the talents and virtues, which Heaven has bestowed on men, given merely to make them more obedient drudges, to be sacrificed to the follies and ambition of a few? or, were not the noble gifts so equally dispensed with a divine purpose and law, that they should as nearly as possible be equally exerted, and the blessings of Providence be equally enjoyed by all? Away then, with those absurd systems, which, to gratify the pride of a few, debase the greatest part of our species below the order of men. What an affront to the King of the universe, to maintain that the happiness of a monster, sunk in debauchery and spreading desolation and murder among men, of a Caligula, a Nero, or a Charles, is more precious in his sight than that of millions of his suppliant creatures, who do justice, love mercy, and walk humbly with their God! No! in the judgment of Heaven there is no other superiority among men, than a superiority in wisdom and virtue. And can we have a safer model in forming ours? The Deity then has not given any order or family of men authority over others, and if any men have given it, they only could give it for themselves. Our forefathers, 'tis said, consented to be subject to the laws of Great Britain. I will not, at present, dispute it, nor mark out the limits and conditions of their submission; but will it be denied that they contracted to pay obedience, and to be under the control of Great Britain, because it appeared to them most beneficial in their then present circumstances and situations? We, my countrymen, have the same right to consult and provide for our happiness, which they had to promote theirs. If they had a view to posterity in their contracts, it must have been to advance the felicity of their descendants. If they erred in their expectations and prospects, we can never be condemned for a conduct which they would have recommended had they foreseen our present condition.

Ye darkeners of counsel, who would make the property, lives, and religion of millions, depend on the evasive interpretations of musty parchments; who would send us to antiquated charters, of uncertain and contradictory meaning, to prove that the present generation are not bound to be victims to cruel and unforgiving despotism, tell us whether our pious and generous ancestors bequeathed to us the miserable privilege of having the rewards of our honest industry, the fruits of those fields which they purchased and bled for, wrested from us at the will of men over whom we have no check? Did they contract for us that, with folded arms, we should expect that justice and mercy from brutal and inflamed invaders which have been denied to our supplications at the foot of the throne? Were we to hear our character as a people ridiculed with indifference? Did they promise for us that our meekness and patience should be insulted; our coasts harassed; our towns demolished and plundered, and our wives and offspring exposed to nakedness, hunger and death, without our feeling the resentment of men, and exerting those powers of self-preservation which God has given us? No man had once a greater veneration for Englishmen than I entertained. They were dear to me as branches of the same parental trunk, and partakers of the same religion and laws; I still view with respect the remains of the constitution as I would a lifeless body which had once been animated by a great and heroic soul. But when I am roused by the din of arms; when I behold legions of foreign assassins, paid by Englishmen to imbrue their hands in our blood; when I tread over the uncoffined bones of my countrymen, neighbors and friends; when I see the locks of a venerable father torn by savage hands, and a feeble mother, clasping her infants to her bosom, and on her knees imploring their lives from her own slaves, whom Englishmen have allured to treachery and murder; when I behold my country, once the seat of industry, peace, and plenty, changed by Englishmen to a theatre of blood and misery, Heaven forgive me, if I cannot root out those passions which it has implanted in my bosom, and detest submission to a people who have either ceased to be human, or have not virtue enough to feel their own wretchedness and servitude.

Men who content themselves with the semblance of truth, and a display of words, talk much of our obligations to Great Britain for protection! Had she a single eye to our advantage? A nation of shopkeepers are very seldom so disinterested. Let us not be so amused with words; the extension of her commerce was her object. When she defended our coasts, she fought for her customers, and convoyed our ships loaded with wealth, which we had acquired for her by our industry. She has treated us as beasts of burden, whom the lordly masters cherish that they may carry a greater load. Let us inquire also against whom she has protected us? Against her own enemies with whom we had no quarrel, or only on her account, and against whom we always readily exerted our wealth and strength when they were required. Were these colonies backward in giving assistance to Great Britain, when they were called upon in 1739, to aid the expedition against Carthagena? They at that time sent three thousand men to join the British army, although the war commenced without their consent. But the last war, 'tis said, was purely American. This is a vulgar error, which, like many others, has gained credit by being confidently repeated. The dispute between the Courts of Great Britain and France related to the limits of Canada and Nova Scotia. The controverted territory was not claimed by any in the colonies, but by the Crown of Great Britain. It was therefore their own quarrel. The infringement of a right which England had, by the treaty of Utrecht, of trading in the Indian country of Ohio, was another cause of the war. The French seized large quantities of British manufactures, and took possession of a fort which a company of British merchants and factors had erected for the security of their commerce. The war was therefore waged in defence of lands claimed by the Crown, and for the protection of British property. The French at that time had no quarrel with America; and, as appears by letters sent from their commander-in-chief, to some of the colonies, wished to remain in peace with us. The part therefore which we then took, and the miseries to which we exposed ourselves, ought to be charged to our affection for Britain. These colonies granted more than their proportion to the support of the war. They raised, clothed, and maintained, nearly twenty-five thousand men, and so sensible were the people of England of our great exertions, that a message was annually sent to the House of Commons purporting: "That His Majesty, being highly satisfied of the zeal and vigor with which his faithful subjects in North America had exerted themselves in defence of His Majesty's just rights and possessions, recommended it to the House, to take the same into consideration, and enable him to give them a proper compensation."

But what purpose can arguments of this kind answer? Did the protection we received annul our rights as men, and lay us under an obligation of being miserable?

Who among you, my countrymen, that is a father, would claim authority to make your child a slave because you had nourished him in his infancy?

It is a strange species of generosity which requires a return infinitely more valuable than anything it could have bestowed; that demands as a reward for a defence of our property, a surrender of those inestimable privileges, to the arbitrary will of vindictive tyrants, which alone give value to that very property.

Political right and public happiness are different words for the same idea. They who wander into metaphysical labyrinths, or have recourse to original contracts, to determine the rights of men, either impose on themselves or mean to delude others. Public utility is the only certain criterion. It is a test which brings disputes to a speedy decision, and makes it appeal to the feelings of mankind. The force of truth has obliged men to use arguments drawn from this principle who were combating it, in practice and speculation. The advocates for a despotic government, and non-resistance to the magistrate, employ reasons in favor of their systems drawn from a consideration of their tendency to promote public happiness.

The Author of Nature directs all his operations to the production of the greatest good, and has made human virtue to consist in a disposition and conduct which tend to the common felicity of his creatures. An abridgement of the natural freedom of man, by the institution of political societies, is vindicable only on this foot. How absurd, then, is it to draw arguments from the nature of civil society for the annihilation of those very ends which society was intended to procure. Men associate for their mutual advantage. Hence the good and happiness of the members, that is, the majority of the members of any state, is the great standard by which everything relating to that state must finally be determined; and though it may be supposed that a body of people may be bound by a voluntary resignation (which they have been so infatuated as to make) of all their interests to a single person, or to a few, it can never be conceived that the resignation is obligatory to their posterity; because it is manifestly contrary to the good of the whole that it should be so.

These are the sentiments of the wisest and most virtuous champions of freedom. Attend to a portion on this subject from a book in our defence, written, I had almost said by the pen of inspiration. "I lay no stress," says he, "on charters—they derive their rights from a higher source. It is inconsistent with common-sense to imagine that any people would ever think of settling in a distant country, on any such condition, or that the people from whom they withdrew should forever be masters of their property, and have power to subject them to any modes of government they pleased. And had there been express stipulations to this purpose in all the charters of the colonies, they would, in my opinion, be no more bound by them than if it had been stipulated with them that they should go naked, or expose themselves to the incursions of wolves and tigers."

Such are the opinions of every virtuous and enlightened patriot in Great Britain. Their petition to Heaven is—"That there may be one free country left upon earth, to which they may fly, when venality, luxury, and vice, shall have completed, the ruin of liberty there."

Courage, then, my countrymen! our contest is not only whether we ourselves shall be free, but whether there shall be left to mankind an asylum on earth, for civil and religious liberty? Dismissing therefore the justice of our cause, as incontestable, the only question is, What is best for us to pursue in our present circumstances?

The doctrine of dependence on Great Britain is, I believe, generally exploded; but as I would attend to the honest weakness of the simplest of men, you will pardon me if I offer a few words on that subject.

We are now on this continent, to the astonishment of the world, three millions of souls united in one common cause. We have large armies, well disciplined and appointed, with commanders inferior to none in military skill, and superior in activity and zeal. We are furnished with arsenals and stores beyond our most sanguine expectations, and foreign nations are waiting to crown our success by their alliances. There are instances of, I would say, an almost astonishing Providence in our favor; our success has staggered our enemies, and almost given faith to infidels; so that we may truly say it is not our own arm which has saved us.

The hand of heaven appears to have led us on to be, perhaps, humble instruments and means in the great providential dispensation which is completing. We have fled from the political Sodom; let us not look back, lest we perish and become a monument of infamy and derision to the world! For can we ever expect more unanimity and a better preparation for defence; more infatuation of counsel among our enemies, and more valor and zeal among ourselves? The same force and resistance which are sufficient to procure us our liberties will secure us a glorious independence and support us in the dignity of free, imperial States. We cannot suppose that our opposition has made a corrupt and dissipated nation more friendly to America, or created in them a greater respect for the rights of mankind. We can therefore expect a restoration and establishment of our privileges, and a compensation for the injuries we have received from their want of power, from their fears, and not from their virtues. The unanimity and valor, which will effect an honorable peace, can render a future contest for our liberties unnecessary. He who has strength to chain down the wolf is a madman if he lets him loose without drawing his teeth and paring his nails.

From the day on which an accommodation takes place between England and America, on any other terms than as independent States, I shall date the ruin of this country. A politic minister will study to lull us into security, by granting us the full extent of our petitions. The warm sunshine of influence would melt down the virtue, which the violence of the storm rendered more firm and unyielding. In a state of tranquillity, wealth and luxury, our descendants would forget the arts of war, and the noble activity and zeal which made their ancestors invincible. Every art of corruption would be employed to loosen the bond of union which renders our assistance formidable. When the spirit of liberty which now animates our hearts and gives success to our arms is extinct, our numbers will accelerate our ruin, and render us easier victims to tyranny. Ye abandoned minions of an infatuated ministry, if peradventure any should yet remain among us!—remember that a Warren and Montgomery are numbered among the dead. Contemplate the mangled bodies of our countrymen, and then say, What should be the reward of such sacrifices? Bid us and our posterity bow the knee, supplicate the friendship, and plough, and sow, and reap, to glut the avarice of the men who have let loose on us the dogs of war to riot in our blood, and hunt us from the face of the earth? If we love wealth better than liberty, the tranquillity of servitude, than the animating contest of freedom—go from us in peace. We ask not your counsels or arms. Crouch down and lick the hands which feed you. May your chains set lightly upon you, and may posterity forget that ye were our countrymen.

To unite the supremacy of Great Britain and the liberty of America, is utterly impossible. So vast a continent and of such a distance from the seat of empire will every day grow more unmanageable. The motion of so unwieldy a body cannot be directed with any despatch and uniformity, without committing to the Parliament of Great Britain powers inconsistent with our freedom. The authority and force which would be absolutely necessary for the preservation of the peace and good order of this continent, would put all our valuable rights within the reach of that nation.

As the administration of government requires firmer and more numerous supports in proportion to its extent, the burdens imposed on us would be excessive, and we should have the melancholy prospect of their increasing on our posterity. The scale of officers, from the rapacious and needy commissioner, to the haughty governor, and from the governor with his hungry train, to perhaps a licentious and prodigal viceroy, must be upheld by you and your children. The fleets and armies which will be employed to silence your murmurs and complaints must be supported by the fruits of your industry.

And yet, with all this enlargement of the expense and powers of government, the administration of it at such a distance, and over so extensive a territory, must necessarily fail of putting the laws into vigorous execution, removing private oppressions, and forming plans for the advancement of agriculture and commerce, and preserving the vast empire in any tolerable peace and security. If our posterity retain any spark of patriotism, they can never tamely submit to such burdens. This country will be made the field of bloody contention till it gains that independence for which nature formed it. It is therefore injustice and cruelty to our offspring, and would stamp us with the character of baseness and cowardice, to leave the salvation of this country to be worked out by them with accumulated difficulty and danger.

Prejudice, I confess, may warp our judgments. Let us hear the decision of Englishmen on this subject, who cannot be suspected of partiality: "The Americans," say they, "are but little short of half our number. To this number they have grown from a small body of original settlers by a very rapid increase. The probability is that they will go on to increase, and that in fifty or sixty years they will be double our number; and form a mighty empire, consisting of a variety of States, all equal or superior to ourselves in all the arts and accomplishments which give dignity and happiness to human life. In that period will they be still bound to acknowledge that supremacy over them which we now claim? Can there be any person who will assert this, or whose mind does not revolt at the idea of a vast continent, holding all that is valuable to it, at the discretion of a handful of people on the other side the Atlantic? But if at that period this would be unreasonable, what makes it otherwise now? Draw the line if you can. But there is still a greater difficulty. Britain is now, I will suppose, the seat of liberty and virtue, and its legislature consists of a body of able and independent men, who govern with wisdom and justice. The time may come when all will be reversed; when its excellent constitution of government will be subverted; when pressed by debts and taxes, it will be greedy to draw to itself an increase of revenue from every distant province, in order to ease its own burdens; when the influence of the Crown, strengthened by luxury and an universal profligacy of manners, will have tainted every heart, broken down every fence of liberty, and rendered us a nation of tame and contented vassals; when a general election will be nothing but a general auction of boroughs, and when the Parliament, the grand council of the nation, and once the faithful guardian of the state, and a terror to evil ministers, will be degenerated into a body of sycophants, dependent and venal, always ready to confirm any measures, and little more than a public court for registering royal edicts. Such, it is possible, may, some time or other, be the state of Great Britain. What will at that period be the duty of the colonies? Will they be still bound to unconditional submission? Must they always continue an appendage to our Government, and follow it implicitly through every change that can happen to it? Wretched condition indeed, of millions of freemen as good as ourselves! Will you say that we now govern equitably, and that there is no danger of such revolution? Would to God that this were true. But will you not always say the same? Who shall judge whether we govern equitably or not? Can you give the colonies any security that such a period will never come?" No! The period, countrymen, is already come. The calamities were at our door. The rod of oppression was raised over us. We were roused from our slumbers, and may we never sink into repose until we can convey a clear and undisputed inheritance to our posterity. This day we are called upon to give a glorious example of what the wisest and best of men were rejoiced to view, only in speculation. This day presents the world with the most august spectacle that its annals ever unfolded. Millions of freemen, deliberately and voluntarily forming themselves into a society for their common defence and common happiness. Immortal spirits of Hampden, Locke, and Sidney! will it not add to your benevolent joys to behold your posterity rising to the dignity of men, and evincing to the world the reality and expediency of your systems, and in the actual enjoyments of that equal liberty, which you were happy, when on earth, in delineating and recommending to mankind!

Other nations have received their laws from conquerors; some are indebted for a constitution to the sufferings of their ancestors through revolving centuries. The people of this country, alone, have formally and deliberately chosen a Government for themselves, and with open and uninfluenced consent, bound themselves into a social compact. Here, no man proclaims his birth or wealth as a title to honorable distinction, or to sanctify ignorance and vice with the name of hereditary authority. He who has most zeal and ability to promote public felicity, let him be the servant of the public. This is the only line of distinction drawn by nature. Leave the bird of night to the obscurity for which nature intended him, and expect only from the eagle to brush the clouds with his wings, and look boldly in the face of the sun.

Some who would persuade us that they have tender feelings for future generations, while they are insensible to the happiness of the present, are perpetually foreboding a train of dissensions under our popular system. Such men's reasoning amounts to this—give up all that is valuable to Great Britain, and then you will have no inducements to quarrel among yourselves; or suffer yourselves to be chained down by your enemies, that you may not be able to fight with your friends.

This is an insult on your virtue as well as your common-sense. Your unanimity this day and through the course of the war, is a decisive refutation of such invidious predictions. Our enemies have already had evidence that our present constitution contains in it the justice and ardor of freedom, and the wisdom and vigor of the most absolute system. When the law is the will of the people, it will be uniform and coherent; but fluctuation, contradiction, and inconsistency of councils must be expected under those governments where every revolution in the ministry of a court produces one in the state. Such being the folly and pride of all ministers, that they ever pursue measures directly opposite to those of their predecessors.

We shall neither be exposed to the necessary convulsions of elective monarchies, nor to the want of wisdom, fortitude, and virtue, to which hereditary succession is liable. In your hands it will be to perpetuate a prudent, active and just legislature, and which will never expire until you yourselves lose the virtues which give it existence.

And, brethren and fellow-countrymen, if it was ever granted to mortals to trace the designs of Providence, and interpret its manifestations in favor of their cause, we may, with humility of soul, cry out, Not unto us, not unto us, but to thy name be the praise. The confusion of the devices among our enemies, and the rage of the elements against them, have done almost as much towards our success as either our councils or our arms.

The time at which this attempt on our liberties was made, when we were ripened into maturity, had acquired a knowledge of war, and were free from the incursions of enemies in this country, the gradual advances of our oppressors enabling us to prepare for our defence, the unusual fertility of our lands and clemency of the seasons, the success which at first attended our feeble arms, producing unanimity among our friends and reducing our internal foes to acquiescence— these are all strong and palpable marks and assurances, that Providence is yet gracious unto Zion, that it will turn away the captivity of Jacob.

Our glorious reformers when they broke through the fetters of superstition, effected more than could be expected from an age so darkened. But they left much to be done by their posterity. They lopped off, indeed, some of the branches of popery, but they left the root and stock when they left us under the domination of human systems and decisions, usurping the infallibility which can be attributed to Revelation alone. They dethroned one usurper only to raise up another; they refused allegiance to the Pope, only to place the civil magistrate in the throne of Christ, vested with authority to enact laws, and inflict penalties in his kingdom. And if we now cast our eyes over the nations of the earth we shall find, that instead of possessing the pure religion of the gospel, they may be divided either into infidels who deny the truth, or politicians who make religion a stalking horse for their ambition, or professors, who walk in the trammels of orthodoxy, and are more attentive to traditions and ordinances of men than to the oracles of truth.

The civil magistrate has everywhere contaminated religion by making it an engine of policy; and freedom of thought and the right of private judgment, in matters of conscience, driven from every other corner of the earth, direct their course to this happy country as their last asylum. Let us cherish the noble guests, and shelter them under the wings of an universal toleration. Be this the seat of unbounded religious freedom. She will bring with her in her train, industry, wisdom, and commerce. She thrives most when left to shoot forth in her natural luxuriance, and asks from human policy, only not to be checked in her growth by artificial encouragements.

Thus by the beneficence of Providence, we shall behold our empire arising, founded on justice and the voluntary consent of the people, and giving full scope to the exercise of those faculties and rights which most ennoble our species. Besides the advantages of liberty and the most equal constitution, heaven has given us a country with every variety of climate and soil, pouring forth in abundance whatever is necessary for the support, comfort, and strength of a nation. Within our own borders we possess all the means of sustenance, defence, and commerce; at the same time, these advantages are so distributed among the different States of this continent, as if nature had in view to proclaim to us—Be united among yourselves, and you will want nothing from the rest of the world.

The more northern States most amply supply us with every necessary, and many of the luxuries of life—with iron, timber, and masts for ships of commerce or of war; with flax for the manufacture of linen, and seed either for oil or exportation.

So abundant are our harvests, that almost every part raises more than double the quantity of grain requisite for the support of the inhabitants. From Georgia and the Carolinas, we have, as well for our own wants as for the purpose of supplying the wants of other powers, indigo, rice, hemp, naval stores, and lumber.

Virginia and Maryland teem with wheat, Indian corn, and tobacco. Every nation whose harvest is precarious, or whose lands yield not those commodities, which we cultivate, will gladly exchange their superfluities and manufactures for ours.

We have already received many and large cargoes of clothing, military stores, etc., from our commerce with foreign powers, and in spite of the efforts of the boasted navy of England, we shall continue to profit by this connection.

The want of our naval stores has already increased the price of these articles to a great height, especially in Britain. Without our lumber, it will be impossible for those haughty islanders to convey the products of the West Indies to their own ports—for a while they may with difficulty effect it, but without our assistance, their resources soon must fail. Indeed, the West India Islands appear as the necessary appendages to this our empire. They must owe their support to it, and ere long, I doubt not, some of them will from necessity wish to enjoy the benefit of our protection.

These natural advantages will enable us to remain independent of the world, or make it the interest of European powers to court our alliance, and aid in protecting us against the invasions of others. What argument therefore do we want, to show the equity of our conduct; or motive of interest to recommend it to our prudence? Nature points out the path, and our enemies have obliged us to pursue it.

If there is any man so base or so weak as to prefer a dependence on Great Britain to the dignity and happiness of living a member of a free and independent nation—let me tell him that necessity now demands what the generous principle of patriotism should have dictated.

We have now no other alternative than independence, or the most ignominious and galling servitude. The legions of our enemies thicken on our plains; desolation and death mark their bloody career; whilst the mangled corpses of our countrymen seem to cry out to us as a voice from heaven—"Will you permit our posterity to groan under the galling chains of our murderers? Has our blood been expended in vain? Is the only reward which our constancy, till death, has obtained for our country, that it should be sunk into a deeper and more ignominious vassalage? Recollect who are the men that demand your submission; to whose decrees you are invited to pay obedience! Men who, unmindful of their relation to you as brethren, of your long implicit submission to their laws; of the sacrifice which you and your forefathers made of your natural advantages for commerce to their avarice—formed a deliberate plan to wrest from you the small pittance of property which they had permitted you to acquire. Remember that the men who wish to rule over you, are they who, in pursuit of this plan of despotism, annulled the sacred contracts which had been made with your ancestors; conveyed into your cities a mercenary soldiery to compel you to submission by insult and murder—who called your patience, cowardice; your piety, hypocrisy."

Countrymen! the men who now invite you to surrender your rights into their hands, are the men who have let loose the merciless savages to riot in the blood of their brethren—who have dared to establish popery triumphant in our land—who have taught treachery to your slaves, and courted them to assassinate your wives and children.

These are the men to whom we are exhorted to sacrifice the blessings which Providence holds out to us—the happiness, the dignity of uncontrolled freedom and independence.

Let not your generous indignation be directed against any among us, who may advise so absurd and maddening a measure. Their number is but few and daily decreases; and the spirit which can render them patient of slavery will render them contemptible enemies.

Our Union is now complete; our constitution composed, established, and approved. You are now the guardians of your own liberties. We may justly address you, as the Decemviri did the Romans, and say—"Nothing that we propose can pass into a law without your consent. Be yourselves, O Americans, the authors of those laws on which your happiness depends."

You have now in the field armies sufficient to repel the whole force of your enemies, and their base and mercenary auxiliaries. The hearts of your soldiers beat high with the spirit of freedom—they are animated with the justice of their cause, and while they grasp their swords, can look up to heaven for assistance. Your adversaries are composed of wretches who laugh at the rights of humanity, who turn religion into derision, and would, for higher wages, direct their swords against their leaders or their country. Go on, then, in your generous enterprise, with gratitude to heaven, for past success, and confidence of it in the future. For my own part, I ask no greater blessing than to share with you the common danger and common glory. If I have a wish dearer to my soul, than that my ashes may be mingled with those of a Warren and Montgomery—it is—that these American States may never cease to be free and independent!

Speech in the Constitutional Convention, at the Conclusion of Its Deliberations

(Delivered in Philadelphia, Pennsylvania, September 17, 1787)

I confess that I do not entirely approve of this Constitution at present, but Sir, I am not sure I shall never approve it: For having lived long, I have experienced many Instances of being oblig'd, by better Information or fuller Consideration, to change Opinions even on important Subjects, which I once thought right, but found to be otherwise. It is therefore that the older I grow the more apt I am to doubt my own Judgment and to pay more Respect to the Judgment of others. Most Men indeed as well as most Sects in Religion, think themselves in Possession of all Truth, and that wherever others differ from them it is so far Error. Steele, a Protestant, in a Dedication tells the Pope, that the only Difference between our two Churches in their Opinions of the Certainty of their Doctrine, is, the Romish Church is infallible, and the Church of England is never in the Wrong. But tho' many private Persons think almost as highly of their own Infallibility, as of that of their Sect, few express it so naturally as a certain French lady, who, in a little Dispute with her Sister, said, I don't know how it happens, Sister, but I meet with no body but myself that's *always* in the right. *Il n'y a que moi que a toujours raison.*

In these Sentiments, Sir, I agree to this Constitution, with all its Faults, if they are such: because I think a General Government necessary for us, and there is no *Form* of Government but what may be a Blessing to the People if well administered; and I believe, farther that this is likely to be well administered for a Course of Years, and can only end in Despotism as other Forms have done before it, when the People shall become so corrupted as to need Despotic Government, being incapable of any other. I doubt too whether any other Convention we can obtain, may be able to make a better Constitution: For when you assemble a Number of Men to have the Advantage of their joint Wisdom, you inevitably assemble with those Men all their Prejudices, their Passions, their Errors of Opinion, their local Interests, and their selfish Views. From such an Assembly can a perfect Production be expected? It therefore astonishes me, Sir, to find this System approaching so near to Perfection as it does; and I think it will astonish our Enemies, who are waiting with Confidence to hear that our Councils are confounded, like those of the Builders of Babel, and that our States are on the Point of Separation, only to meet hereafter for the Purpose of cutting one another's Throats. Thus I consent, Sir, to this Constitution because I expect no better, and because I am not sure that it is not the best. The Opinions I have had of its Errors, I sacrifice to the Public Good. I have never whisper'd a Syllable of them abroad. Within these Walls they were born, & here they shall die. If every one of us in returning to our Constituents were to report the Objections he has had to it, and endeavour to gain Partizans in support of them, we might prevent its being generally received, and thereby lose all the salutary Effects & great Advantages resulting naturally in our favour among foreign Nations, as well as among ourselves, from our real or apparent Unanimity. Much of the Strength and Efficiency of any Government, in procuring & securing Happiness to the People depends on Opinion, on the general Opinion of the Goodness of that Government as well as of the Wisdom & Integrity of its Governors. I hope therefore for our own Sakes, as a Part of the People, and for the Sake of our Posterity, we shall act heartily & unanimously in recommending this Constitution, wherever our Influence may extend, and turn our future Thoughts and Endeavours to the Means of having it well administered.—

On the whole, Sir, I cannot help expressing a Wish, that every Member of the Convention, who may still have Objections to it, would with me on this Occasion doubt a little of his own Infallibility, and, to make *manifest* our *Unanimity,* put his name to this Instrument.

Alexander Hamilton

On the Expediency of Adopting the Federal Constitution

(Delivered at the New York Constitutional Convention, June 27, 1788)

This is one of those subjects, Mr. Chairman, on which objections very naturally arise, and assume the most plausible shape. Its address is to the passions, and its first impressions create a prejudice, before cool examination has an opportunity for exertion. It is more easy for the human mind to calculate the evils, than the advantages of a measure; and vastly more natural to apprehend the danger, than to see the necessity, of giving powers to our rulers. Hence, I may justly expect, that those who hear me, will place less confidence in those arguments which oppose, than in those which favor, their prepossessions.

After all our doubts, our suspicions and speculations, on the subject of government, we must return, at last, to this important truth—that when we have formed a constitution upon free principles; when we have given a proper balance to the different branches of administration, and fixed representation upon pure and equal principles, we may, with safety, furnish it with all the powers necessary to answer, in the most ample manner, the purposes of government. The great desiderata are a free representation, and mutual checks. When these are obtained, all our apprehensions of the extent of powers are unjust and imaginary. What then is the structure of this constitution. One branch of the legislature is to be elected by the people—by the same people, who choose your state representatives. It members are to hold their office two years, and then return to their constituents. Here, sir, the people govern: here they act by their immediate representatives. You have also a senate, constituted by your state legislatures—by men in whom you place the highest confidence, and forming another representative branch. Then, again, you have an executive magistrate, created by a form of election, which merits universal admiration. In the form of this government, and in the mode of legislation, you find all the checks which the greatest politicians and the best writers, have ever conceived. What more can reasonable men desire? Is there any one branch in which the whole legislative and executive branch is lodged? No. The legislative authority is lodged in three distinct branches, properly balanced:

the executive authority is divided between two branches; and the judicial is still reserved for an independent body, who hold their offices during good behavior. This organization is so complex, so skillfully contrived, that it is next to impossible that an impolitic or wicked measure should pass the great scrutiny with success. Now, what do gentlemen mean, by coming forward and declaiming against this government? Why do they say we ought to limit its powers, to disable it, and to destroy its capacity of blessing the people? Has philosophy suggested—has experience taught, that such a government ought not to be trust with every thing necessary for the good of society. Sir, when you have divided and nicely balanced the departments of government; when you have strongly connected the virtue of your rulers with their interest; when, in short, you have rendered your system as perfect as human forms can be—you must place a confidence; you must give power.

We have heard a great deal of the sword and the purse: it is said, our liberties are in danger, if both are possessed by Congress. Let us see what is the true meaning of this maxim, which has been so much used, and so little understood. It is, that you shall not place these powers in either the legislative or executive singly: neither one nor the other shall have both; because this would destroy that division of powers, on which political liberty is founded; and would furnish one body with all the means of tyranny. But, where the purse is lodged in one branch, and the sword in another, there can be no danger. All governments have possessed these powers: they would be monsters without them, and incapable of exertion. What is your state government? Does not your legislature command what money it pleases? Does not your executive execute the laws without restraint? These distinctions between the purse and the sword have no application to the system, but only to its separate branches. Sir, when we reason about the great interests of a great people, it is high time that we dismiss our prejudices and banish declamation.

In order to induce us to consider the powers, given by this constitution, as dangerous—in order to render plausible an attempt to take away the life and spirit of the most important power in government, the gentleman complains that we shall not have a true and safe representation. I asked him what a safe representation was, and he has given no satisfactory answer. The assembly of New York has been mentioned as a proper standard; but, if we apply this standard to the general government, our Congress will become a mere mob, exposed to every irregular impulse, and subject to every breeze of faction. Can such a system afford security? Can you have confidence in such a body? The idea of taking the ration of representation, in a small society, for the ration of a great one, is a fallacy which ought to be exposed. It is impossible to ascertain to what point our representation will increase: it may vary from one, to two, three, or four hundred; it depends upon the progress of population. Suppose it to rest at two hundred; is not this number sufficient to secure it against corruption? Human nature must be a much more weak and despicable thing, than I apprehend it to be, if two hundred of our fellow-citizens can be corrupted in two years. But, suppose they are corrupted; can they, in two years, accomplish their designs? Can they form a combination, and even lay a foundation for a system of tyranny, in so short a period? It is far from my intention to wound the feelings of any gentleman; but I must, in this most interesting discussion, speak of things as they are; and hold up opinions in the light in which they out to appear: and I maintain, that all that has been said of corruption, of the purse and the sword, and the danger of giving powers, is not supported by principle or fact: that it is mere verbiage, and idle decimation. The true principle of government is this: make the system complete in its structure; give a perfect proportion and balance to its parts; and the powers you give it will never afflict your security. The question, then, or the division of powers between the general and state governments, is a question of convenience: it becomes a prudential inquiry, what powers are proper to be reserved to the latter; and this immediately involves another inquiry into the proper objects of the two governments. This is the criterion by which we shall determine the just distribution of powers.

The great leading objects of the federal government, in which revenue is concerned, are to maintain domestic peace, and provide for the common defence. In these are comprehended the regulation of commerce, that is, the whole system of foreign intercourse; the support of armies and navies, and of the civil administration. It is useless to go into detail. Every one knows that the objects of the general government are numerous, extensive and important. Every one must acknowledge the necessity of giving powers, in all respects, and in every degree, equal to these objects. This principle assented to, let us inquire what are the objects of the state governments. Have they to provide against foreign invasion? Have they to maintain fleets and armies? Have they any concern in the regulation of commerce, the procuring alliances, or forming treaties of peace? No. Their objects are merely civil and domestic; to support the legislative establishment, and to provide for the administration of the laws. Let any one compare the expense of supporting the civil list in a state, with the expense of providing for the defence of the union. The difference is almost beyond calculation. The experience of Great Britain will throw some light on this subject. In that kingdom, the ordinary expenses of peace to those of war, are as one to fourteen: but there they have a monarch, with his splendid court, and an enormous civil establishment, with which we have nothing in this country to compare. If, in Great Britain, the expenses of war and peace are so disproportioned, how wide will be their disparity in the United States; how infinitely wider between the general government and each individual state! Now, sir, where ought the great resources to be lodged? Every rational man will give an immediate answer. To what extent shall these resources be possessed? Reason says, as far as possible exigencies can require; that is, without limitation. A constitution cannot set bounds to a nation's wants; it ought not, therefore, to set bounds to its resources. Unexpected invasions, long and ruinous wars, may demand all the possible abilities of the country. Shall not your government have power to call these abilities into action? The contingencies of society are not reduceable to calculations. They cannot be fixed or bounded, even in imagination. Will you limit the means of your defence, when you cannot ascertain the force or extent of the invasion? Even in ordinary wars, a government is frequently obliged to call for supplies, to the temporary oppression of the people.

Sir, if we adopt the idea of exclusive revenues, we shall be obliged to fix some distinguished line, which neither government shall overpass. The inconveniences of this measure must appear evident, on the slightest examination. The resources appropriated to one, may diminish or fail, while those of the other may increase, beyond the wants of government. One may be destitute of revenues, while the other shall possess an unnecessary abundance, and the constitution will be an eternal barrier to a mutual intercourse and relief. In this case, will the individual states stand on so good a ground, as if the objects of taxation were left free and open to the embrace of both the governments? Possibly, in the advancement of commerce, the imposts may increase to such a degree, as to render direct taxes unnecessary. These resources, then, as the constitution stands, may be occasionally relinquished to the states; but on the gentleman's idea of prescribing exclusive limits, and precluding all reciprocal communication, this would be entirely improper. The laws of the states must not touch the appropriated resources of the United States, whatever may be their wants. Would it not be of more advantage to the states, to have a concurrent jurisdiction extending to all the sources of revenue, than to be confined to such a small resource, as, on calculation of the objects of the two governments, should appear to be their due proportion? Certainly you cannot hesitate on this question. The gentleman's plan would have a further ill effect; it would tend to dissolve the connexion and correspondence of the two governments, to estrange them from each other, and to destroy that mutual dependence, which forms the essence of union. Sir, a number of arguments have been advanced by an honorable member from New York, which, to every unclouded mind, must carry conviction. He has stated, that in sudden emergencies, it may be necessary to borrow; and that it is impossible to borrow, unless you have funds to pledge for payment of your debts. Limiting the powers of government to certain resources, is rendering the fund precarious; and obliging the government to ask, instead of empowering it to command, is to destroy all confidence and credit. If the power of taxing is restricted, the consequence is, that on the breaking out of a war, you must divert the funds appropriated to the payment of debts, to answer immediate exigencies. Thus, you violate your engagements at the very time you increase the burden of them. Besides, sound policy condemns the practice of accumulating debts. A government, to act with energy, should have the possession of all its revenues to answer present purposes. The principle, for which I contend, is recognized, in all its extent, by our old constitution. Congress is authorized to raise troops, to call for supplies without limitation, and to borrow money to any amount. It is true, they must used the form of recommendations and requisitions: but the states are bound by the solemn ties of honor, of justice, or religion, to comply without reserve.

Mr. Chairman, it has been advanced as a principle, that no government but a despotism, can exist in a very extensive country. This is a melancholy consideration indeed. If it were founded on truth, we ought to dismiss the idea of a republican government, even for the state of New York. This idea has been taken from a celebrated writer, who by being misunderstood, has been the occasion of frequent fallacies in our reasoning on political subjects. But the position has been misapprehended; and its application is entirely false and unwarrantable: it relates only to democracies, where the whole body of the people meet to transact business: and where representation is unknown. Such were a number of ancient, and some modern independent cities. Men who read without attention, have taken these maxims respecting the extent of country; and, contrary to their proper meaning, have applied them to republics in general. This application is wrong in respect to all representative governments; but especially in relation to a confederacy of states, in which the supreme legislature has only general powers, and the civil and domestic concerns of the people are regulated by the laws of the several states. This distinction being kept in view, all the difficulty will vanish, and we may easily conceive, that the people of a large country may be represented, as truly as those of a small one. An assembly constituted for general purposes, may be fully competent to every federal regulation, without being too numerous for deliberate conduct. If the state governments were to be abolished, the question would wear a different face: but this idea is inadmissible. They are absolutely necessary to the system. Their existence must form a leading principle in the most perfect constitution we could form. I insist, that it never can be the interest or desire of the national legislature, to destroy the state governments. It can derive no advantage from such an event; but, on the contrary, would lose an indispensable support, a necessary aid in executing the laws, and conveying the influence of government to the doors of the people. The union is dependent on the will of the state governments for its chief magistrate, and for its senate. The blow aimed at the members, must give a fatal wound to the head; and the destruction of the states must be at once a political suicide. Can the national government be guilty of this madness? What inducements, what temptations can they have? Will they attach new honors to their station; will they increase the national strength; will they multiply the national resources; will they make themselves more respectable in the view of foreign nations, or of their fellow-citizens, by robbing the states of their constitutional privileges? But imagine, for a moment, that a political frenzy should seize the government; suppose they should make the attempt—certainly, sir, it would be for ever impracticable. This has been sufficiently demonstrated by reason and experience. It has been proved, that the members of republics have been, and ever will be, stronger than the head. Let us attend to one general historical example. In the ancient feudal governments of Europe, there were, in the first place, a monarch; subordinate to him, a body of nobles; and subject to these, the vassals, or the whole body of the people. The authority of the kings was limited, and that of the barons considerably independent. A great part of the early wars in Europe were contests between the king and his nobility. In these contests, the latter possessed many advantages derived from their influence, and the immediate command they had over the people; and they generally prevailed. The history of the feudal wars exhibits little more than a series of successful encroachments on the prerogatives of monarchy. Here, sir, is one great proof of the superiority, which the members in limited governments possess over their head. As long as the barons enjoyed the confidence and attachment of the people, they had the strength of the country on their side, and were irresistible. I may be told, that in some instances the barons were overcome: but how did this happen? Sir, they took advantage of the depression of the royal authority, and the establishment of their own power, to oppress and tyrannize over their vassal. As commerce enlarged, and as wealth and civilization increased, the people began to feel their own weight and consequence: they grew tired of their oppressions; united their strength with that of the prince, and threw off the yoke of aristocracy. These very instances prove what I contend for. They prove, that in whatever direction the popular weight leans, the current of power will flow: wherever the popular attachments lie, there will rest the political superiority. Sir, can it be supposed that the state governments will become the oppressors of the people? Will they forfeit their affections? Will they combine to destroy the liberties and happiness of their fellow-citizens, for the sole purpose of involving themselves in ruin? God forbid! The idea, sir, is shocking! It outrages every feeling of humanity, and every dictate of common sense!

There are certain social principles in human nature, from which we may draw the most solid conclusions, with respect to the conduct of individuals and of communities. We love our families more than our neighbors: we love our neighbors more than our countrymen in general. The human affections, like the solar heat, lose their intensity, as they depart from the centre, and become languid, in proportion to the expansion of the circle, on which they act. On these principles, the attachment of the individual will be first and for ever secured by the state governments: they will be a mutual protection and support. Another source of influence, which has already been pointed out, is the various official connexions in the states. Gentlemen endeavor to evade the force of this, by saying that these offices will be insignificant. This is by no means true. The state officers will ever be important, because they are necessary and useful. Their powers are such as are extremely interesting to the people; such as affect their property, their liberty and life. What is more important than the administration of justice, and the execution of the civil and criminal laws? Can the state governments become insignificant, while they have the power of raising money independently, and without control? If they are really useful; if they are calculated to promote the essential interests of the people; they must have their confidence and support. The states can never lose their powers, till the whole people of America are robbed of their liberties. These must go together; they must support each other, or meet one common fate. On the gentleman's principle, we may safely trust the state governments, though we have no means of resisting them: but we cannot confide in the national government, though we have an effectual constitutional guard against every encroachment. This is the essence of their argument, and it is false and fallacious beyond conception.

With regard to the jurisdiction of the two governments, I shall certainly admit that the constitution ought to be so formed, as not to prevent the states from providing for their own existence; and I maintain that it is so formed; and their power of providing for themselves is sufficiently established. This is conceded by one gentleman, and in the next breath, the concession is retracted. He says, Congress have but one exclusive right in taxation; that of duties on imports: certainly, then, their other powers are only concurrent. But to take off the force of this obvious conclusion, he immediately says, that the laws of the United States are supreme; and that where there is one supreme, there cannot be a concurrent authority; and further, that where the laws of the union are supreme, those of the states must be subordinate; because, there cannot be two supremes. This is curious sophistry. That two supreme powers cannot act together, is false. They are inconsistent only when they are aimed at each other, or at one indivisible object. The laws of the United States are supreme, as to all their proper, constitutional objects: the laws of the states are supreme in the same way. These supreme laws may act on different objects, without clashing; or they may operate on different parts of the same common object, with perfect harmony. Suppose both governments should lay a tax, of a penny, on a certain article: has not each independent and uncontrollable power to collect its own tax? The meaning of the maxim, there cannot be two supremes, is simply this—two powers cannot be supreme over each other. This meaning is entirely perverted by the gentlemen. But, it is said, disputes between collectors are to be referred to the federal courts. This is again wandering in the field of conjecture. But suppose the fact certain: is it not to be presumed, that they will express the true meaning of the constitution and the laws? Will they not be bound to consider the concurrent jurisdiction; to declare that both the taxes shall have equal operation; that both the powers, in that respect, are sovereign and co-extensive? If they transgress their duty, we are to hope that they will be punished. Sir, we can reason from probabilities alone. When we leave common sense, and give ourselves up to conjecture, there can be no certainty, no security in our reasonings.

I imagine I have stated to the committee, abundant reasons to prove the entire safety of the state governments, and of the people. I would go into a more minute consideration of the nature of the concurrent jurisdiction, and the operation of the laws, in relation to revenue; but at present, I feel too much indisposed to proceed. I shall, with the leave of the committee, improve another opportunity of expressing to them more fully my ideas on this point. I wish the committee to remember, that the constitution under examination, is framed upon truly republican principles; and that, as it is expressly designed to provide for the common protection and the general welfare of the United States, it must be utterly repugnant to this constitution, to subvert the state governments, or oppress the people.

George Washington

First Inaugural Address

(Delivered at Federal Hall in New York City, April 30, 1789)

Among the vicissitudes incident to life, no event could have filled me with greater anxieties than that of which the notification was transmitted by your order, and received on the 14th day of the present month. On the one hand, I was summoned by my country, whose voice I can never hear but with veneration and love, from a retreat which I had chosen with the fondest predilection, and, in my flattering hopes, with an immutable decision, as the asylum of my declining years—a retreat which was rendered every day more necessary as well as more dear to me by the addition of habit to inclination, and of frequent interruptions in my health to the gradual waste committed on it by time. On the other hand, the magnitude and difficulty of the trust to which the voice of my country called me, being sufficient to awaken in the wisest and most experienced of her citizens a distrustful scrutiny into his qualifications, could not but overwhelm with despondence one who, inheriting inferior endowments from nature, and unpractised in the duties of civil administration, ought to be peculiarly conscious of his own deficiencies. In this conflict of emotions, all I dare aver is, that it has been my faithful study to collect my duty from a just appreciation of every circumstance by which it might be affected. All I dare hope is, that if, in accepting this task, I have been too much swayed by a grateful remembrance of former instances, or by an affectionate sensibility to this transcendant proof of the confidence of my fellow-citizens, and have thence too little consulted my incapacity as well as disinclination for the weighty and untried cares before me, my error will be palliated by the motives which misled me, and its consequences be judged by my country with some share of the partiality with which they originated.

Such being the impressions under which I have, in obedience to the public summons, repaired to the present station, it would be peculiarly improper to omit, in this first official act, my fervent supplications to that Almighty Being who rules over the universe, who presides in the councils of nations, and whose providential aids can supply every human defect, that his benediction may consecrate to the liberties and happiness of the people of the United States a government instituted by themselves for these essential purposes, and may enable every instrument employed in its administration to execute with success the functions allotted to his charge. In tendering this homage to the great Author of every public and private good, I assure myself that it expresses your sentiments not less than my own, nor those of my fellow-citizens at large less than either. No people can be bound to acknowledge and adore the invisible Hand which conducts the affairs of men, more than the people of the United States. Every step by which they have advanced to the character of an independent nation seems to have been distinguished by some token of providential agency; and in the important revolution just accomplished in the system of their united government, the tranquil deliberations and voluntary consent of so many distinct communities from which the event has resulted, can not be compared with the means by which most governments have been established, without some return of pious gratitude, along with an humble anticipation of the future blessings which the past seem to presage. These reflections, arising out of the present crisis, have forced themselves too strongly on my mind to be suppressed. You will join with me, I trust, in thinking that there are none under the influence of which the proceedings of a new and free government can more auspiciously commence.

By the article establishing the executive department, it is made the duty of the president "to recommend to your consideration such measures as he shall judge necessary and expedient." The circumstances under which I now meet you will acquit me from entering into that subject farther than to refer to the great constitutional charter under which you are assembled, and which, in defining your powers, designates the objects to which your attention is to be given. It will be more consistent with those circumstances, and far more congenial with the feelings which actuate me, to substitute, in place of a recommendation of particular measures, the tribute that is due to the talents, the rectitude, and the patriotism which adorn the characters selected to devise and adopt them. In these honorable qualifications I behold the surest pledges that, as on one side, no local prejudices or attachments, no separate views, no party animosities, will misdirect the comprehensive and equal eye which ought to watch over this great assemblage of communities and interests, so, on another, that the foundations of our national policy will be laid in the pure and immutable principles of private morality, and the pre-eminence of free government be exemplified by all the attributes which can win the affections of its citizens and command the respect of the world. I dwell on this prospect with every satisfaction which an ardent love for my country can inspire, since there is no truth more thoroughly established than that there exists in the economy and course of nature an indissoluble union between virtue and happiness, between duty and advantage, between the genuine maxims of an honest and magnanimous policy and the solid rewards of public prosperity and felicity; since we ought to be no less persuaded that the propitious smiles of Heaven can never be expected on a nation that disregards the eternal rules of order and right which Heaven itself has ordained, and since the preservation of the sacred fire of liberty and the destiny of the republican model of government are justly considered as deeply, perhaps as finally, staked on the experiment intrusted to the hands of the American people.

Besides the ordinary objects submitted to your care, it will remain with your judgment to decide how far an exercise of the occasional power delegated by the fifth article of the constitution is rendered expedient at the present juncture by the nature of the objections which have been urged against the system, or by the degree of inquietude which has given birth to them. Instead of undertaking particular recommendations on this subject, in which I could be guided by no lights derived from official opportunities, I shall again give way to my entire confidence in your discernment and pursuit of the public good; for I assure myself that while you carefully avoid every alteration which might endanger the benefits of a united and effective government, or which ought to await the future lessons of experience, a reverence for the characteristic rights of freemen, and a regard for the public harmony will sufficiently influence your deliberations on the question how far the former can be more impregnably fortified, or the latter be safely and advantageously promoted.

To the preceding observations I have one to add which will be most properly addressed to the house of representatives. It concerns myself, and will therefore be as brief as possible. When I was first honored with a call into the service of my country, then on the eve of an arduous struggle for its liberties, the light in which I contemplated my duty required that I should renounce every pecuniary compensation. From this resolution I have in no instance departed; and being still under the impressions which produced it, I must decline as inapplicable to myself any share in the personal emoluments which may be indispensably included in a permanent provision for the executive department, and must accordingly pray that the pecuniary estimates for the station in which I am placed may, during my continuance in it, be limited to such actual expenditures as the public good may be thought to require.

Having thus imparted to you my sentiments as they have been awakened by the occasion which brings us together, I shall take my present leave; but not without resorting once more to the benign Parent of the human race in humble supplication that, since he has been pleased to favor the American people with opportunities for deliberating in perfect tranquillity, and dispositions for deciding with unparalleled unanimity on a form of government for the security of their union and the advancement of their happiness, so his divine blessing may be equally conspicuous in the enlarged views, the temperate consultations, and the wise measures, on which the success of this government must depend.

John Quincy Adams

On American Independence

(Delivered in Boston, Massachusetts, July 4, 1793, in commemoration of the
anniversary of American independence)

It has been a custom, sanctioned by the universal practice of civilized nations, to celebrate, with anniversary solemnities, the return of the days which have been distinguished by events the most important to the happiness of the people. In countries where the natural dignity of mankind, has been degraded by the weakness of bigotry, or debased by the miseries of despotism, this customary celebration has degenerated into a servile mockery of festivity upon the birthday of a sceptred tyrant, or has dwindled to an unmeaning revel, in honor of some canonized fanatic, of whom nothing now remains but the name, in the calendar of antiquated superstition. In those more fortunate regions of the earth where liberty has condescended to reside, the cheerful gratitude of her favored people has devoted to innocent gayety and useful relaxation from the toils of virtuous industry the periodical revolution of those days which have been rendered illustrious by the triumphs of freedom.

Americans! such is the nature of the institution which again calls your attention to celebrate the establishment of your national independence. And surely since the creation of the heavenly orb which separated the day from the night, amid the unnumbered events which have diversified the history of the human race, none has ever occurred more highly deserving of celebration, by every species of ceremonial, that can testify a sense of gratitude to the Deity, and of happiness, derived from his transcendent favors.

It is a wise and salutary institution, which forcibly recalls to the memory of freemen, the principles upon which they originally founded their laboring plan of state. It is a sacrifice at the altar of liberty herself; a renewal of homage to the sovereign, who alone is worthy of our veneration; a profession of political fidelity, expressive of our adherence to those maxims of liberal submission and obedient freedom, which in these favored climes, have harmonized the long-contending claims of liberty and law. By a frequent recurrence to those sentiments and actions upon which the glory and felicity of the nation rest supported, we are enabled to renew the moments of bliss which we are not permitted to retain; we secure a permanency to the exaltation of what the constitution of nature has rendered fleeting, and a perennial existence to enjoyments which the lot of humanity has made transitory.

The "feelings, manners, and principles" which led to the independence of our country: such, my friends and fellow-citizens, is the theme of our present commemoration. The field is extensive; it is fruitful; but the copious treasures of its fragrance have already been gathered by the hands of genius; and there now remains for the gleaning of mental indigence nought but the thinly scattered sweets which have escaped the vigilance of their industry.

They were the same feelings, manners, and principles which conducted our venerable forefathers from the unhallowed shores of oppression; which inspired them with the sublime purpose of converting the forests of a wilderness into the favorite mansion of liberty, of unfolding the gates of a new world as a refuge for the victims of persecution in the old—the feelings of injured freedom, the manners of social equality, and the principles of eternal justice.

Had the sovereigns of England pursued the policy prescribed by their interest; had they not provoked the hostilities of their colonies against the feeble fortress of their authority; they might perhaps have retained to this day an empire which would have been but the more durable for resting only upon the foundation of immemorial custom and national affection.

Incumbered, however, with the oppressive glory of a successful war, which had enriched the pride of Britain with the spoils of her own opulence and replenished the arrogance in proportion as it had exhausted the resources of the nation, an adventurous ministry, catching at every desperate expedient to support the ponderous burden of the national dignity and stimulated by the perfidious instigations of their dependents in America, abandoned the profitable commercial policy of their predecessors, and superadded to the lucrative system of monopoly which we had always tolerated as the price of their protection a system of internal taxation from which they hoped to derive a fund for future corruption and a supply for future extravagance.

The nation eagerly grasped at the proposal. The situation, the condition, the sentiments of the colonies were subjects upon which the people of Britain were divided between ignorance and error. The endearing ties of consanguinity, which had connected their ancestors with those of the Americans, had been gradually loosened to the verge of dissolution by the slow but ceaseless hand of time. Instead of returning the sentiments of fraternal affection which animated the Americans, they indulged their vanity with preposterous opinions of insulting superiority;

they considered us, not as fellow-subjects, equally entitled with themselves to every privilege of Englishmen, but as wretched outcasts, upon whom they might safely load the burden while they reserved to themselves the advantages of the national grandeur. It has been observed that nations most highly favored with freedom have not always been the most friendly to the liberty of others. The people of Britain expected to feel none of the oppression which a parliamentary tyranny might impose upon the Americans; on the contrary, they expected an alleviation of their burden from the accumulation of ours, and vainly hoped that by the stripes inflicted upon us their wounds would be healed.

The king—need it be said that he adopted the offspring of his own affections, a plan so favorable to the natural propensity of royalty towards arbitrary power? Depending upon the prostituted valor of his mercenary legions, he was deaf to the complaints, he was inexorable to the remonstrances of violated freedom. Born and educated to the usual prejudices of hereditary dominion and habitually accustomed to the syren song of adulation, he was ready to believe what the courtly tribe about his throne did not fail to assure him—that complaint was nothing more than the murmur of sedition, and remonstrance the clamor of rebellion.

But they knew not the people with whom they had to contend. A people sagacious and enlightened to discern, cool and deliberate to discuss, firm and resolute to maintain their rights. From the first appearance of the system of parliamentary oppression under the form of a stamp-act, it was met by the determined opposition of the whole American continent. The annals of other nations have produced instances of successful struggles to break a yoke previously imposed; but the records of history did not, perhaps, furnish an example of a people whose penetration had anticipated the operations of tyranny, and whose spirit had disdained to suffer an experiment upon their liberties. The ministerial partizans had flattered themselves with the expectation that the Act would execute itself; that before the hands of freedom could be raised to repel the usurpation, they would be loaded with fetters; that the American Samson would be shorn of his locks while asleep, and, when thus bereaved of his strength, might be made their sport with impunity. Vain illusion! Instantaneous and forceful as an electric spark, the fervid spirit of resistance pervaded every part of the country; and at the moment when the operation of the system was intended to commence, it was indignantly rejected by three millions of men; high-minded men, determined to sacrifice their existence rather than resign the liberty from which all its enjoyments were derived.

It is unnecessary to pursue the detail of obstinacy and cruelty on the one part, of perseverance and fortitude on the other, until the period when every cord which had bound the two countries together was destroyed by the violence of reciprocal hostilities, and the representatives of America adopted the measure which was already dictated by the wishes of their constituents; they declared the United Colonies free, sovereign, and independent States.

Americans! let us pause for a moment to consider the situation of our country at that eventful day when our national existence commenced. In the full possession and enjoyment of all those prerogatives for which you then dared to adventure upon "all the varieties of untried being," the calm and settled moderation of the mind is scarcely competent to conceive the tone of heroism to which the souls of freemen were exalted in that hour of perilous magnanimity. Seventeen times has the sun, in the progress of his annual revolutions, diffused his prolific radiance over the plains of independent America. Millions of hearts, which then palpitated with the rapturous glow of patriotism have already been translated to brighter worlds—to the abodes of more than mortal freedom. Other millions have arisen to receive from their parents and benefactors the inestimable recompense of their achievements. A large proportion of the audience whose benevolence is at this moment listening to the speaker of the day, like him were at that period too little advanced beyond the threshold of life to partake of the divine enthusiasm which inspired the American bosom; which prompted her voice to proclaim defiance to the thunders of Britain; which consecrated the banners of her armies, and finally erected the holy temple of American liberty over the tomb of departed tyranny. It is from those who have already passed the meridian of life, it is from you, ye venerable asserters of the rights of mankind, that we are to be informed what were the feelings which swayed within your breasts and impelled you to action when, like the stripling of Israel, with scarce a weapon to attack and without a shield for your defence, you met and undismayed engaged with the greatness of the British power. Untutored in the disgraceful science of human butchery; destitute of the fatal materials which the ingenuity of man has combined to sharpen the scythe of death; unsupported by the arm of any friendly alliance, and unfortified against the powerful assaults of an unrelenting enemy, you did not hesitate at that moment when your coasts were infested by a formidable fleet, when your territories were invaded by a numerous and veteran army, to pronounce the sentence of eternal separation from Britain, and to throw the gauntlet to a power, the terror of whose recent triumphs was almost coextensive with the earth. The interested and selfish propensities which in times of prosperous tranquillity have such powerful dominion over the heart were all expelled; and, in their stead, the public virtues, the spirit of personal devotion to the common cause, a contempt of every danger in comparison with the subserviency of the country, had assumed an unlimited control. The passion for the republic had absorbed all the rest, as the glorious luminary of heaven extinguishes in a flood of refulgence the twinkling splendor of every inferior planet. Those of you, my countrymen, who were actors in those interesting scenes will best know how feeble and impotent is the language of this description to express the impassioned emotions of the soul with which you were then agitated; yet it were injustice to conclude from thence, or from the greater prevalence of private and personal motives in these days of calm serenity, that your sons have degenerated from the virtues of their fathers. Let it rather be a subject of pleasing reflection to you that the generous and disinterested energies which you were summoned to display are permitted by the bountiful indulgence of Heaven to remain latent in the bosoms of your children. From the present prosperous appearance of our public affairs, we may admit a rational hope that our country will have no occasion to require of us those extraordinary and heroic exertions which it was your fortune to exhibit. But, from the common versatility of all human destiny, should the prospect hereafter darken and the clouds of public misfortune thicken to a tempest, should the voice of our country's calamity ever call us to her relief, we swear by the precious memory of the sages who toiled and of the heroes who bled in her defence that we will prove ourselves not unworthy the prize which they so dearly purchased, that we will act as the faithful disciples of those who so magnanimously taught us the instructive lesson of republican virtue.

Seven years of ineffectual hostility, a hundred millions of treasure fruitlessly expended, and uncounted thousands of human lives sacrificed to no purpose at length taught the dreadful lesson of wisdom to the British Government, and compelled them to relinquish a claim which they had long since been unable to maintain. The pride of Britain, which should have been humbled, was only mortified. With sullen impotence, she yielded to the pressure of accumulated calamity and closed with reluctance an inglorious war, in which she had often been the object, and rarely the actor, of a triumph.

The various occurrences of our national history since that period are within the recollection of all my hearers. The relaxation and debility of the political body which succeeded the violent exertions it had made during the war; the total inefficacy of the recommendatory federal system, which had been formed in the bosom of contention; the peaceable and deliberate adoption of a more effectual national Constitution by the people, of the Union, and the prosperous administration of that government, which has repaired the shattered fabric of public confidence, which has strengthened the salutary bands of national union and restored the bloom and vigor of impartial justice to the public countenance, afford a subject of pleasing contemplation to the patriotic mind. The repeated unanimity of the nation has placed at the head of the American councils the heroic leader whose prudence and valor conducted to victory the armies of freedom; and the two first offices of the commonwealth still exhibit the virtues and employ the talents of the venerable patriots,* whose firm and disinterested devotion to the cause of liberty was rewarded by the honorable distinction of a British proscription. Americans! the voice of grateful freedom is a stranger to the language of adulation. While we wish these illustrious sages to be assured that the memory of their services is impressed upon all our hearts in characters indelible to the latest period of time, we trust that the most acceptable tribute of respect which can be offered to their virtues is found in the confidence of their countrymen. From the fervent admiration of future ages, when the historians of America shall trace from their examples the splendid pattern of public virtue, their merits will receive a recompense of much more precious estimation than can be conferred by the most flattering testimonials of contemporaneous applause.

The magnitude and importance of the great event which we commemorate derives a vast accession from its influence upon the affairs of the world and its operation upon the history of mankind. It has already been observed that the origin of the American Revolution bears a character different from that of any other civil contest that has ever arisen among men. It was not the convulsive struggle of slavery to throw off the burden of accumulated oppression, but the deliberate, though energetic, effort of freemen to repel the insidious approaches of tyranny. It was a contest involving the elementary principles of government—a question of right between the sovereign and the subject, which in its progress had a tendency to introduce among the civilized nations of Europe the discussion of a topic, the first in magnitude which can attract the attention of mankind, but which for many centuries the gloomy shades of despotism had overspread with impenetrable darkness. The French nation cheerfully supported an alliance with the United States and a war with Britain, during the course of which a large body of troops and considerable fleets were sent by the French Government to act in conjunction with their new allies. The union, which had at first been formed by the coalescence of a common enmity, was soon strengthened by the bonds of a friendly intercourse, and the subjects of an arbitrary prince, in fighting the battles of freedom, soon learned to cherish the cause of liberty itself. By a natural and easy application to themselves of the principles upon which the Americans asserted the justice of their warfare, they were led to inquire into the nature of the obligation which prescribed their submission to their own sovereign; and when

---

* John Hancock and Samuel Adams.

they discovered that the consent of the people is the only legitimate source of authority, they necessarily drew the conclusion that their own obedience was no more than the compulsive acquiescence of servitude, and they waited only for a favorable opportunity to recover the possession of those enjoyments to which they had never forfeited the right. Sentiments of a similar nature, by a gradual and imperceptible progress, secretly undermined all the foundations of their government; and when the necessities of the sovereign reduced him to the inevitable expedient of appealing to the benevolence of the people, the magic talisman of despotism was broken, the spell of prescriptive tyranny was dissolved, and the pompous pageant of their monarchy instantaneously crumbled to atoms.

The subsequent European events, which have let slip the dogs of war to prey upon the vitals of humanity; which have poured the torrent of destruction over the fairest harvests of European fertility; which have unbound the pinions of desolation, and sent her forth to scatter pestilence and death among the nations; the scaffold smoking with the blood of a fallen monarch; the corpse-covered field, where agonized nature struggles with the pangs of dissolution—permit me, my happy countrymen, to throw a pall over objects like these, which could only spread a gloom upon the face of our festivity. Let us rather indulge the pleasing and rational anticipation of the period when all the nations of Europe shall partake of the blessings of equal liberty and universal peace. Whatever issue may be destined by the will of Heaven to await the termination of the present European commotions, the system of feudal absurdity has received an irrevocable wound, and every symptom indicates its approaching dissolution. The seeds of liberty are plentifully sown. However severe the climate, however barren the soil, of the regions in which they have been received, such is the native exuberance of the plant that it must eventually flourish with luxuriant profusion. The governments of Europe must fall; and the only remaining expedient in their power is to gather up their garments and fall with decency. The bonds of civil subjection must be loosened by the discretion of civil authority, or they will be shivered by the convulsive efforts of slavery itself. The feelings of benevolence involuntarily make themselves a party to every circumstance that can affect the happiness of mankind; they are ever ready to realize the sanguine hope that the governments to rise upon the ruins of the present system will be immutably founded upon the principles of freedom and administered by the genuine maxims of moral subordination and political equality. We cherish, with a fondness which cannot be chilled by the cold, unanimated philosophy of scepticism, the delightful expectation that the cancer of arbitrary power will be radically extracted from the human constitution ; that the passions which have hitherto made the misery of mankind will be disarmed of all their violence and give place to the soft control of mild and amiable sentiments, which shall unite in social harmony the innumerable varieties of the human race. Then shall the nerveless arm of superstition no longer interpose an impious barrier between the beneficence of Heaven and the adoration of its votaries; then shall the most distant regions of the earth be approximated by the gentle attraction of a liberal intercourse ; then shall the fair fabric of universal liberty rise upon the durable foundation of social equality; and the long-expected era of human felicity, which has been announced by prophetic inspiration and described in the most enraptured language of the muses, shall commence its splendid progress. Visions of bliss! with every breath to Heaven we speed an ejaculation that the time may hasten when your reality shall be no longer the ground of votive supplication, but the theme of grateful acknowledgment; when the choral gratulations of the liberated myriads of the elder world, in symphony sweeter than the music of the spheres, shall hail your country, Americans, as the youngest daughter of Nature, and the first-born of Freedom!

George Washington

Farewell Address to the People of the United States

(From the Philadelphia Daily American Advertiser, *September 17, 1796)*

The period for a new election of a citizen to administer the executive government of the United States being not far distant, and the time actually arrived when your thoughts must be employed in designating the person who is to be clothed with that important trust, it appears to me proper, especially as it may conduce to a more distinct expression of the public voice, that I should now apprise you of the resolution I have formed, to decline being considered among the number of those out of whom the choice is to be made.

I beg you at the same time to do me the justice to be assured that this resolution has not been taken without a strict regard to all the considerations appertaining to the relation which binds a dutiful citizen to his country—and that, in withdrawing the tender of service which silence in my situation might imply, I am influenced by no diminution of zeal for your future interest, no deficiency of grateful respect for your past kindness, but am supported by a full conviction that the step is compatible with both.

The acceptance of, and continuance hitherto in, the office to which your suffrages have twice called me have been a uniform sacrifice of inclination to the opinion of duty and to a deference for what appeared to be your desire. I constantly hoped that it would have been much earlier in my power, consistently with motives which I was not at liberty to disregard, to return to that retirement from which I had been reluctantly drawn. The strength of my inclination to do this, previous to the last election, had even led to the preparation of an address to declare it to you; but mature reflection on the then perplexed and critical posture of our affairs with foreign nations, and the unanimous advice of persons entitled to my confidence, impelled me to abandon the idea.

I rejoice that the state of your concerns, external as well as internal, no longer renders the pursuit of inclination incompatible with the sentiment of duty or propriety and am persuaded, whatever partiality may be retained for my services, that in the present circumstances of our country you will not disapprove of my determination to retire.

The impressions with which I first undertook the arduous trust were explained on the proper occasion. In the discharge of this trust, I will only say that I have, with good intentions, contributed towards the organization and administration of the government the best exertions of which a very fallible judgment was capable. Not unconscious in the outset of the inferiority of my qualifications, experience in my own eyes, perhaps still more in the eyes of others, has strengthened the motives to diffidence of myself, and every day the increasing weight of years admonishes me more and more that the shade of retirement is as necessary to me as it will be welcome. Satisfied that if any circumstances have given peculiar value to my services, they were temporary, I have the consolation to believe that, while choice and prudence invite me to quit the political scene, patriotism does not forbid it.

In looking forward to the moment which is intended to terminate the career of my political life, my feelings do not permit me to suspend the deep acknowledgment of that debt of gratitude which I owe to my beloved country for the many honors it has conferred upon me; still more for the steadfast confidence with which it has supported me, and for the opportunities I have thence enjoyed of manifesting my inviolable attachment by services faithful and persevering, though in usefulness unequal to my zeal. If benefits have resulted to our country from these services, let it always be remembered to your praise and as an instructive example in our annals that, under circumstances in which the passions agitated in every direction were liable to mislead, amidst appearances sometimes dubious, vicissitudes of fortune often discouraging, in situations in which not unfrequently want of success has countenanced the spirit of criticism, the constancy of your support was the essential prop of the efforts and a guarantee of the plans by which they were effected. Profoundly penetrated with this idea, I shall carry it with me to my grave as a strong incitement to unceasing vows that Heaven may continue to you the choicest tokens of its beneficence; that your union and brotherly affection may be perpetual; that the free constitution, which is the work of your hands, may be sacredly maintained; that its administration in every department may be stamped with wisdom and virtue; that, in fine, the happiness of the people of these states, under the auspices of liberty, may be made complete by so careful a preservation and so prudent a use of this blessing as will acquire to them the glory of recommending it to the applause, the affection, and adoption, of every nation which is yet a stranger to it.

Here, perhaps, I ought to stop. But a solicitude for your welfare, which can not end but with my life, and the apprehension of danger natural to that solicitude, urge me on an occasion like the present to offer to your solemn contemplation, and to recommend to your frequent review, some sentiments which are the result of much reflection, of no inconsiderable observation, and which appear to me all important to the permanency of your felicity as a people. These will be offered to you with the more freedom as you can only see in them the disinterested warnings of a parting friend, who can possibly have no personal motive to bias his counsel. Nor can I forget, as an encouragement to it, your indulgent reception of my sentiments on a former and not dissimilar occasion.

Interwoven as is the love of liberty with every ligament of your hearts, no recommendation of mine is necessary to fortify or confirm the attachment.

The unity of government which constitutes you one people is also now dear to you. It is justly so; for it is a main pillar in the edifice of your real independence, the support of your tranquillity at home, your peace abroad, of your safety, of your prosperity, of that very liberty which you so highly prize. But as it is easy to foresee that, from different causes and from different quarters, much pains will be taken, many artifices employed, to weaken in your minds the conviction of this truth; as this is the point in your political fortress against which the batteries of internal and external enemies will be most constantly and actively (though often covertly and insidiously) directed, it is of infinite moment that you should properly estimate the immense value of your national Union to your collective and individual happiness; that you should cherish a cordial, habitual, and immovable attachment to it; accustoming yourselves to think and to speak of it as of the palladium of your political safety and prosperity; watching for its preservation with jealous anxiety; discountenancing whatever may suggest even a suspicion that it can in any event be abandoned; and indignantly frowning upon the first dawning of every attempt to alienate any portion of our country from the rest, or to enfeeble the sacred ties which now link together the various parts.

For this you have every inducement of sympathy and interest. Citizens by birth or choice of a common country, that country has a right to concentrate your affections. The name of American, which belongs to you in your national capacity, must always exalt the just pride of patriotism more than any appellation derived from local discriminations. With slight shades of difference, you have the same religion, manners, habits, and political principles. You have in a common cause fought and triumphed together. The independence and liberty you possess are the work of joint councils and joint efforts—of common dangers, sufferings, and successes.

But these considerations, however powerfully they address themselves to your sensibility, are greatly outweighed by those which apply more immediately to your interest. Here every portion of our country finds the most commanding motives for carefully guarding and preserving the Union of the whole.

The *North,* in an unrestrained intercourse with the *South,* protected by the equal laws of a common government, finds in the productions of the latter great additional resources of maritime and commercial enterprise and precious materials of manufacturing industry. The *South* in the same intercourse, benefitting by the same agency of the *North,* sees its agriculture grow and its commerce expand. Turning partly into its own channels the seamen of the *North,* it finds its particular navigation invigorated; and while it contributes, in different ways, to nourish and increase the general mass of the national navigation, it looks forward to the protection of a maritime strength to which itself is unequally adapted. The *East,* in like intercourse with the *West,* already finds, and in the progressive improvement of interior communications by land and water will more and more find a valuable vent for the commodities which it brings from abroad or manufactures at home. The *West* derives from the *East* supplies requisite to its growth and comfort—and what is perhaps of still greater consequence, it must of necessity owe the *secure* enjoyment of the indispensable *outlets* for its own productions to the weight, influence, and future maritime strength of the Atlantic side of the Union, directed by an indissoluble community of interest, as *one nation.* Any other tenure by which the *West* can hold this essential advantage, whether derived from its own separate strength or from an apostate and unnatural connection with any foreign power, must be intrinsically precarious.

While then every part of our country thus feels an immediate and particular interest in union, all the parts combined cannot fail to find in the united mass of means and efforts greater strength, greater resource, proportionably greater security from external danger, a less frequent interruption of their peace by foreign nations; and, what is of inestimable value! they must derive from union an exemption from those broils and wars between themselves which so frequently afflict neighboring countries not tied together by the same government, which their own rivalships alone would be sufficient to produce, but which opposite foreign alliances, attachments, and intrigues, would stimulate and embitter. Hence likewise they will avoid the necessity of those overgrown military establishments, which under any form of government are inauspicious to liberty, and which are to be regarded as particularly hostile to republican liberty. In this sense it is, that your Union ought to be considered as a main prop of your liberty, and that the love of the one ought to endear to you the preservation of the other.

These considerations speak a persuasive language to every reflecting and virtuous mind and exhibit the continuance of the Union as a primary object of patriotic desire. Is there a doubt whether a common government can embrace so large a sphere? Let experience solve it. To listen to mere speculation in such a case were criminal. We are authorized to hope that a proper organization of the whole, with the auxiliary agency of governments for the respective subdivisions, will afford a happy issue to the experiment. It is well worth a fair and full experiment. With such powerful and obvious motives to union affecting all parts of our country, while experience shall not have demonstrated its impracticability, there will always be reason to distrust the patriotism of those who in any quarter may endeavor to weaken its bands.

In contemplating the causes which may disturb our Union, it occurs as matter of serious concern that any ground should have been furnished for characterizing parties by *geographical discriminations—northern* and *southern, Atlantic* and *western;* whence designing men may endeavor to excite a belief that there is a real difference of local interests and views. One of the expedients of party to acquire influence within particular districts is to misrepresent the opinions and aims of other districts. You cannot shield yourselves too much against the jealousies and heartburnings which spring from these misrepresentations. They tend to render alien to each other those who ought to be bound together by fraternal affection. The inhabitants of our western country have lately had a useful lesson on this head. They have seen in the negotiation by the executive—and in the unanimous ratification by the Senate of the treaty with Spain, and in the universal satisfaction at that event throughout the United States, a decisive proof how unfounded were the suspicions propagated among them of a policy in the general government and in the Atlantic states unfriendly to their interests in regard to the Mississippi. They have been witnesses to the formation of two treaties, that with Great Britain and that with Spain, which secure to them everything they could desire, in respect to our foreign relations, towards confirming their prosperity. Will it not be their wisdom to rely for the preservation of these advantages on the Union by which they were procured? Will they not henceforth be deaf to those advisers, if such there are, who would sever them from their brethren and connect them with aliens?

To the efficacy and permanency of your Union, a government for the whole is indispensable. No alliances, however strict, between the parts can be an adequate substitute. They must inevitably experience the infractions and interruptions which alliances in all times have experienced. Sensible of this momentous truth, you have improved upon your first essay by the adoption of a Constitution of government better calculated than your former for an intimate Union and for the efficacious management of your common concerns. This government, the offspring of our own choice uninfluenced and unawed, adopted upon full investigation and mature deliberation, completely free in its principles, in the distribution of its powers uniting security with energy, and containing within itself a provision for its own amendment, has a just claim to your confidence and your support. Respect for its authority, compliance with its laws, acquiescence in its measures, are duties enjoined by the fundamental maxims of true liberty. The basis of our political system is the right of the people to make and to alter their constitutions of government. But the Constitution which at any time exists, until changed by an explicit and authentic act of the whole people, is sacredly obligatory upon all. The very idea of the power and the right of the people to establish government presupposes the duty of every individual to obey the established government.

All obstructions to the execution of the laws, all combinations and associations under whatever plausible character with the real design to direct, control, counteract, or awe the regular deliberation and action of the constituted authorities, are destructive of this fundamental principle and of fatal tendency. They serve to organize faction; to give it an artificial and extraordinary force; to put in the place of the delegated will of the nation the will of a party, often a small but artful and enterprising minority of the community; and, according to the alternate triumphs of different parties, to make the public administration the mirror of the ill concerted and incongruous projects of faction, rather than the organ of consistent and wholesome plans digested by common councils and modified by mutual interests. However combinations or associations of the above description may now and then answer popular ends, they are likely, in the course of time and things, to become potent engines by which cunning, ambitious, and unprincipled men will be enabled to subvert the power of the people and to usurp for themselves the reins of government, destroying afterward the very engines which have lifted them to unjust dominion.

Towards the preservation of your government and the permanency of your present happy state, it is requisite not only that you steadily discountenance irregular opposition to its acknowledged authority, but also that you resist with care the spirit of innovation upon its principles, however specious the pretexts. One method of assault may be to effect in the forms of the Constitution alterations which will impair the energy of the system and thus to undermine what cannot be directly overthrown. In all the changes to which you may be invited, remember that time and habit are at least as necessary to fix the true character of governments as of other human institutions, that experience is the surest standard by which to test the real tendency of the existing constitution of a country, that facility in changes upon the credit of mere hypotheses and opinion exposes to perpetual change from the endless variety of hypotheses and opinion; and remember, especially, that for the efficient management of your common interests in a country so extensive as ours, a government of as much vigor as is consistent with the perfect security of liberty is indispensable; liberty itself will find in such a government, with powers properly distributed and adjusted, its surest guardian. It is indeed little else than a name, where the government is too feeble to withstand the enterprises of faction, to confine each member of society within the limits prescribed by the laws, and to maintain all in the secure and tranquil enjoyment of the rights of person and property.

I have already intimated to you the danger of parties in the state, with particular reference to the founding of them upon geographical discriminations. Let me now take a more comprehensive view and warn you in the most solemn manner against the baneful effects of the spirit of party, generally.

This spirit, unfortunately, is inseparable from our nature, having its root in the strongest passions of the human mind. It exists under different shapes in all governments, more or less stifled, controlled, or repressed; but in those of the popular form, it is seen in its greatest rankness and is truly their worst enemy.

The alternate domination of one faction over another, sharpened by the spirit of revenge natural to party dissension, which in different ages and countries has perpetrated the most horrid enormities, is itself a frightful despotism. But this leads at length to a more formal and permanent despotism. The disorders and miseries which result gradually incline the minds of men to seek security and repose in the absolute power of an individual; and sooner or later the chief of some prevailing faction, more able or more fortunate than his competitors, turns this disposition to the purposes of his own elevation on the ruins of public liberty.

Without looking forward to an extremity of this kind (which nevertheless ought not to be entirely out of sight) the common and continual mischiefs of the spirit of party are sufficient to make it the interest and the duty of a wise people to discourage and restrain it.

It serves always to distract the public councils and enfeeble the public administration. It agitates the community with ill founded jealousies and false alarms, kindles the animosity of one part against another, foments occasional riot and insurrection. It opens the door to foreign influence and corruption, which finds a facilitated access to the government itself through the channels of party passion. Thus the policy and the will of one country are subjected to the policy and will of another.

There is an opinion that parties in free countries are useful checks upon the administration of the government and serve to keep alive the spirit of liberty. This within certain limits is probably true—and in governments of a monarchical cast patriotism may look with indulgence, if not with favor, upon the spirit of party. But in those of the popular character, in governments purely elective, it is a spirit not to be encouraged. From their natural tendency, it is certain there will always be enough of that spirit for every salutary purpose. And there being constant danger of excess, the effort ought to be by force of public opinion to mitigate and assuage it. A fire not to be quenched, it demands a uniform vigilance to prevent its bursting into a flame, lest instead of warming it should consume.

It is important, likewise, that the habits of thinking in a free country should inspire caution in those intrusted with its administration to confine themselves within their respective constitutional spheres, avoiding in the exercise of the powers of one department to encroach upon another. The spirit of encroachment tends to consolidate the powers of all the departments in one and thus to create, whatever the form of government, a real despotism. A just estimate of that love of power and proneness to abuse it which predominates in the human heart is sufficient to satisfy us of the truth of this position. The necessity of reciprocal checks in the exercise of political power, by dividing and distributing it into different depositories and constituting each the guardian of the public weal against invasions by the others, has been evinced by experiments ancient and modern, some of them in our country and under our own eyes. To preserve them must be as necessary as to institute them. If in the opinion of the people the distribution or modification of the constitutional powers be in any particular wrong, let it be corrected by an amendment in the way in which the Constitution designates. But let there be no change by usurpation; for though this, in one instance, may be the instrument of good, it is the customary weapon by which free governments are destroyed. The precedent must always greatly overbalance in permanent evil any partial or transient benefit which the use can at any time yield.

Of all the dispositions and habits which lead to political prosperity, religion and morality are indispensable supports. In vain would that man claim the tribute of patriotism who should labor to subvert these great pillars of human happiness, these firmest props of the duties of men and citizens. The mere politician, equally with the pious man, ought to respect and to cherish them. A volume could not trace all their connections with private and public felicity. Let it be simply asked where is the security for property, for reputation, for life, if the sense of religious obligation *desert* the oaths which are the instruments of investigation in courts of justice? And let us with caution indulge the supposition that morality can be maintained without religion. Whatever may be conceded to the influence of refined education on minds of peculiar structure, reason and experience both forbid us to expect that national morality can prevail in exclusion of religious principles.

It is substantially true that virtue or morality is a necessary spring of popular government. The rule indeed extends with more or less force to every species of free government. Who that is a sincere friend to it can look with indifference upon attempts to shake the foundation of the fabric?

Promote then, as an object of primary importance, institutions for the general diffusion of knowledge. In proportion as the structure of a government gives force to public opinion, it is essential that public opinion should be enlightened.

As a very important source of strength and security, cherish public credit. One method of preserving it is to use it as sparingly as possible, avoiding occasions of expense by cultivating peace, but remembering also that timely disbursements to prepare for danger frequently prevent much greater disbursements to repel it; avoiding likewise the accumulation of debt, not only by shunning occasions of expense, but by vigorous exertions in time of peace to discharge the debts which unavoidable wars have occasioned, not ungenerously throwing upon posterity the burden which we ourselves ought to bear. The execution of these maxims belongs to your representatives, but it is necessary that public opinion should cooperate. To facilitate to them the performance of their duty, it is essential you should practically bear in mind that towards the payment of debts there must be revenue; that to have revenue there must be taxes; that no taxes can be devised which are not more or less inconvenient and unpleasant; that the intrinsic embarrassment inseparable from the selection of the proper objects (which is always a choice of difficulties) ought to be a decisive motive for a candid construction of the conduct of the government in making it, and for a spirit of acquiescence in the measures for obtaining revenue which the public exigencies may at any time dictate.

Observe good faith and justice towards all nations; cultivate peace and harmony with all; religion and morality enjoin this conduct; and can it be that good policy does not equally enjoin it? It will be worthy of a free, enlightened, and, at no distant period, a great nation, to give to mankind the magnanimous and too novel example of a people always guided by an exalted justice and benevolence. Who can doubt that in the course of time and things the fruits of such a plan would richly repay any temporary advantages which might be lost by a steady adherence to it? Can it be, that Providence has connected the permanent felicity of a nation with its virtue? The experiment, at least, is recommended by every sentiment which ennobles human nature. Alas! is it rendered impossible by its vices?

In the execution of such a plan nothing is more essential than that permanent, inveterate antipathies against particular nations and passionate attachments for others should be excluded and that in place of them just and amicable feelings towards all should be cultivated. The nation which indulges towards another an habitual hatred, or an habitual fondness, is in some degree a slave. It is a slave to its animosity or to its affection, either of which is sufficient to lead it astray from its duty and its interest. Antipathy in one nation against another disposes each more readily to offer insult and injury, to lay hold of slight causes of umbrage, and to be haughty and intractable when accidental or trifling occasions of dispute occur. Hence, frequent collisions, obstinate, envenomed, and bloody contests. The nation, prompted by ill will and resentment, sometimes impels to war the government, contrary to the best calculations of policy. The government sometimes participates in the national propensity and adopts through passion what reason would reject; at other times, it makes the animosity of the nation subservient to projects of hostility instigated by pride, ambition, and other sinister and pernicious motives. The peace often, sometimes perhaps the liberty, of nations has been the victim.

So likewise, a passionate attachment of one nation for another produces a variety of evils. Sympathy for the favorite nation, facilitating the illusion of an imaginary common interest in cases where no real common interest exists and infusing into one the enmities of the other, betrays the former into a participation in the quarrels and the wars of the latter, without adequate inducements or justification. It leads also to concessions to the favorite nation of privileges denied to others, which is apt doubly to injure the nation making the concessions, by unnecessarily parting with what ought to have been retained and by exciting jealousy, ill will, and a disposition to retaliate in the parties from whom equal privileges are withheld. And it gives to ambitious, corrupted, or deluded citizens (who devote themselves to the favorite nation) facility to betray or sacrifice the interests of their own country without odium, sometimes even with popularity, gilding with the appearances of a virtuous sense of obligation, a commendable deference for public opinion, or a laudable zeal for public good, the base or foolish compliances of ambition, corruption, or infatuation.

As avenues to foreign influence in innumerable ways, such attachments are particularly alarming to the truly enlightened and independent patriot. How many opportunities do they afford to tamper with domestic factions, to practice the arts of seduction, to mislead public opinion, to influence or awe the public councils! Such an attachment of a small or weak nation towards a great and powerful nation dooms the former to be the satellite of the latter.

Against the insidious wiles of foreign influence (I conjure you to believe me, fellow-citizens), the jealousy of a free people ought to be constantly awake, since history and experience prove that foreign influence is one of the most baneful foes of republican government. But that jealousy to be useful must be impartial; else it becomes the instrument of the very influence to be avoided, instead of a defense against it. Excessive partiality for one foreign nation and excessive dislike of another cause those whom they actuate to see danger only on one side, and serve to veil and even second the arts of influence on the other. Real patriots, who may resist the intrigues of the favorite, are liable to become suspected and odious, while its tools and dupes usurp the applause and confidence of the people to surrender their interests.

The great rule of conduct for us in regard to foreign nations is, in extending our commercial relations, to have with them as little political connection as possible. So far as we have already formed engagements, let them be fulfilled with perfect good faith. Here let us stop.

Europe has a set of primary interests, which to us have none or a very remote relation. Hence she must be engaged in frequent controversies, the causes of which are essentially foreign to our concerns. Hence therefore it must be unwise in us to implicate ourselves, by artificial ties, in the ordinary vicissitudes of her politics, or the ordinary combinations and collisions of her friendships or enmities.

Our detached and distant situation invites and enables us to pursue a different course. If we remain one people under an efficient government, the period is not far off when we may defy material injury from external annoyance; when we may take such an attitude as will cause the neutrality we may at any time resolve upon to be scrupulously respected; when belligerent nations, under the impossibility of making acquisitions upon us, will not lightly hazard the giving us provocation; when we may choose peace or war, as our interest guided by justice shall counsel.

Why forgo the advantages of so peculiar a situation? Why quit our own to stand upon foreign ground? Why, by interweaving our destiny with that of any part of Europe, entangle our peace and prosperity in the toils of European ambition, rivalship, interest, humor, or caprice?

It is our true policy to steer clear of permanent alliances with any portion of the foreign world—so far, I mean, as we are now at liberty to do it, for let me not be understood as capable of patronizing infidelity to existing engagements (I hold the maxim no less applicable to public than to private affairs, that honesty is always the best policy)—I repeat it therefore, let those engagements be observed in their genuine sense. But in my opinion it is unnecessary and would be unwise to extend them.

Taking care always to keep ourselves, by suitable establishments, on a respectable defensive posture, we may safely trust to temporary alliances for extraordinary emergencies.

Harmony, liberal intercourse with all nations, are recommended by policy, humanity, and interest. But even our commercial policy should hold an equal and impartial hand: neither seeking nor granting exclusive favors or preferences; consulting the natural course of things; diffusing and diversifying by gentle means the stream of commerce but forcing nothing; establishing with powers so disposed—in order to give trade a stable course, to define the rights of our merchants, and to enable the government to support them—conventional rules of intercourse, the best that present circumstances and mutual opinion will permit, but temporary, and liable to be from time to time abandoned or varied, as experience and circumstances shall dictate; constantly keeping in view, that it is folly in one nation to look for disinterested favors from another—that it must pay with a portion of its independence for whatever it may accept under that character—that by such acceptance it may place itself in the condition of giving equivalents for nominal favors and yet of being reproached with ingratitude for not having given more. There can be no greater error than to expect or calculate upon real favors from nation to nation. It is an illusion which experience must cure, which a just pride ought to discard.

In offering to you, my countrymen, these counsels of an old and affectionate friend, I dare not hope they will make the strong and lasting impression I could wish—that they will control the usual current of the passions or prevent our nation from running the course which has hitherto marked the destiny of nations. But if I may even flatter myself that they may be productive of some partial benefit, some occasional good, that they may now and then recur to moderate the fury of party spirit, to warn against the mischiefs of foreign intrigue, to guard against the impostures of pretended patriotism—this hope will be a full recompense for the solicitude for your welfare by which they have been dictated.

How far in the discharge of my official duties I have been guided by the principles which have been delineated, the public records and the other evidences of my conduct must witness to you and to the world. To myself, the assurance of my own conscience is that I have at least believed myself to be guided by them.

In relation to the still subsisting war in Europe, my proclamation of the 22d of April 1793 is the index to my plan. Sanctioned by your approving voice and by that of your representatives in both houses of Congress, the spirit of that measure has continually governed me, uninfluenced by any attempts to deter or divert me from it.

After deliberate examination with the aid of the best lights I could obtain, I was well satisfied that our country, under all the circumstances of the case, had a right to take—and was bound in duty and interest to take—a neutral position. Having taken it, I determined, as far as should depend upon me, to maintain it with moderation, perseverance, and firmness.

The considerations which respect the right to hold this conduct it is not necessary on this occasion to detail. I will only observe that, according to my understanding of the matter, that right, so far from being denied by any of the belligerent powers, has been virtually admitted by all.

The duty of holding a neutral conduct may be inferred, without anything more, from the obligation which justice and humanity impose on every nation, in cases in which it is free to act, to maintain inviolate the relations of peace and amity towards other nations.

The inducements of interest for observing that conduct will best be referred to your own reflections and experience. With me, a predominant motive has been to endeavor to gain time to our country to settle and mature its yet recent institutions and to progress without interruption to that degree of strength and constancy which is necessary to give it, humanly speaking, the command of its own fortunes.

Though in reviewing the incidents of my administration I am unconscious of intentional error, I am nevertheless too sensible of my defects not to think it probable that I may have committed many errors. Whatever they may be, I fervently beseech the Almighty to avert or mitigate the evils to which they may tend. I shall also carry with me the hope that my country will never cease to view them with indulgence and that, after forty-five years of my life dedicated to its service with an upright zeal, the faults of incompetent abilities will be consigned to oblivion, as myself must soon be to the mansions of rest.

Relying on its kindness in this as in other things, and actuated by that fervent love towards it which is so natural to a man who views in it the native soil of himself and his progenitors for several generations, I anticipate with pleasing expectation that retreat, in which I promise myself to realize without alloy the sweet enjoyment of partaking in the midst of my fellow citizens the benign influence of good laws under a free government—the ever favorite object of my heart, and the happy reward, as I trust, of our mutual cares, labors, and dangers.

Eulogy on George Washington

(Delivered in Philadelphia, Pennsylvania, December 26, 1799)

In obedience to your will, I rise your humble organ, with the hope of executing a part of the system of public mourning which you have been pleased to adopt, commemorative of the death of the most illustrious and most beloved personage this country has ever produced; and which, while it transmits to posterity your sense of the awful event, faintly represents your knowledge of the consummate excellence you so cordially honor.

Desperate indeed is any attempt on earth to meet correspondently this dispensation of Heaven; for, while with pious resignation we submit to the will of an all-gracious Providence, we can never cease lamenting in our finite view of Omnipotent Wisdom, the heart-rending privation for which our nation weeps. When the civilized world shakes to its centre; when every moment gives birth to strange and momentous changes; when our peaceful quarter of the globe, exempt as it happily has been from any share in the slaughter of the human race, may yet be compelled to abandon her pacific policy, and to risk the doleful casualties of war, what limit is there to the extent of our loss! None within the reach of my words to express; none which your feelings will not disavow.

The founder of our federate republic, our bulwark in war, our guide in peace, is no more. Oh that this was but questionable! Hope, the comforter of the wretched, would pour into our agonized hearts its balmy dew. But, alas! there is no hope for us: our Washington is removed forever. Possessing the stoutest frame, and purest mind, he had passed nearly to his sixty-eighth year, in the enjoyment of high health; when, habituated by his care of us to neglect himself, a slight cold, disregarded, became inconvenient on Friday, oppressive on Saturday, and, defying every medical interposition, before the morning of Sunday put an end to the best of men. An end did I say—his fame survives! bounded only by the limits of the earth, and by the extent of the human mind. He survives in our hearts, in the growing knowledge of our children, in the affection of the good throughout the world; and when our monuments shall be done away, when nations now existing shall be no more, when even our young and far-spreading empire shall have perished, still will our Washington's glory unfaded shine, and die not, until love of virtue cease on earth, or earth itself sink into chaos.

How, my fellow-citizens, shall I single to your grateful hearts his pre-eminent worth! Where shall I begin in opening to your view a character throughout sublime! Shall I speak of his warlike achievements, all springing from obedience to his country's will—all directed to his country's good!

Will you go with me to the banks of the Monongahela, to see your youthful Washington, supporting, in the dismal hour of Indian victory, the ill-fated Braddock, and saving, by his judgment and by his valor, the remains of a defeated army, pressed by the conquering savage foe? Or, when oppressed America, nobly resolving to risk her all in defence of her violated rights, he was elevated by the unanimous voice of Congress to the command of her armies? Will you follow him to the high grounds of Boston, where to an undisciplined, courageous, and virtuous yeomanry, his presence gave the stability of system, and infused the invincibility of love of country? Or shall I carry you to the painful scenes of Long Island, York Island, and New Jersey; when, combating superior and gallant armies, aided by powerful fleets, and led by chiefs high in the roll of fame, he stood the bulwark of our safety; undismayed by disaster; unchanged by change of fortune? Or will you view him in the precarious fields of Trenton, where deep gloom unnerving every arm, reigned triumphant through our thinned, worn down, unaided ranks, himself unmoved? Dreadful was the night it was about this time of winter—the storm raged—the Delaware, rolling furiously with floating ice, forbade the approach of man. Washington, self-collected, viewed the tremendous scene; his country called; unappalled by surrounding dangers, he passed to the hostile shore: he fought; he conquered. The morning sun cheered the American world. Our country rose on the event; and her dauntless chief, pursuing his blow, completed in the lawns of Princeton what his vast soul had conceived on the shores of Delaware.

Thence to the strong ground of Morristown he led his small but gallant band; and through an eventful winter, by the high efforts of his genius, whose matchless force was measurable only by the growth of difficulties, he held in check formidable hostile legions, conducted by a chief experienced in the art of war, and famed for his valor on the ever-memorable Heights of Abraham, where fell Wolfe, Montcalm, and since our much-lamented Montgomery, all covered with glory. In this fortunate interval, produced by his masterly conduct, our fathers, ourselves, animated by his resistless example, rallied around our country's standard, and continued to follow her beloved chief through the various and trying scenes to which the destinies of our Union led.

Who is there that has forgotten the vales of Brandywine, the fields of Germantown, or the plains of Monmouth? Every where present, wants of every kind obstructing, numerous and valiant armies encountering, himself a host, he assuaged our sufferings, limited our privations, and upheld our tottering republic. Shall I display to you the spread of the tire of his soul, by rehearsing the praises of the hero of Saratoga, and his much-loved compeer of the Carolinas? No; our Washington wears not borrowed glory. To Gates—to Green—he gave without reserve the applause due to their eminent merit; and long may the chiefs of Saratoga and of Eutaw receive the grateful respect of a grateful people.

Moving in his own orbit, he imparted heat and light to his most distant satellites; and combining the physical and moral force of all within his sphere, with irresistible weight he took his course, commiserating folly, disdaining vice, dismaying treason, and invigorating despondency, until the auspicious hour arrived; when, united with the intrepid forces of a potent and magnanimous ally, he brought to submission the since conqueror of India; thus finishing his long career of military glory with a lustre corresponding to his great name, and in this his last act of war affixing the seal of fate to our nation's birth.

To the horrid din of battle sweet peace succeeded; and our virtuous chief, mindful only of the common good, in a moment tempting personal aggrandizement, hushed the discontents of growing sedition, and surrendering his power into the hands from which he had received it, converted his sword into a plough-share, teaching an admiring world that to be truly great you must be truly good.

Were I to stop here, the picture would be incomplete, and the task imposed unfinished. Great as was our Washington in war, and much as did that greatness contribute to produce the American republic, it is not in war alone his pre-eminence stands conspicuous: his various talents combining all the capacities of the statesman with those of the soldier, fitted him alike to guide the councils and the armies of our nation. Scarcely had he rested from his martial toils, while his invaluable parental advice was still sounding in our ears, when he who had been our shield and our sword was called forth to act a loss splendid but a more important part.

Possessing a clear and penetrating mind, a strong and a sound judgment, calmness and temper for deliberation, with invincible firmness and perseverance in resolutions maturely formed, drawing information from all, acting from himself, with incorruptible integrity and unvarying patriotism; his own superiority and the public confidence alike marked him as the man designed by Heaven to lead in the great political as well as military events which have distinguished the era of his life.

The finger of an overruling Providence, pointing at Washington, was neither mistaken nor unobserved; when, to realize the vast hopes to which our revolution had given birth, a change of political system became indispensable.

How novel—how grand the spectacle! independent States stretched over an immense territory, and known only by common difficulty, clinging to their Union as the rock of their safety, deciding by frank comparison of their relative condition, to rear on that rock, under the guidance of reason, a common Government, through whose commanding protection, liberty and order, with their long train of blessings, should be safe to themselves, and the sure inheritance of their posterity.

This arduous task devolved on citizens selected by the people, from knowledge of their wisdom and confidence in their virtue. In this august assembly of sages and of patriots, Washington of course was found; and, as if acknowledged to be most wise, where all were wise, with one voice he was declared their chief. How well he merited this rare distinction, how faithful were the labors of himself and his compatriots, the work of their hands and our Union, strength and prosperity, the fruits of that work, best attest.

But to have essentially aided in presenting to his country this consummation of her hopes, neither satisfied the claims of his fellow-citizens on his talents, nor those duties which the possession of those talents imposed. Heaven had not infused into his mind such an uncommon share of its ethereal spirit to remain unemployed, nor bestowed on him his genius unaccompanied with the corresponding duty of devoting it to the common good. To have framed a constitution, was showing only, without realizing, the general happiness. This great work remained to be done, and America, steadfast in her preference, with one voice summoned her beloved Washington, unpractised as he was in the duties of civil administration, to execute this last act in the completion of the national felicity. obedient to her call, he assumed the high office with that self-distrust peculiar to his innate modesty, the constant attendant of pre-eminent virtue. What was the burst of joy through our anxious land on this exhilarating event is known to us all. The aged, the young, the brave, the fair, rivalled each other in demonstrations of their gratitude; and this high-wrought delightful scene was heightened in its effect, by the singular contest between the zeal of the bestowers, and the avoidance of the receiver of the honors bestowed. Commencing his administration, what heart is not charmed with the recollection of the pure and wise principles announced by himself, as the basis of his political life. He best understood the indissoluble union between virtue and happiness, between duty and advantage, between the genuine maxims of an honest and magnanimous policy, and the solid rewards of public prosperity and individual felicity: watching with an equal and comprehensive eye over this great assemblage of communities and interests, he laid the foundation of our national policy in the unerring immutable principles of morality, based on religion, exemplifying the pre-eminence of free Government, by all the attributes which win the affections of its citizens, or command the respect of the world.

O fortunatos nimium, sua si bona norint!

Leading through the complicated difficulties produced by previous obligations and conflicting interests, seconded by succeeding Houses of Congress, enlightened and patriotic, he surmounted all original obstructions, and brightened the path of our national felicity.

The Presidential term expiring, his solicitude to exchange exaltation for humility returned with a force increased with increase of age, and he had prepared his farewell address to his countrymen, proclaiming his intention, when the united interposition of all around him, enforced by the eventful prospects of the epoch, produced a further sacrifice of inclination to duty. The election of President followed; and Washington, by the unanimous vote of the nation, was called to resume the Chief Magistracy. What a wonderful fixture of confidence! Which attracts most our admiration—a people so correct, or a citizen combining an assemblage of talents forbidding rivalry, and stifling even envy itself? Such a nation ought to be happy; such a chief must be forever revered.

War, long menaced by the Indian tribes, now broke out; and the terrible conflict, deluging Europe with blood, began to shed its baneful influence over our happy land. To the first, outstretching his invincible arm, under the orders of the gallant Wayne, the American eagle soared triumphant through distant forests. Peace followed victory, and the melioration of the condition of the enemy followed peace. Godlike virtue, which uplifts even the subdued savage.

To the second he opposed himself. New and delicate was the conjuncture, and great was the stake. Soon did his penetrating mind discern and seize the only course; continuing to us all the felicity enjoyed. He issued his proclamation of neutrality. This index to his whole subsequent conduct was sanctioned by the approbation of both Houses of Congress, and by the approving voice of the people.

To this sublime policy he inviolably adhered, unmoved by foreign intrusion, unshaken by domestic turbulence.

Justum et tenacem propositi virum,
Non civium ardor prava jubentium,
Non vultus instantis tyranni,
Mente quatit solida.

Maintaining his pacific system at the expense of no duty, America, faithful to herself and unstained in her honor, continued to enjoy the delights of peace, while afflicted Europe mourns in every quarter, under the accumulated miseries of an unexampled war; miseries in which our happy country must have shared, had not our pro-eminent Washington been as firm in council as he was brave in the field.

Pursuing steadfastly his course, he held safe the public happiness, preventing foreign war, and quelling internal discord, till the revolving period of a third election approached, when he executed his interrupted but inextinguishable desire of returning to the humble walks of private life.

The promulgation of his fixed resolution stopped the anxious wishes of an affectionate people from adding a third unanimous testimonial of their unabated confidence in the man so long enthroned in their hearts. When, before, was affection like this exhibited on earth? Turn over the records of ancient Greece—review the annals of mighty Rome—examine the volumes of modern Europe—you search in vain. America and her Washington only afford the dignified exemplification.

The illustrious personage called by the national voice in succession to the arduous office of guiding a free people, had new difficulties to encounter; the amicable effort of settling our difficulties with France, begun by Washington, and pursued by his successor in virtue as in station, proving abortive, America took measures of self-defence. No sooner was the public mind roused by prospect of danger, than every eye was turned to the friend of all, though secluded from public view, and grey in public service; the virtuous veteran, following his plough, it received the unexpected summons with mingled emotions of indignation at the unmeritcd ill-treatment of his country, and of a determination once more to risk his all in her defence.

The annunciation of these feelings, in his affecting letter to the President accepting the command of the army, concludes his official conduct.

First in war—first in peace—and first in the hearts of his countrymen, he was second to none in the humble and endearing scenes of private life; pious, just, humane, temperate, and sincere; uniform, dignified, and commanding; his example was as edifying to all around him, as were the effects of that example lasting.

To his equals he was condescending, to his inferiors kind, and to the dear object of his affections exemplarily tender; correct throughout, vice shuddered in his presence, and virtue always felt his fostering hand; the purity of his private character gave effulgence to his public virtues.

His last scene comported with the whole tenor of his life. Although in extreme pain, not a sigh, not a groan escaped him; and with undisturbed serenity he closed his well-spent life. Such was the man America has lost such was the man for whom our nation mourns.

Methinks I see his august image, and hear falling from his venerable lips these deep sinking words:

"Cease, sons of America, lamenting our separation: go on, and confirm by your wisdom the fruits of our joint councils, joint efforts, and common dangers; reverence religion, diffuse knowledge throughout your land, patronize the arts and sciences; let liberty and order be inseparable companions; control party spirit, the bane of free Governments; observe good faith to, and cultivate peace with, all nations; shut up every avenue to foreign influence; contract rather than extend national connexion; rely on yourselves only; be American in thought, word, and deed: thus will you give immortality to that Union, which was the constant object of my terrestrial labors; thus will you preserve, undisturbed, to the latest posterity, the felicity of a people to me most dear; and thus will you supply (if my happiness is now aught to you) the only vacancy in the round of pure bliss high Heaven bestows."

Thomas Jefferson

First Inaugural Address

(Delivered in Washington, D.C., March 4, 1801)

Called upon to undertake the duties of the first executive office of our country, I avail myself of the presence of that portion of my fellow-citizens which is here assembled, to express my grateful thanks for the favor with which they have been pleased to look toward me, to declare a sincere consciousness that the task is above my talents, and that I approach it with those anxious and awful presentiments which the greatness of the charge and the weakness of my powers so justly inspire. A rising nation, spread over a wide and fruitful land, traversing all the seas with the rich productions of their industry, engaged in commerce with nations who feel power and forget right, advancing rapidly to destinies beyond the reach of mortal eye—when I contemplate these transcendent objects, and see the honor, the happiness, and the hopes of this beloved country committed to the issue and the auspices of this day, I shrink from the contemplation, and humble myself before the magnitude of the undertaking. Utterly indeed, should I despair, did not the presence of many whom I here see remind me, that in the other high authorities provided by our constitution I shall find resources of wisdom, of virtue, and of zeal, on which to rely under all difficulties. To you, then, gentlemen, who are charged with the sovereign functions of legislation, and to those associated with you, I look with encouragement for that guidance and support which may enable us to steer with safety the vessel in which we are all embarked amid the conflicting elements of a troubled world.

During the contest of opinion through which we have passed, the animation of discussion and of exertions has sometimes worn an aspect which might impose on strangers unused to think freely and to speak and to write what they think; but this being now decided by the voice of the nation, announced according to the rules of the constitution, all will, of course, arrange themselves under the will of the law, and unite in common efforts for the common good. All, too, will bear in mind this sacred principle, that though the will of the majority is in all cases to prevail, that will, to be rightful, must be reasonable; that the minority possess their equal rights, which equal laws must protect, and to violate which would be oppression. Let us, then, fellow-citizens, unite with one heart and one mind. Let us restore to social intercourse that harmony and affection without which liberty and even life itself are but dreary things. And let us reflect that having banished from our land that religious intolerance under which mankind so long bled and suffered, we have yet gained little if we countenance a political intolerance as despotic, as wicked, and capable of as bitter and bloody persecutions. During the throes and convulsions of the ancient world, during the agonizing spasms of infuriated man, seeking through blood and slaughter his long-lost liberty, it was not wonderful that the agitation of the billows should reach even this distant and peaceful shore; that this should be more felt and feared by some and less by others; that this should divide opinions as to measures of safety. But every difference of opinion is not a difference of principle. We have called by different names brethren of the same principle. We are all republicans—we are all federalists. If there be any among us who would wish to dissolve this Union or to change its republican form, let them stand undisturbed as monuments of the safety with which error of opinion may be tolerated where reason is left free to combat it. I know, indeed, that some honest men fear that a republican government can not be strong; that this government is not strong enough. But would the honest patriot, in the full tide of successful experiment, abandon a government which has so far kept us free and firm, on the theoretic and visionary fear that this government, the world's best hope, may by possibility want energy to preserve itself? I trust not. I believe this, on the contrary, the strongest government on earth. I believe it the only one where every man, at the call of the laws, would fly to the standard of the law, and would meet invasions of the public order as his own personal concern. Sometimes it is said that man can not be trusted with the government of himself. Can he, then, be trusted with the government of others? Or have we found angels in the forms of kings to govern him? Let history answer this question.

Let us, then, with courage and confidence pursue our own federal and republican principles, our attachment to our union and representative government. Kindly separated by nature and a wide ocean from the exterminating havoc of one quarter of the globe; too high-minded to endure the degradations of the others; possessing a chosen country, with room enough for our descendants to the hundredth and thousandth generation; entertaining a due sense of our equal right to the use of our own faculties, to the acquisitions of our industry, to honor and confidence from our fellow-citizens, resulting not from birth but from our actions and their sense of them; enlightened by a benign religion, professed, indeed, and practised in various forms, yet all of them including honesty, truth, temperance, gratitude, and the love of man; acknowledging and adoring an overruling Providence, which by all its dispensations proves that it delights in the happiness of man here and his greater happiness hereafter; with all these blessings, what more is necessary to make us a happy and prosperous people? Still one thing more, fellow-citizens—a wise and frugal government, which shall restrain men from injuring one another, which shall leave them otherwise free to regulate their own pursuits of industry and improvement, and shall not take from the mouth of labor the bread it has earned. This is the sum of good government, and this is necessary to close the circle of our felicities.

About to enter, fellow-citizens, on the exercise of duties which comprehend everything dear and valuable to you, it is proper that you should understand what I deem the essential principles of our government, and consequently those which ought to shape its administration. I will compress them within the narrowest compass they will bear, stating the general principle, but not all its limitations. Equal and exact justice to all men, of whatever state or persuasion, religious or political; peace, commerce, and honest friendship, with all nations—entangling alliances with none; the support of the state governments in all their rights, as the most competent administrations for our domestic concerns and the surest bulwarks against anti-republican tendencies; the preservation of the general government in its whole constitutional vigor, as the sheet anchor of our peace at home and safety abroad; a jealous care of the right of election by the people—a mild and safe corrective of abuses which are lopped by the sword of revolution where peaceable remedies are unprovided; absolute acquiescence in the decisions of the majority— the vital principle of republics, from which there is no appeal but to force, the vital principle and immediate parent of despotism; a well-disciplined militia—our best reliance in peace and for the first moments of war, till regulars may relieve them; the supremacy of the civil over the military authority; economy in the public expense, that labor may be lightly burdened; the honest payment of our debts and sacred preservation of the public faith; encouragement of agriculture, and of commerce as its handmaid; the diffusion of information and the arraignment of all abuses at the bar of public reason; freedom of religion; freedom of the press; freedom of person under the protection of the habeas corpus; and trial by juries impartially selected—these principles form the bright constellation which has gone before us, and guided our steps through an age of revolution and reformation. The wisdom of our sages and the blood of our heroes have been devoted to their attainment. They should be the creed of our political faith—the text of civil instruction—the touchstone by which to try the services of those we trust; and should we wander from them in moments of error or alarm, let us hasten to retrace our steps and to regain the road which alone leads to peace, liberty, and safety.

I repair, then, fellow-citizens, to the post you have assigned me. With experience enough in subordinate offices to have seen the difficulties of this, the greatest of all, I have learned to expect that it will rarely fall to the lot of imperfect man to retire from this station with the reputation and the favor which bring him into it. Without pretensions to that high confidence reposed in our first and great revolutionary character, whose preeminent services had entitled him to the first place in his country's love, and destined for him the fairest page in the volume of faithful history, I ask so much confidence only as may give firmness and effect to the legal administration of your affairs. I shall often go wrong through defect of judgment. When right, I shall often be thought wrong by those whose positions will not command a view of the whole ground. I ask your indulgence for my own errors, which will never be intentional; and your support against the errors of others, who may condemn what they would not if seen in all its parts. The approbation implied by your suffrage is a consolation to me for the past; and my future solicitude will be to retain the good opinion of those who have bestowed it in advance, to conciliate that of others by doing them all the good in my power, and to be instrumental to the happiness and freedom of all.

Relying, then, on the patronage of your good will, I advance with obedience to the work, ready to retire from it whenever you become sensible how much better choice it is in your power to make. And may that Infinite Power which rules the destinies of the universe, lead our councils to what is best, and give them a favorable issue for your peace and prosperity.

Thomas Jefferson

Second Inaugural Address

(Delivered in Washington, D.C., March 4, 1805)

Proceeding, fellow-citizens, to that qualification which the constitution requires, before my entrance on the charge again conferred on me, it is my duty to express the deep sense I entertain of this new proof of confidence from my fellow-citizens at large, and the zeal with which it inspires me, so to conduct myself as may best satisfy their just expectations.

On taking this station on a former occasion, I declared the principles on which I believed it my duty to administer the affairs of our commonwealth. My conscience tells me that I have, on every occasion, acted up to that declaration, according to its obvious import, and to the understanding of every candid mind.

In the transaction of your foreign affairs, we have endeavored to cultivate the friendship of all nations, and especially of those with which we have the most important relations. We have done them justice on all occasions, favored where favor was lawful, and cherished mutual interests and intercourse on fair and equal terms. We are firmly convinced, and we act on that conviction, that with nations, as with individuals, our interests soundly calculated will ever be found inseparable from our moral duties; and history bears witness to the fact, that a just nation is trusted on its word, when resource is had to armaments and wars to bridle others.

At home, fellow-citizens, you best know whether we have done well or ill. The suppression of unnecessary offices, of useless establishments and expenses, enabled us to discontinue our internal taxes. These covering our land with officers, and opening our doors to their intrusions, had already begun that process of domiciliary vexation, which, once entered, is scarcely to be restrained from reaching successively every article of produce and property. If among these taxes some minor ones fell which had not been inconvenient, it was because their amount would not have paid the officers who collected them, and because, if they had any merit, the state authorities might adopt them, instead of others less approved.

The remaining revenue on the consumption of foreign articles, is paid cheerfully by those who can afford to add foreign luxuries to domestic comforts, being collected on our seaboard and frontiers only, and incorporated with the transactions of our mercantile citizens, it may be the pleasure and the pride of an American to ask, what farmer, what mechanic, what laborer, ever sees a taxgatherer of the United States? These contributions enable us to support the current expenses of the government, to fulfil contracts with foreign nations, to extinguish the native right of soil within our limits, to extend those limits, and to apply such a surplus to our public debts, as places at a short day their final redemption, and that redemption once effected, the revenue thereby liberated may, by a just repartition among the states, and a corresponding amendment of the constitution, be applied, *in time of peace,* to rivers, canals, roads, arts, manufactures, education, and other great objects within each state. *In time of war,* if injustice, by ourselves or others, must sometimes produce war, increased as the same revenue will be increased by population and consumption, and aided by other resources reserved for that crisis, it may meet within the year all the expenses of the year, without encroaching on the rights of future generations by burdening them with the debts of the past. War will then be but a suspension of useful works, and a return to a state of peace, a return to the progress of improvement.

I have said, fellow-citizens, that the income reserved had enabled us to extend our limits; but that extension may possibly pay for itself before we are called on, and in the meantime, may keep down the accruing interest; in all events, it will repay the advances we have made. I know that the acquisition of Louisiana has been disapproved by some, from a candid apprehension that the enlargement of our territory would endanger its union. But who can limit the extent to which the federative principle may operate effectively? The larger our association, the less will it be shaken by local passions; and in any view, is it not better that the opposite bank of the Mississippi should be settled by our own brethren and children, than by strangers of another family? With which shall we be most likely to live in harmony and friendly intercourse?

In matters of religion, I have considered that its free exercise is placed by the constitution independent of the powers of the general government. I have therefore undertaken, on no occasion, to prescribe the religious exercises suited to it; but have left them, as the constitution found them, under the direction and discipline of state or church authorities acknowledged by the several religious societies.

The aboriginal inhabitants of these countries I have regarded with the commiseration their history inspires. Endowed with the faculties and the rights of men, breathing an ardent love of liberty and independence, and occupying a country which left them no desire but to be undisturbed, the stream of overflowing population from other regions directed itself on these shores; without power to divert, or habits to contend against, they have been overwhelmed by the current, or driven before it; now reduced within limits too narrow for the hunter's state, humanity enjoins us to teach them agriculture and the domestic arts; to encourage them to that industry which alone can enable them to maintain their place in existence, and to prepare them in time for that state of society, which to bodily comforts adds the improvement of the mind and morals. We have therefore liberally furnished them with the implements of husbandry and household use; we have placed among them instructors in the arts of first necessity; and they are covered with the ægis of the law against aggressors from among ourselves.

But the endeavors to enlighten them on the fate which awaits their present course of life, to induce them to exercise their reason, follow its dictates, and change their pursuits with the change of circumstances, have powerful obstacles to encounter; they are combated by the habits of their bodies, prejudice of their minds, ignorance, pride, and the influence of interested and crafty individuals among them, who feel themselves something in the present order of things, and fear to become nothing in any other. These persons inculcate a sanctimonious reverence for the customs of their ancestors; that whatsoever they did, must be done through all time; that reason is a false guide, and to advance under its counsel, in their physical, moral, or political condition, is perilous innovation; that their duty is to remain as their Creator made them, ignorance being safety, and knowledge full of danger; in short, my friends, among them is seen the action and counteraction of good sense and bigotry; they too have their anti-philosophers, who find an interest in keeping things in their present state, who dread reformation, and exert all their faculties to maintain the ascendency of habit over the duty of improving our reason and obeying its mandates.

In giving these outlines, I do not mean, fellow-citizens, to arrogate to myself the merit of the measures; that is due, in the first place, to the reflecting character of our citizens at large, who, by the weight of public opinion, influence and strengthen the public measures; it is due to the sound discretion with which they select from among themselves those to whom they confide the legislative duties; it is due to the zeal and wisdom of the characters thus selected, who lay the foundations of public happiness in wholesome laws, the execution of which alone remains for others; and it is due to the able and faithful auxiliaries, whose patriotism has associated with me in the executive functions.

During this course of administration, and in order to disturb it, the artillery of the press has been levelled against us, charged with whatsoever its licentiousness could devise or dare. These abuses of an institution so important to freedom and science, are deeply to be regretted, inasmuch as they tend to lessen its usefulness, and to sap its safety; they might, indeed, have been corrected by the wholesome punishments reserved and provided by the laws of the several states against false-hood and defamation; but public duties more urgent press on the time of public servants, and the offenders have therefore been left to find their punishment in the public indignation.

Nor was it uninteresting to the world, that an experiment should be fairly and fully made, whether freedom of discussion, unaided by power, is not sufficient for the propagation and protection of truth—whether a government, conduct-ing itself in the true spirit of its constitution, with zeal and purity, and doing no act which it would be unwilling the whole world should witness, can be written down by falsehood and defamation. The experiment has been tried; you have witnessed the scene; our fellow-citizens have looked on, cool and collected; they saw the latent source from which these outrages proceeded; they gathered around their public functionaries, and when the constitution called them to the decision by suffrage, they pronounced their verdict, honorable to those who had served them, and consolatory to the friend of man, who believes he may be intrusted with his own affairs.

No inference is here intended, that the laws, provided by the state against false and defamatory publications, should not be enforced; he who has time, ren-ders a service to public morals and public tranquillity, in reforming these abuses by the salutary coercions of the law; but the experiment is noted, to prove that, since truth and reason have maintained their ground against false opinions in league with false facts, the press, confined to truth, needs no other legal restraint; the public judgment will correct false reasonings and opinions, on a full hearing of all parties; and no other definite line can be drawn between the inestimable lib-erty of the press and its demoralizing licentiousness. If there be still improprieties which this rule would not restrain, its supplement must be sought in the censor-ship of public opinion.

Contemplating the union of sentiment now manifested so generally, as augur-ing harmony and happiness to our future course, I offer to our country sincere congratulations. With those, too, not yet rallied to the same point, the disposition to do so is gaining strength; facts are piercing through the veil drawn over them; and our doubting brethren will at length see, that the mass of their fellow-citizens, with whom they can not yet resolve to act, as to principles and measures, think as they think, and desire what they desire; that our wish, as well as theirs, is, that the public efforts may be directed honestly to the public good, that peace be cul-tivated, civil and religious liberty unassailed, law and order preserved, equality of rights maintained, and that state of property, equal or unequal, which results to every man from his own industry, or that of his fathers. When satisfied of these views, it is not in human nature that they should not approve and support them; in the meantime, let us cherish them with patient affection; let us do them justice, and more than justice, in all competitions of interest; and we need not doubt that truth, reason, and their own interests, will at length prevail, will gather them into the fold of their country, and will complete their entire union of opinion, which gives to a nation the blessing of harmony, and the benefit of all its strength.

I shall now enter on the duties to which my fellow-citizens have again called me, and shall proceed in the spirit of those principles which they have approved. I fear not that any motives of interest may lead me astray; I am sensible of no passion which could seduce me knowingly from the path of justice; but the weakness of human nature, and the limits of my own understanding, will produce errors of judgment sometimes injurious to your interests. I shall need, therefore, all the indulgence I have heretofore experienced—the want of it will certainly not lessen with increasing years. I shall need, too, the favor of that Being in whose hands we are, who led our forefathers, as Israel of old, from their native land, and planted them in a country flowing with all the necessaries and comforts of life; who has covered our infancy with his providence, and our riper years with his wisdom and power; and to whose goodness I ask you to join with me in supplications, that he will so enlighten the minds of your servants, guide their councils, and prosper their measures that whatsoever they do, shall result in your good, and shall secure to you the peace, friendship, and approbation of all nations.

Speech at Vincennes

*(Delivered in Vincennes, Indiana, August 12, 1810, in response to
Governor William Henry Harrison's purchase of lands from the
Delawares and other Native American tribes)*

It is true I am a Shawanee. My forefathers were warriors. Their son is a warrior. From them I only take my existence; from my tribe I take nothing. I am the maker of my own fortune; and oh! that I could make that of my red people, and of my country, as great as the conceptions of my mind, when I think of the Spirit that rules the universe. I would not then come to Governor Harrison, to ask him to tear the treaty and to obliterate the landmark; but I would say to him, sir you have liberty to return to your own country. The being within, communing with past ages, tells me that once, nor until lately, there was no white man on this continent. That it then all belonged to red men, children of the same parents, placed on it by the Great Spirit that made them, to keep it, to traverse it, to enjoy its productions, and to fill it with the same race. Once a happy race. Since made miserable by the white people, who are never contented, but always encroaching. The way, and the only way to check and to stop this evil, is for all the red men to unite in claiming a common and equal right in the land as it was at first, and should be yet; for it never was divided, but belongs to all for the use of each. That no part has a right to sell, even to each other, much less to strangers; those who want all, and will not do with less.

The white people have no right to take the land from the Indians, because they had it first; it is theirs. They may sell, but all must join. Any sale not made by all is not valid. The late sale is bad. It was made by a part only. Part do not know how to sell. It requires all to make a bargain for all. All red men have equal rights to the unoccupied land. The right of occupancy is as good in one place as in another. There cannot be two occupations in the same place. The first excludes all others. It is not so in hunting or travelling; for there the same ground will serve many, as they may follow each other all day; but the camp is stationary, and that is occupancy. It belongs to the first who sits down on his blanket or skins which he has thrown upon the ground; and till he leaves it no other has a right.

DANIEL WEBSTER

The Bunker Hill Monument

*(Delivered June 17, 1825, at the laying of the cornerstone of the
Bunker Hill Monument in Charlestown, Massachusetts)*

This uncounted multitude before me and around me proves the feeling which the occasion has excited. These thousands of human faces, glowing with sympathy and joy, and from the impulses of a common gratitude turned reverently to heaven in this spacious temple of the firmament, proclaim that the day, the place, and the purpose of our assembling have made a deep impression on our hearts.

If, indeed, there be any thing in local association fit to affect the mind of man, we need not strive to repress the emotions which agitate us here. We are among the sepulchres of our fathers. We are on ground, distinguished by their valor, their constancy, and the shedding of their blood. We are here, not to fix an uncertain date in our annals, nor so draw into notice an obscure and unknown spot. If our humble purpose had never been conceived, if we ourselves had never been born, the 17th of June, 1775, would have been a day on which all subsequent history would have poured its light, and the eminence where we stand a point of attraction to the eyes of successive generations. But we are Americans. We live in what may be called the early age of this great continent; and we know that our posterity, through all time, are here to enjoy and suffer the allotments of humanity. We see before us a probable train of great events; we know that our own fortunes have been happily cast; and it is natural, therefore, that we should be moved by the contemplation of occurrences which have guided our destiny before many of us were born, and settled the condition in which we should pass that portion of our existence which God allows to men on earth.

We do not read even of the discovery of this continent, without feeling something of a personal interest in the event; without being reminded how much it has affected our own fortunes and our own existence. It would be still more unnatural for us, therefore, than for others, to contemplate with unaffected minds that interesting, I may say that most touching and pathetic scene, when the great discoverer of America stood on the deck of his shattered bark, the shades of night falling on the sea, yet no man sleeping; tossed on the billows of an unknown ocean, yet the stronger billows of alternate hope and despair tossing his own troubled thoughts; extending forward his harassed frame, straining westward his anxious and eager eyes, till Heaven at last granted him a moment of rapture and ecstasy, in blessing his vision with the sight of the unknown world.

Nearer to our times, more closely connected with our fates, and therefore still more interesting to our feelings and affections, is the settlement of our own country by colonists from England. We cherish every memorial of these worthy ancestors; we celebrate their patience and fortitude; we admire their daring enterprise; we teach our children to venerate their piety; and we are justly proud of being descended from men who have set the world an example of founding civil institutions on the great and united principles of human freedom and human knowledge. To us, their children, the story of their labors and sufferings can never be without its interest. We shall not stand unmoved on the shore of Plymouth, while the sea continues to wash it; nor will our brethren in another early and ancient Colony forget the place of its first establishment, till their river shall cease to flow by it. No vigor of youth, no maturity of manhood, will lead the nation to forget the spots where its infancy was cradled and defended.

But the great event in the history of the continent, which we are now met here to commemorate, that prodigy of modern times, at once the wonder and the blessing of the world, is the American Revolution. In a day of extraordinary prosperity and happiness, of high national honor, distinction, and power, we are brought together, in this place, by our love of country, by our admiration of exalted character, by our gratitude for signal services and patriotic devotion.

The Society whose organ I am was formed for the purpose of rearing some honorable and durable monument to the memory of the early friends of American Independence. They have thought, that for this object no time could be more propitious than the present prosperous and peaceful period; that no place could claim preference over this memorable spot; and that no day could be more auspicious to the undertaking, than the anniversary of the battle which was here fought. The foundation of that monument we have now laid. With solemnities suited to the occasion, with prayers to Almighty God for his blessing, and in the midst of this cloud of witnesses, we have begun the work. We trust it will be prosecuted, and that, springing from a broad foundation, rising high in massive solidity and unadorned grandeur, it may remain as long as Heaven permits the work of man to last, a fit emblem, both of the events in memory of which it is raised, and of the gratitude of those who have reared it.

We know, indeed, that the record of illustrious actions is most safely deposited in the universal remembrance of mankind. We know, that if we could cause this structure to ascend, not only till it reached the skies, but till it pierced them, its broad surfaces could still contain but part of that which, in an age of knowledge, hath already been spread over the earth, and which history charges itself with making known to all future times. We know that no inscription on entablatures less broad than the earth itself can carry information of the events we commemorate where it had not already gone; and that no structure, which shall not outlive the duration of letters and knowledge among men, can prolong the memorial. But our object is, by this edifice, to show our own deep sense of the value and importance of the achievements of our ancestors; and, by presenting this work of gratitude to the eye, to keep alive similar sentiments, and to foster a constant regard for the principles of the Revolution. Human beings are composed, not of reason only, but of imagination also, and sentiment; and that is neither wasted nor misapplied which is appropriated to the purpose of giving right direction to sentiments, and opening proper springs of feeling in the heart. Let it not be supposed that our object is to perpetuate national hostility, or even to cherish a mere military spirit. It is higher, purer, nobler. We consecrate our work to the spirit of national independence, and we wish that the light of peace may rest upon it for ever. We rear a memorial of our conviction of that unmeasured benefit which has been conferred on our own land, and of the happy influences which have been produced, by the same events, on the general interests of mankind. We come, as Americans, to mark a spot which must for ever be dear to us and our posterity. We wish that whosoever, in all coming time, shall turn his eye hither, may behold that the place is not undistinguished where the first great battle of the Revolution was fought. We wish that this structure may proclaim the magnitude and importance of that event to every class and every age. We wish that infancy may learn the purpose of its erection from maternal lips, and that weary and withered age may behold it, and be solaced by the recollections which it suggests. We wish that labor may look up here, and be proud, in the midst of its toil. We wish that, in those days of disaster, which, as they come upon all nations, must be expected to come upon us also, desponding patriotism may turn its eyes hitherward, and be assured that the foundations of our national power are still strong. We wish that this column, rising towards heaven among the pointed spires of so many temples dedicated to God, may contribute also to produce, in all minds, a pious feeling of dependence and gratitude. We wish, finally, that the last object to the sight of him who leaves his native shore, and the first to gladden his who revisits it, may be something which shall remind him of the liberty and the glory of his country. Let it rise! let it rise, till it meet the sun in his coming; let the earliest light of the morning gild it, and parting day linger and play on its summit.

We live in a most extraordinary age. Events so various and so important that they might crowd and distinguish centuries are, in our times, compressed within the compass of a single life. When has it happened that history has had so much to record, in the same term of years, as since the 17th of June, 1775? Our own Revolution, which, under other circumstances, might itself have been expected to occasion a war of half a century, has been achieved; twenty-four sovereign and independent States erected; and a general government established over them, so safe, so wise, so free, so practical, that we might well wonder its establishment should have been accomplished so soon, were it not far the greater the wonder that it should have been established at all. Two or three millions of people have been augmented to twelve, the great forests of the West prostrated beneath the arm of successful industry, and the dwellers on the banks of the Ohio and the Mississippi become the fellow-citizens and neighbors of those who cultivate the hills of New England. We have a commerce, that leaves no sea unexplored; navies, which take no law from superior force; revenues, adequate to all the exigencies of government, almost without taxation; and peace with all nations, founded on equal rights and mutual respect.

Europe, within the same period, has been agitated by a mighty revolution, which, while it has been felt in the individual condition and happiness of almost every man, has shaken to the centre her political fabric, and dashed against one another thrones which had stood tranquil for ages. On this, our continent, our own example has been followed, and colonies have sprung up to be nations. Unaccustomed sounds of liberty and free government have reached us from beyond the track of the sun; and at this moment the dominion of European power in this continent, from the place where we stand to the south pole, is annihilated for ever.

In the mean time, both in Europe and America, such has been the general progress of knowledge, such the improvement in legislation, in commerce, in the arts, in letters, and, above all, in liberal ideas and the general spirit of the age, that the whole world seems changed.

Yet, notwithstanding that this is but a faint abstract of the things which have happened since the day of the battle of Bunker Hill, we are but fifty years removed from it; and we now stand here to enjoy all the blessings of our own condition, and to look abroad on the brightened prospects of the world, while we still have among us some of those who were active agents in the scenes of 1775, and who are now here, from every quarter of New England, to visit once more, and under circumstances so affecting, I had almost said so overwhelming, this renowned theatre of their courage and patriotism.

Venerable Men! you have come down to us from a former generation. Heaven has bounteously lengthened out your lives, that you might behold this joyous day. You are now where you stood fifty years ago, this very hour, with your brothers and your neighbors, shoulder to shoulder, in the strife for your country. Behold, how altered! The same heavens are indeed over your heads; the same ocean rolls at your feet; but all else how changed! You hear now no roar of hostile cannon, you see no mixed volumes of smoke and flame rising from burning Charlestown. The ground strewed with the dead and the dying; the impetuous charge; the steady and successful repulse; the loud call to repeated assault; the summoning of all that is manly to repeated resistance; a thousand bosoms freely and fearlessly bared in an instant to whatever of terror there may be in war and death;—all these you have witnessed, but you witness them no more. All is peace. The heights of yonder metropolis, its towers and roofs, which you then saw filled with wives and children and countrymen in distress and terror, and looking with unutterable emotions for the issue of the combat, have presented you to-day with the sight of its whole happy population, come out to welcome and greet you with a universal jubilee. Yonder proud ships, by a felicity of position appropriately lying at the foot of this mount, and seeming fondly to cling around it, are not means of annoyance to you, but your country's own means of distinction and defence. All is peace; and God has granted you this sight of your country's happiness, ere you slumber in the grave. He has allowed you to behold and to partake the reward of your patriotic toils; and he has allowed us, your sons and countrymen, to meet you here, and in the name of the present generation, in the name of your country, in the name of liberty, to thank you!

But, alas! you are not all here! Time and the sword have thinned your ranks. Prescott, Putnam, Stark, Brooks, Read, Pomeroy, Bridge! our eyes seek for you in vain amid this broken band. You are gathered to your fathers, and live only to your country in her grateful remembrance and your own bright example. But let us not too much grieve, that you have met the common fate of men. You lived at least long enough to know that your work had been nobly and successfully accomplished. You lived to see your country's independence established, and to sheathe your swords from war. On the light of Liberty you saw arise the light of Peace, like

> another morn,
> Risen on mid-noon

and the sky on which you closed your eyes was cloudless.

But ah! Him! the first great martyr in this great cause! Him! the premature victim of his own self-devoting heart! Him! the head of our civil councils, and the destined leader of our military bands, whom nothing brought hither but the unquenchable fire of his own spirit! Him! cut off by Providence in the hour of overwhelming anxiety and thick gloom; falling ere he saw the star of his country rise; pouring out his generous blood like water, before he knew whether it would fertilize a land of freedom or of bondage!—how shall I struggle with the emotions that stifle the utterance of thy name? Our poor work may perish; but thine shall endure! This monument may moulder away; the solid ground it rests upon may sink down to a level with the sea; but thy memory shall not fail! Wheresoever among men a heart shall be found that beats to the transports of patriotism and liberty, its aspirations shall be to claim kindred with thy spirit!

But the scene amidst which we stand does not permit us to confine our thoughts or our sympathies to those fearless spirits who hazarded or lost their lives on this consecrated spot. We have the happiness to rejoice here in the presence of a most worthy representation of the survivors of the whole Revolutionary army.

VETERANS! you are the remnant of many a well-fought field. You bring with you marks of honor from Trenton and Monmouth, from Yorktown, Camden, Bennington, and Saratoga. VETERANS OF HALF A CENTURY! when in your youthful days you put every thing at hazard in your country's cause, good as that cause was, and sanguine as youth is, still your fondest hopes did not stretch onward to an hour like this! At a period to which you could not reasonably have expected to arrive, at a moment of national prosperity such as you could never have foreseen, you are now met here to enjoy the fellowship of old soldiers, and to receive the overflowing of a universal gratitude.

But your agitated countenances and your heaving breasts inform me that even this is not an unmixed joy. I perceive that a tumult of contending feelings rushes upon you. The images of the dead, as well as the persons of the living, present themselves before you. The scene overwhelms you, and I turn from it. May the Father of all mercies smile upon your declining years, and bless them! And when you shall here have exchanged your embraces, when you shall once more have pressed the hands which have been so often extended to give succor in adversity, or grasped in the exultation of victory, then look abroad upon this lovely land which your young valor defended, and mark the happiness with which it is filled; yea, look abroad upon the whole earth, and see what a name you have contributed to give to your country, and what a praise you have added to freedom, and then rejoice in the sympathy and gratitude which beam upon your last days from the improved condition of mankind!

The occasion does not require of me any particular account of the battle of the 17th of June, 1775, nor any detailed narrative of the events which immediately preceded it. These are familiarly known to all. In the progress of the great and interesting controversy, Massachusetts and the town of Boston had become early and marked objects of the displeasure of the British Parliament. This had been manifested in the act for altering the government of the Province, and in that for shutting up the port of Boston. Nothing sheds more honor on our early history, and nothing better shows how little the feelings and sentiments of the Colonies were known or regarded in England, than the impression which these measures everywhere produced in America. It had been anticipated, that, while the Colonies in general would be terrified by the severity of the punishment inflicted on Massachusetts, the other seaports would be governed by a mere spirit of gain; and that, as Boston was now cut off from all commerce, the unexpected advantage which this blow on her was calculated to confer on other towns would be greedily enjoyed. How miserably such reasoners deceived themselves! How little they knew of the depth, and the strength, and the intenseness of that feeling of resistance to illegal acts of power, which possessed the whole American people! Everywhere the unworthy boon was rejected with scorn. The fortunate occasion was seized, everywhere, to show to the whole world that the Colonies were swayed by no local interest, no partial interest, no selfish interest. The temptation to profit by the punishment of Boston was strongest to our neighbors of Salem. Yet Salem was precisely the place where this miserable proffer was spurned, in a tone of the most lofty self-respect and the most indignant patriotism. "We are deeply affected," said its inhabitants, "with the sense of our public calamities; but the miseries that are now rapidly hastening on our brethren in the capital of the Province greatly excite our commiseration. By shutting up the port of Boston, some imagine that the course of trade might be turned hither and to our benefit; but we must be dead to every idea of justice, lost to all feelings of humanity, could we indulge a thought to seize on wealth and raise our fortunes on the ruin of our suffering neighbors." These noble sentiments were not confined to our immediate vicinity. In that day of general affection and brotherhood, the blow given to Boston smote on every patriotic heart from one end of the country to the other. Virginia and the Carolinas, as well as Connecticut and New Hampshire, felt and proclaimed the cause to be their own. The Continental Congress, then holding its first session in Philadelphia, expressed its sympathy for the suffering inhabitants of Boston, and addresses were received from all quarters, assuring them that the cause was a common one, and should be met by common efforts and common sacrifices. The Congress of Massachusetts responded to these assurances; and in an address to the Congress at Philadelphia, bearing the official signature, perhaps among the last, of the immortal Warren, notwithstanding the severity of its suffering and the magnitude of the dangers which threatened it, it was declared, that this Colony "is ready, at all times, to spend and be spent in the cause of America."

But the hour drew nigh which was to put professions to the proof, and to determine whether the authors of these mutual pledges were ready to seal them in blood. The tidings of Lexington and Concord had no sooner spread, than it was universally felt that the time was at last come for action. A spirit pervaded all ranks, not transient, not boisterous, but deep, solemn, determined,

> totamque infusa per artus
> Mens agitat molem, et magno se corpore miscet.

War, on their own soil and at their own doors, was, indeed, a strange work to the yeomanry of New England; but their consciences were convinced of its necessity, their country called them to it, and they did not withhold themselves from the perilous trial. The ordinary occupations of life were abandoned; the plough was staid in the unfinished furrow; wives gave up their husbands, and mothers gave up their sons, to the battles of a civil war. Death might come, in honor, on the field; it might come, in disgrace, on the scaffold. For either and for both they were prepared. The sentiment of Quincy was full in their hearts. "Blandishments," said that distinguished son of genius and patriotism, "will not fascinate us, nor will threats of a halter intimidate; for, under God, we are determined that, wheresoever, whensoever, or howsoever we shall be called to make our exit, we will die free men."

The 17th of June saw the four New England Colonies standing here, side by side, to triumph or to fall together; and there was with them from that moment to the end of the war, what I hope will remain with them for ever, one cause, one country, one heart.

The battle of Bunker Hill was attended with the most important effects beyond its immediate results as a military engagement. It created at once a state of open, public war. There could now be no longer a question of proceeding against individuals, as guilty of treason or rebellion. That fearful crisis was past. The appeal lay to the sword, and the only question was, whether the spirit and the resources of the people would hold out, till the object should be accomplished. Nor were its general consequences confined to our own country. The previous proceedings of the Colonies, their appeals, resolutions, and addresses, had made their cause known in Europe. Without boasting, we may say, that in no age or country has the public cause been maintained with more force of argument, more power of illustration, or more of that persuasion which excited feeling and elevated principle can alone bestow, than the Revolutionary state papers exhibit. These papers will for ever deserve to be studied, not only for the spirit which they breathe, but for the ability with which they were written.

To this able vindication of their cause, the Colonies had now added a practical and severe proof of their own true devotion to it, and given evidence also of the power which they could bring to its support. All now saw, that, if America fell, she would not fall without a struggle. Men felt sympathy and regard, as well as surprise, when they beheld these infant states, remote, unknown, unaided, encounter the power of England, and, in the first considerable battle, leave more of their enemies dead on the field, in proportion to the number of combatants, than had been recently known to fall in the wars of Europe.

Information of these events, circulating throughout the world, at length reached the ears of one who now hears me.* He has not forgotten the emotion which the fame of Bunker Hill, and the name of Warren, excited in his youthful breast.

Sir, we are assembled to commemorate the establishment of great public principles of liberty, and to do honor to the distinguished dead. The occasion is too severe for eulogy of the living. But, Sir, your interesting relation to this country, the peculiar circumstances which surround you and surround us, call on me to express the happiness which we derive from your presence and aid in this solemn commemoration.

Fortunate, fortunate man! with what measure of devotion will you not thank God for the circumstances of your extraordinary life! You are connected with both hemispheres and with two generations. Heaven saw fit to ordain, that the electric spark of liberty should be conducted, through you, from the New World to the Old; and we, who are now here to perform this duty of patriotism, have all of us long ago received it in charge from our fathers to cherish your name and your virtues. You will account it an instance of your good fortune, Sir, that you crossed the seas to visit us at a time which enables you to be present at this solemnity. You now behold the field, the renown of which reached you in the heart of France, and caused a thrill in your ardent bosom. You see the lines of the little redoubt thrown up by the incredible diligence of Prescott; defended, to the last extremity, by his lion-hearted valor; and within which the corner-stone of our monument has now taken its position. You see where Warren fell, and where Parker, Gardner, McCleary, Moore, and other early patriots, fell with him. Those who survived that

* General Lafayette.

day, and whose lives have been prolonged to the present hour, are now around you. Some of them you have known in the trying scenes of the war. Behold! they now stretch forth their feeble arms to embrace you. Behold! they raise their trembling voices to invoke the blessing of God on you and yours for ever.

Sir, you have assisted us in laying the foundation of this structure. You have heard us rehearse, with our feeble commendation, the names of departed patriots. Monuments and eulogy belong to the dead. We give them this day to Warren and his associates. On other occasions they have been given to your more immediate companions in arms, to Washington, to Greene, to Gates, to Sullivan, and to Lincoln. We have become reluctant to grant these, our highest and last honors, further. We would gladly hold them yet back from the little remnant of that immortal band. *Serus in cælum redeas.* Illustrious as are your merits, yet far, O, very far distant be the day, when any inscription shall bear your name, or any tongue pronounce its eulogy!

The leading reflection to which this occasion seems to invite us, respects the great changes which have happened in the fifty years since the battle of Bunker Hill was fought. And it peculiarly marks the character of the present age, that, in looking at these changes, and in estimating their effect on our condition, we are obliged to consider, not what has been done in our own country only, but in others also. In these interesting times, while nations are making separate and individual advances in improvement, they make, too, a common progress; like vessels on a common tide, propelled by the gales at different rates, according to their several structure and management, but all moved forward by one mighty current, strong enough to bear onward whatever does not sink beneath it.

A chief distinction of the present day is a community of opinions and knowledge amongst men in different nations, existing in a degree heretofore unknown. Knowledge has, in our time, triumphed, and is triumphing, over distance, over difference of languages, over diversity of habits, over prejudice, and over bigotry. The civilized and Christian world is fast learning the great lesson, that difference of nation does not imply necessary hostility, and that all contact need not be war. The whole world is becoming a common field for intellect to act in. Energy of mind, genius, power, wheresoever it exists, may speak out in any tongue, and the *world* will hear it. A great chord of sentiment and feeling runs through two continents, and vibrates over both. Every breeze wafts intelligence from country to country; every wave rolls it; all give it forth, and all in turn receive it. There is a vast commerce of ideas; there are marts and exchanges for intellectual discoveries, and a wonderful fellowship of those individual intelligences which make up the mind and opinion of the age. Mind is the great lever of all things; human thought is the process by which human ends are ultimately answered; and the diffusion of knowledge, so astonishing in the last half-century, has rendered innumerable minds, variously gifted by nature, competent to be competitors or fellow-workers on the theatre of intellectual operation.

From these causes important improvements have taken place in the personal condition of individuals. Generally speaking, mankind are not only better fed and better clothed, but they are able also to enjoy more leisure; they possess more refinement and more self-respect. A superior tone of education, manners, and habits prevails. This remark, most true in its application to our own country, is also partly true when applied elsewhere. It is proved by the vastly augmented consumption of those articles of manufacture and of commerce which contribute to the comforts and the decencies of life; an augmentation which has far outrun the progress of population. And while the unexampled and almost incredible use of machinery would seem to supply the place of labor, labor still finds its occupation and its reward; so wisely has Providence adjusted men's wants and desires to their condition and their capacity.

Any adequate survey, however, of the progress made during the last half-century in the polite and the mechanic arts, in machinery and manufactures, in commerce and agriculture, in letters and in science, would require volumes. I must abstain wholly from these subjects, and turn for a moment to the contemplation of what has been done on the great question of politics and government. This is the master topic of the age; and during the whole fifty years it has intensely occupied the thoughts of men. The nature of civil government, its ends and uses, have been canvassed and investigated; ancient opinions attacked and defended; new ideas recommended and resisted, by whatever power the mind of man could bring to the controversy. From the closet and the public halls the debate has been transferred to the field; and the world has been shaken by wars of unexampled magnitude, and the greatest variety of fortune. A day of peace has at length succeeded; and now that the strife has subsided, and the smoke cleared away, we may begin to see what has actually been done, permanently changing the state and condition of human society. And, without dwelling on particular circumstances, it is most apparent, that, from the before-mentioned causes of augmented knowledge and improved individual condition, a real, substantial, and important change has taken place, and is taking place, highly favorable, on the whole, to human liberty and human happiness.

The great wheel of political revolution began to move in America. Here its rotation was guarded, regular, and safe. Transferred to the other continent, from unfortunate but natural causes, it received an irregular and violent impulse; it whirled along with a fearful celerity; till at length, like the chariot-wheels in the races of antiquity, it took fire from the rapidity of its own motion, and blazed onward, spreading conflagration and terror around.

We learn from the result of this experiment, how fortunate was our own condition, and how admirably the character of our people was calculated for setting the great example of popular governments. The possession of power did not turn the heads of the American people, for they had long been in the habit of exercising a great degree of self-control. Although the paramount authority of the parent state existed over them, yet a large field of legislation had always been open to our Colonial assemblies. They were accustomed to representative bodies and the forms of free government; they understood the doctrine of the division of power among different branches, and the necessity of checks on each. The character of our countrymen, moreover, was sober, moral, and religious; and there was little in the change to shock their feelings of justice and humanity, or even to disturb an honest prejudice. We had no domestic throne to overturn, no privileged orders to cast down, no violent changes of property to encounter. In the American Revolution, no man sought or wished for more than to defend and enjoy his own. None hoped for plunder or for spoil. Rapacity was unknown to it; the axe was not among the instruments of its accomplishment; and we all know that it could not have lived a single day under any well-founded imputation of possessing a tendency adverse to the Christian religion.

It need not surprise us, that, under circumstances less auspicious, political revolutions elsewhere, even when well intended, have terminated differently. It is, indeed, a great achievement, it is the master-work of the world, to establish governments entirely popular on lasting foundations; nor is it easy, indeed, to introduce the popular principle at all into governments to which it has been altogether a stranger. It cannot be doubted, however, that Europe has come out of the contest, in which she has been so long engaged, with greatly superior knowledge, and, in many respects, in a highly improved condition. Whatever benefit has been acquired, is likely to be retained, for it consists mainly in the acquisition of more enlightened ideas. And although kingdoms and provinces may be wrested from the hands that hold them, in the same manner they were obtained; although ordinary and vulgar power may, in human affairs, be lost as it has been won; yet it is the glorious prerogative of the empire of knowledge, that what it gains it never loses. On the contrary, it increases by the multiple of its own power; all its ends become means; all its attainments, helps to new conquests. Its whole abundant harvest is but so much seed wheat, and nothing has limited, and nothing can limit, the amount of ultimate product.

Under the influence of this rapidly increasing knowledge, the people have begun, in all forms of government, to think and to reason, on affairs of state. Regarding government as an institution for the public good, they demand a knowledge of its operations, and a participation in its exercise. A call for the representative system, wherever it is not enjoyed, and where there is already intelligence enough to estimate its value, is perseveringly made. Where men may speak out, they demand it; where the bayonet is at their throats, they pray for it.

When Louis the Fourteenth said, "I am the state," he expressed the essence of the doctrine of unlimited power. By the rules of that system, the people are disconnected from the state; they are its subjects; it is their lord. These ideas, founded in the love of power, and long supported by the excess and the abuse of it, are yielding, in our age, to other opinions; and the civilized world seems at last to be proceeding to the conviction of that fundamental and manifest truth, that the powers of government are but a trust, and that they cannot be lawfully exercised but for the good of the community. As knowledge is more and more extended, this conviction becomes more and more general. Knowledge, in truth, is the great sun in the firmament. Life and power are scattered with all its beams. The prayer of the Grecian champion, when enveloped in unnatural clouds and darkness, is the appropriate political supplication for the people of every country not yet blessed with free institutions:—

Dispel this cloud, the light of heaven restore,
Give me TO SEE,—and Ajax asks no more.

We may hope that the growing influence of enlightened sentiment will promote the permanent peace of the world. Wars to maintain family alliances, to uphold or to cast down dynasties, and to regulate successions to thrones, which have occupied so much room in the history of modern times, if not less likely to happen at all, will be less likely to become general and involve many nations, as the great principle shall be more and more established, that the interest of the world is peace, and its first great statute, that every nation possesses the power of establishing a government for itself. But public opinion has attained also an influence over governments which do not admit the popular principle into their organization. A necessary respect for the judgment of the world operates, in some measure, as a control over the most unlimited forms of authority. It is owing, perhaps, to this truth, that the interesting struggle of the Greeks has been suffered to go on so long, without a direct interference, either to wrest that country from its present masters, or to execute the system of pacification by force, and, with united strength, lay the neck of Christian and civilized Greek at the foot of the barbarian Turk. Let us thank God that we live in an age when something has influence besides the bayonet, and when the sternest authority does not venture to encounter the scorching power of public reproach. Any attempt of the kind I have mentioned should be met by one universal burst of indignation; the air of the civilized world ought to be made too warm to be comfortably breathed by any one who would hazard it.

It is, indeed, a touching reflection, that, while, in the fulness of our country's happiness, we rear this monument to her honor, we look for instruction in our undertaking to a country which is now in fearful contest, not for works of art or memorials of glory, but for her own existence. Let her be assured, that she is not forgotten in the world; that her efforts are applauded, and that constant prayers ascend for her success. And let us cherish a confident hope for her final triumph. If the true spark of religious and civil liberty be kindled, it will burn. Human agency cannot extinguish it. Like the earth's central fire, it may be smothered for a time; the ocean may overwhelm it; mountains may press it down; but its inherent and unconquerable force will heave both the ocean and the land, and at some time or other, in some place or other, the volcano will break out and flame up to heaven.

Among the great events of the half-century, we must reckon, certainly, the revolution of South America; and we are not likely to overrate the importance of that revolution, either to the people of the country itself or to the rest of the world. The late Spanish colonies, now independent states, under circumstances less favorable, doubtless, than attended our own revolution, have yet successfully commenced their national existence. They have accomplished the great object of establishing their independence; they are known and acknowledged in the world; and although in regard to their systems of government, their sentiments on religious toleration, and their provisions for public instruction, they may yet have much to learn, it must be admitted that they have risen to the condition of settled and established states more rapidly than could have been reasonably anticipated. They already furnish an exhilarating example of the difference between free governments, and despotic misrule. Their commerce, at this moment, creates a new activity in all the great marts of the world. They show themselves able, by an exchange of commodities, to bear a useful part in the intercourse of nations.

A new spirit of enterprise and industry begins to prevail; all the great interests of society receive a salutary impulse; and the progress of information not only testifies to an improved condition, but itself constitutes the highest and most essential improvement.

When the battle of Bunker Hill was fought, the existence of South America was scarcely felt in the civilized world. The thirteen little Colonies of North America habitually called themselves the "Continent." Borne down by colonial subjugation, monopoly, and bigotry, these vast regions of the South were hardly visible above the horizon. But in our day there has been, as it were, a new creation. The southern hemisphere emerges from the sea. Its lofty mountains begin to lift themselves into the light of heaven; its broad and fertile plains stretch out, in beauty, to the eye of civilized man, and at the mighty bidding of the voice of political liberty, the waters of darkness retire.

And, now, let us indulge an honest exultation in the conviction of the benefit which the example of our country has produced, and is likely to produce, on human freedom and human happiness. Let us endeavor to comprehend in all its magnitude, and to feel in all its importance, the part assigned to us in the great drama of human affairs. We are placed at the head of the system of representative and popular governments. Thus far our example shows that such governments are compatible, not only with respectability and power, but with repose, with peace, with security of personal rights, with good laws, and a just administration.

We are not propagandists. Wherever other systems are preferred, either as being thought better in themselves, or as better suited to existing condition, we leave the preference to be enjoyed. Our history hitherto proves, however, that the popular form is practicable, and that with wisdom and knowledge men may govern themselves; and the duty incumbent on us is, to preserve the consistency of this cheering example, and take care that nothing may weaken its authority with the world. If, in our case, the representative system ultimately fail, popular governments must be pronounced impossible. No combination of circumstances more favorable to the experiment can ever be expected to occur. The last hopes of mankind, therefore, rest with us; and if it should be proclaimed, that our example had become an argument against the experiment, the knell of popular liberty would be sounded throughout the earth.

These are excitements to duty; but they are not suggestions of doubt. Our history and our condition, all that is gone before us, and all that surrounds us, authorize the belief, that popular governments, though subject to occasional variations, in form perhaps not always for the better, may yet, in their general character, be as durable and permanent as other systems. We know, indeed, that in our country any other is impossible. The *principle* of free governments adheres to the American soil. It is bedded in it, immovable as its mountains.

And let the sacred obligations which have devolved on this generation, and on us, sink deep into our hearts. Those who established our liberty and our government are daily dropping from among us. The great trust now descends to new hands. Let us apply ourselves to that which is presented to us, as our appropriate object. We can win no laurels in a war for independence. Earlier and worthier hands have gathered them all. Nor are there places for us by the side of Solon, and Alfred, and other founders of states. Our fathers have filled them. But there remains to us a great duty of defence and preservation; and there is opened to us, also, a noble pursuit, to which the spirit of the times strongly invites us. Our proper business is improvement. Let our age be the age of improvement. In a day of peace, let us advance the arts of peace and the works of peace. Let us develop the resources of our land, call forth its powers, build up its institutions, promote all its great interests, and see whether we also, in our day and generation, may not perform something worthy to be remembered. Let us cultivate a true spirit of union and harmony. In pursuing the great objects which our condition points out to us, let us act under a settled conviction, and an habitual feeling, that these twenty-four States are one country. Let our conceptions be enlarged to the circle of our duties. Let us extend our ideas over the whole of the vast field in which we are called to act. Let our object be, OUR COUNTRY, OUR WHOLE COUNTRY, AND NOTHING BUT OUR COUNTRY. And, by the blessing of God, may that country itself become a vast and splendid monument, not of oppression and terror, but of Wisdom, of Peace, and of Liberty, upon which the world may gaze with admiration for ever!

EDWARD EVERETT

The History of Liberty

(Delivered at Charlestown, Massachusetts, July 4, 1828)

The event which we commemorate is all-important, not merely in our own annals, but in those of the world. The sententious English poet has declared that "the proper study of mankind is man," and of all inquiries of a temporal nature, the history of our fellow-beings is unquestionably among the most interesting. But not all the chapters of human history are alike important. The annals of our race have been filled up with incidents which concern not, or at least ought not to concern, the great company of mankind. History, as it has often been written, is the genealogy of princes, the field-book of conquerors; and the fortunes of our fellow-men have been treated only so far as they have been affected by the influence of the great masters and destroyers of our race. Such history is, I will not say a worthless study, for it is necessary for us to know the dark side as well as the bright side of our condition. But it is a melancholy study which fills the bosom of the philanthropist and the friend of liberty with sorrow.

But the history of liberty—the history of men struggling to be free—the history of men who have acquired and are exercising their freedom—the history of those great movements in the world, by which liberty has been established and perpetuated, forms a subject which we cannot contemplate too closely. This is the real history of man, of the human family, of rational immortal beings.

This theme is one—the free of all climes and nations are themselves a people. Their annals are the history of freedom. Those who fell victims to their principles in the civil convulsions of the short-lived republics of Greece, or who sunk beneath the power of her invading foes; those who shed their blood for liberty amidst the ruins of the Roman republic; the victims of Austrian tyranny in Switzerland and of Spanish tyranny in the Netherlands; the solitary champions or the united bands of high-minded and patriotic men who have, in any region or age, struggled and suffered in this great cause, belong to that people of the free whose fortunes and progress are the most noble theme man can contemplate.

The theme belongs to us. We inhabit a country which has been signalized in the great history of freedom. We live under forms of government more favorable to its diffusion than any the world has elsewhere known. A succession of incidents, of rare curiosity, and almost mysterious connection, has marked out America as a great theatre of political reform. Many circumstances stand recorded in our annals, connected with the assertion of human rights, which, were we not familiar with them, would fill even our own minds with amazement.

The theme belongs to the day. We celebrate the return of the day on which our separate national existence was declared—the day when the momentous experiment was commenced, by which the world, and posterity, and we ourselves were to be taught how far a nation of men can be trusted with self-government— how far life, liberty, and property are safe, and the progress of social improvement is secure, under the influence of laws made by those who are to obey them—the day when, for the first time in the world, a numerous people was ushered into the family of nations, organized on the principle of the political equality of all the citizens.

Let us, then, fellow-citizens, devote the time which has been set apart for this portion of the duties of the day, to a hasty review of the history of liberty, especially to a contemplation of some of those astounding incidents which preceded, accompanied, or have followed the settlement of America, and the establishment of our constitutions, and which plainly indicate a general tendency and co-operation of things towards the erection, in this country, of the great monitorial school of political freedom.

We hear much at school of the liberty of Greece and Rome—a great and complicated subject, which this is not the occasion to attempt to disentangle. True it is that we find, in the annals of both these nations, bright examples of public virtue—the record of faithful friends of their country—of strenuous foes of oppression at home or abroad—and admirable precedents of popular strength. But we nowhere find in them the account of a populous and extensive region, blessed with institutions securing the enjoyment and transmission of regulated liberty. In freedom, as in most other things, the ancient nations, while they made surprisingly close approaches to the truth, yet, for want of some one great and essential principle or instrument, they came utterly short of it in practice. They had profound and elegant scholars; but, for want of the art of printing, they could not send information out among the people, where alone it is of great use in reference to human happiness. Some of them ventured boldly out to sea, and possessed an aptitude for foreign commerce; yet, for want of the mariner's compass, they could not navigate distant seas, but crept for ages along the shores of the Mediterranean. In respect to freedom, they established popular governments in single cities; but, for want of the representative principle, they could not extend these institutions over a large and populous country. But as a large and populous country, generally speaking, can alone possess strength enough for self-defence, this want was fatal. The freest of their cities accordingly fell a prey, sooner of later, either to a foreign invader or to domestic traitors.

In this way, liberty made no firm progress in the ancient states. It was a speculation of the philosopher, and an experiment of the patriot, but not an established state of society. The patriots of Greece and Rome had indeed succeeded in enlightening the public mind on one of the cardinal points of freedom—the necessity of an elected executive. The name and the office of a king were long esteemed not only something to be rejected, but something rude and uncivilized, belonging to savage nations, ignorant of the rights of man, as understood in cultivated states. The word " tyrant," which originally meant no more than monarch, soon became with the Greeks synonymous with oppressor and despot, as it has continued to be ever since. When the first Cæsar made his encroachments on the liberties of Rome, the patriots even of that age boasted that they had

> ——heard their fathers say,
> There was a Brutus once, that would have brooked
> The eternal devil, to keep his state in Rome,
> As easily as a king.

So deeply rooted was this horror of the very name of king in the bosom of the Romans, that under their worst tyrants, and in the darkest days, the forms of the republic were preserved. There was no name under Nero and Caligula for the office of monarch. The individual who filled the office was called Cæsar and Augustus, after the first and second of the line. The word "emperor" *(imperator)* implied no more than general. The offices of consul and tribune were kept up; although, if the choice did not fall, as it frequently did, on the emperor, it was conferred on his favorite general, and sometimes on his favorite horse. The Senate continued to meet, and affected to deliberate; and, in short, the empire began and continued a pure military despotism, ingrafted, by a sort of permanent usurpation, on the forms and names of the ancient republic. The spirit, indeed, of liberty had long since ceased to animate these ancient forms, and when the barbarous tribes of Central Asia and Northern Europe burst into the Roman empire, they swept away the poor remnant of these forms, and established upon their ruins the system of feudal monarchy from which all modern kingdoms are descended. Efforts were made in the Middle Ages by the petty republics of Italy to regain the political rights which a long proscription had wrested from them. But the remedy of bloody civil wars between neighboring cities was plainly more disastrous than the disease of subjection. The struggles of freedom in these little states resulted much as they had done in Greece, exhibiting brilliant examples of individual character, and short intervals of public prosperity, but no permanent progress in the organization of liberal governments.

At length a new era seemed to begin. The art of printing was invented. The capture of Constantinople by the Turks drove the learned Greeks of that city into Italy, and letters revived. A general agitation of public sentiment in various parts of Europe ended in the religious reformation. A spirit of adventure had been awakened in the maritime nations, projects of remote discovery were started, and the signs of the times seemed to augur a great political regeneration. But, as if to blast this hope in its bud; as if to counterbalance at once the operations of these springs of improvement; as if to secure the permanence of the arbitrary institutions which existed in every part of the continent, at the moment when it was most threatened, the last blow at the same time was given to the remaining power of the great barons, the sole check on the despotism of the monarch which the feudal system provided was removed, and a new institution was firmly established in Europe, prompt, efficient, and terrible in its operation beyond anything which the modern world has seen—I mean the system of standing armies; in other words, a military force organized and paid to support the king on his throne and retain the people in their subjection.

From this moment the fate of freedom in Europe was sealed. Something might be hoped from the amelioration of manners in softening down the more barbarous parts of political despotism, but nothing was to be expected in the form of liberal institutions, founded on principle.

The ancient and the modern forms of political servitude were thus combined. The Roman emperors, as I have hinted, maintained themselves simply by military force, in nominal accordance with the forms of the republic. Their power (to speak in modern terms) was no part of the constitution. The feudal sovereigns possessed a constitutional precedence in the state, which, after the diffusion of Christianity, they claimed by the grace of God; but their power, in point of fact, was circumscribed by that of their brother barons. With the firm establishment of standing armies was consummated a system of avowed despotism, paralyzing all expression of the popular will, existing by divine right, and unbalanced by any effectual check in the state. It needs but a glance at the state of Europe, in the beginning of the sixteenth century, to see, that, notwithstanding the revival and diffusion of letters, the progress of the reformation, and the improvement of the manners, the tone of the people, in the most enlightened countries, was more abject than it had been since the days of the Cæsars. The state of England certainly compared favorably with that of any other part of Europe; but who can patiently listen to the language with which Henry VII chides, and Elizabeth scolds the Lords and Commons of the Parliament of Great Britain?

All hope of liberty then seemed lost; in Europe all hope was lost. A disastrous turn has been given to the general movement of things; and in the disclosure of the fatal secret of standing armies, the future political servitude of man was apparently decided.

But a change is destined to come over the face of things, as romantic in its origin as it is wonderful in its progress. All is not lost; on the contrary, all is saved, at the moment when all seemed involved in ruin. Let me just allude to the incidents connected with this change, as they have lately been described by an accomplished countryman, now beyond the sea.

About half a league from the little port of Palos, in the province of Andalusia, in Spain, stands a convent dedicated to St. Mary. Some time in the year 1486, a poor, wayfaring stranger, accompanied by a small boy, makes his appearance on foot at the gate of this convent, and begs of the porter a little bread and water for his child. This friendless stranger is Columbus. Brought up in the hardy pursuit of a mariner—occasionally serving in the fleets of his native country—with the burden of fifty years upon his frame, the unprotected foreigner makes his suit to the sovereigns of Portugal and Spain. He tells them that the broad, flat earth on which we tread is round; and he proposes, with what seems a sacrilegious hand, to lift the veil which has hung from the creation of the world over the bounds of the ocean. He promises, by a western course, to reach the eastern shores of Asia, the region of gold, diamonds, and spices; to extend the sovereignty of Christian kings over the realms and nations hitherto unapproached and unknown; and, ultimately, to perform a new crusade to the Holy Land, and ransom the sepulchre of our Saviour with the new-found gold of the East.

Who shall believe the chimerical pretension? The learned men examine it and pronounce it futile. The royal pilots have ascertained by their own experience that it is groundless. The priesthood have considered it, and have pronounced that sentence, so terrific where the Inquisition reigns, that it is a wicked heresy. The common-sense and popular feeling of men have been kindled into disdain and indignation towards a project, which, by a strange, new chimera, represented one-half of mankind walking with their feet towards the other half.

Such is the reception which his proposal meets. For a long time the great cause of humanity, depending on the discovery of this fair continent, is involved in the fortitude, perseverance, and spirit of the solitary stranger, already past the time of life when the pulse of adventure beats full and high. If, sinking beneath the indifference of the great, the sneers of the wise, the enmity of the mass, and the persecution of a host of adversaries, high and low, he give up the thankless pursuit of his noble vision, what a hope for mankind is blasted! But he does not sink. He shakes off his enemies, as the lion shakes the dewdrops from his mane. That consciousness of motive and of strength, which always supports the man who is worthy to be supported, sustains him in his hour of trial; and, at length, after years of expectation, importunity, and hope deferred, he launches forth upon the unknown deep, to discover a new world under the patronage of Ferdinand and Isabella.

The patronage of Ferdinand and Isabella! Let us dwell for a moment on the auspices under which our country was discovered. The patronage of Ferdinand and Isabella! Yes, doubtless, they have fitted out a convoy worthy the noble temper of the man and the grandeur of his project. Convinced at length that it is no day-dream of a heated visionary, the fortunate sovereigns of Castile and Aragon, returning from their triumph over the last of the Moors, and putting a victorious close to a war of seven centuries' duration, have no doubt prepared an expedition of well-appointed magnificence to go out upon this splendid search for other worlds. They have made ready, no doubt, their proudest galleon to waft the heroic adventurer upon his path of glory, with a whole armada of kindred spirits to accompany him.

Alas! from his ancient resort of Palos—which he first visited as a mendicant—in three frail barks, of which two were without decks, the great discoverer of America sails forth on the first voyage across the unexplored ocean! Such is the patronage of kings! A few years pass by; he discovers a new hemisphere; the wildest of his visions fade into insignificance before the reality of their fulfilment; he finds a new world for Castile and Leon, and comes back to Spain loaded with chains. Republics, it is said, are ungrateful. Such are the rewards of monarchies!

With this humble instrumentality did it please Providence to prepare the theatre for those events by which a new dispensation of liberty was to be communicated to man. But much is yet to transpire before even the commencement can be made in the establishment of those institutions by which this great advance in human affairs was to be affected. The discovery of America had taken place under the auspices of the government most disposed for maritime adventure, and best enabled to extend a helping arm, such as it was, to the enterprise of the great discoverer. But it was not from the same quarter that the elements of liberty could be introduced into the New World. Causes, upon which I need not dwell, made it impossible that the great political reform should go forth from Spain. For this object, a new train of incidents was preparing in another quarter.

The only real advance which modern Europe had made in freedom had been made in England. The cause of constitutional liberty in that country was persecuted, was subdued, but not annihilated, nor trampled out of being. From the choicest of its suffering champions were collected the brave band of emigrants who first went out on the second, the more precious voyage of discovery—the discovery of a land where liberty and its consequent blessings might be established.

A late English writer has permitted himself to say that the original establishment of the United States, and that of the colony of Botany Bay, were modelled nearly on the same plan. The meaning of this slanderous insinuation is, that the United States was settled by deported convicts, as New South Wales has been settled by transported felons. It is doubtless true that at one period the English government was in the habit of condemning to hard labor, as servants in the colonies, a portion of those who had received a sentence of the law. If this practice makes it proper to compare America with Botany Bay, the same comparison might be made of England herself, before the practice of transportation began, and even now, inasmuch as a considerable number of convicts are at all times retained at home. In one sense, indeed, we might doubt whether the allegation were more of a reproach or a compliment. During the time that the colonization of America was going on most rapidly, some of the best citizens of England, if it be any part of good citizenship to resist oppression, were immured in her prisons of state or lying at the mercy of the law.

Such were some of the convicts by whom America was settled—men convicted of fearing God more than they feared man; of sacrificing property, ease, and all the comforts of life, to a sense of duty and to the dictates of conscience; men convicted of pure lives, brave hearts, and simple manners. The enterprise was led by Raleigh, the chivalrous convict, who unfortunately believed that his royal master had the heart of a man, and would not let a sentence of death, which had slumbered for sixteen years, revive and take effect after so long an interval of employment and favor. But *nullum tempus occurrit regi*. The felons who followed next were the heroic and long-suffering church of Robinson, at Leyden—Carver, Brewster, Bradford, Winslow, and their pious associates, convicted of worshipping God according to the dictates of their consciences, and of giving up all—country, property, and the tombs of their fathers—that they might do it unmolested. Not content with having driven the Puritans from her soil, England next enacted or put in force the oppressive laws which colonized Maryland with Catholics, and Pennsylvania with Quakers. Nor was it long before the American plantations were recruited by the Germans, convicted of inhabiting the Palatinate, when the merciless armies of Louis XIV were turned into that devoted region, and by the Huguenots, convicted of holding what they deemed the simple truth of Christianity, when it pleased the mistress of Louis XIV to be very zealous for the Catholic faith. These were followed, in the next century, by the Highlanders, convicted of the enormous crime, under a monarchical government, of loyalty to their hereditary prince on the plains of Culloden, and the Irish, convicted of supporting the rights of their country against what they deemed an oppressive external power. Such are the convicts by whom America was settled.

In this way, a fair representation of whatsoever was most valuable in European character—the resolute industry of one nation, the inventive skill and curious arts of another, the courage, conscience, principle, self-denial of all—was winnowed out, by the policy of the prevailing governments, as a precious seed wherewith to plant the American soil. By this singular coincidence of events, our country was constituted the great asylum of suffering virtue and oppressed humanity. It could now no longer be said—as it was of the Roman empire—that mankind was shut up, as if in a vast prison house, from whence there was no escape. The political and ecclesiastical oppressors of the world allowed their persecution to find a limit at the shores of the Atlantic. They scarcely ever attempted to pursue their victims beyond its protecting waters. It is plain that in this way alone the design of Providence could be accomplished, which provided for one catholic school of freedom in the western hemisphere. For it must not be a freedom of too sectional and peculiar a cast. On the stock of the English civilization, as the general basis, were to be ingrafted the languages, the arts, and the tastes of the other civilized nations. A tie of consanguinity must connect the members of every family of Europe with some portion of our happy land; so that in all their trials and disasters they may look safely beyond the ocean for a refuge. The victims of power, of intolerance, of war, of disaster, in every other part of the world, must feel that they may find a kindred home within our limits. Kings, whom the perilous convulsions of the day have shaken from their thrones, must find a safe retreat; and the needy emigrant must at least not fail of his bread and water, were it not only for the sake of the great discoverer, who was himself obliged to beg them. On this corner-stone the temple of our freedom was laid from the first—

> For here the exile met from every clime,
> And spoke in friendship every distant tongue;
> Men, from the blood of warring Europe sprung,
> Were here divided by the running brook.

This peculiarity of our population, which some have thought a misfortune, is in reality one of the happiest circumstances attending the settlement of the country. It assures the exile from every part of Europe a kind reception from men of his own tongue and race. Had we been the unmixed descendants of any one nation of Europe, we should have retained a moral and intellectual dependence on that nation, even after the dissolution of our political connection had taken place. It was sufficient for the great purpose in view that the earliest settlements were made by men who had fought the battles of liberty in England, and who brought with them the rudiments of constitutional freedom to a region where no deep-rooted proscriptions would prevent their development. Instead of marring the symmetry of our social system, it is one of the most attractive and beautiful peculiarities, that, with the prominent qualities of the Anglo-Saxon character inherited from our English fathers, we have an admixture of almost everything that is valuable in the character of most of the other states of Europe.

Such was the first preparation for the great political reform, of which America was to be the theatre. The colonies of England—of a country where the supremacy of laws and the constitution is best recognized—the North American colonies—were protected from the first against the introduction of the unmitigated despotism which prevailed in the Spanish settlements—the continuance of which, down to the moment of their late revolt, prevented the education of these provinces in the exercise of political rights, and in that way has thrown them into the revolution inexperienced and unprepared—victims, some of them, to a domestic anarchy scarcely less grievous than the foreign yoke they have thrown off. While, however, the settlers of America brought with them the principles and feelings, the political habits and temper, which defied the encroachment of arbitrary power, and made it necessary, when they were to be oppressed under the forms of law, it was an unavoidable consequence of the state of things—a result, perhaps, of the very nature of a colonial government—that they should be thrown into a position of whole controversy with the mother-country, and thus become familiar with the whole energetic doctrine and discipline of resistance. This formed and hardened the temper of the colonists, and trained them up to a spirit meet for the struggles of separation.

On the other hand, by what I had almost called an accidental circumstance, but one which ought rather to be considered as a leading incident in the great train of events connected with the establishment of constitutional freedom in this country, it came to pass that nearly all the colonies (founded as they were on the charters granted to corporate institutions in England, which had for their object the pursuit of the branches of industry and trade pertinent to a new plantation) adopted a regular representative system, by which, as in ordinary civil corporations, the affairs of the community are decided by the will and the voices of its members, or those authorized by them. It was no device of the parent government which gave us our colonial assemblies. It was no refinement of philosophical statesmen to which we are indebted for our republican institutions of government. They grew up, as it were, by accident, on the simple foundation I have named. "A House of Burgesses," says Hutchinson, "broke out in Virginia, in 1620"; and, "although there was no color for it in the charter of Massachusetts, a House of Deputies appeared suddenly in 1634." "Lord Say," observes the same historian, "tempted the principal men of Massachusetts to make themselves and their heirs nobles and absolute governors of a new colony, but, under this plan, they could find no people to follow them."

At this early period, and in this simple, unpretending manner, was introduced to the world that greatest discovery in political science, or political practice, a representative republican system. "The discovery of the system of the representative republic," says M. de Chateâubriand, "is one of the greatest political events that ever occurred." But it is not one of the greatest, it is the very greatest, and, combined with another principle, to which I shall presently avert, and which is also the invention of the United States, it marks an era in human affairs—a discovery in the great science of social life, compared with which everything else that terminates in the temporal interests of man, sinks into insignificance.

Thus, then, was the foundation laid, and thus was the preparation commenced, of the world's grand political regeneration. For about a century and a half this preparation was carried on. Without any of the temptations which drew the Spanish adventurers to Mexico and Peru the colonies throve almost beyond example, and in the face of neglect, contempt, and persecution. Their numbers, in the substantial, middle classes of life, increased with regular rapidity. They had no materials out of which an aristocracy could be formed, and no great eleemosynary establishments to cause an influx of paupers. There was nothing but the rewards of labor and the hope of freedom.

But at length this hope, never adequately satisfied, began to turn into doubt and despair. The colonies had become too important to be overlooked; their government was a prerogative too important to be left in their own hands; and the legislation of the mother-country decidedly assumed a form which announced to the patriots that the hour at length had come when the chains of the great discoverer were to be avenged, the sufferings of the first settlers to be compensated, and the long-deferred hopes of humanity to be fulfilled.

You need not, friends and fellow-citizens, that I should dwell upon the incidents of the last great acts in the colonial drama. This very place was the scene of some of the earliest and the most memorable of them, and their recollection in a part of your inheritance of honor. In the early councils and first struggles of the great revolutionary enterprise, the citizens of this place were among the most prominent. The measures of resistance which were projected by the patriots of Charlestown were opposed by but one individual. An active co-operation existed between the political leaders in Boston and this place. The beacon light which was kindled in the towers of Christ Church in Boston, on the night of April 18, 1775, was answered from the steeple of the church in which we are now assembled. The intrepid messenger who was sent forward to convey to Hancock and Adams the intelligence of the approach of the British troops was furnished with a horse, for his eventful errand, by a respected citizen of this place. At the close of the following momentous day, the British forces—the remnant of its disasters—found refuge, under the shades of night, upon the heights of Charlestown; and there, on the ever-memorable seventeenth of June, that great and costly sacrifice in the cause of freedom was consummated with fire and blood. Your hilltops were strewed with illustrious dead; your homes were wrapped in flames; the fair fruits of a century and a half of civilized culture were reduced to a heap of bloody ashes, and two thousand men, women, and children turned houseless on the world. With the exception of the ravages of the nineteenth of April, the chalice of woe and desolation was in this manner first presented to the lips of the citizens of Charlestown. Thus devoted, as it were, to the cause, it is no wonder that the spirit of the Revolution should have taken possession of their bosoms, and been transmitted to their children. The American, who, in any part of the Union, could forget the scenes and the principles of the Revolution, would thereby prove himself unworthy of the blessings which he enjoys; but the citizen of Charlestown, who could be cold on this momentous theme, must hear a voice of reproach from the walls which were reared on the ashes of the seventeenth of June—a piercing cry from the very sods of yonder hill.

The Revolution was at length accomplished. The political separation of the country of Great Britain was effected, and it now remained to organize the liberty which had been reaped on bloody fields—to establish, in the place of the government whose yoke had been thrown off, a government at home, which should fulfil the great design of the Revolution and satisfy the demands of the friends of liberty at large. What manifold perils awaited the step! The danger was great that too little or too much would be done. Smarting under the oppressions of a distant government, whose spirit was alien to their feelings, there was great danger that the colonies, in the act of declaring themselves sovereign and independent states, would push to an extreme the prerogative of their separate independence, and refuse to admit any authority beyond the limits of each particular commonwealth. On the other hand, achieving their independence under the banners of the Continental Army, ascribing, and justly, a large portion of their success to the personal qualities of the beloved father of his country, there was danger not less imminent, that those who perceived the evils of the opposite extreme, would be disposed to confer too much strength on one general government, and would, perhaps, even fancy the necessity of investing the hero of the Revolution, in form, with that sovereign power which his personal ascendancy gave him in the hearts of his countrymen. Such and so critical was the alternative which the organization of the new government presented, and on the successful issue of which the entire benefit of this great movement in human affairs was to depend.

The first effort to solve the great problem was made in the course of the Revolution, and was without success. The Articles of Confederation verged to the extreme of a union too weak for its great purposes; and the moment the pressure of this war was withdrawn, the inadequacy of this first project of a government was felt. The United States found themselves overwhelmed with debt, without the means of paying it. Rich in the materials of an extensive commerce, they found their ports crowded with foreign ships, and themselves without the power to raise a revenue. Abounding in all the elements of national wealth, they wanted resources to defray the ordinary expenses of government.

For a moment, and to the hasty observer, this last effort for the establishment of freedom had failed. No fruit had sprung from this lavish expenditure of treasure and blood. We had changed the powerful protection of the mother-country into a cold and jealous amity, if not into a slumbering hostility. The oppressive principles against which our fathers had struggled were succeeded by more oppressive realities. The burden of the British Navigation Act, as it operated on the colonies, was removed, but it was followed by the impossibility of protecting our shipping by a navigation act of our own. A state of material prosperity, existing before the Revolution, was succeeded by universal exhaustion; and a high and indignant tone of militant patriotism, by universal despondency.

It remained, then, to give its last great effort to all that had been done since the discovery of America for the establishment of the cause of liberty in the western hemisphere, and by another more deliberate effort to organize a government by which not only the present evils under which the country was suffering should be remedied, but the final design of Providence should be fulfilled. Such was the task that devolved on the statesmen who convened at Philadelphia on May 2, 1787, in the assembly of which General Washington was elected president, and over whose debates your townsman, Mr. Gorham, presided for two or three months as chairman of the committee of the whole, during the discussion of the plan of the federal constitution.

The very first step to be taken was one of pain and regret. The old confederation was to be given up. What misgivings and grief must not this preliminary sacrifice have occasioned to the patriotic members of the convention! They were attached, and with reason, to its simple majesty. It was weak then, but it had been strong enough to carry the colonies through the storms of Revolution. Some of the great men who led up the forlorn hope of their country in the hour of her direst peril, had died in its defence. Could not a little inefficiency be pardoned to a Union with which France had made an alliance, and England had made peace? Could the proposed new government do more or better things than this had done? Who could give assurance, when the flag of the old thirteen was struck, that the hearts of the people could be rallied to another banner?

Such were the misgivings of some of the great men of that day—the Henrys, the Gerrys, and other eminent anti-federalists, to whose scruples it is time that justice should be done. They were the sagacious misgivings of wise men, the just forebodings of brave men, who were determined not to defraud posterity of the blessings for which they had all suffered, and for which some of them had fought.

The members of that convention, in going about the great work before them, deliberately laid aside the means by which all preceding legislators had aimed to accomplish a like work. In founding a strong and efficient government, adequate to the raising up of a powerful and prosperous people, their first step was to reject the institutions in which other governments traced their strength and prosperity, or had, at least, regarded as the necessary conditions of stability and order. The world had settled down into the belief that an hereditary monarch was necessary to give strength to the executive power. The framers of our constitution provided for an elective chief magistrate, chosen every four years. Every other country had been betrayed into the admission of a distinction of ranks in society, under the absurd impression that privileged orders are necessary to the permanence of the social system. The framers of our constitution established everything on the purely natural basis of a uniform equality of the elective franchise, to be exercised by all the citizens at fixed and short intervals. In other countries it had been thought necessary to constitute some one political centre, towards which all political power should tend, and at which, in the last resort, it should be exercised. The framers of the constitution devised a scheme of confederate and representative sovereign republics, united in a happy distribution of powers, which, reserving to the separate states all the political functions essential to local administrations and private justice, bestowed upon the general government those, and those only, required for the service of the whole.

Thus was completed the great revolutionary movement; thus was perfected that mature organization of a free system, destined, as we trust, to stand forever, as the exemplar of popular government. Thus was discharged the duty of our fathers to themselves, to the country, and to the world.

The power of the example thus set up, in the eyes of the nations, was instantly and widely felt. It was immediately made visible to sagacious observers that a constitutional age had begun. It was in the nature of things, that, where the former evil existed in its most inveterate form, the reaction should also be the most violent. Hence, the dreadful excesses that marked the progress of the French Revolution, and, for a while, almost made the name of liberty odious. But it is not less in the nature of things, that, when the most indisputable and enviable political blessings stand illustrated before the world—not merely in speculation and in theory, but in living practice and bright example—the nations of the earth, in proportion as they have eyes to see, and ears to hear, and hands to grasp, should insist on imitating the example. France clung to the hope of constitutional liberty through thirty years of appalling tribulation, and now enjoys the freest constitution in Europe. Spain, Portugal, the two Italian kingdoms, and several of the German states, have entered on the same path. Their progress has been and must be various, modified by circumstances, by the interests and passions of governments and men, and, in some cases, seemingly arrested. But their march is as sure as fate. If we believe at all in the political revival of Europe, there can be no really retrograde movement in this cause; and that which seems so in the revolutions of government, is, like that of the heavenly bodies, a part of their eternal orbit.

There can be no retreat, for the great exemplar must stand, to convince the hesitating nations, under every reverse, that the reform they strive at is real, is practicable, is within their reach. Efforts at reform, by the power of action and reaction, may fluctuate; but there is an element of popular strength abroad in the world, stronger than forms and institutions, and daily growing in power. A public opinion of a new kind has risen among men—the opinion of the civilized world. Springing into existence on the shores of our own continent, it has grown with our growth and strengthened with our strength, till now, this moral giant, like that of the ancient poet, marches along the earth and across the ocean, but his front is among the stars. The course of the day does not weary, nor the darkness of the night arrest him. He grasps the pillars of the temple where Oppression sits enthroned, not groping and benighted, like the strong man of old, to be crushed, himself, beneath the fall, but trampling, in his strength, on the massy ruins.

Under the influence, I might almost say the unaided influence, of public opinion, formed and nourished by our example, three wonderful revolutions have broken out in a generation. That of France, not yet consummated, has left that country (which it found in a condition scarcely better than Turkey) in the possession of the blessings of a representative constitutional government. Another revolution has emancipated the American possessions of Spain, by an almost unassisted action of moral causes. Nothing but the strong sense of the age, that a government like that of Ferdinand ought not to subsist over regions like those which stretch to the south of us on the continent, could have sufficed to bring about their emancipation, against all the obstacles which the state of society among them opposes at present to regulated liberty and safe independence. When an eminent British statesman (Mr. Canning) said of the emancipation of these states, that "he had called into existence a new world in the West," he spoke as wisely as the artist who, having tipped the forks of a conductor with silver, should boast that he had created the lightning which it calls down from the clouds. But the greatest triumph of public opinion is the revolution of Greece. The spontaneous sense of the friends of liberty, at home and abroad—without armies, without navies, without concert, and acting only through the simple channels of ordinary communication, principally the press—has rallied the governments of Europe to this ancient and favored soil of freedom. Pledged to remain at peace, they have been driven by the force of public sentiment into war. Leagued against the cause of revolution, as such, they have been compelled to send their armies and navies to fight the battles of revolt. Dignifying the barbarous oppressor of Christian Greece with the title of "ancient and faithful ally," they have been constrained, by the outraged feelings of the civilized world, to burn up, in time of peace, the navy of their ally, with all his antiquity and all his fidelity; and to cast the broad shield of the Holy Alliance over a young and turbulent republic.

This bright prospect may be clouded in; the powers of Europe, which have reluctantly taken, may speedily abandon the field. Some inglorious composition may yet save the Ottoman Empire from dissolution, at the sacrifice of the liberty of Greece, and the power of Europe. But such are not the indications of things. The prospect is fair that the political regeneration, which commenced in the West, is now going backward to resuscitate the once happy and long-deserted regions of the older world. The hope is not now chimerical, that those lovely islands, the flower of the Levant—the shores of that renowned sea, around which all associations of antiquity are concentrated—are again to be brought back to the sway of civilization and Christianity. Happily, the interest of the great powers of Europe seems to beckon them onward in the path of humanity. The half-deserted coasts of Syria and Egypt, the fertile but almost desolated archipelago, the empty shores of Africa, the granary of ancient Rome, seem to offer themselves as a ready refuge for the crowded, starving, discontented millions of Western Europe. No natural nor political obstacle opposes itself to their occupation. France has long cast a wistful eye on Egypt. Napoleon derived the idea of his expedition, which was set down to the unchastened ambition of a revolutionary soldier, from a memoir found in the cabinet of Louis XIV. England has already laid her hand—an arbitrary, but a civilized and a Christian hand—on Malta; and the Ionian isles, and Cyprus, Rhodes, and Claudia must soon follow. It is not beyond the reach of hope, that a representative republic may be established in Central Greece and the adjacent islands. In this way, and with the example of what has been done, it is not too much to anticipate that many generations will not pass, before the same benignant influence will revisit the awakened East, and thus fulfil, in the happiest sense, the vision of Columbus, by restoring a civilized population to the primitive seats of our holy faith.

Fellow-citizens, the eventful pages in the volume of human fortune are opening upon us with sublime rapidity of succession. It is two hundred years this summer since a few of that party who, in 1628, commenced in Salem the first settlement of Massachusetts, were sent by Governor Endicott to explore the spot where we stand. They found that one pioneer of the name of Walford had gone before them, and had planted himself among the numerous and warlike savages in this quarter. From them, the native lords of the soil, these first hardy adventurers derived their title to the lands on which they settled, and, in some degree, prepared the way by the arts of civilization and peace; for the main body of the colonists of Massachusetts came under Governor Winthrop, who, two years afterward, by a coincidence which you will think worth naming, arrived in Mystic River, and pitched his patriarchal tent on Ten Hills, on June 17, 1630. Massachusetts at that moment consisted of six huts at Salem and one at this place. It seems but a span of time as the mind ranges over it. A venerable individual is living, at the seat of the first settlement, whose life covers one-half of the entire period; but what a destiny has been unfolded before our country! what events have crowded your annals! what scenes of thrilling interest and eternal glory have signalized the very spot where we stand!

In that unceasing march of things, which calls forward the successive generations of men to perform their part on the stage of life, we at length are summoned to appear. Our fathers have passed their hour of visitation—how worthily, let the growth and prosperity of our happy land and the security of our firesides attest. Or, if this appeal be too weak to move us, let the eloquent silence of yonder famous heights—let the column which is there rising in simple majesty—recall their venerable forms, as they toiled in the hasty trenches through the dreary watches of that night of expectation, heaving up the sods, where many of them lay in peace and honor before the following sun had set. The turn has come to us. The trial of adversity was theirs; the trial of prosperity is ours. Let us meet it as men who know their duty and prize their blessings. Our position is the most enviable, the most responsible, which men can fill. If this generation does its duty, the cause of constitutional freedom is safe. If we fail—if we fail, not only do we defraud our children of the inheritance which we received from our fathers, but we blast the hopes of the friends of liberty throughout our continent, throughout Europe, throughout the world, to the end of time.

History is not without her examples of hard-fought fields, where the banner of liberty has floated triumphantly on the wildest storm of battle. She is without her examples of a people by whom the dear-bought treasure has been wisely employed and safely handed down. The eyes of the world are turned for that example to us. It is related by an ancient historian, of that Brutus who slew Cæsar, that he threw himself on his sword, after the disastrous battle of Philippi, with the bitter exclamation, that he had followed virtue as a substance, but found it a name. It is not too much to say, that there are, at this moment, noble spirits in the elder world, who are anxiously watching the practical operation of our institutions, to learn whether liberty, as they have been told, is a mockery, a pretence, a curse—or a blessing, for which it became them to brave the scaffold and the scimitar.

Let us, then, as we assemble on the birthday of the nation, as we gather upon the green turf, once wet with precious blood—let us devote ourselves to the sacred cause of constitutional liberty! Let us abjure the interests and passions which divide the great family of American freemen! Let the range of party spirit sleep to-day! Let us resolve that our children shall have cause to bless the memory of their fathers, as we have cause to bless the memory of ours!

RALPH WALDO EMERSON

Man the Reformer

*(Delivered Before the Mechanics' Apprentices' Library Association
in Boston, Massachusetts, January 25, 1841)*

I wish to offer to your consideration some thoughts on the particular and general relations of man as a reformer. I shall assume that the aim of each young man in this association is the very highest that belongs to a rational mind. Let it be granted that our life, as we lead it, is common and mean; that some of those offices and functions for which we were mainly created are grown so rare in society that the memory of them is only kept alive in old books and in dim traditions; that prophets and poets, that beautiful and perfect men we are not now, no, nor have even seen such; that some sources of human instruction are almost unnamed and unknown among us; that the community in which we live will hardly bear to be told that every man should be open to ecstacy or a divine illumination, and his daily walk elevated by intercourse with the spiritual world. Grant all this, as we must, yet I suppose none of my auditors will deny that we ought to seek to establish ourselves in such disciplines and courses as will deserve that guidance and clearer communication with the spiritual nature. And further, I will not dissemble my hope that each person whom I address has felt his own call to cast aside all evil customs, timidities, and limitations, and to be in his place a free and helpful man, a reformer, a benefactor, not content to slip along through the world like a footman or a spy, escaping by his nimbleness and apologies as many knocks as he can, but a brave and upright man, who must find or cut a straight road to everything excellent in the earth, and not only go honorably himself, but make it easier for all who follow him to go in honor and with benefit.

In the history of the world the doctrine of Reform had never such scope as at the present hour. Lutherans, Herrnhutters, Jesuits, Monks, Quakers, Knox, Wesley, Swedenborg, Bentham, in their accusations of society, all respected something,—church or state, literature or history, domestic usages, the market town, the dinner table, coined money. But now all these and all things else hear the trumpet, and must rush to judgment,—Christianity, the laws, commerce, schools, the farm, the laboratory; and not a kingdom, town, statute, rite, calling, man, or woman, but is threatened by the new spirit.

What if some of the objections whereby our institutions are assailed are extreme and speculative, and the reformers tend to idealism? That only shows the extravagance of the abuses which have driven the mind into the opposite extreme. It is when your facts and persons grow unreal and fantastic by too much falsehood, that the scholar flies for refuge to the world of ideas, and aims to recruit and replenish nature from that source. Let ideas establish their legitimate sway again in society, let life be fair and poetic, and the scholars will gladly be lovers, citizens, and philanthropists.

It will afford no security from the new ideas, that the old nations, the laws of centuries, the property and institutions of a hundred cities, are built on other foundations. The demon of reform has a secret door into the heart of every lawmaker, of every inhabitant of every city. The fact that a new thought and hope have dawned in your breast, should apprize you that in the same hour a new light broke in upon a thousand private hearts. That secret which you would fain keep,—as soon as you go abroad, lo! there is one standing on the doorstep to tell you the same. There is not the most bronzed and sharpened money-catcher who does not, to your consternation almost, quail and shake the moment he hears a question prompted by the new ideas. We thought he had some semblance of ground to stand upon, that such as he at least would die hard; but he trembles and flees. Then the scholar says, "Cities and coaches shall never impose on me again; for behold every solitary dream of mine is rushing to fulfilment. That fancy I had, and hesitated to utter because you would laugh,—the broker, the attorney, the market-man are saying the same thing. Had I waited a day longer to speak, I had been too late. Behold, State Street thinks, and Wall Street doubts, and begins to prophesy!"

It cannot be wondered at that this general inquest into abuses should arise in the bosom of society, when one considers the practical impediments that stand in the way of virtuous young men. The young man, on entering life, finds the way to lucrative employments blocked with abuses. The ways of trade are grown selfish to the borders of theft, and supple to the borders (if not beyond the borders) of fraud. The employments of commerce are not intrinsically unfit for a man, or less genial to his faculties; but these are now in their general course so vitiated by derelictions and abuses at which all connive, that it requires more vigor and resources than can be expected of every young man, to right himself in them; he is lost in them; he cannot move hand or foot in them. Has he genius and virtue? the less does he find them fit for him to grow in, and if he would thrive in them, he must sacrifice all the brilliant dreams of boyhood and youth as dreams; he must forget the prayers of his childhood and must take on him the harness of routine and obsequiousness. If not so minded, nothing is left him but to begin the world anew, as he does who puts the spade into the ground for food. We are all implicated of course in this charge; it is only necessary to ask a few questions as to the progress of the articles of commerce from the fields where they grew, to our houses, to become aware that we eat and drink and wear perjury and fraud in a hundred commodities. How many articles of daily consumption are furnished us from the West Indies; yet it is said that in the Spanish islands the venality of the officers of the government has passed into usage, and that no article passes into our ships which has not been fraudulently cheapened. In the Spanish islands, every agent or factor of the Americans, unless he be a consul, has taken oath that he is a Catholic, or has caused a priest to make that declaration for him. The abolitionist has shown us our dreadful debt to the southern negro. In the island of Cuba, in addition to the ordinary abominations of slavery, it appears only men are bought for the plantations, and one dies in ten every year, of these miserable bachelors, to yield us sugar. I leave for those who have the knowledge the part of sifting the oaths of our custom-houses; I will not inquire into the oppression of the sailors; I will not pry into the usages of our retail trade. I content myself with the fact that the general system of our trade (apart from the blacker traits, which, I hope, are exceptions denounced and unshared by all reputable men) is a system of selfishness; is not dictated by the high sentiments of human nature; is not measured by the exact law of reciprocity, much less by the sentiments of love and heroism, but is a system of distrust, of concealment, of superior keenness, not of giving but of taking advantage. It is not that which a man delights to unlock to a noble friend; which he meditates on with joy and self-approval in his hour of love and aspiration; but rather what he then puts out of sight, only showing the brilliant result, and atoning for the manner of acquiring, by the manner of expending it. I do not charge the merchant or the manufacturer. The sins of our trade belong to no class, to no individual. One plucks, one distributes, one eats. Every body partakes, every body confesses,—with cap and knee volunteers his confession, yet none feels himself accountable. He did not create the abuse; he cannot alter it. What is he? an obscure private person who must get his bread. That is the vice,—that no one feels himself called to act for man, but only as a fraction of man. It happens therefore that all such ingenuous souls as feel within themselves the irrepressible strivings of a noble aim, who by the law of their nature must act simply, find these ways of trade unfit for them, and they come forth from it. Such cases are becoming more numerous every year.

But by coming out of trade you have not cleared yourself. The trail of the serpent reaches into all the lucrative professions and practices of man. Each has

its own wrongs. Each finds a tender and very intelligent conscience a disqualifica-
tion for success. Each requires of the practitioner a certain shutting of the eyes,
a certain dapperness and compliance, an acceptance of customs, a sequestration
from the sentiments of generosity and love, a compromise of private opinion and
lofty integrity. Nay, the evil custom reaches into the whole institution of property,
until our laws which establish and protect it seem not to be the issue of love and
reason, but of selfishness. Suppose a man is so unhappy as to be born a saint, with
keen perceptions but with the conscience and love of an angel, and he is to get
his living in the world; he finds himself excluded from all lucrative works; he has
no farm, and he cannot get one; for to earn money enough to buy one requires a
sort of concentration toward money, which is the selling himself for a number of
years, and to him the present hour is as sacred and inviolable as any future hour.
Of course, whilst another man has no land, my title to mine, your title to yours,
is at once vitiated. Inextricable seem to be the twinings and tendrils of this evil,
and we all involve ourselves in it the deeper by forming connections, by wives and
children, by benefits and debts.

Considerations of this kind have turned the attention of many philanthropic
and intelligent persons to the claims of manual labor, as a part of the education
of every young man. If the accumulated wealth of the past generation is thus
tainted,—no matter how much of it is offered to us,—we must begin to consider
if it were not the nobler part to renounce it, and to put ourselves into primary
relations with the soil and nature, and abstaining from whatever is dishonest and
unclean, to take each of us bravely his part, with his own hands, in the manual
labor of the world.

But it is said, "What! will you give up the immense advantages reaped from
the division of labor, and set every man to make his own shoes, bureau, knife,
wagon, sails, and needle? This would be to put men back into barbarism by their
own act." I see no instant prospect of a virtuous revolution; yet I confess I should
not be pained at a change which threatened a loss of some of the luxuries or
conveniences of society, if it proceeded from a preference of the agricultural life
out of the belief that our primary duties as men could be better discharged in
that calling. Who could regret to see a high conscience and a purer taste exercising a sensible effect on young men in their choice of occupation, and thinning
the ranks of competition in the labors of commerce, of law, and of state? It is
easy to see that the inconvenience would last but a short time. This would be
great action, which always opens the eyes of men. When many persons shall have
done this, when the majority shall admit the necessity of reform in all these institutions, their abuses will be redressed, and the way will be open again to the

advantages which arise from the division of labor, and a man may select the fittest employment for his peculiar talent again, without compromise.

But quite apart from the emphasis which the times give to the doctrine that the manual labor of society ought to be shared among all the members, there are reasons proper to every individual why he should not be deprived of it. The use of manual labor is one which never grows obsolete, and which is inapplicable to no person. A man should have a farm or a mechanical craft for his culture. We must have a basis for our higher accomplishments, our delicate entertainments of poetry and philosophy, in the work of our hands. We must have an antagonism in the tough world for all the variety of our spiritual faculties, or they will not be born. Manual labor is the study of the external world. The advantage of riches remains with him who procured them, not with the heir. When I go into my garden with a spade, and dig a bed, I feel such an exhilaration and health that I discover that I have been defrauding myself all this time in letting others do for me what I should have done with my own hands. But not only health, but education is in the work. Is it possible that I, who get indefinite quantities of sugar, hominy, cotton, buckets, crockery-ware, and letter-paper, by simply signing my name once in three months to a cheque in favor of John Smith & Co. traders, get the fair share of exercise to my faculties by that act which nature intended for me in making all these far-fetched matters important to my comfort? It is Smith himself, and his carriers, and dealers, and manufacturers; it is the sailor, the hide-drogher, the butcher, the negro, the hunter, and the planter, who have intercepted the sugar of the sugar, and the cotton of the cotton. They have got the education, I only the commodity. This were all very well if I were necessarily absent, being detained by work of my own, like theirs, work of the same faculties; then should I be sure of my hands and feet; but now I feel some shame before my wood-chopper, my ploughman, and my cook, for they have some sort of self-sufficiency, they can contrive without my aid to bring the day and year round, but I depend on them, and have not earned by use a right to my arms and feet.

Consider further the difference between the first and second owner of property. Every species of property is preyed on by its own enemies, as iron by rust; timber by rot; cloth by moths; provisions by mould, putridity, or vermin; money by thieves; an orchard by insects; a planted field by weeds and the inroad of cattle; a stock of cattle by hunger; a road by rain and frost; a bridge by freshets. And whoever takes any of these things into his possession, takes the charge of defending them from this troop of enemies, or of keeping them in repair. A man who supplies his own want, who builds a raft or a boat to go a-fishing, finds it easy to caulk it, or put in a thole-pin, or mend the rudder. What he gets only as fast as he wants for his own ends, does not embarrass him, or take away his sleep with looking after. But when he comes to give all the goods he has year after year collected, in one estate to his son,—house, orchard, ploughed land, cattle, bridges, hardware, wooden-ware, carpets, cloths, provisions, books, money,—and cannot give him the skill and experience which made or collected these, and the method and place they have in his own life, the son finds his hands full,—not to use these things, but to look after them and defend them from their natural enemies. To him they are not means, but masters. Their enemies will not remit; rust, mould, vermin, rain, sun, freshet, fire, all seize their own, fill him with vexation, and he is converted from the owner into a watchman or a watch-dog to this magazine of old and new chattels. What a change! Instead of the masterly good humor and sense of power and fertility of resource in himself; instead of those strong and learned hands, those piercing and learned eyes, that supple body, and that mighty and prevailing heart which the father had, whom nature loved and feared, whom snow and rain, water and land, beast and fish seemed all to know and to serve,—we have now a puny, protected person, guarded by walls and curtains, stoves and down beds, coaches, and men-servants and women-servants from the earth and the sky, and who, bred to depend on all these, is made anxious by all that endangers those possessions, and is forced to spend so much time in guarding them, that he has quite lost sight of their original use, namely, to help him to his ends,—to the prosecution of his love; to the helping of his friend, to the worship of his God, to the enlargement of his knowledge, to the serving of his country, to the indulgence of his sentiment; and he is now what is called a rich man,—the menial and runner of his riches.

Hence it happens that the whole interest of history lies in the fortunes of the poor. Knowledge, Virtue, Power are the victories of man over his necessities, his march to the dominion of the world. Every man ought to have this opportunity to conquer the world for himself. Only such persons interest us, Spartans, Romans, Saracens, English, Americans, who have stood in the jaws of need, and have by their own wit and might extricated themselves, and made man victorious.

I do not wish to overstate this doctrine of labor, or insist that every man should be a farmer, any more than that every man should be a lexicographer. In general one may say that the husbandman's is the oldest and most universal profession, and that where a man does not yet discover in himself any fitness for one work more than another, this may be preferred. But the doctrine of the Farm is merely this, that every man ought to stand in primary relations with the work of the world; ought to do it himself, and not to suffer the accident of his having a purse in his pocket, or his having been bred to some dishonorable and injurious craft, to sever him from those duties; and for this reason, that labor is God's education; that he only is a sincere learner, he only can become a master, who learns the secrets of labor, and who by real cunning extorts from nature its sceptre.

Neither would I shut my ears to the plea of the learned professions, of the poet, the priest, the law-giver, and men of study generally; namely, that in the experience of all men of that class, the amount of manual labor which is necessary to the maintenance of a family, indisposes and disqualifies for intellectual exertion. I know it often, perhaps usually, happens that where there is a fine organization, apt for poetry and philosophy, that individual finds himself compelled to wait on his thoughts; to waste several days that he may enhance and glorify one; and is better taught by a moderate and dainty exercise, such as rambling in the fields, rowing, skating, hunting, than by the downright drudgery of the farmer and the smith. I would not quite forget the venerable counsel of the Egyptian mysteries, which declared that "there were two pairs of eyes in man, and it is requisite that the pair which are beneath should be closed, when the pair that are above them perceive, and that when the pair above are closed, those which are beneath should be opened." Yet I will suggest that no separation from labor can be without some loss of power and of truth to the seer himself; that, I doubt not, the faults and vices of our literature and philosophy, their too great fineness, effeminacy, and melancholy, are attributable to the enervated and sickly habits of the literary class. Better that the book should not be quite so good, and the book-maker abler and better, and not himself often a ludicrous contrast to all that he has written.

But granting that for ends so sacred and dear some relaxation must be had, I think that if a man find in himself any strong bias to poetry, to art, to the contemplative life, drawing him to these things with a devotion incompatible with good husbandry, that man ought to reckon early with himself, and, respecting the compensations of the Universe, ought to ransom himself from the duties of economy by a certain rigor and privation in his habits. For privileges so rare and grand, let him not stint to pay a great tax. Let him be a cænobite, a pauper, and if need be, celibate also. Let him learn to eat his meals standing, and to relish the taste of fair water and black bread. He may leave to others the costly conveniences of housekeeping, and large hospitality, and the possession of works of art. Let him feel that genius is a hospitality, and that he who can create works of art needs not collect them. He must live in a chamber, and postpone his self-indulgence, forewarned and forearmed against that frequent misfortune of men of genius,—the taste for luxury. This is the tragedy of genius;—attempting to drive along the ecliptic with one horse of the heavens and one horse of the earth, there is only discord and ruin and downfall to chariot and charioteer.

The duty that every man should assume his own vows, should call the institutions of society to account, and examine their fitness to him, gains in emphasis if
we look at our modes of living. Is our housekeeping sacred and honorable? Does
it raise and inspire us, or does it cripple us instead? I ought to be armed by every
part and function of my household, by all my social function, by my economy,
by my feasting, by my voting, by my traffic. Yet I am almost no party to any of
these things. Custom does it for me, gives me no power therefrom, and runs
me in debt to boot. We spend our incomes for paint and paper, for a hundred
trifles, I know not what, and not for the things of a man. Our expense is almost
all for conformity. It is for cake that we run in debt; it is not the intellect, not the
heart, not beauty, not worship, that costs so much. Why needs any man be rich?
Why must he have horses, fine garments, handsome apartments, access to public
houses and places of amusement? Only for want of thought. Give his mind a new
image, and he flees into a solitary garden or garret to enjoy it, and is richer with
that dream than the fee of a county could make him. But we are first thoughtless,
and then find that we are moneyless. We are first sensual, and then must be rich.
We dare not trust our wit for making our house pleasant to our friend, and so we
buy ice-creams. He is accustomed to carpets, and we have not sufficient character
to put floor cloths out of his mind whilst he stays in the house, and so we pile the
floor with carpets. Let the house rather be a temple of the Furies of Lacedæmon,
formidable and holy to all, which none but a Spartan may enter or so much as
behold. As soon as there is faith, as soon as there is society, comfits and cushions
will be left to slaves. Expense will be inventive and heroic. We shall eat hard and
lie hard, we shall dwell like the ancient Romans in narrow tenements, whilst our
public edifices, like theirs, will be worthy for their proportion of the landscape in
which we set them, for conversation, for art, for music, for worship. We shall be
rich to great purposes; poor only for selfish ones.

Now what help for these evils? How can the man who has learned but one art,
procure all the conveniences of life honestly? Shall we say all we think ?—Perhaps
with his own hands. Suppose he collects or makes them ill;—yet he has learned
their lesson. If he cannot do that?—Then perhaps he can go without. Immense
wisdom and riches are in that. It is better to go without, than to have them at too
great a cost. Let us learn the meaning of economy. Economy is a high, humane
office, a sacrament, when its aim is grand; when it is the prudence of simple tastes,
when it is practised for freedom, or love, or devotion. Much of the economy
which we see in houses is of a base origin, and is best kept out of sight. Parched
corn eaten to-day, that I may have roast fowl to my dinner Sunday, is a baseness; but parched corn and a house with one apartment, that I may be free of all

perturbations, that I may be serene and docile to what the mind shall speak, and girt and road-ready for the lowest mission of knowledge or goodwill, is frugality for gods and heroes.

Can we not learn the lesson of self-help? Society is full of infirm people, who incessantly summon others to serve them. They contrive everywhere to exhaust for their single comfort the entire means and appliances of that luxury to which our invention has yet attained. Sofas, ottomans, stoves, wine, game-fowl, spices, perfumes, rides, the theatre, entertainments,—all these they want, they need, and whatever can be suggested more than these they crave also, as if it was the bread which should keep them from starving; and if they miss any one, they represent themselves as the most wronged and most wretched persons on earth. One must have been born and bred with them to know how to prepare a meal for their learned stomach. Meantime they never bestir themselves to serve another person; not they! they have a great deal more to do for themselves than they can possibly perform, nor do they once perceive the cruel joke of their lives, but the more odious they grow, the sharper is the tone of their complaining and craving. Can anything be so elegant as to have few wants and to serve them one's self, so as to have somewhat left to give, instead of being always prompt to grab? It is more elegant to answer one's own needs than to be richly served; inelegant perhaps it may look to-day, and to a few, but it is an elegance forever and to all.

I do not wish to be absurd and pedantic in reform. I do not wish to push my criticism on the state of things around me to that extravagant mark that shall compel me to suicide, or to an absolute isolation from the advantages of civil society. If we suddenly plant our foot and say,—I will neither eat nor drink nor wear nor touch any food or fabric which I do not know to be innocent, or deal with any person whose whole manner of life is not clear and rational, we shall stand still. Whose is so? Not mine; not thine; not his. But I think we must clear ourselves each one by the interrogation, whether we have earned our bread to-day by the hearty contribution of our energies to the common benefit; and we must not cease to *tend* to the correction of flagrant wrongs, by laying one stone aright every day.

But the idea which now begins to agitate society has a wider scope than our daily employments, our households, and the institutions of property. We are to revise the whole of our social structure, the State, the school, religion, marriage, trade, science, and explore their foundations in our own nature; we are to see that the world not only fitted the former men, but fits us, and to clear ourselves of every usage which has not its roots in our own mind. What is a man born for but to be a Reformer, a Remaker of what man has made; a renouncer of lies; a restorer of truth and good, imitating that great Nature which embosoms us all,

and which sleeps no moment on an old past, but every hour repairs herself, yielding us every morning a new day, and with every pulsation a new life? Let him
renounce everything which is not true to him, and put all his practices back on
their first thoughts, and do nothing for which he has not the whole world for his
reason. If there are inconveniences and what is called ruin in the way, because we
have so enervated and maimed ourselves, yet it would be like dying of perfumes
to sink in the effort to re-attach the deeds of every day to the holy and mysterious
recesses of life.

The power which is at once spring and regulator in all efforts of reform is the
conviction that there is an infinite worthiness in man, which will appear at the call
of worth, and that all particular reforms are the removing of some impediment. Is
it not the highest duty that man should be honored in us? I ought not to allow any
man, because he has broad lands, to feel that he is rich in my presence. I ought to
make him feel that I can do without his riches, that I cannot be bought,—neither
by comfort, neither by pride,—and though I be utterly penniless, and receiving
bread from him, that he is the poor man beside me. And if, at the same time, a
woman or a child discovers a sentiment of piety, or a juster way of thinking than
mine, I ought to confess it by my respect and obedience, though it go to alter my
whole way of life.

The Americans have many virtues, but they have not Faith and Hope. I know
no two words whose meaning is more lost sight of. We use these words as if they
were as obsolete as Selah and Amen. And yet they have the broadest meaning,
and the most cogent application to Boston in this year. The Americans have little
faith. They rely on the power of a dollar; they are deaf to a sentiment. They think
you may talk the north wind down as easily as raise society; and no class more
faithless than the scholars or intellectual men. Now if I talk with a sincere wise
man, and my friend, with a poet, with a conscientious youth who is still under the
dominion of his own wild thoughts, and not yet harnessed in the team of society
to drag with us all in the ruts of custom, I see at once how paltry is all this generation of unbelievers, and what a house of cards their institutions are, and I see
what one brave man, what one great thought executed might effect. I see that the
reason of the distrust of the practical man in all theory, is his inability to perceive
the means whereby we work. Look, he says, at the tools with which this world of
yours is to be built. As we cannot make a planet, with atmosphere, rivers, and forests, by means of the best carpenters' or engineers' tools, with chemist's laboratory
and smith's forge to boot,—so neither can we ever construct that heavenly society
you prate of out of foolish, sick, selfish men and women, such as we know them
to be. But the believer not only beholds his heaven to be possible, but already

to begin to exist,—not by the men or materials the statesman uses, but by men transfigured and raised above themselves by the power of principles. To principles something else is possible that transcends all the power of expedients.

Every great and commanding moment in the annals of the world is the triumph of some enthusiasm. The victories of the Arabs after Mahomet, who, in a few years, from a small and mean beginning, established a larger empire than that of Rome, is an example. They did they knew not what. The naked Derar, horsed on an idea, was found an overmatch for a troop of Roman cavalry. The women fought like men, and conquered the Roman men. They were miserably equipped, miserably fed. They were Temperance troops. There was neither brandy nor flesh needed to feed them. They conquered Asia and Africa and Spain on barley. The Caliph Omar's walking-stick struck more terror into those who saw it than another man's sword. His diet was barley bread; his sauce was salt; and oftentimes, by way of abstinence, he ate his bread without salt. His drink was water. His palace was built of mud; and when he left Medina to go to the conquest of Jerusalem, he rode on a red camel, with a wooden platter hanging at his saddle, with a bottle of water and two sacks, one holding barley and the other dried fruits.

But there will dawn ere long on our politics, on our modes of living, a nobler morning than that Arabian faith, in the sentiment of love. This is the one remedy for all ills, the panacea of nature. We must be lovers, and at once the impossible becomes possible. Our age and history, for these thousand years, has not been the history of kindness, but of selfishness. Our distrust is very expensive. The money we spend for courts and prisons is very ill laid out. We make, by distrust, the thief, and burglar, and incendiary, and by our court and jail we keep him so. An acceptance of the sentiment of love throughout Christendom for a season would bring the felon and the outcast to our side in tears, with the devotion of his faculties to our service. See this wide society of laboring men and women. We allow ourselves to be served by them, we live apart from them, and meet them without a salute in the streets. We do not greet their talents, nor rejoice in their good fortune, nor foster their hopes, nor in the assembly of the people vote for what is dear to them. Thus we enact the part of the selfish noble and king from the foundation of the world. See, this tree always bears one fruit. In every household, the peace of a pair is poisoned by the malice, slyness, indolence, and alienation of domestics. Let any two matrons meet, and observe how soon their conversation turns on the troubles from their "help," as our phrase is. In every knot of laborers, the rich man does not feel himself among his friends,—and at the polls he finds them arrayed in a mass in distinct opposition to him. We complain that the politics of masses of the people are controlled by designing men, and led in opposition to manifest justice and the common weal, and to their own interest. But the people do not wish to be represented or ruled by the ignorant and base. They only vote for these, because they were asked with the voice and semblance of kindness. They will not vote for them long. They inevitably prefer wit and probity. To use an Egyptian metaphor, it is not their will for any long time "to raise the nails of wild beasts, and to depress the heads of the sacred birds." Let our affection flow out to our fellows; it would operate in a day the greatest of all revolutions. It is better to work on institutions by the sun than by the wind. The State must consider the poor man, and all voices must speak for him. Every child that is born must have a just chance for his bread. Let the amelioration in our laws of property proceed from the concession of the rich, not from the grasping of the poor. Let us begin by habitual imparting. Let us understand that the equitable rule is, that no one should take more than his share, let him be ever so rich. Let me feel that I am to be a lover. I am to see to it that the world is the better for me, and to find my reward in the act. Love would put a new face on this weary old world in which we dwell as pagans and enemies too long, and it would warm the heart to see how fast the vain diplomacy of statesmen, the impotence of armies, and navies, and lines of defence, would be superseded by this unarmed child. Love will creep where it cannot go, will accomplish that by imperceptible methods,—being its own lever, fulcrum, and power,—which force could never achieve. Have you not seen in the woods, in a late autumn morning, a poor fungus or mushroom,—a plant without any solidity, nay, that seemed nothing but a soft mush or jelly,—by its constant, total, and inconceivably gentle pushing, manage to break its way up through the frosty ground, and actually to lift a hard crust on its head? It is the symbol of the power of kindness. The virtue of this principle in human society in application to great interests is obsolete and forgotten. Once or twice in history it has been tried in illustrious instances, with signal success. This great, overgrown, dead Christendom of ours still keeps alive at least the name of a lover of mankind. But one day all men will be lovers; and every calamity will be dissolved in the universal sunshine.

Will you suffer me to add one trait more to this portrait of man the reformer? The mediator between the spiritual and the actual world should have a great prospective prudence. An Arabian poet describes his hero by saying,

> Sunshine was he
> In the winter day;
> And in the midsummer
> Coolness and shade.

He who would help himself and others should not be a subject of irregular and interrupted impulses of virtue, but a continent, persisting, immovable person,— such as we have seen a few scattered up and down in time for the blessing of the world; men who have in the gravity of their nature a quality which answers to the fly-wheel in a mill, which distributes the motion equably over all the wheels and hinders it from falling unequally and suddenly in destructive shocks. It is better that joy should be spread over all the day in the form of strength, than that it should be concentrated into ecstasies, full of danger and followed by reactions. There is a sublime prudence which is the very highest that we know of man, which, believing in a vast future,—sure of more to come than is yet seen,—postpones always the present hour to the whole life; postpones talent to genius, and special results to character. As the merchant gladly takes money from his income to add to his capital, so is the great man very willing to lose particular powers and talents, so that he gain in the elevation of his life. The opening of the spiritual senses disposes men ever to greater sacrifices, to leave their signal talents, their best means and skill of procuring a present success, their power and their fame,—to cast all things behind, in the insatiable thirst for divine communications. A purer fame, a greater power rewards the sacrifice. It is the conversion of our harvest into seed. As the farmer casts into the ground the finest ears of his grain, the time will come when we too shall hold nothing back, but shall eagerly convert more than we now possess into means and powers, when we shall be willing to sow the sun and the moon for seeds.

Frederick Douglass

What to the Slave Is the 4th of July?

(Delivered in Rochester, New York, July 5, 1852)

He who could address this audience without a quailing sensation, has stronger nerves than I have. I do not remember ever to have appeared as a speaker before any assembly more shrinkingly, nor with greater distrust of my ability, than I do this day. A feeling has crept over me, quite unfavorable to the exercise of my limited powers of speech. The task before me is one which requires much previous thought and study for its proper performance. I know that apologies of this sort are generally considered flat and unmeaning. I trust, however, that mine will not be so considered. Should I seem at ease, my appearance would much misrepresent me. The little experience I have had in addressing public meetings, in country school houses, avails me nothing on the present occasion.

The papers and placards say, that I am to deliver a 4th of July oration. This certainly sounds large, and out of the common way, for me. It is true that I have often had the privilege to speak in this beautiful Hall, and to address many who now honor me with their presence. But neither their familiar faces, nor the perfect gage I think I have of Corinthian Hall, seems to free me from embarrassment.

The fact is, ladies and gentlemen, the distance between this platform and the slave plantation, from which I escaped, is considerable—and the difficulties to be overcome in getting from the latter to the former, are by no means slight. That I am here to-day is, to me, a matter of astonishment as well as of gratitude. You will not, therefore, be surprised, if in what I have to say, I evince no elaborate preparation, nor grace my speech with any high sounding exordium. With little experience and with less learning, I have been able to throw my thoughts hastily and imperfectly together; and trusting to your patient and generous indulgence, I will proceed to lay them before you.

This, for the purpose of this celebration, is the 4th of July. It is the birthday of your National Independence, and of your political freedom. This, to you, is what the Passover was to the emancipated people of God. It carries your minds back to the day, and to the act of your great deliverance; and to the signs, and to the wonders, associated with that act, and that day. This celebration also marks the beginning of another year of your national life; and reminds you that the Republic of America is now seventy-six years old. I am glad, fellow-citizens, that your nation is so young. Seventy-six years, though a good old age for a man, is but a mere speck in the life of a nation. Three score years and ten is the allotted time for individual men; but nations number their years by thousands. According to this fact, you are, even now, only in the beginning of your national career, still lingering in the period of childhood. I repeat, I am glad this is so. There is hope in the thought, and hope is much needed, under the dark clouds which lower above the horizon. The eye of the reformer is met with angry flashes, portending disastrous times; but his heart may well beat lighter at the thought that America is young, and that she is still in the impressible stage of her existence. May he not hope that high lessons of wisdom, of justice and of truth, will yet give direction to her destiny? Were the nation older, the patriot's heart might be sadder, and the reformer's brow heavier. Its future might be shrouded in gloom, and the hope of its prophets go out in sorrow. There is consolation in the thought that America is young. Great streams are not easily turned from channels, worn deep in the course of ages. They may sometimes rise in quiet and stately majesty, and inundate the land, refreshing and fertilizing the earth with their mysterious properties. They may also rise in wrath and fury, and bear away, on their angry waves, the accumulated wealth of years of toil and hardship. They, however, gradually flow back to the same old channel, and flow on as serenely as ever. But, while the river may not be turned aside, it may dry up, and leave nothing behind but the withered branch, and the unsightly rock, to howl in the abyss-sweeping wind, the sad tale of departed glory. As with rivers so with nations.

Fellow-citizens, I shall not presume to dwell at length on the associations that cluster about this day. The simple story of it is that, seventy-six years ago, the people of this country were British subjects. The style and title of your "sovereign people" (in which you now glory) was not then born. You were under the British Crown. Your fathers esteemed the English Government as the home government, and England as the fatherland. This home government, you know, although a considerable distance from your home, did, in the exercise of its parental prerogatives, impose upon its colonial children, such restraints, burdens and limitations, as, in its mature judgment, it deemed wise, right and proper.

But, your fathers, who had not adopted the fashionable idea of this day, of the infallibility of government, and the absolute character of its acts, presumed to differ from the home government in respect to the wisdom and the justice of some of those burdens and restraints. They went so far in their excitement as to pronounce the measures of government unjust, unreasonable, and oppressive, and altogether such as ought not to be quietly submitted to. I scarcely need say, fellow-citizens, that my opinion of those measures fully accords with that of your fathers. Such a declaration of agreement on my part would not be worth much to anybody. It would, certainly, prove nothing, as to what part I might have taken, had I lived during the great controversy of 1776. To say *now* that America was right, and England wrong, is exceedingly easy. Everybody can say it; the dastard, not less than the noble brave, can flippantly discant on the tyranny of England towards the American Colonies. It is fashionable to do so; but there was a time when to pronounce against England, and in favor of the cause of the colonies, tried men's souls. They who did so were accounted in their day, plotters of mischief, agitators and rebels, dangerous men. To side with the right, against the wrong, with the weak against the strong, and with the oppressed against the oppressor! *here* lies the merit, and the one which, of all others, seems unfashionable in our day. The cause of liberty may be stabbed by the men who glory in the deeds of your fathers. But, to proceed.

Feeling themselves harshly and unjustly treated by the home government, your fathers, like men of honesty, and men of spirit, earnestly sought redress. They petitioned and remonstrated; they did so in a decorous, respectful, and loyal manner. Their conduct was wholly unexceptionable. This, however, did not answer the purpose. They saw themselves treated with sovereign indifference, coldness and scorn. Yet they persevered. They were not the men to look back.

As the sheet anchor takes a firmer hold, when the ship is tossed by the storm, so did the cause of your fathers grow stronger, as it breasted the chilling blasts of kingly displeasure. The greatest and best of British statesmen admitted its justice, and the loftiest eloquence of the British Senate came to its support. But, with that blindness which seems to be the unvarying characteristic of tyrants, since Pharoah and his hosts were drowned in the Red Sea, the British Government persisted in the exactions complained of.

The madness of this course, we believe, is admitted now, even by England; but, we fear the lesson is wholly lost on our present rulers.

Oppression makes a wise man mad. Your fathers were wise men, and if they did not go mad, they became restive under this treatment. They felt themselves the victims of grievous wrongs, wholly incurable in their colonial capacity. With brave men there is always a remedy for oppression. Just here, the idea of a total separation of the colonies from the crown was born! It was a startling idea, much more so, than we, at this distance of time, regard it. The timid and the prudent (as has been intimated) of that day, were, of course, shocked and alarmed by it.

Such people lived then, had lived before, and will, probably, ever have a place on this planet; and their course, in respect to any great change, (no matter how

great the good to be attained, or the wrong to be redressed by it), may be calculated with as much precision as can be the course of the stars. They hate all
changes, but silver, gold and copper change! Of this sort of change they are always
strongly in favor.

These people were called tories in the days of your fathers; and the appellation, probably, conveyed the same idea that is meant by a more modern, though
a somewhat less euphonious term, which we often find in our papers, applied to
some of our old politicians.

Their opposition to the then dangerous thought was earnest and powerful;
but, amid all their terror and affrighted vociferations against it, the alarming and
revolutionary idea moved on, and the country with it.

On the 2d of July, 1776, the old Continental Congress, to the dismay of the
lovers of ease, and the worshippers of property, clothed that dreadful idea with all
the authority of national sanction. They did so in the form of a resolution; and as
we seldom hit upon resolutions, drawn up in our day, whose transparency is at all
equal to this, it may refresh your minds and help my story if I read it.

> Resolved, That these united colonies *are,* and of right, ought to
> be free and Independent States; that they are absolved from all
> allegiance to the British Crown; and that all political connection
> between them and the State of Great Britain *is,* and ought to be,
> dissolved.

Citizens, your fathers made good that resolution. They succeeded; and to-day
you reap the fruits of their success. The freedom gained is yours; and you, therefore,
may properly celebrate this anniversary. The 4th of July is the first great fact in your
nation's history—the very ring-bolt in the chain of your yet undeveloped destiny.

Pride and patriotism, not less than gratitude, prompt you to celebrate
and to hold it in perpetual remembrance. I have said that the Declaration of
Independence is the RING-BOLT to the chain of your nation's destiny; so, indeed, I
regard it. The principles contained in that instrument are saving principles. Stand
by those principles, be true to them on all occasions, in all places, against all foes,
and at whatever cost.

From the round top of your ship of state, dark and threatening clouds may be
seen. Heavy billows, like mountains in the distance, disclose to the leeward huge
forms of flinty rocks! That *bolt* drawn, that *chain* broken, and all is lost. *Cling to
this day—cling to it,* and to its principles, with the grasp of a storm-tossed mariner
to a spar at midnight.

The coming into being of a nation, in any circumstances, is an interesting event. But, besides general considerations, there were peculiar circumstances which make the advent of this republic an event of special attractiveness.

The whole scene, as I look back to it, was simple, dignified and sublime.

The population of the country, at the time, stood at the insignificant number of three millions. The country was poor in the munitions of war. The population was weak and scattered, and the country a wilderness unsubdued. There were then no means of concert and combination, such as exist now. Neither steam nor lightning had then been reduced to order and discipline. From the Potomac to the Delaware was a journey of many days. Under these, and innumerable other disadvantages, your fathers declared for liberty and independence and triumphed.

Fellow Citizens, I am not wanting in respect for the fathers of this republic. The signers of the Declaration of Independence were brave men. They were great men too—great enough to give fame to a great age. It does not often happen to a nation to raise, at one time, such a number of truly great men. The point from which I am compelled to view them is not, certainly, the most favorable; and yet I cannot contemplate their great deeds with less than admiration. They were statesmen, patriots and heroes, and for the good they did, and the principles they contended for, I will unite with you to honor their memory.

They loved their country better than their own private interests; and, though this is not the highest form of human excellence, all will concede that it is a rare virtue, and that when it is exhibited, it ought to command respect. He who will, intelligently, lay down his life for his country, is a man whom it is not in human nature to despise. Your fathers staked their lives, their fortunes, and their sacred honor, on the cause of their country. In their admiration of liberty, they lost sight of all other interests.

They were peace men; but they preferred revolution to peaceful submission to bondage. They were quiet men; but they did not shrink from agitating against oppression. They showed forbearance; but that they knew its limits. They believed in order; but not in the order of tyranny. With them, nothing was "*settled*" that was not right. With them, justice, liberty and humanity were "*final*"; not slavery and oppression. You may well cherish the memory of such men. They were great in their day and generation. Their solid manhood stands out the more as we contrast it with these degenerate times.

How circumspect, exact and proportionate were all their movements! How unlike the politicians of an hour! Their statesmanship looked beyond the passing moment, and stretched away in strength into the distant future. They seized upon eternal principles, and set a glorious example in their defence. Mark them!

Fully appreciating the hardship to be encountered, firmly believing in the right of their cause, honorably inviting the scrutiny of an on-looking world, reverently appealing to heaven to attest their sincerity, soundly comprehending the solemn responsibility they were about to assume, wisely measuring the terrible odds against them, your fathers, the fathers of this republic, did, most deliberately, under the inspiration of a glorious patriotism, and with a sublime faith in the great principles of justice and freedom, lay deep the corner-stone of the national superstructure, which has risen and still rises in grandeur around you.

Of this fundamental work, this day is the anniversary. Our eyes are met with demonstrations of joyous enthusiasm. Banners and pennants wave exultingly on the breeze. The din of business, too, is hushed. Even Mammon seems to have quitted his grasp on this day. The ear-piercing fife and the stirring drum unite their accents with the ascending peal of a thousand church bells. Prayers are made, hymns are sung, and sermons are preached in honor of this day; while the quick martial tramp of a great and multitudinous nation, echoed back by all the hills, valleys and mountains of a vast continent, bespeak the occasion one of thrilling and universal interest—a nation's jubilee.

Friends and citizens, I need not enter further into the causes which led to this anniversary. Many of you understand them better than I do. You could instruct me in regard to them. That is a branch of knowledge in which you feel, perhaps, a much deeper interest than your speaker. The causes which led to the separation of the colonies from the British crown have never lacked for a tongue. They have all been taught in your common schools, narrated at your firesides, unfolded from your pulpits, and thundered from your legislative halls, and are as familiar to you as household words. They form the staple of your national poetry and eloquence.

I remember, also, that, as a people, Americans are remarkably familiar with all facts which make in their own favor. This is esteemed by some as a national trait— perhaps a national weakness. It is a fact, that whatever makes for the wealth or for the reputation of Americans, and can be had *cheap!* will be found by Americans. I shall not be charged with slandering Americans, if I say I think the Americans can side of any question may be safely left in American hands.

I leave, therefore, the great deeds of your fathers to other gentlemen whose claim to have been regularly descended will be less likely to be disputed than mine!

My business, if I have any here to-day, is with the present. The accepted time with God and his cause is the ever-living now.

> Trust no future, however pleasant,
>   Let the dead past bury its dead;
> Act, act in the living present,
>   Heart within, and God overhead.

We have to do with the past only as we can make it useful to the present and to the future. To all inspiring motives, to noble deeds which can be gained from the past, we are welcome. But now is the time, the important time. Your fathers have lived, died, and have done their work, and have done much of it well. You live and must die, and you must do your work. You have no right to enjoy a child's share in the labor of your fathers, unless your children are to be blest by your labors. You have no right to wear out and waste the hard-earned fame of your fathers to cover your indolence. Sydney Smith tells us that men seldom eulogize the wisdom and virtues of their fathers, but to excuse some folly or wickedness of their own. This truth is not a doubtful one. There are illustrations of it near and remote, ancient and modern. It was fashionable, hundreds of years ago, for the children of Jacob to boast, we have "Abraham to our father," when they had long lost Abraham's faith and spirit. That people contented themselves under the shadow of Abraham's great name, while they repudiated the deeds which made his name great. Need I remind you that a similar thing is being done all over this country to-day? Need I tell you that the Jews are not the only people who built the tombs of the prophets, and garnished the sepulchres of the righteous? Washington could not die till he had broken the chains of his slaves. Yet his monument is built up by the price of human blood, and the traders in the bodies and souls of men, shout—"We have Washington to *our father*." Alas! that it should be so; yet so it is.

> The evil that men do, lives after them,
> The good is oft' interred with their bones.

Fellow-citizens, pardon me, allow me to ask, why am I called upon to speak here to-day? What have I, or those I represent, to do with your national independence? Are the great principles of political freedom and of natural justice, embodied in that Declaration of Independence, extended to us? and am I, therefore, called upon to bring our humble offering to the national altar, and to confess the benefits and express devout gratitude for the blessings resulting from your independence to us?

Would to God, both for your sakes and ours, that an affirmative answer could be truthfully returned to these questions! Then would my task be light, and my burden easy and delightful. For *who* is there so cold, that a nation's sympathy could not warm him? Who so obdurate and dead to the claims of gratitude, that would not thankfully acknowledge such priceless benefits? Who so stolid and self-ish, that would not give his voice to swell the hallelujahs of a nation's jubilee, when the chains of servitude had been torn from his limbs? I am not that man. In a case like that, the dumb might eloquently speak, and the "lame man leap as an hart."

But, such is not the state of the case. I say it with a sad sense of the disparity between us. I am not included within the pale of this glorious anniversary! Your high independence only reveals the immeasurable distance between us. The blessings in which you, this day, rejoice, are not enjoyed in common. The rich inheritance of justice, liberty, prosperity and independence, bequeathed by your fathers, is shared by you, not by me. The sunlight that brought life and healing to you, has brought stripes and death to me. This Fourth July is *yours,* not *mine. You* may rejoice, *I* must mourn. To drag a man in fetters into the grand illuminated temple of liberty, and call upon him to join you in joyous anthems, were inhuman mockery and sacrilegious irony. Do you mean, citizens, to mock me, by asking me to speak to-day? If so, there is a parallel to your conduct. And let me warn you that it is dangerous to copy the example of a nation whose crimes, towering up to heaven, were thrown down by the breath of the Almighty, burying that nation in irrecoverable ruin! I can to-day take up the plaintive lament of a peeled and woe-smitten people!

"By the rivers of Babylon, there we sat down. Yea! we wept when we remembered Zion. We hanged our harps upon the willows in the midst thereof. For there, they that carried us away captive, required of us a song; and they who wasted us required of us mirth, saying, Sing us one of the songs of Zion. How can we sing the Lord's song in a strange land? If I forget thee, O Jerusalem, let my right hand forget her cunning. If I do not remember thee, let my tongue cleave to the roof of my mouth."

Fellow citizens; above your national, tumultuous joy, I hear the mournful wail of millions! whose chains, heavy and grievous yesterday, are, to-day, rendered more intolerable by the jubilee shouts that reach them. If I do forget, if I do not faithfully remember those bleeding children of sorrow this day, "may my right hand forget her cunning, and may my tongue cleave to the roof of my mouth!" To forget them, to pass lightly over their wrongs, and to chime in with the popular theme, would be treason most scandalous and shocking, and would make me a reproach before God and the world. My subject, then, fellow-citizens, is AMERICAN SLAVERY. I shall see, this day, and its popular characteristics, from the slave's point of view. Standing, there, identified with the American bondman, making his wrongs mine, I do not hesitate to declare, with all my soul, that the character and conduct of this nation never looked blacker to me than on this 4th of July! Whether we turn to the declarations of the past, or to the professions of the present, the conduct of the nation seems equally hideous and revolting. America is false to the past, false to the present, and solemnly binds herself to be false to the future. Standing with God and the crushed and bleeding slave on this occasion, I will, in the name of humanity which is outraged, in the name of liberty which is fettered, in the name of the constitution and the Bible, which are disregarded and trampled upon, dare to call in question and to denounce, with all the emphasis I can command, everything that serves to perpetuate slavery—the great sin and shame of America! "I will not equivocate; I will not excuse"; I will use the severest language I can command; and yet not one word shall escape me that any man, whose judgement is not blinded by prejudice, or who is not at heart a slaveholder, shall not confess to be right and just.

But I fancy I hear some one of my audience say, it is just in this circumstance that you and your brother abolitionists fail to make a favorable impression on the public mind. Would you argue more, and denounce less, would you persuade more, and rebuke less, your cause would be much more likely to succeed. But, I submit, where all is plain there is nothing to be argued. What point in the anti-slavery creed would you have me argue? On what branch of the subject do the people of this country need light? Must I undertake to prove that the slave is a man? That point is conceded already. Nobody doubts it. The slaveholders themselves acknowledge it in the enactment of laws for their government. They acknowledge it when they punish disobedience on the part of the slave. There are seventy-two crimes in the State of Virginia, which, if committed by a black man, (no matter how ignorant he be), subject him to the punishment of death; while only two of the same crimes will subject a white man to the like punishment. What is this but the acknowledgement that the slave is a moral, intellectual and responsible being. The manhood of the slave is conceded. It is admitted in the fact that Southern statute books are covered with enactments forbidding, under severe fines and penalties, the teaching of the slave to read or to write. When you can point to any such laws, in reference to the beasts of the field, then I may consent to argue the manhood of the slave. When the dogs in your streets, when the fowls of the air, when the cattle on your hills, when the fish of the sea, and the reptiles that crawl, shall be unable to distinguish the slave from a brute, *then* will I argue with you that the slave is a man!

For the present, it is enough to affirm the equal manhood of the negro race. Is it not astonishing that, while we are ploughing, planting and reaping, using all kinds of mechanical tools, erecting houses, constructing bridges, building ships, working in metals of brass, iron, copper, silver and gold; that, while we are reading, writing and cyphering, acting as clerks, merchants and secretaries, having among us lawyers, doctors, ministers, poets, authors, editors, orators and teachers; that, while we are engaged in all manner of enterprises common to other men, digging gold in California, capturing the whale in the Pacific, feeding sheep and cattle on the hill-side, living, moving, acting, thinking, planning, living in families as husbands, wives and children, and, above all, confessing and worshipping the Christian's God, and looking hopefully for life and immortality beyond the grave, we are called upon to prove that we are men!

Would you have me argue that man is entitled to liberty? that he is the rightful owner of his own body? You have already declared it. Must I argue the wrongfulness of slavery? Is that a question for Republicans? Is it to be settled by the rules of logic and argumentation, as a matter beset with great difficulty, involving a doubtful application of the principle of justice, hard to be understood? How should I look to-day, in the presence of Americans, dividing, and subdividing a discourse, to show that men have a natural right to freedom? speaking of it relatively, and positively, negatively, and affirmatively. To do so, would be to make myself ridiculous, and to offer an insult to your understanding. There is not a man beneath the canopy of heaven, that does not know that slavery is wrong *for him.*

What, am I to argue that it is wrong to make men brutes, to rob them of their liberty, to work them without wages, to keep them ignorant of their relations to their fellow men, to beat them with sticks, to flay their flesh with the lash, to load their limbs with irons, to hunt them with dogs, to sell them at auction, to sunder their families, to knock out their teeth, to burn their flesh, to starve them into obedience and submission to their masters? Must I argue that a system thus marked with blood, and stained with pollution, is *wrong*? No! I will not. I have better employments for my time and strength, than such arguments would imply.

What, then, remains to be argued? Is it that slavery is not divine; that God did not establish it; that our doctors of divinity are mistaken? There is blasphemy in the thought. That which is inhuman, cannot be divine! *Who* can reason on such a proposition? They that can, may; I cannot. The time for such argument is past.

At a time like this, scorching irony, not convincing argument, is needed. O! had I the ability, and could I reach the nation's ear, I would, to-day, pour out a fiery stream of biting ridicule, blasting reproach, withering sarcasm, and stern rebuke. For it is not light that is needed, but fire; it is not the gentle shower, but thunder. We need the storm, the whirlwind, and the earthquake. The feeling of the nation must be quickened; the conscience of the nation must be roused; the propriety of the nation must be startled; the hypocrisy of the nation must be exposed; and its crimes against God and man must be proclaimed and denounced.

What, to the American slave, is your 4th of July? I answer: a day that reveals to him, more than all other days in the year, the gross injustice and cruelty to which he is the constant victim. To him, your celebration is a sham; your boasted liberty, an unholy license; your national greatness, swelling vanity; your sounds of rejoicing are empty and heartless; your denunciations of tyrants, brass fronted impudence; your shouts of liberty and equality, hollow mockery; your prayers and hymns, your sermons and thanksgivings, with all your religious parade, and solemnity, are, to him, mere bombast, fraud, deception, impiety, and hypocrisy—a thin veil to cover up crimes which would disgrace a nation of savages. There is not a nation on the earth guilty of practices, more shocking and bloody, than are the people of these United States, at this very hour.

Go where you may, search where you will, roam through all the monarchies and despotisms of the old world, travel through South America, search out every abuse, and when you have found the last, lay your facts by the side of the everyday practices of this nation, and you will say with me, that, for revolting barbarity and shameless hypocrisy, America reigns without a rival.

Take the American slave-trade, which, we are told by the papers, is especially prosperous just now. Ex-Senator Benton tells us that the price of men was never higher than now. He mentions the fact to show that slavery is in no danger. This trade is one of the peculiarities of American institutions. It is carried on in all the large towns and cities in one-half of this confederacy; and millions are pocketed every year, by dealers in this horrid traffic. In several states, this trade is a chief source of wealth. It is called (in contradistinction to the foreign slave-trade) "*the internal slave-trade.*" It is, probably, called so, too, in order to divert from it the horror with which the foreign slave-trade is contemplated. That trade has long since been denounced by this government, as piracy. It has been denounced with burning words, from the high places of the nation, as an execrable traffic. To arrest it, to put an end to it, this nation keeps a squadron, at immense cost, on the coast of Africa. Everywhere, in this country, it is safe to speak of this foreign slave-trade, as a most inhuman traffic, opposed alike to the laws of God and of man. The duty to extirpate and destroy it, is admitted even by our DOCTORS OF DIVINITY. In order to put an end to it, some of these last have consented that their colored brethren (nominally free) should leave this country, and establish themselves on the western coast of Africa! It is, however, a notable fact that, while so much execration is poured out by Americans upon those engaged in the foreign slave-trade, the men engaged in the slave-trade between the states pass without condemnation, and their business is deemed honorable.

Behold the practical operation of this internal slave-trade, the American slave-trade, sustained by American politics and American religion. Here you will see men and women reared like swine for the market. You know what is a swine-drover? I will show you a man-drover. They inhabit all our Southern States. They perambulate the country, and crowd the highways of the nation, with droves of human stock. You will see one of these human flesh-jobbers, armed with pistol, whip and bowie-knife, driving a company of a hundred men, women, and children, from the Potomac to the slave market at New Orleans. These wretched people are to be sold singly, or in lots, to suit purchasers. They are food for the cotton-field, and the deadly sugar-mill. Mark the sad procession, as it moves wearily along, and the inhuman wretch who drives them. Hear his savage yells and his blood-chilling oaths, as he hurries on his affrighted captives! There, see the old man, with locks thinned and gray. Cast one glance, if you please, upon that young mother, whose shoulders are bare to the scorching sun, her briny tears falling on the brow of the babe in her arms. See, too, that girl of thirteen, weeping, *yes*! weeping, as she thinks of the mother from whom she has been torn! The drove moves tardily. Heat and sorrow have nearly consumed their strength; suddenly you hear a quick snap, like the discharge of a rifle; the fetters clank, and the chain rattles simultaneously; your ears are saluted with a scream, that seems to have torn its way to the centre of your soul! The crack you heard, was the sound of the slave-whip; the scream you heard, was from the woman you saw with the babe. Her speed had faltered under the weight of her child and her chains! that gash on her shoulder tells her to move on. Follow this drove to New Orleans. Attend the auction; see men examined like horses; see the forms of women rudely and brutally exposed to the shocking gaze of American slave-buyers. See this drove sold and separated forever; and never forget the deep, sad sobs that arose from that scattered multitude. Tell me citizens, WHERE, under the sun, you can witness a spectacle more fiendish and shocking. Yet this is but a glance at the American slave-trade, as it exists, at this moment, in the ruling part of the United States.

I was born amid such sights and scenes. To me the American slave-trade is a terrible reality. When a child, my soul was often pierced with a sense of its horrors. I lived on Philpot Street, Fell's Point, Baltimore, and have watched from the wharves, the slave ships in the Basin, anchored from the shore, with their cargoes of human flesh, waiting for favorable winds to waft them down the Chesapeake. There was, at that time, a grand slave mart kept at the head of Pratt Street, by Austin Woldfolk. His agents were sent into every town and county in Maryland, announcing their arrival, through the papers, and on flaming "*hand-bills*," headed CASH FOR NEGROES. These men were generally well dressed men, and very captivating in their manners. Ever ready to drink, to treat, and to gamble. The fate of many a slave has depended upon the turn of a single card; and many a child has been snatched from the arms of its mother by bargains arranged in a state of brutal drunkenness.

The flesh-mongers gather up their victims by dozens, and drive them, chained, to the general depot at Baltimore. When a sufficient number have been collected here, a ship is chartered, for the purpose of conveying the forlorn crew to Mobile, or to New Orleans. From the slave prison to the ship, they are usually driven in the darkness of night; for since the anti-slavery agitation, a certain caution is observed.

In the deep still darkness of midnight, I have been often aroused by the dead heavy footsteps, and the pitious cries of the chained gangs that passed our door. The anguish of my boyish heart was intense; and I was often consoled, when speaking to my mistress in the morning, to hear her say that the custom was very wicked; that she hated to hear the rattle of the chains, and the heart-rending cries. I was glad to find one who sympathized with me in my horror.

Fellow-citizens, this murderous traffic is, to-day, in active operation in this boasted republic. In the solitude of my spirit, I see clouds of dust raised on the highways of the South; I see the bleeding footsteps; I hear the doleful wail of fettered humanity, on the way to the slave-markets, where the victims are to be sold like *horses*, *sheep*, and *swine*, knocked off to the highest bidder. There I see the tenderest ties ruthlessly broken, to gratify the lust, caprice and rapacity of the buyers and sellers of men. My soul sickens at the sight.

> Is this the land your Fathers loved,
>   The freedom which they toiled to win?
> Is this the earth whereon they moved?
>   Are these the graves they slumber in?

But a still more inhuman, disgraceful, and scandalous state of things remains to be presented.

By an act of the American Congress, not yet two years old, slavery has been nationalized in its most horrible and revolting form. By that act, Mason & Dixon's line has been obliterated; New York has become as Virginia; and the power to hold, hunt, and sell men, women and children as slaves remains no longer a mere state institution, but is now an institution of the whole United

States. The power is co-extensive with the star-spangled banner and American Christianity. Where these go, may also go the merciless slave-hunter. Where these are, man is not sacred. He is a bird for the sportsman's gun. By that most foul and fiendish of all human decrees, the liberty and person of every man are put in peril. Your broad republican domain is hunting ground for *men. Not* for thieves and robbers, enemies of society, merely, but for men guilty of no crime. Your law-makers have commanded all good citizens to engage in this hellish sport. Your President, your Secretary of State, your *lords, nobles,* and ecclesiastics, enforce, as a duty you owe to your free and glorious country, and to your God, that you do this accursed thing. Not fewer than forty Americans have, within the past two years, been hunted down and, without a moment's warning, hurried away in chains, and consigned to slavery and excruciating torture. Some of these have had wives and children, dependent on them for bread; but of this, no account was made. The right of the hunter to his prey stands superior to the right of marriage, and to *all* rights in this republic, the rights of God included! For black men there are neither law, justice, humanity, nor religion. The Fugitive Slave *Law* makes MERCY TO THEM, A CRIME; and bribes the judge who tries them. An American JUDGE GETS TEN DOLLARS FOR EVERY VICTIM HE CONSIGNS to slavery, and five, when he fails to do so. The oath of any two villains is sufficient, under this hell-black enactment, to send the most pious and exemplary black man into the remorseless jaws of slavery! His own testimony is nothing. He can bring no witnesses for himself. The minister of American justice is bound, by the law to hear but *one* side; and *that* side, is the side of the oppressor. Let this damning fact be perpetually told. Let it be thundered around the world, that, in tyrant-killing, king-hating, people-loving, democratic, Christian America, the seats of justice are filled with judges, who hold their offices under an open and palpable *bribe,* and are bound, in deciding in the case of a man's liberty, *to hear only his accusers*!

In glaring violation of justice, in shameless disregard of the forms of administering law, in cunning arrangement to entrap the defenceless, and in diabolical intent, this Fugitive Slave Law stands alone in the annals of tyrannical legislation. I doubt if there be another nation on the globe, having the brass and the baseness to put such a law on the statute-book. If any man in this assembly thinks differently from me in this matter, and feels able to disprove my statements, I will gladly confront him at any suitable time and place he may select.

I take this law to be one of the grossest infringements of Christian Liberty, and, if the churches and ministers of our country were not stupidly blind, or most wickedly indifferent, they, too, would so regard it.

At the very moment that they are thanking God for the enjoyment of civil and religious liberty, and for the right to worship God according to the dictates of their own consciences, they are utterly silent in respect to a law which robs religion of its chief significance, and makes it utterly worthless to a world lying in wickedness. Did this law concern the "*mint, anise* and *cummin*"—abridge the right to sing psalms, to partake of the sacrament, or to engage in any of the ceremonies of religion, it would be smitten by the thunder of a thousand pulpits. A general shout would go up from the church, demanding *repeal, repeal, instant repeal!* And it would go hard with that politician who presumed to solicit the votes of the people without inscribing this motto on his banner. Further, if this demand were not complied with, another Scotland would be added to the history of religious liberty, and the stern old Covenanters would be thrown into the shade. A John Knox would be seen at every church door, and heard from every pulpit, and Fillmore would have no more quarter than was shown by Knox, to the beautiful, but treacherous Queen Mary of Scotland. The fact that the church of our country, (with fractional exceptions), does not esteem "the Fugitive Slave Law" as a declaration of war against religious liberty, implies that that church regards religion simply as a form of worship, an empty ceremony, and *not* a vital principle, requiring active benevolence, justice, love and good will towards man. It esteems sacrifice above mercy; psalm-singing above right doing; solemn meetings above practical righteousness. A worship that can be conducted by persons who refuse to give shelter to the houseless, to give bread to the hungry, clothing to the naked, and who enjoin obedience to a law forbidding these acts of mercy, is a curse, not a blessing to mankind. The Bible addresses all such persons as "scribes, pharisees, hypocrites, who pay tithe of *mint, anise,* and *cummin,* and have omitted the weightier matters of the law, judgement, mercy and faith."

But the church of this country is not only indifferent to the wrongs of the slave, it actually takes sides with the oppressors. It has made itself the bulwark of American slavery, and the shield of American slave-hunters. Many of its most eloquent Divines, who stand as the very lights of the church, have shamelessly given the sanction of religion and the Bible to the whole slave system. They have taught that man may, properly, be a slave; that the relation of master and slave is ordained of God; that to send back an escaped bondman to his master is clearly the duty of all the followers of the Lord Jesus Christ; and this horrible blasphemy is palmed off upon the world for Christianity.

For my part, I would say, welcome infidelity! welcome atheism! welcome anything! in preference to the gospel, *as preached by those Divines!* They convert the very name of religion into an engine of tyranny, and barbarous cruelty, and serve to confirm more infidels, in this age, than all the infidel writings of Thomas Paine, Voltaire, and Bolingbroke, put together, have done! These ministers make religion a cold and flinty-hearted thing, having neither principles of right action, nor bowels of compassion. They strip the love of God of its beauty, and leave the throne of religion a huge, horrible, repulsive form. It is a religion for oppressors, tyrants, man-stealers, and *thugs*. It is not that "*pure and undefiled religion*" which is from above, and which is "*first pure, then peaceable, easy to be entreated,* full of mercy and good fruits, *without partiality, and without hypocrisy.*" But a religion which favors the rich against the poor; which exalts the proud above the humble; which divides mankind into two classes, tyrants and slaves; which says to the man in chains, *stay there*; and to the oppressor, *oppress on*; it is a religion which may be professed and enjoyed by all the robbers and enslavers of mankind; it makes God a respecter of persons, denies his fatherhood of the race, and tramples in the dust the great truth of the brotherhood of man. All this we affirm to be true of the popular church, and the popular worship of our land and nation—a religion, a church, and a worship which, on the authority of inspired wisdom, we pronounce to be an abomination in the sight of God. In the language of Isaiah, the American church might be well addressed, "Bring no more vain oblations; incense is an abomination unto me: the new moons and Sabbaths, the calling of assemblies, I cannot away with; it is iniquity, even the solemn meeting. Your new moons and your appointed feasts my soul hateth. They are a trouble to me; I am weary to bear them; and when ye spread forth your hands I will hide mine eyes from you. Yea! when ye make many prayers, I will not hear. YOUR HANDS ARE FULL OF BLOOD; cease to do evil, learn to do well; seek judgement; relieve the oppressed; judge for the fatherless; plead for the widow."

The American church is guilty, when viewed in connection with what it is doing to uphold slavery; but it is superlatively guilty when viewed in connection with its ability to abolish slavery.

The sin of which it is guilty is one of omission as well as of commission. Albert Barnes but uttered what the common sense of every man at all observant of the actual state of the case will receive as truth, when he declared that "There is no power out of the church that could sustain slavery an hour, if it were not sustained in it."

Let the religious press, the pulpit, the Sunday school, the conference meeting, the great ecclesiastical, missionary, Bible and tract associations of the land array their immense powers against slavery, and slave-holding; and the whole system of crime and blood would be scattered to the winds; and that they do not do this involves them in the most awful responsibility of which the mind can conceive.

In prosecuting the anti-slavery enterprise, we have been asked to spare the church, to spare the ministry; but *how*, we ask, could such a thing be done? We are met on the threshold of our efforts for the redemption of the slave, by the church and ministry of the country, in battle arrayed against us; and we are compelled to fight or flee. From what *quarter*, I beg to know, has proceeded a fire so deadly upon our ranks, during the last two years, as from the Northern pulpit? As the champions of oppressors, the chosen men of American theology have appeared—men, honored for their so-called piety, and their real learning. The LORDS of Buffalo, the SPRINGS of New York, the LATHROPS of Auburn, the COXES and SPENCERS of Brooklyn, the GANNETS and SHARPS of Boston, the DEWEYS of Washington, and other great religious lights of the land, have, in utter denial of the authority of *Him*, by whom they professed to be called to the ministry, deliberately taught us, against the example of the Hebrews and against the remonstrance of the Apostles, they teach "*that we ought to obey man's law before the law of God.*"

My spirit wearies of such blasphemy; and how such men can be supported, as the "standing types and representatives of Jesus Christ," is a mystery which I leave others to penetrate. In speaking of the American church, however, let it be distinctly understood that I mean the *great mass* of the religious organizations of our land. There are exceptions, and I thank God that there are. Noble men may be found, scattered all over these Northern States, of whom Henry Ward Beecher of Brooklyn, Samuel J. May of Syracuse, and my esteemed friend on the platform [Reverend R. R. Raymond], are shining examples; and let me say further, that upon these men lies the duty to inspire our ranks with high religious faith and zeal, and to cheer us on in the great mission of the slave's redemption from his chains.

One is struck with the difference between the attitude of the American church towards the anti-slavery movement, and that occupied by the churches in England towards a similar movement in that country. There, the church, true to its mission of ameliorating, elevating, and improving the condition of mankind, came forward promptly, bound up the wounds of the West Indian slave, and restored him to his liberty. There, the question of emancipation was a highly religious question. It was demanded, in the name of humanity, and according to the law of the living God. The Sharps, the Clarksons, the Wilberforces, the Buxtons, the Burchells and the Knibbs, were alike famous for their piety, and for their philanthropy. The anti-slavery movement *there* was not an anti-church movement, for the reason that the church took its full share in prosecuting that movement: and the anti-slavery movement in this country will cease to be an anti-church movement, when the church of this country shall assume a favorable, instead of a hostile position towards that movement.

Americans! your republican politics, not less than your republican religion, are flagrantly inconsistent. You boast of your love of liberty, your superior civilization, and your pure Christianity, while the whole political power of the nation, (as embodied in the two great political parties), is solemnly pledged to support and perpetuate the enslavement of three millions of your countrymen. You hurl your anathemas at the crowned headed tyrants of Russia and Austria, and pride yourselves on your Democratic institutions, while you yourselves consent to be the mere *tools* and *bodyguards* of the tyrants of Virginia and Carolina. You invite to your shores fugitives of oppression from abroad, honor them with banquets, greet them with ovations, cheer them, toast them, salute them, protect them, and pour out your money to them like water; but the fugitives from your own land you advertise, hunt, arrest, shoot and kill. You glory in your refinement and your universal education; yet you maintain a system as barbarous and dreadful as ever stained the character of a nation—a system begun in avarice, supported in pride, and perpetuated in cruelty. You shed tears over fallen Hungary, and make the sad story of her wrongs the theme of your poets, statesmen and orators, till your gallant sons are ready to fly to arms to vindicate her cause against her oppressors; but, in regard to the ten thousand wrongs of the American slave, you would enforce the strictest silence, and would hail him as an enemy of the nation who dares to make those wrongs the subject of public discourse! You are all on fire at the mention of liberty for France or for Ireland; but are as cold as an iceberg at the thought of liberty for the enslaved of America. You discourse eloquently on the dignity of labor; yet, you sustain a system which, in its very essence, casts a stigma upon labor. You can bare your bosom to the storm of British artillery to throw off a threepenny tax on tea; and yet wring the last hard-earned farthing from the grasp of the black laborers of your country. You profess to believe "that, of one blood, God made all nations of men to dwell on the face of all the earth," and hath commanded all men, everywhere to love one another; yet you notoriously hate, (and glory in your hatred), all men whose skins are not colored like your own. You declare, before the world, and are understood by the world to declare, that you *"hold these truths to be self evident, that all men are created equal; and are endowed by their Creator with certain inalienable rights; and that, among these are, life, liberty, and the pursuit of happiness;"* and yet, you hold securely, in a bondage which, according to your own Thomas Jefferson, *"is worse than ages of that which your fathers rose in rebellion to oppose,"* a *seventh part* of the inhabitants of your country.

Fellow-citizens! I will not enlarge further on your national inconsistencies. The existence of slavery in this country brands your republicanism as a sham, your humanity as a base pretence, and your Christianity as a lie. It destroys your moral power abroad, it corrupts your politicians at home. It saps the foundation of religion; it makes your name a hissing, and a by-word to a mocking earth. It is the antagonistic force in your government, the only thing that seriously disturbs and endangers your *Union*. It fetters your progress; it is the enemy of improvement, the deadly foe of education; it fosters pride; it breeds insolence; it promotes vice; it shelters crime; it is a curse to the earth that supports it; and yet, you cling to it, as if it were the sheet anchor of all your hopes. Oh! be warned! be warned! a horrible reptile is coiled up in your nation's bosom; the venomous creature is nursing at the tender breast of your youthful republic; *for the love of God, tear away*, and fling from you the hideous monster, and *let the weight of twenty millions crush and destroy it forever*!

But it is answered in reply to all this, that precisely what I have now denounced is, in fact, guaranteed and sanctioned by the Constitution of the United States; that, the right to hold and to hunt slaves is a part of that Constitution framed by the illustrious Fathers of this Republic.

Then, I dare to affirm, notwithstanding all I have said before, your fathers stooped, basely stooped

> To palter with us in a double sense:
> And keep the word of promise to the ear,
> But break it to the heart.

And instead of being the honest men I have before declared them to be, they were the veriest imposters that ever practised on mankind. *This* is the inevitable conclusion, and from it there is no escape. But I differ from those who charge this baseness on the framers of the Constitution of the United States. *It is a slander upon their memory*, at least, so I believe. There is not time now to argue the constitutional question at length; nor have I the ability to discuss it as it ought to be discussed. The subject has been handled with masterly power by Lysander Spooner, Esq., by William Goodell, by Samuel E. Sewall, Esq., and last, though not least, by Gerritt Smith, Esq. These gentlemen have, as I think, fully and clearly vindicated the Constitution from any design to support slavery for an hour.

Fellow-citizens! there is no matter in respect to which, the people of the North have allowed themselves to be so ruinously imposed upon, as that of the pro-slavery character of the Constitution. In *that* instrument I hold there is neither warrant, license, nor sanction of the hateful thing; but interpreted, as it *ought* to be interpreted, the Constitution is a GLORIOUS LIBERTY DOCUMENT. Read its preamble, consider its purposes. Is slavery among them? Is it at the gateway? or is it in the temple? It is neither. While I do not intend to argue this question on the present occasion, let me ask, if it be not somewhat singular that, if the Constitution were intended to be, by its framers and adopters, a slave-holding instrument, why neither *slavery, slaveholding,* nor *slave* can anywhere be found in it. What would be thought of an instrument, drawn up, *legally* drawn up, for the purpose of entitling the city of Rochester to a track of land, in which no mention of land was made? Now, there are certain rules of interpretation, for the proper understanding of all legal instruments. These rules are well established. They are plain, common-sense rules, such as you and I, and all of us, can understand and apply, without having passed years in the study of law. I scout the idea that the question of the constitutionality, or unconstitutionality of slavery, is not a question for the people. I hold that every American citizen has a right to form an opinion of the constitution, and to propagate that opinion, and to use all honorable means to make his opinion the prevailing one. Without this right, the liberty of an American citizen would be as insecure as that of a Frenchman. Ex-Vice-President Dallas tells us that the constitution is an object to which no American mind can be too attentive, and no American heart too devoted. He further says, the constitution, in its words, is plain and intelligible, and is meant for the home-bred, unsophisticated understandings of our fellow-citizens. Senator Berrien tells us that the Constitution is the fundamental law, that which controls all others. The charter of our liberties, which every citizen has a personal interest in understanding thoroughly. The testimony of Senator Breese, Lewis Cass, and many others that might be named, who are everywhere esteemed as sound lawyers, so regard the constitution. I take it, therefore, that it is not presumption in a private citizen to form an opinion of that instrument.

Now, take the constitution according to its plain reading, and I defy the presentation of a single pro-slavery clause in it. On the other hand it will be found to contain principles and purposes, entirely hostile to the existence of slavery.

I have detained my audience entirely too long already. At some future period I will gladly avail myself of an opportunity to give this subject a full and fair discussion.

Allow me to say, in conclusion, notwithstanding the dark picture I have this day presented of the state of the nation, I do not despair of this country. There are forces in operation, which must inevitably work the downfall of slavery. "*The arm of the Lord is not shortened,*" and the doom of slavery is certain. I, therefore, leave off where I began, with *hope.* While drawing encouragement from "the Declaration of Independence," the great principles it contains, and the genius of American Institutions, my spirit is also cheered by the obvious tendencies of the age. Nations do not now stand in the same relation to each other that they did ages ago. No nation can now shut itself up from the surrounding world, and trot round in the same old path of its fathers without interference. The time *was* when such could be done. Long established customs of hurtful character could formerly fence themselves in, and do their evil work with social impunity. Knowledge was then confined and enjoyed by the privileged few, and the multitude walked on in mental darkness. But a change has now come over the affairs of mankind. Walled cities and empires have become unfashionable. The arm of commerce has borne away the gates of the strong city. Intelligence is penetrating the darkest corners of the globe. It makes its pathway over and under the sea, as well as on the earth. Wind, steam, and lightning are its chartered agents. Oceans no longer divide, but link nations together. From Boston to London is now a holiday excursion. Space is comparatively annihilated. Thoughts expressed on one side of the Atlantic are distinctly heard on the other.

The far off and almost fabulous Pacific rolls in grandeur at our feet. The Celestial Empire, the mystery of ages, is being solved. The fiat of the Almighty, "*Let there be Light*," has not yet spent its force. No abuse, no outrage whether in taste, sport or avarice, can now hide itself from the all-pervading light. The iron shoe, and crippled foot of China must be seen, in contrast with nature. *Africa must rise and put on her yet unwoven garment. "Ethiopia shall stretch out her hand unto God."* In the fervent aspirations of William Lloyd Garrison, I say, and let every heart join in saying it:

> God speed the year of jubilee
> 　　The wide world o'er!
> When from their galling chains set free,
> Th' oppress'd shall vilely bend the knee,
> And wear the yoke of tyranny
> 　　Like brutes no more.
> That year will come, and freedom's reign,
> To man his plundered rights again
> 　　Restore.
>
> God speed the day when human blood
> 　　Shall cease to flow!
> In every clime be understood,
> The claims of human brotherhood,
> And each return for evil, good,
> 　　Not blow for blow;
> That day will come all feuds to end,

And change into a faithful friend
  Each foe.

God speed the hour, the glorious hour,
  When none on earth
Shall exercise a lordly power,
Nor in a tyrant's presence cower;
But all to manhood's stature tower,
  By equal birth!
THAT HOUR WILL COME, to each, to all,
And from his prison-house, the thrall
  Go forth.

Until that year, day, hour, arrive,
With head, and heart, and hand I'll strive,
To break the rod, and rend the gyve,
The spoiler of his prey deprive—
  So witness Heaven!
And never from my chosen post,
Whate'er the peril or the cost,
  Be driven.

Elizabeth Cady Stanton

Address to the Legislature of the State of New York

(Delivered in Albany, New York, February 14, 1854)

"The thinking minds of all nations call for change. There is a
deep-lying struggle in the whole fabric of society; a boundless,
grinding collision of the New with the Old."

The tyrant, Custom, has been summoned before the bar of Common-Sense. His majesty no longer awes the multitude—his sceptre is broken—his crown is trampled in the dust—the sentence of death is pronounced upon him. All nations, ranks, and classes have, in turn, questioned and repudiated his authority; and now, that the monster is chained and caged, timid woman, on tiptoe, comes to look him in the fare, and to demand of her brave sires and sons, who have struck stout blows for liberty, if, in this change of dynasty, she, too, shall find relief. Yes, gentlemen, in republican America, in the nineteenth century, we, the daughters of the revolutionary heroes of '76, demand at your hands the redress of our grievances—a revision of your State Constitution—a new code of laws. Permit us then, as briefly as possible, to call your attention to the legal disabilities under which we labor.

1st. Look at the position of woman as woman. It is not enough for us that by your laws we are permitted to live and breathe, to claim the necessaries of life from our legal protectors—to pay the penalty of our crimes; we demand the full recognition of all our rights as citizens of the Empire State. We are persons; native, free-born citizens; property-holders, tax-payers; yet are we denied the exercise of our right to the elective franchise. We support ourselves, and, in part, your schools, colleges, churches, your poor-houses, jails, prisons, the army, the navy, the whole machinery of government, and yet we have no voice in your councils. We have every qualification required by the Constitution, necessary to the legal voter, but the one of sex. We are moral, virtuous, and intelligent, and in all respects quite equal to the proud white man himself, and yet by your laws we are classed with idiots, lunatics, and negroes; and though we do not feel honored by the place assigned us, yet, in fact, our legal position is lower than that of either; for the negro can be raised to the dignity of a voter if he possess himself of $250; the lunatic can vote in his moments of sanity, and the idiot, too, if he be a male one, and not more than nine-tenths a fool; but we, who have guided great movements of charity, established missions, edited journals, published works on history, economy, and statistics; who have governed nations, led armies, filled the professor's chair, taught philosophy and mathematics to the savants of our age, discovered planets, piloted ships across the sea, are denied the most sacred rights of citizens, because, forsooth, we came not into this republic crowned with the dignity of manhood! Woman is theoretically absolved from all allegiance to the laws of the State. Sec. 1, Bill of Rights, 2 R. S., 801, says that no authority can, on any pretence whatever, be exercised over the citizens of this State but such as is or shall be derived from, and granted by the people of this State.

Now, gentlemen, we would fain know by what authority you have disfranchised one-half the people of this State? You who have so boldly taken possession of the bulwarks of this republic, show us your credentials, and thus prove your exclusive right to govern, not only yourselves, but us. Judge Hurlburt, who has long occupied a high place at the bar in this State, and who recently retired with honor from the bench of the Supreme Court, in his profound work on Human Rights, has pronounced your present position rank usurpation. Can it be that here, where we acknowledge no royal blood, no apostolic descent, that you, who have declared that all men were created equal—that governments derive their just powers from the consent of the governed, would willingly build up an aristocracy that places the ignorant and vulgar above the educated and refined—the alien and the ditch-digger above the authors and poets of the day—an aristocracy that would raise the sons above the mothers that bore them? Would that the men who can sanction a Constitution so opposed to the genius of this government, who can enact and execute laws so degrading to womankind, had sprung, Minerva-like, from the brains of their fathers, that the matrons of this republic need not blush to own their sons!

Woman's position, under our free institutions, is much lower than under the monarchy of England. "In England the idea of woman holding official station is not so strange as in the United States. The Countess of Pembroke, Dorset, and Montgomery held the office of hereditary sheriff of Westmoreland, and exercised it in person. At the assizes at Appleby, she sat with the judges on the bench. In a reported case, it is stated by counsel, and substantially assented to by the court, that a woman is capable of serving in almost all the offices of the kingdom, such as those of queen, marshal, great chamberlain and constable of England, the champion of England, commissioner of sewers, governor of work-house, sexton, keeper of the prison, of the gate-house of the dean and chapter of Westminster, returning officer for members of Parliament, and constable, the latter of which is in some respects judicial. The office of jailor is frequently exercised by a woman.

"In the United States a woman may administer on the effects of her deceased husband, and she has occasionally held a subordinate place in the post-office department. She has therefore a sort of post mortem, post-mistress notoriety; but with the exception of handling letters of administration and letters mailed, she is the submissive creature of the old common law." True, the unmarried woman has a right to the property she inherits and the money she earns, but she is taxed without representation. And here again you place the negro, so unjustly degraded by you, in a superior position to your own wives and mothers; for colored males, if possessed of a certain amount of property and certain other qualifications, can vote, but if they do not have these qualifications they are not subject to direct taxation; wherein they have the advantage of woman, she being subject to taxation for whatever amount she may possess. (Constitution of New York, Article 2, Sec. 2). But, say you, are not all women sufficiently represented by their fathers, husbands, and brothers? Let your statute books answer the question.

Again we demand in criminal cases that most sacred of all rights, trial by a jury of our own peers. The establishment of trial by jury is of so early a date that its beginning is lost in antiquity; but the right of trial by a jury of one's own peers is a great progressive step of advanced civilization. No rank of men have ever been satisfied with being tried by jurors higher or lower in the civil or political scale than themselves; for jealousy on the one hand, and contempt on the other, has ever effectually blinded the eyes of justice. Hence, all along the pages of history, we find the king, the noble, the peasant, the cardinal, the priest, the layman, each in turn protesting against the authority of the tribunal before which they were summoned to appear. Charles the First refused to recognize the competency of the tribunal which condemned him: For how, said he, can subjects judge a king? The stern descendants of our Pilgrim Fathers refused to answer for their crimes before an English Parliament. For how, said they, can a king judge rebels? And shall woman here consent to be tried by her liege lord, who has dubbed himself law-maker, judge, juror, and sheriff too?—whose power, though sanctioned by Church and State, has no foundation in justice and equity, and is a bold assumption of our inalienable rights. In England a Parliament-lord could challenge a jury where a knight was not empanneled; an alien could demand a jury composed half of his own countrymen; or, in some special cases, juries were even constituted entirely of women. Having seen that man fails to do justice to woman in her best estate, to the virtuous, the noble, the true of our sex, should we trust to his tender mercies the weak, the ignorant, the morally insane? It is not to be denied that the interests of man and woman in the present undeveloped state of the race, and under the existing social arrangements, are and must be antagonistic. The nobleman can not make just laws for the peasant; the slaveholder for the slave; neither can man make and execute just laws for woman, because in each case, the one in power fails to apply the immutable principles of right to any grade but his own.

Shall an erring woman be dragged before a bar of grim-visaged judges, lawyers, and jurors, there to be grossly questioned in public on subjects which women scarce breathe in secret to one another? Shall the most sacred relations of life be called up and rudely scanned by men who, by their own admission, are so coarse that women could not meet them even at the polls without contamination? and yet shall she find there no woman's face or voice to pity and defend? Shall the frenzied mother, who, to save herself and child from exposure and disgrace, ended the life that had but just began, be dragged before such a tribunal to answer for her crime? How can man enter into the feelings of that mother? How can he judge of the agonies of soul that impelled her to such an outrage of maternal instincts? How can he weigh the mountain of sorrow that crushed that mother's heart when she wildly tossed her helpless babe into the cold waters of the midnight sea? Where is he who by false vows thus blasted this trusting woman? Had that helpless child no claims on his protection? Ah, he is freely abroad in the dignity of manhood, in the pulpit, on the bench, in the professor's chair. The imprisonment of his victim and the death of his child, detract not a tithe from his standing and complacency. His peers made the law, and shall law-makers lay nets for those of their own rank? Shall laws which come from the logical brain of man take cognizance of violence done to the moral and affectional nature which predominates, as is said, in woman?

Statesmen of New York, whose daughters, guarded by your affection, and lapped amidst luxuries which your indulgence spreads, care more for their nodding plumes and velvet trains than for the statute laws by which their persons and properties are held—who, blinded by custom and prejudice to the degraded position which they and their sisters occupy in the civil scale, haughtily claim that they already have all the rights they want, how, think ye, you would feel to see a daughter summoned for such a crime—and remember these daughters are but human—before such a tribunal? Would it not, in that hour, be some consolation to see that she was surrounded by the wise and virtuous of her own sex; by those who had known the depth of a mother's love and the misery of a lover's falsehood; to know that to these she could make her confession, and from them receive her sentence? If so, then listen to our just demands and make such a change in your laws as will secure to every woman tried in your courts, an impartial jury. At this moment among the hundreds of women who are shut up in prisons in this State, not one has enjoyed that most sacred of all rights—that right which you would die to defend for yourselves—trial by a jury of one's peers.

2d. Look at the position of woman as wife. Your laws relating to marriage—founded as they are on the old common law of England, a compound of barbarous usages, but partially modified by progressive civilization—are in open violation of our enlightened ideas of justice, and of the holiest feelings of our nature. If you take the highest view of marriage, as a Divine relation, which love alone can constitute and sanctify, then of course human legislation can only recognize it. Men can neither bind nor loose its ties, for that prerogative belongs to God alone, who makes man and woman, and the laws of attraction by which they are united. But if you regard marriage as a civil contract, then let it be subject to the same laws which control all other contracts. Do not make it a kind of half-human, half-divine institution, which you may build up, but can not regulate. Do not, by your special legislation for this one kind of contract, involve yourselves in the grossest absurdities and contradictions.

So long as by your laws no man can make a contract for a horse or piece of land until he is twenty-one years of age, and by which contract he is not bound if any deception has been practiced, or if the party contracting has not fulfilled his part of the agreement—so long as the parties in all mere civil contracts retain their identity and all the power and independence they had before contracting, with the full right to dissolve all partnerships and contracts for any reason, at the will and option of the parties themselves, upon what principle of civil jurisprudence do you permit the boy of fourteen and the girl of twelve, in violation of every natural law, to make a contract more momentous in importance than any other, and then hold them to it, come what may, the whole of their natural lives, in spite of disappointment, deception, and misery? Then, too, the signing of this contract is instant civil death to one of the parties. The woman who but yesterday was sued on bended knee, who stood so high in the scale of being as to make an agreement on equal terms with a proud Saxon man, to-day has no civil existence, no social freedom. The wife who inherits no property holds about the same legal position that does the slave on the Southern plantation. She can own nothing, sell nothing. She has no right even to the wages she earns; her person, her time, her services are the property of another. She can not testify, in many cases, against her husband. She can get no redress for wrongs in her own name in any court of justice. She can neither sue nor be sued. She is not held morally responsible for any crime committed in the presence of her husband, so completely is her very existence supposed by the law to be merged in that of another. Think of it; your wives may be thieves, libelers, burglars, incendiaries, and for crimes like these they are not held amenable to the laws of the land, if they but commit them in your dread presence. For them, alas! there is no higher law than the will of man. Herein behold the bloated conceit of these Petruchios of the law, who seem to say:

> Nay, look not big, nor stamp, nor stare, nor fret;
> I will be master of what is mine own;
> She is my goods, my chattels; she is my house,
> My household stuff, my field, my barn,
> My horse, my ox, my ass, my anything;
> And here she stands, touch her whoever dare;
> I'll bring my action on the proudest he,
> That stops my way, in Padua.

How could man ever look thus on woman? She, at whose feet Socrates learned wisdom—she, who gave to the world a Saviour, and witnessed alike the adoration of the Magi and the agonies of the cross. How could such a being, so blessed and honored, ever become the ignoble, servile, cringing slave, with whom the fear of man could be paramount to the sacred dictates of conscience and the holy love of Heaven? By the common law of England, the spirit of which has been but too faithfully incorporated into our statute law, a husband has a right to whip his wife with a rod not larger than his thumb, to shut her up in a room, and administer whatever moderate chastisement he may deem necessary to insure obedience to his wishes, and for her healthful moral development! He can forbid all persons harboring or trusting her on his account. He can deprive her of all social intercourse with her nearest and dearest friends. If by great economy she accumulates a small sum, which for future need she deposit, little by little, in a savings bank, the husband has a right to draw it out, at his option, to use it, as he may see fit.

"Husband is entitled to wife's credit or business talents (whenever their intermarriage may have occurred); and goods purchased by her on her own credit, with his consent, while cohabiting with him, can be seized and sold in execution against him for his own debts, and this, though she carry on business in her own name."—7 *Howard's Practice Reports*, 105, *Lovett agt. Robinson and Whitbeck, sheriff, etc.*

"No letters of administration shall be granted to a person convicted of infamous crime; nor to any one incapable by law of making a contract; nor to a person not a citizen of the United States, unless such person reside within this

State; nor to any one who is under twenty-one years of age; nor to any person who shall be adjudged incompetent by the surrogate to execute duties of such trust, by reason of drunkenness, improvidence, or want of understanding, nor to any married woman; but where a married woman is entitled to administration, the same may be granted to her husband in her right and behalf."

There is nothing that an unruly wife might do against which the husband has not sufficient protection in the law. But not so with the wife. If she have a worthless husband, a confirmed drunkard, a villain, or a vagrant, he has still all the rights of a man, a husband, and a father. Though the whole support of the family be thrown upon the wife, if the wages she earns be paid to her by her employer, the husband can receive them again. If, by unwearied industry and perseverance, she can earn for herself and children a patch of ground and a shed to cover them, the husband can strip her of all her hard earnings, turn her and her little ones out in the cold northern blast, take the clothes from their backs, the bread from their mouths; all this by your laws may he do, and has he done, oft and again, to satisfy the rapacity of that monster in human form, the rum-seller.

But the wife who is so fortunate as to have inherited property, has, by the new law in this State, been redeemed from her lost condition. She is no longer a legal nonentity. This property law, if fairly construed, will overturn the whole code relating to woman and property. The right to property implies the right to buy and sell, to will and bequeath, and herein is the dawning of a civil existence for woman, for now the "femme covert" must have the right to make contracts. So, get ready, gentlemen; the "little justice" will be coming to you one day, deed in hand, for your acknowledgment. When he asks you "if you sign without fear or compulsion," say yes, boldly, as we do. Then, too, the right to will is ours. Now what becomes of the "tenant for life"? Shall he, the happy husband of a millionaire, who has lived in yonder princely mansion in the midst of plenty and elegance, be cut down in a day to the use of one-third of this estate and a few hundred a year, as long he remains her widower? And should he, in spite of this bounty on celibacy, impelled by his affections, marry again, choosing for a wife a woman as poor as himself, shall he be thrown penniless on the cold world—this child of fortune, enervated by ease and luxury, henceforth to be dependent wholly on his own resources? Poor man! He would be rich, though, in the sympathies of many women who have passed through just such an ordeal. But what is property without the right to protect that property by law? It is mockery to say a certain estate is mine, if, without my consent, you have the right to tax me when and how you please, while I have no voice in making the tax-gatherer, the legislator, or the law. The right to property will, of necessity, compel us in due time to the exercise of our right to the elective franchise, and then naturally follows the right to hold office.

3d. Look at the position of woman as widow. Whenever we attempt to point out the wrongs of the wife, those who would have us believe that the laws can not be improved, point us to the privileges, powers, and claims of the widow. Let us look into these a little. Behold in yonder humble house a married pair, who, for long years, have lived together, childless and alone. Those few acres of well-tilled land, with the small, white house that looks so cheerful through its vines and flowers, attest the honest thrift and simple taste of its owners. This man and woman, by their hard days' labor, have made this home their own. Here they live in peace and plenty, happy in the hope that they may dwell together securely under their own vine and fig-tree for the few years that remain to them, and that under the shadow of these trees, planted by their own hands, and in the midst of their household gods, so loved and familiar, they may take their last farewell of earth. But, alas for human hopes! the husband dies, and without a will, and the stricken widow, at one fell blow, loses the companion of her youth, her house and home, and half the little sum she had in bank. For the law, which takes no cognizance of widows left with twelve children and not one cent, instantly spies out this widow, takes account of her effects, and announces to her the startling intelligence that but one-third of the house and lot, and one-half the personal property, are hers. The law has other favorites with whom she must share the hard-earned savings of years. In this dark hour of grief, the coarse minions of the law gather round the widow's hearth-stone, and, in the name of justice, outrage all natural sense of right; mock at the sacredness of human love, and with cold familiarity proceed to place a moneyed value on the old arm-chair, in which, but a few brief hours since, she closed the eyes that had ever beamed on her with kindness and affection; on the solemn clock in the corner, that told the hour he passed away; on every garment with which his form and presence were associated, and on every article of comfort and convenience that the house contained, even down to the knives and forks and spoons—and the widow saw it all—and when the work was done, she gathered up what the law allowed her and went forth to seek another home! This is the much-talked-of widow's dower. Behold the magnanimity of the law in allowing the widow to retain a life interest in one-third the landed estate, and one-half the personal property of her husband, and taking the lion's share to itself! Had she died first, the house and land would all have been the husband's still. No one would have dared to intrude upon the privacy of his home, or to molest him in his sacred retreat of sorrow. How, I ask you, can that be called justice, which makes such a distinction as this between man and woman?

By management, economy, and industry, our widow is able, in a few years, to redeem her house and home. But the law never loses sight of the purse, no matter how low in the scale of being its owner may be. It sends its officers round every year to gather in the harvest for the public crib, and no widow who owns a piece of land two feet square ever escapes this reckoning. Our widow, too, who has now twice earned her home, has her annual tax to pay also—a tribute of gratitude that she is permitted to breathe the free air of this republic, where "taxation without representation," by such worthies as John Hancock and Samuel Adams, has been declared "intolerable tyranny." Having glanced at the magnanimity of the law in its dealings with the widow, let us see how the individual man, under the influence of such laws, doles out justice to his helpmate. The husband has the absolute right to will away his property as he may see fit. If he has children, he can divide his property among them, leaving his wife her third only of the landed estate, thus making her a dependent on the bounty of her own children. A man with thirty thousand dollars in personal property, may leave his wife but a few hundred a year, as long as she remains his widow.

The cases are without number where women, who have lived in ease and elegance, at the death of their husbands have, by will, been reduced to the bare necessaries of life. The man who leaves his wife the sole guardian of his property and children is an exception to the general rule. Man has ever manifested a wish that the world should indeed be a blank to the companion whom he leaves behind him. The Hindoo makes that wish a law, and burns the widow on the funeral pyre of her husband; but the civilized man, impressed with a different view of the sacredness of life, takes a less summary mode of drawing his beloved partner after him; he does it by the deprivation and starvation of the flesh, and the humiliation and mortification of the spirit. In bequeathing to the wife just enough to keep soul and body together, man seems to lose sight of the fact that woman, like himself, takes great pleasure in acts of benevolence and charity. It is but just, therefore, that she should have it in her power to give during her life, and to will away at her death, as her benevolence or obligations might prompt her to do.

4th. Look at the position of woman as mother. There is no human love so strong and steadfast as that of the mother for her child; yet behold how ruthless are your laws touching this most sacred relation. Nature has clearly made the mother the guardian of the child; but man, in his inordinate love of power, does continually set nature and nature's laws at open defiance. The father may apprentice his child, bind him out to a trade, without the mother's consent—yea, in direct opposition to her most earnest entreaties, prayers and tears.

He may apprentice his son to a gamester or rum-seller, and thus cancel his debts of *honor*. By the abuse of this absolute power, he may bind his daughter to the owner of a brothel, and, by the degradation of his child, supply his daily wants: and such things, gentlemen, have been done in our very midst. Moreover, the father, about to die, may bind out all his children wherever and to whom-soever he may see fit, and thus, in fact, will away the guardianship of all his children from the mother. The Revised Statutes of New York provide that "every father, whether of full age or a minor, of a child to be born, or of any living child under the age of twenty-one years, and unmarried, may by his deed or last will, duly executed, dispose of the custody and tuition of such child during its minor-ity, or for any less time, to any person or persons, in possession or remainder." 2 R. S., page 150, sec. 1. Thus, by your laws, the child is the absolute property of the father, wholly at his disposal in life or at death.

In case of separation, the law gives the children to the father; no matter what his character or condition. At this very time we can point you to noble, virtuous, well-educated mothers in this State, who have abandoned their husbands for their profligacy and confirmed drunkenness. All these have been robbed of their chil-dren, who are in the custody of the husband, under the care of his relatives, whilst the mothers are permitted to see them but at stated intervals. But, said one of these mothers, with a grandeur of attitude and manner worthy the noble Roman matron in the palmiest days of that republic, I would rather never see my child again, than be the medium to hand down the low animal nature of its father, to stamp degradation on the brow of another innocent being. It is enough that one child of his shall call me mother.

If you are far-sighted statesmen, and do wisely judge of the interests of this commonwealth, you will so shape your future laws as to encourage woman to take the high moral ground that the father of her children must be great and good. Instead of your present laws, which make the mother and her children the vic-tims of vice and license, you might rather pass laws prohibiting to all drunkards, libertines, and fools, the rights of husbands and fathers. Do not the hundreds of laughing idiots that are crowding into our asylums, appeal to the wisdom of our statesmen for some new laws on marriage—to the mothers of this day for a higher, purer morality?

Again, as the condition of the child always follows that of the mother, and as by the sanction of your laws the father may beat the mother, so may he the child. What mother can not bear me witness to untold sufferings which cruel, vindic-tive fathers have visited upon their helpless children? Who ever saw a human being that would not abuse unlimited power? Base and ignoble must that man be who, let the provocation be what it may, would strike a woman: but he who would lacerate a trembling child is unworthy the name of man. A mother's love can be no protection to a child; she can not appeal to you to save it from a father's cruelty, for the laws take no cognizance of the mother's most grievous wrongs. Neither at home nor abroad can a mother protect her son. Look at the temptations that surround the paths of our youth at every step; look at the gambling and drinking saloons, the club rooms, the dens of infamy and abomination that infest all our villages and cities—slowly but surely sapping the very foundations of all virtue and strength.

By your laws, all these abominable resorts are permitted. It is folly to talk of a mother moulding the character of her son, when all mankind, backed up by law and public sentiment, conspire to destroy her influence. But when woman's moral power shall speak through the ballot-box, then shall her influence be seen and felt; then, in our legislative debates, such questions as the canal tolls on salt, the improvement of rivers and harbors, and the claims of Mr. Smith for damages against the State, would be secondary to the consideration of the legal existence of all these public resorts, which lure our youth on to excessive indulgence and destruction.

Many times and oft it has been asked us, with unaffected seriousness, "What do you women want? What are you aiming at?" Many have manifested a laudable curiosity to know what the wives and daughters could complain of in republican America, where their sires and sons have so bravely fought for freedom and gloriously secured their independence, trampling all tyranny, bigotry, and caste in the dust, and declaring to a waiting world the divine truth that all men are created equal. What can woman want under such a government? Admit a radical difference in sex, and you demand different spheres—water for fish, and air for birds.

It is impossible to make the Southern planter believe that his slave feels and reasons just as he does—that injustice and subjection are as galling as to him—that the degradation of living by the will of another, the mere dependent on his caprice, at the mercy of his passions, is as keenly felt by him as his master. If you can force on his unwilling vision a vivid picture of the negro's wrongs, and for a moment touch his soul, his logic brings him instant consolation. He says, the slave does not feel this as I would. Here, gentlemen, is our difficulty: When we plead our cause before the law-makers and savants of the republic, they can not take in the idea that men and women are alike; and so long as the mass rest in this delusion, the public mind will not be so much startled by the revelations made of the injustice and degradation of woman's position as by the fact that she should at length wake up to a sense of it.

If you, too, are thus deluded, what avails it that we show by your statute books that your laws are unjust—that woman is the victim of avarice and power? What avails it that we point out the wrongs of woman in social life; the victim of passion and lust? You scorn the thought that she has any natural love of freedom burning in her breast, any clear perception of justice urging her on to demand her rights.

Would to God you could know the burning indignation that fills woman's soul when she turns over the pages of your statute books, and sees there how like feudal barons you freemen hold your women. Would that you could know the humiliation she feels for sex, when she thinks of all the beardless boys in your law offices, learning these ideas of one-sided justice—taking their first lessons in contempt for all womankind—being indoctrinated into the incapacities of their mothers, and the lordly, absolute rights of man over all women, children, and property, and to know that these are to be our future presidents, judges, husbands, and fathers; in sorrow we exclaim, alas! for that nation whose sons bow not in loyalty to woman. The mother is the first object of the child's veneration and love, and they who root out this holy sentiment, dream not of the blighting effect it has on the boy and the man. The impression left on law students, fresh from your statute books, is most unfavorable to woman's influence; hence you see but few lawyers chivalrous and high-toned in their sentiments toward woman. They can not escape the legal view which, by constant reading, has become familiarized to their minds: "*Femme covert*," "dower," "widow's claims," "protection," "incapacities," "incumbrance," is written on the brow of every woman they meet.

But if, gentlemen, you take the ground that the sexes are alike, and, therefore, you are our faithful representatives—then why all these special laws for woman? Would not one code answer for all of like needs and wants? Christ's golden rule is better than all the special legislation that the ingenuity of man can devise: "Do unto others as you would have others do unto you." This, men and brethren, is all we ask at your hands. We ask no better laws than those you have made for yourselves. We need no other protection than that which your present laws secure to you.

In conclusion, then, let us say, in behalf of the women of this State, we ask for all that you have asked for yourselves in the progress of your development, since the *Mayflower* cast anchor beside Plymouth rock; and simply on the ground that the rights of every human being are the same and identical. You may say that the mass of the women of this State do not make the demand; it comes from a few sour, disappointed old maids and childless women.

You are mistaken; the mass speak through us. A very large majority of the women of this State support themselves and their children, and many their husbands too. Go into any village you please, of three or four thousand inhabitants, and you will find as many as fifty men or more, whose only business is to discuss religion and politics, as they watch the trains come and go at the depot, or the passage of a canal boat through a lock; to laugh at the vagaries of some drunken brother, or the capers of a monkey dancing to the music of his master's organ. All these are supported by their mothers, wives, or sisters.

Now, do you candidly think these wives do not wish to control the wages they earn—to own the land they buy—the houses they build? to have at their disposal their own children, without being subject to the constant interference and tyranny of an idle, worthless profligate?) Do you suppose that any woman is such a pattern of devotion and submission that she willingly stitches all day for the small sum of fifty cents, that she may enjoy the unspeakable privilege, in obedience to your laws, of paying for her husband's tobacco and rum? Think you the wife of the confirmed, beastly drunkard would consent to share with him her home and bed, if law and public sentiment would release her from such gross companionship? Verily, no! Think you the wife with whom endurance has ceased to be a virtue, who, through much suffering, has lost all faith in the justice of both heaven and earth, takes the law in her own hand, severs the unholy bond, and turns her back forever upon him whom she once called husband, consents to the law that in such an hour tears her child from her—all that she has left on earth to love and cherish? The drunkards' wives speak through us, and they number 50,000. Think you that the woman who has worked hard all her days in helping her husband to accumulate a large property, consents to the law that places this wholly at his disposal? Would not the mother whose only child is bound out for a term of years against her expressed wish, deprive the father of this absolute power if she could?

For all these, then, we speak. If to this long list you add the laboring women who are loudly demanding remuneration for their unending toil; those women who teach in our seminaries, academies, and public schools for a miserable pittance; the widows who are taxed without mercy; the unfortunate ones in our work-houses, poor-houses, and prisons; who are they that we do not now represent? But a small class of the fashionable butterflies, who, through the short summer days, seek the sunshine and the flowers; but the cool breezes of autumn and the hoary frosts of winter will soon chase all these away; then they, too, will need and seek protection, and through other lips demand in their turn justice and equity at your hands.

Abraham Lincoln

On the Dred Scott Decision

(Delivered at Springfield, Illinois, June 26, 1857)

I am here to-night, partly by the invitation of some of you, and partly by my own inclination. Two weeks ago Judge Douglas spoke here on the several subjects of Kansas, the Dred Scott decision, and Utah. I listened to the speech at the time, and have read the report of it since. It was intended to controvert opinions which I think just, and to assail (politically, not personally,) those men who, in common with me, entertain those opinions. For this reason I wished then, and still wish, to make some answer to it, which I now take the opportunity of doing.

I begin with Utah. If it prove to be true, as is probable, that the people of Utah are in open rebellion to the United States, then Judge Douglas is in favor of repealing their territorial organization, and attaching them to the adjoining States for judicial purposes. I say, too, if they are in rebellion, they ought to be somehow coerced to obedience; and I am not now prepared to admit or deny that the Judge's mode of coercing them is not as good as any. The Republicans can fall in with it without taking back anything they have ever said. To be sure, it would be a considerable backing down by Judge Douglas from his much vaunted doctrine of self-government for the territories; but this is only additional proof of what was very plain from the beginning, that that doctrine was a mere deceitful pretense for the benefit of slavery. Those who could not see that much in the Nebraska act itself, which forced Governors, and Secretaries, and Judges on the people of the territories, without their choice or consent, could not be made to see, though one should rise from the dead to testify.

But in all this, it is very plain the Judge evades the only question the Republicans have ever pressed upon the Democracy in regard to Utah. That question the Judge well knows to be this: "If the people of Utah shall peacefully form a State Constitution tolerating polygamy, will the Democracy admit them into the Union?" There is nothing in the United States Constitution or law against polygamy; and why is it not a part of the Judge's "sacred right of self-government" for that people to have it, or rather to *keep* it, if they choose? These questions, so far as I know, the Judge never answers. It might involve the Democracy to answer them either way, and they go unanswered.

As to Kansas. The substance of the Judge's speech on Kansas is an effort to put the free State men in the wrong for not voting at the election of delegates to the Constitutional Convention. He says: *"There is every reason to hope and believe that the law will be fairly interpreted and impartially executed, so as to insure to every bona fide inhabitant the free and quiet exercise of the elective franchise."*

It appears extraordinary that Judge Douglas should make such a statement. He knows that, by the law, no one can vote who has not been registered; and he knows that the free State men place their refusal to vote on the ground that but few of them have been registered. It is *possible* this is not true, but Judge Douglas knows it is asserted to be true in letters, newspapers and public speeches, and borne by every mail, and blown by every breeze to the eyes and ears of the world. He knows it is boldly declared that the people of many whole counties, and many whole neighborhoods in others, are left unregistered; yet, he does not venture to contradict the declaration, nor to point out how they *can* vote without being registered; but he just slips along, not seeming to know there is any such question of fact, and complacently declares: "There is every reason to hope and believe that the law will be fairly and impartially executed, so as to insure to every *bona fide* inhabitant the free and quiet exercise of the elective franchise."

I readily agree that if all had a chance to vote, they ought to have voted. If, on the contrary, as they allege, and Judge Douglas ventures not to particularly contradict, few only of the free State men had a chance to vote, they were perfectly right in staying from the polls in a body.

By the way since the Judge spoke, the Kansas election has come off. The Judge expressed his confidence that all the Democrats in Kansas would do their duty—including "free state Democrats" of course. The returns received here as yet are very incomplete; but so far as they go, they indicate that only about one sixth of the registered voters, have really voted; and this too, when not more, perhaps, than one half of the rightful voters have been registered, thus showing the thing to have been altogether the most exquisite farce ever enacted. I am watching with considerable interest, to ascertain what figure "the free state Democrats" cut in the concern. Of course they voted—all democrats do their duty—and of course they did not vote for slave-state candidates. We soon shall know how many delegates *they* elected, how many candidates they had, pledged for a free state; and how many votes were cast for them.

Allow me to barely whisper my suspicion that there were no such things in Kansas as "free state Democrats"—that they were altogether mythical, good only to figure in newspapers and speeches in the free states. If there should prove to be one real living free state Democrat in Kansas, I suggest that it might be well to catch him, and stuff and preserve his skin, as an interesting specimen of that soon to be extinct variety of the genus, Democrat.

And now as to the Dred Scott decision. That decision declares two propositions—first, that a negro cannot sue in the U.S. Courts; and secondly, that Congress cannot prohibit slavery in the Territories. It was made by a divided court—dividing differently on the different points. Judge Douglas does not discuss the merits of the decision; and, in that respect, I shall follow his example, believing I could no more improve on McLean and Curtis, than he could on Taney.

He denounces all who question the correctness of that decision, as offering violent resistance to it. But who resists it? Who has, in spite of the decision, declared Dred Scott free, and resisted the authority of his master over him?

Judicial decisions have two uses—first, to absolutely determine the case decided, and secondly, to indicate to the public how other similar cases will be decided when they arise. For the latter use, they are called "precedents" and "authorities."

We believe, as much as Judge Douglas, (perhaps more) in obedience to, and respect for the judicial department of government. We think its decisions on Constitutional questions, when fully settled, should control, not only the particular cases decided, but the general policy of the country, subject to be disturbed only by amendments of the Constitution as provided in that instrument itself. More than this would be revolution. But we think the Dred Scott decision is erroneous. We know the court that made it, has often over-ruled its own decisions, and we shall do what we can to have it to over-rule this. We offer no *resistance* to it.

Judicial decisions are of greater or less authority as precedents, according to circumstances. That this should be so, accords both with common sense, and the customary understanding of the legal profession.

If this important decision had been made by the unanimous concurrence of the judges, and without any apparent partisan bias, and in accordance with legal public expectation, and with the steady practice of the departments throughout our history, and had been in no part, based on assumed historical facts which are not really true; or, if wanting in some of these, it had been before the court more than once, and had there been affirmed and re-affirmed through a course of years, it then might be, perhaps would be, factious, nay, even revolutionary, to not acquiesce in it as a precedent.

But when, as it is true we find it wanting in all these claims to the public confidence, it is not resistance, it is not factious, it is not even disrespectful, to treat it as not having yet quite established a settled doctrine for the country—But Judge Douglas considers this view awful. Hear him:

"The courts are the tribunals prescribed by the Constitution and created by the authority of the people to determine, expound and enforce the law. Hence, whoever resists the final decision of the highest judicial tribunal, aims a deadly blow to our whole Republican system of government—a blow, which if successful would place all our rights and liberties at the mercy of passion, anarchy and violence. I repeat, therefore, that if resistance to the decisions of the Supreme Court of the United States, in a matter like the points decided in the Dred Scott case, clearly within their jurisdiction as defined by the Constitution, shall be forced upon the country as a political issue, it will become a distinct and naked issue between the friends and the enemies of the Constitution—the friends and the enemies of the supremacy of the laws."

Why this same Supreme court once decided a national bank to be constitutional; but Gen. Jackson, as President of the United States, disregarded the decision, and vetoed a bill for a re-charter, partly on constitutional ground, declaring that each public functionary must support the Constitution, "*as he understands it.*" But hear the General's own words. Here they are, taken from his veto message:

"It is maintained by the advocates of the bank, that its constitutionality, in all its features, ought to be considered as settled by precedent, and by the decision of the Supreme Court. To this conclusion I cannot assent. Mere precedent is a dangerous source of authority, and should not be regarded as deciding questions of constitutional power, except where the acquiescence of the people and the States can be considered as well settled. So far from this being the case on this subject, an argument against the bank might be based on precedent. One Congress in 1791, decided in favor of a bank; another in 1811, decided against it. One Congress in 1815 decided against a bank; another in 1816 decided in its favor. Prior to the present Congress, therefore the precedents drawn from that source were equal. If we resort to the States, the expressions of legislative, judicial and executive opinions against the bank have been probably to those in its favor as four to one. There is nothing in precedent, therefore, which if its authority were admitted, ought to weigh in favor of the act before me."

I drop the quotations merely to remark that all there ever was, in the way of precedent up to the Dred Scott decision, on the points therein decided, had been against that decision. But hear Gen. Jackson further—

"If the opinion of the Supreme court covered the whole ground of this act, it ought not to control the co-ordinate authorities of this Government. The Congress, the executive and the court, must each for itself be guided by its own opinion of the Constitution. Each public officer, who takes an oath to support the Constitution, swears that he will support it as he understands it, and not as it is understood by others."

Again and again have I heard Judge Douglas denounce that bank decision, and applaud Gen. Jackson for disregarding it. It would be interesting for him to look over his recent speech, and see how exactly his fierce philippics against us for resisting Supreme Court decisions, fall upon his own head. It will call to his mind a long and fierce political war in this country, upon an issue which, in his own language, and, of course, in his own changeless estimation, was "a distinct and naked issue between the friends and the enemies of the Constitution," and in which war he fought in the ranks of the enemies of the Constitution.

I have said, in substance, that the Dred Scott decision was, in part, based on assumed historical facts which were not really true; and I ought not to leave the subject without giving some reasons for saying this; I therefore give an instance or two, which I think fully sustain me. Chief Justice Taney, in delivering the opinion of the majority of the Court, insists at great length that negroes were no part of the people who made, or for whom was made, the Declaration of Independence, or the Constitution of the United States.

On the contrary, Judge Curtis, in his dissenting opinion, shows that in five of the then thirteen states, to wit, New Hampshire, Massachusetts, New York, New Jersey and North Carolina, free negroes were voters, and, in proportion to their numbers, had the same part in making the Constitution that the white people had. He shows this with so much particularity as to leave no doubt of its truth; and, as a sort of conclusion on that point, holds the following language:

"The Constitution was ordained and established by the people of the United States, through the action, in each State, of those persons who were qualified by its laws to act thereon in behalf of themselves and all other citizens of the State. In some of the States, as we have seen, colored persons were among those qualified by law to act on the subject. These colored persons were not only included in the body of 'the people of the United States,' by whom the Constitution was ordained and established; but in at least five of the States they had the power to act, and, doubtless, did act, by their suffrages, upon the question of its adoption."

Again, Chief Justice Taney says: "It is difficult, at this day to realize the state of public opinion in relation to that unfortunate race, which prevailed in the civilized and enlightened portions of the world at the time of the Declaration of

Independence, and when the Constitution of the United States was framed and adopted." And again, after quoting from the Declaration, he says: "The general words above quoted would seem to include the whole human family, and if they were used in a similar instrument at this day, would be so understood."

In these the Chief Justice does not directly assert, but plainly assumes, as a fact, that the public estimate of the black man is more favorable *now* than it was in the days of the Revolution. This assumption is a mistake. In some trifling particulars, the condition of that race has been ameliorated; but, as a whole, in this country, the change between then and now is decidedly the other way; and their ultimate destiny has never appeared so hopeless as in the last three or four years. In two of the five States—New Jersey and North Carolina—that then gave the free negro the right of voting, the right has since been taken away; and in a third—New York—it has been greatly abridged; while it has not been extended, so far as I know, to a single additional State, though the number of the States has more than doubled. In those days, as I understand, masters could, at their own pleasure, emancipate their slaves; but since then, such legal restraints have been made upon emancipation, as to amount almost to prohibition. In those days, Legislatures held the unquestioned power to abolish slavery in their respective States; but now it is becoming quite fashionable for State Constitutions to withhold that power from the Legislatures. In those days, by common consent, the spread of the black man's bondage to new countries was prohibited; but now, Congress decides that it *will* not continue the prohibition, and the Supreme Court decides that it *could* not if it would. In those days, our Declaration of Independence was held sacred by all, and thought to include all; but now, to aid in making the bondage of the negro universal and eternal, it is assailed, and sneered at, and construed, and hawked at, and torn, till, if its framers could rise from their graves, they could not at all recognize it. All the powers of earth seem rapidly combining against him. Mammon is after him; ambition follows, and philosophy follows, and the Theology of the day is fast joining the cry. They have him in his prison house; they have searched his person, and left no prying instrument with him. One after another they have closed the heavy iron doors upon him, and now they have him, as it were, bolted in with a lock of a hundred keys, which can never be unlocked without the concurrent of every key; the keys in the hands of a hundred different men, and they scattered to a hundred different and distant places; and they stand musing as to what invention, in all the dominions of mind and matter, can be produced to make the impossibility of his escape more complete than it is.

It is grossly incorrect to say or assume, that the public estimate of the negro is more favorable now than it was at the origin of the government.

Three years and a half ago, Judge Douglas brought forward his famous Nebraska bill. The country was at once in a blaze. He scorned all opposition, and carried it through Congress. Since then he has seen himself superseded in a Presidential nomination, by one indorsing the general doctrine of his measure, but at the same time standing clear of the odium of its untimely agitation, and its gross breach of national faith; and he has seen that successful rival Constitutionally elected, not by the strength of friends, but by the division of adversaries, being in a popular minority of nearly four hundred thousand votes. He has seen his chief aids in his own State, Shields and Richardson, politically speaking, successively tried, convicted, and executed, for an offense not their own, but his. And now he sees his own case, standing next on the docket for trial.

There is a natural disgust in the minds of nearly all white people, to the idea of an indiscriminate amalgamation of the white and black races; and Judge Douglas evidently is basing his chief hope, upon the chances of being able to appropriate the benefit of this disgust to himself. If he can, by much drumming and repeating, fasten the odium of that idea upon his adversaries, he thinks he can struggle through the storm. He therefore clings to this hope, as a drowning man to the last plank. He makes an occasion for lugging it in from the opposition to the Dred Scott decision. He finds the Republicans insisting that the Declaration of Independence includes ALL men, black as well as white; and forthwith he boldly denies that it includes negroes at all, and proceeds to argue gravely that all who contend it does, do so only because they want to vote, and eat, and sleep, and marry with negroes! He will have it that they cannot be consistent else. Now I protest against that counterfeit logic which concludes that, because I do not want a black woman for a *slave* I must necessarily want her for a *wife*. I need not have her for either, I can just leave her alone. In some respects she certainly is not my equal; but in her natural right to eat the bread she earns with her own hands without asking leave of any one else, she is my equal, and the equal of all others.

Chief Justice Taney, in his opinion in the Dred Scott case, admits that the language of the Declaration is broad enough to include the whole human family, but he and Judge Douglas argue that the authors of that instrument did not intend to include negroes, by the fact that they did not at once, actually place them on an equality with the whites. Now this grave argument comes to just nothing at all, by the other fact, that they did not at once, *or ever afterwards,* actually place all white people on an equality with one or another. And this is the staple argument of both the Chief Justice and the Senator, for doing this obvious violence to the plain unmistakable language of the Declaration. I think the authors of that notable instrument intended to include *all* men, but they did not intend to declare all men equal *in all respects*. They did not mean to say all were equal in color, size, intellect, moral developments, or social capacity. They defined with tolerable distinctness, in what respects they did consider all men created equal—equal in "certain inalienable rights, among which are life, liberty, and the pursuit of happiness." This they said, and this meant. They did not mean to assert the obvious untruth, that all were then actually enjoying that equality, nor yet, that they were about to confer it immediately upon them. In fact they had no power to confer such a boon. They meant simply to declare the *right*, so that the *enforcement* of it might follow as fast as circumstances should permit. They meant to set up a standard maxim for free society, which should be familiar to all, and revered by all; constantly looked to, constantly labored for, and even though never perfectly attained, constantly approximated, and thereby constantly spreading and deepening its influence, and augmenting the happiness and value of life to all people of all colors everywhere. The assertion that "all men are created equal" was of no practical use in effecting our separation from Great Britain; and it was placed in the Declaration, not for that, but for future use. Its authors meant it to be, thank God, it is now proving itself, a stumbling block to those who in after times might seek to turn a free people back into the hateful paths of despotism. They knew the proneness of prosperity to breed tyrants, and they meant when such should re-appear in this fair land and commence their vocation they should find left for them at least one hard nut to crack.

I have now briefly expressed my view of the *meaning* and *objects* of that part of the Declaration of Independence which declares that "all men are created equal."

Now let us hear Judge Douglas' view of the same subject, as I find it in the printed report of his late speech. Here it is:

"No man can vindicate the character, motives and conduct of the signers of the Declaration of Independence, except upon the hypothesis that they referred to the white race alone, and not to the African, when they declared all men to have been created equal—that they were speaking of British subjects on this continent being equal to British subjects born and residing in Great Britain—that they were entitled to the same inalienable rights, and among them were enumerated life, liberty and the pursuit of happiness. The Declaration was adopted for the purpose of justifying the colonists in the eyes of the civilized world in withdrawing their allegiance from the British crown, and dissolving their connection with the mother country."

My good friends, read that carefully over some leisure hour, and ponder well upon it—see what a mere wreck—mangled ruin—it makes of our once glorious Declaration.

"They were speaking of British subjects on this continent being equal to British subjects born and residing in Great Britain!" Why, according to this, not only negroes but white people outside of Great Britain and America are not spoken of in that instrument. The English, Irish and Scotch, along with white Americans, were included to be sure, but the French, Germans and other white people of the world are all gone to pot along with the Judge's inferior races.

I had thought the Declaration promised something better than the condition of British subjects; but no, it only meant that we should be *equal* to them in their own oppressed and *unequal* condition. According to that, it gave no promise that having kicked off the King and Lords of Great Britain, we should not at once be saddled with a King and Lords of our own.

I had thought the Declaration contemplated the progressive improvement in the condition of all men everywhere; but no, it merely "was adopted for the purpose of justifying the colonists in the eyes of the civilized world in withdrawing their allegiance from the British crown, and dissolving their connection with the mother country." Why, that object having been effected some eighty years ago, the Declaration is of no practical use now—mere rubbish—old wadding left to rot on the battle-field after the victory is won.

I understand you are preparing to celebrate the "Fourth," to-morrow week. What for? The doings of that day had no reference to the present; and quite half of you are not even descendants of those who were referred to at that day. But I suppose you will celebrate; and will even go so far as to read the Declaration. Suppose after you read it once in the old fashioned way, you read it once more with Judge Douglas's version. It will then run thus: "We hold these truths to be self-evident that all British subjects who were on this continent eighty-one years ago, were created equal to all British subjects born and then residing in Great Britain."

And now I appeal to all—to Democrats as well as others,—are you really willing that the Declaration shall be thus frittered away?—thus left no more at most, than an interesting memorial of the dead past? thus shorn of its vitality, and practical value; and left without the *germ* or even the *suggestion* of the individual rights of man in it?

But Judge Douglas is especially horrified at the thought of the mixing blood by the white and black races: agreed for once—a thousand times agreed. There are white men enough to marry all the white women, and black men enough to marry all the black women; and so let them be married. On this point we fully agree with the Judge; and when he shall show that his policy is better adapted to prevent amalgamation than ours we shall drop ours, and adopt his. Let us see. In 1850 there were in the United States, 405,751, mulattoes. Very few of these are the offspring of whites and *free* blacks; nearly all have sprung from black *slaves* and white masters. A separation of the races is the only perfect preventive of amalgamation but as all immediate separation is impossible the next best thing is to *keep* them apart *where* they are not already together. If white and black people never get together in Kansas, they will never mix blood in Kansas. That is at least one self-evident truth. A few free colored persons may get into the free States, in any event; but their number is too insignificant to amount to much in the way of mixing blood. In 1850 there were in the free states, 56,649 mulattoes; but for the most part they were not born there—they came from the slave States, ready made up. In the same year the slave States had 348,874 mulattoes all of home production. The proportion of free mulattoes to free blacks—the only colored classes in the free states—is much greater in the slave than in the free states. It is worthy of note too, that among the free states those which make the colored man the nearest to equal the white, have, proportionally the fewest mulattoes the least of amalgamation. In New Hampshire, the State which goes farthest towards equality between the races, there are just 184 Mulattoes while there are in Virginia—how many do you think? 79,775, being 23,126 more than in all the free States together.

These statistics show that slavery is the greatest source of amalgamation; and next to it, not the elevation, but the degeneration of the free blacks. Yet Judge Douglas dreads the slightest restraints on the spread of slavery, and the slightest human recognition of the negro, as tending horribly to amalgamation.

This very Dred Scott case affords a strong test as to which party most favors amalgamation, the Republicans or the dear Union-saving Democracy. Dred Scott, his wife and two daughters were all involved in the suit. We desired the court to have held that they were citizens so far at least as to entitle them to a hearing as to whether they were free or not; and then, also, that they were in fact and in law really free. Could we have had our way, the chances of these black girls, ever mixing their blood with that of white people, would have been diminished at least to the extent that it could not have been without their consent. But Judge Douglas is delighted to have them decided to be slaves, and not human enough to have a hearing, even if they were free, and thus left subject to the forced concubinage of their masters, and liable to become the mothers of mulattoes in spite of themselves—the very state of case that produces nine tenths of all the mulattoes—all the mixing of blood in the nation.

Of course, I state this case as an illustration only, not meaning to say or intimate that the master of Dred Scott and his family, or any more than a per centage of masters generally, are inclined to exercise this particular power which they hold over their female slaves.

I have said that the separation of the races is the only perfect preventive of amalgamation. I have no right to say all the members of the Republican party are in favor of this, nor to say that as a party they are in favor of it. There is nothing in their platform directly on the subject. But I can say a very large proportion of its members are for it, and that the chief plank in their platform—opposition to the spread of slavery—is most favorable to that separation.

Such separation, if ever effected at all, must be effected by colonization; and no political party, as such, is now doing anything directly for colonization. Party operations at present only favor or retard colonization incidentally. The enterprise is a difficult one; but "when there is a will there is a way"; and what colonization needs most is a hearty will. Will springs from the two elements of moral sense and self-interest. Let us be brought to believe it is morally right, and, at the same time, favorable to, or, at least, not against, our interest, to transfer the African to his native clime, and we shall find a way to do it, however great the task may be. The children of Israel, to such numbers as to include four hundred thousand fighting men, went out of Egyptian bondage in a body.

How differently the respective courses of the Democratic and Republican parties incidentally bear on the question of forming a will—a public sentiment—for colonization, is easy to see. The Republicans inculcate, with whatever of ability they can, that the negro is a man; that his bondage is cruelly wrong, and that the field of his oppression ought not to be enlarged. The Democrats deny his manhood; deny, or dwarf to insignificance, the wrong of his bondage; so far as possible, crush all sympathy for him, and cultivate and excite hatred and disgust against him; compliment themselves as Union-savers for doing so; and call the indefinite outspreading of his bondage "a sacred right of self-government."

The plainest print cannot be read through a gold eagle; and it will be ever hard to find many men who will send a slave to Liberia, and pay his passage while they can send him to a new country, Kansas for instance, and sell him for fifteen hundred dollars, and the rise.

Abraham Lincoln

"A House Divided" Speech

(Delivered at the close of the Republican State Convention in
Springfield, Illinois, June 16, 1858)

If we could first know *where* we are, and *whither* we are tending, we could then better judge *what* to do, and *how* to do it.

We are now far into the *fifth* year, since a policy was initiated, with the *avowed* object, and *confident* promise, of putting an end to slavery agitation.

Under the operation of that policy, that agitation has not only, *not ceased*, but has *constantly augmented*.

In *my* opinion, it will not cease, until a *crisis* shall have been reached, and passed.

"A house divided against itself cannot stand."

I believe this government cannot endure, permanently half *slave* and half *free*.

I do not expect the Union to be *dissolved*—I do not expect the house to *fall*—but I *do* expect it will cease to be divided.

It will become *all* one thing, or *all* the other.

Either the *opponents* of slavery, will arrest the further spread of it, and place it where the public mind shall rest in the belief that it is in course of ultimate extinction; or its *advocates* will push it forward, till it shall become alike lawful in *all* the States, *old* as well as *new*—*North* as well as *South*.

Have we no *tendency* to the latter condition?

Let any one who doubts, carefully contemplate that now almost complete legal combination—piece of *machinery* so to speak—compounded of the Nebraska doctrine, and the Dred Scott decision. Let him consider not only *what work* the machinery is adapted to do, and *how well* adapted; but also, let him study the *history* of its construction, and trace, if he can, or rather *fail*, if he can, to trace the evidences of design, and concert of action, among its chief bosses, from the beginning.

The new year of 1854 found slavery excluded from more than half the States by State Constitutions, and from most of the national territory by Congressional prohibition.

Four days later, commenced the struggle, which ended in repealing that Congressional prohibition.

This opened all the national territory to slavery; and was the first point gained.

But, so far, *Congress* only, had acted; and an *indorsement* by the people, *real* or apparent, was indispensable, to *save* the point already gained, and give chance for more.

This necessity had not been overlooked; but had been provided for, as well as might be, in the notable argument of "*squatter sovereignty*," otherwise called "*sacred right of self government*," which latter phrase, though expressive of the only rightful basis of any government, was so perverted in this attempted use of it as to amount to just this: That if any *one* man, choose to enslave *another*, no *third* man shall be allowed to object.

That argument was incorporated into the Nebraska bill itself, in the language which follows: "*It being the true intent and meaning of this act not to legislate slavery into any Territory or state, nor to exclude it therefrom; but to leave the people thereof perfectly free to form and regulate their domestic institutions in their own way, subject only to the Constitution of the United States.*"

Then opened the roar of loose declamation in favor of "Squatter Sovereignty," and "Sacred right of self government."

"But," said opposition members, "let us be more *specific*—let us *amend* the bill so as to expressly declare that the people of the territory *may* exclude slavery." "Not we," said the friends of the measure; and down they voted the amendment.

While the Nebraska bill was passing through congress, a *law case*, involving the question of a negroe's freedom, by reason of his owner having voluntarily taken him first into a free state and then a territory covered by the congressional prohibition, and held him as a slave, for a long time in each, was passing through the U.S. Circuit Court for the District of Missouri; and both Nebraska bill and law suit were brought to a decision in the same month of May, 1854. The negroe's name was "Dred Scott," which name now designates the decision finally made in the case.

Before the *then* next Presidential election, the law case came to, and was argued in the Supreme Court of the United States; but the *decision* of it was deferred until *after* the election. Still, *before* the election, Senator Trumbull, on the floor of the Senate, requests the leading advocate of the Nebraska bill to state *his opinion* whether the people of a territory can constitutionally exclude slavery from their limits; and the latter answers, "That is a question for the Supreme Court."

The election came. Mr. Buchanan was elected, and the *indorsement*, such as it was, secured. That was the *second* point gained. The indorsement, however, fell short of a clear popular majority by nearly four hundred thousand votes, and so, perhaps, was not overwhelmingly reliable and satisfactory.

The *outgoing* President, in his last annual message, as impressively as possible *echoed* back upon the people the *weight* and *authority* of the indorsement.

The Supreme Court met again; *did not* announce their decision, but ordered a re-argument.

The Presidential inauguration came, and still no decision of the court; but the *incoming* President, in his inaugural address, fervently exhorted the people to abide by the forthcoming decision, *whatever it might be.*

Then, in a few days, came the decision.

The reputed author of the Nebraska bill finds an early occasion to make a speech at this capitol indorsing the Dred Scott Decision, and vehemently denouncing all opposition to it.

The new President, too, seizes the early occasion of the Silliman letter to *indorse* and strongly *construe* that decision, and to express his *astonishment* that any different view had ever been entertained.

At length a squabble springs up between the President and the author of the Nebraska bill, on the *mere* question of *fact*, whether the Lecompton constitution was or was not, in any just sense, made by the people of Kansas; and in that squabble the latter declares that all he wants is a fair vote for the people, and that he *cares* not whether slavery be voted *down* or voted *up*. I do not understand his declaration that he cares not whether slavery be voted down or voted up, to be intended by him other than as an *apt definition* of the *policy* he would impress upon the public mind—the *principle* for which he declares he has suffered much, and is ready to suffer to the end.

And well may he cling to that principle. If he has any parental feeling, well may he cling to it. That principle, is the only *shred* left of his original Nebraska doctrine. Under the Dred Scott decision, "squatter sovereignty" squatted out of existence, tumbled down like temporary scaffolding—like the mould at the foundry served through one blast and fell back into loose sand—helped to carry an election, and then was kicked to the winds. His late *joint* struggle with the Republicans, against the Lecompton Constitution, involves nothing of the original Nebraska doctrine. That struggle was made on a point, the right of a people to make their own constitution, upon which he and the Republicans have never differed.

The several points of the Dred Scott decision, in connection with Senator Douglas' "care not" policy, constitute the piece of machinery, in its *present* state of advancement. This was the third point gained.

The *working* points of that machinery are:

First, that no negro slave, imported as such from Africa, and no descendant of such slave can ever be a *citizen* of any State, in the sense of that term as used in the Constitution of the United States.

This point is made in order to deprive the negro, in every possible event, of the benefit of this provision of the United States Constitution, which declares that—

"The citizens of each State shall be entitled to all privileges and immunities of citizens in the several States."

Secondly, that "subject to the Constitution of the United States," neither *Congress* nor a *Territorial Legislature* can exclude slavery from any United States territory.

This point is made in order that individual men may *fill up* the territories with slaves, without danger of losing them as property, and thus to enhance the chances of *permanency* to the institution through all the future.

Thirdly, that whether the holding a negro in actual slavery in a free State, makes him free, as against the holder, the United States courts will not decide, but will leave to be decided by the courts of any slave State the negro may be forced into by the master.

This point is made, not to be pressed *immediately*; but, if acquiesced in for a while, and apparently *indorsed* by the people at an election, then to sustain the logical conclusion that what Dred Scott's master might lawfully do with Dred Scott, in the free State of Illinois, every other master may lawfully do with any other *one*, or one *thousand* slaves, in Illinois, or in any other free State.

Auxiliary to all this, and working hand in hand with it, the Nebraska doctrine, or what is left of it, is to *educate* and *mould* public opinion, at least Northern public opinion, to not care whether slavery is voted down or voted up.

This shows exactly where we now *are*; and *partially* also, whither we are tending.

It will throw additional light on the latter, to go back, and run the mind over the string of historical facts already stated. Several things will *now* appear less *dark* and *mysterious* than they did *when* they were transpiring. The people were to be left "perfectly free" "subject only to the Constitution." What the *Constitution* had to do with it, outsiders could not *then* see. Plainly enough now, it was an exactly fitted *niche*, for the Dred Scott decision to afterwards come in, and declare the *perfect freedom* of the people, to be just no freedom at all.

Why was the amendment, expressly declaring the right of the people to exclude slavery, voted down? Plainly enough *now*, the adoption of it, would have spoiled the niche for the Dred Scott decision.

Why was the court decision held up? Why, even a Senator's individual opinion withheld, till *after* the Presidential election? Plainly enough *now*, the speaking out then would have damaged the "*perfectly free*" argument upon which the election was to be carried.

Why the *outgoing* President's felicitation on the indorsement? Why the delay of a reargument? Why the incoming President's *advance* exhortation in favor of the decision?

These things *look* like the cautious *patting* and *petting* a spirited horse, preparatory to mounting him, when it is dreaded that he may give the rider a fall.

And why the hasty after indorsements of the decision by the President and others?

We can not absolutely *know* that all these exact adaptations are the result of preconcert. But when we see a lot of framed timbers, different portions of which we know have been gotten out at different times and places and by different workmen—Stephen, Franklin, Roger and James, for instance—and when we see these timbers joined together, and see they exactly make the frame of a house or a mill, all the tenons and mortices exactly fitting, and all the lengths and proportions of the different pieces exactly adapted to their respective places, and not a piece too many or too few—not omitting even scaffolding—or, if a single piece be lacking, we can see the place in the frame exactly fitted and prepared to yet bring such piece in—in *such* a case, we find it impossible to not believe that Stephen and Franklin and Roger and James all understood one another from the beginning, and all worked upon a common *plan* or *draft* drawn up before the first lick was struck.

It should not be overlooked that, by the Nebraska bill, the people of a *State* as well as *Territory*, were to be left "*perfectly free*" "*subject only to the Constitution.*"

Why mention a *State*? They were legislating for *territories*, and not *for* or *about* States. Certainly the people of a State *are* and *ought to be* subject to the Constitution of the United States; but why is mention of this *lugged* into this merely *territorial* law? Why are the people of a *territory* and the people of a *state* therein *lumped* together, and their relation to the Constitution therein treated as being *precisely* the same?

While the opinion of *the Court*, by Chief Justice Taney, in the Dred Scott case, and the separate opinions of all the concurring Judges, expressly declare that the Constitution of the United States neither permits Congress nor a Territorial legislature to exclude slavery from any United States territory, they all *omit* to declare whether or not the same Constitution permits a *state*, or the people of a State, to exclude it.

Possibly, this was a mere *omission*; but who can be *quite* sure, if McLean or Curtis had sought to get into the opinion a declaration of unlimited power in the people of a *state* to exclude slavery from their limits, just as Chase and Macy sought to get such declaration, in behalf of the people of a territory, into the Nebraska bill—I ask, who can be quite *sure* that it would not have been voted down, in the one case, as it had been in the other.

The nearest approach to the point of declaring the power of a State over slavery, is made by Judge Nelson. He approaches it more than once, using the precise idea, and *almost* the language too, of the Nebraska act. On one occasion his exact language is, "except in cases where the power is restrained by the Constitution of the United States, the law of the State is supreme over the subject of slavery within its jurisdiction."

In what cases the power of the *states is* so restrained by the U.S. Constitution, is left an *open* question, precisely as the same question, as to the restraint on the power of the *territories* was left open in the Nebraska act. Put *that* and *that* together, and we have another nice little niche, which we may, ere long, see filled with another Supreme Court decision, declaring that the Constitution of the United States does not permit a *state* to exclude slavery from its limits.

And this may especially be expected if the doctrine of "care not whether slavery be voted *down* or voted *up*," shall gain upon the public mind sufficiently to give promise that such a decision can be maintained when made.

Such a decision is all that slavery now lacks of being alike lawful in all the States.

Welcome or unwelcome, such decision *is* probably coming, and will soon be upon us, unless the power of the present political dynasty shall be met and over-thrown.

We shall *lie down* pleasantly dreaming that the people of *Missouri* are on the verge of making their State *free*; and we shall *awake* to the *reality*, instead, that the *Supreme* Court has made *Illinois* a *slave* State.

To meet and overthrow the power of that dynasty, is the work now before all those who would prevent that consummation.

That is *what* we have to do.

But *how* can we best do it?

There are those who denounce us *openly* to their *own* friends, and yet whisper *us softly*, that *Senator Douglas* is the *aptest* instrument there is, with which to effect that object. *They* do *not* tell us, nor has *he* told us, that he *wishes* any such object to be effected. They wish us to *infer* all, from the facts, that he now has a little quarrel with the present head of the dynasty; and that he has regularly voted with us, on a single point, upon which, he and we, have never differed.

They remind us that *he* is a very *great man*, and that the largest of us are very small ones. Let this be granted. But "a *living dog* is better than a *dead lion*." Judge Douglas, if not a *dead* lion for *this work*, is at least a *caged* and *toothless* one. How can he oppose the advances of slavery? He don't *care* anything about it. His avowed *mission is impressing* the "public heart" to *care* nothing about it.

A leading Douglas Democratic newspaper thinks Douglas' superior talent will be needed to resist the revival of the African slave trade.

Does Douglas believe an effort to revive that trade is approaching? He has not said so. Does he *really* think so? But if it is, how can he resist it? For years he has labored to prove it a *sacred right* of white men to take negro slaves into the new territories. Can he possibly show that it is *less* a sacred right to *buy* them where they can be bought cheapest? And, unquestionably they can be bought *cheaper in Africa* than in *Virginia*.

He has done all in his power to reduce the whole question of slavery to one of a mere *right of property*; and as such, how can *he* oppose the foreign slave trade—how can he refuse that trade in that "property" shall be "perfectly free"—unless he does it as a *protection* to the home production? And as the home *producers* will probably not *ask* the protection, he will be wholly without a ground of opposition.

Senator Douglas holds, we know, that a man may rightfully be *wiser to-day* than he was *yesterday*—that he may rightfully change when he finds himself wrong.

But, can we for that reason, run ahead, and *infer* that he *will* make any particular change, of which he, himself, has given no intimation? Can we *safely* base *our* action upon any such *vague* inference?

Now, as ever, I wish to not *misrepresent* Judge Douglas' *position*, question his *motives*, or do ought that can be personally offensive to him.

Whenever, *if ever*, he and we can come together on *principle* so that *our great cause* may have assistance from *his great ability*, I hope to have interposed no adventitious obstacle.

But clearly, he is not *now* with us—he does not *pretend* to be—he does not *promise* to *ever* be.

Our cause, then, must be intrusted to, and conducted by its own undoubted friends—those whose hands are free, whose hearts are in the work—who do *care* for the result.

Two years ago the Republicans of the nation mustered over thirteen hundred thousand strong.

We did this under the single impulse of resistance to a common danger, with every external circumstance against us.

Of *strange*, *discordant*, and even, *hostile* elements, we gathered from the four winds, and *formed* and fought the battle through, under the constant hot fire of a disciplined, proud, and pampered enemy.

Did we brave all *then*, to *falter* now?—*now*—when that same enemy is *wavering*, dissevered and belligerent?

The result is not doubtful. We shall not fail—if we stand firm, we shall not fail.

Wise councils may *accelerate* or *mistakes delay* it, but, sooner or later the victory is *sure* to come.

Carl Schurz

True Americanism

(Delivered at Faneuil Hall in Boston, Massachusetts, April 18, 1859)

A few days ago I stood on the cupola of your Statehouse, and overlooked for the first time this venerable city and the country surrounding it. Then the streets, and hills, and waters around me began to teem with the life of historical recollections, recollections dear to all mankind, and a feeling of pride arose in my heart, and I said to myself, I, too, am an American citizen. [Applause.] There was Bunker Hill, there Charlestown, Lexington, and Dorchester Heights not far off; there the harbor into which the British tea was sunk; there the place where the old liberty-tree stood; there John Hancock's house; there Benjamin Franklin's birth-place—and now I stand in this grand old hall, which so often resounded with the noblest appeals that ever thrilled American hearts, and where I am almost afraid to hear the echo of my own feeble voice;—oh, sir, no man that loves liberty, wherever he may have first seen the light of day, can fail on this sacred spot to pay his tribute to Americanism. And here, with all these glorious memories crowding upon my heart, I will offer mine. I, born in a foreign land, pay my tribute to Americanism? Yes, for to me the word Americanism, *true* Americanism, comprehends the noblest ideas which ever swelled a human heart with noble pride. [Applause.]

It is one of the earliest recollections of my boyhood, that one summer night our whole village was stirred up by an uncommon occurrence. I say our village, for I was born not far from that beautiful spot where the Rhine rolls his green waters out of the wonderful gate of the Seven Mountains, and then meanders with majestic tranquillity through one of the most glorious valleys of the world. That night our neighbors were pressing around a few wagons covered with linen sheets and loaded with household utensils and boxes and trunks to their utmost capacity. One of our neighboring families were moving far away across a great water, and it was said that they would never again return. And I saw silent tears trickling down weather-beaten cheeks, and the hands of rough peasants firmly pressing each other, and some of the men and women hardly able to speak when they nodded to one another a last farewell. At last the train started into motion, they gave three cheers for *America*, and then in the first gray dawn of the morning I saw them wending their way over the hill until they disappeared in the shadow of the forest. And I heard many a man say, how happy he would be if he could go with them to that great and free country, where a man could be himself. [Applause.]

That was the first time that I heard of America, and my childish imagination took possession of a land covered partly with majestic trees, partly with flowery prairies, immeasurable to the eye, and intersected with large rivers and broad lakes—a land where everybody could do what he thought best, and where nobody need be poor, because everybody was free.

And later, when I was old enough to read, and descriptions of this country and books on American history fell into my hands, the offspring of my imagination acquired the colors of reality, and I began to exercise my brain with the thought of what man might be and become, when left perfectly free to himself. And still later, when ripening into manhood, I looked up from my school-books into the stir and bustle of the world, and the trumpet-tones of struggling humanity struck my ear and thrilled my heart, and I saw my nation shake her chains in order to burst them, and I heard a gigantic, universal shout for Liberty rising up to the skies; and at last, after having struggled manfully and drenched the earth of Fatherland with the blood of thousands of noble beings, I saw that nation crushed down again, not only by overwhelming armies, but by the dead weight of customs and institutions and notions and prejudices, which past centuries had heaped upon them, and which a moment of enthusiasm, however sublime, could not destroy; then I consoled an almost despondent heart with the idea of a youthful people and of original institutions clearing the way for an untrammeled development of the ideal nature of man. Then I turned my eyes instinctively across the Atlantic Ocean, and America and Americanism, as I fancied them, appeared to me as the last depositories of the hopes of all true friends of humanity. [Applause.]

I say all this, not as though I indulged in the presumptuous delusion that my personal feelings and experience would be of any interest to you, but in order to show you what America is to the thousands of thinking men in the old world, who, disappointed in their fondest hopes and depressed by the saddest experience, cling with their last remnant of confidence in human nature, to the last spot on earth where man is free to follow the road to attainable perfection, and where, unbiassed by the disastrous influence of traditional notions, customs, and institutions, he acts on his own responsibility. They ask themselves: Was it but a wild delusion when we thought that man has the faculty to be free and to govern himself? Have we been fighting, were we ready to die, for a mere phantom, for a mere product of a morbid imagination? This question downtrodden humanity cries out into the world, and from this country it expects an answer.

As its advocate I speak to you. I will speak of Americanism as the great representative of the reformatory age, as the great champion of the dignity of human nature, as the great repository of the last hopes of suffering mankind. I will speak of the ideal mission of this country and of this people.

You may tell me that these views are visionary, that the destiny of this country is less exalted, that the American people are less great than I think they are or ought to be. I answer, ideals are like stars; you will not succeed in touching them with your hands. But like the seafaring man on the desert of waters, you choose them as your guides, and following them you will reach your destiny. I invite you to ascend with me the watchtower of history, overlooking the grand panorama of the development of human affairs, in which the American Republic stands in so bold and prominent relief.

He who reviews the past of this country in connection with the history of the world besides, cannot fail to discover a wonderful coincidence of great events and fortunate circumstances, which were destined to produce everlasting results, unless recklessly thrown away by imbecile generations.

Look back with me four or five centuries. The dark period of the middle ages is drawing near its close. The accidental explosion of that mysterious black powder, discovered by an obscure German monk, is the first flash of lightning preluding that gigantic thunder-storm which is to shatter the edifice of feudal society to pieces. The invention of gunpowder strips the feudal lord of his prestige as a *warrior*; another discovery is to strip him of his prestige as a *man!* Guttenberg, another obscure German, invents the printing-press, and as gunpowder blows the castles of the small feudal tyrants into the air, so the formidable artillery of printed letters batters down the citadels of ignorance and superstition. [Loud applause.] Soul and body take up arms and prepare themselves for the great battle of the Reformation. Now the mighty volcano of the German mind bursts the crust of indolence which has covered it. Luther's triumphant thunder rattles against the holy see of Rome. [Applause.] The world is ablaze, all the elements of society are rising up in boiling commotion—two ages are battling against each other.

This is the time, when the regeneration of the old world is to take place. But the old order of things, fortified in customs and prejudices and deeply-rooted institutions, does not surrender at the first blast of trumpets. The grand but fearful struggle of the reformatory movement plunges all Europe into endless confusion. The very wheel of progress seems to grind and crush one generation after another. The ideas which concerned the highest and most sacred relations of humanity, seem at the same time to call into their service the basest and most violent passions of the human heart, and in all Europe the wars of great principles degenerate into wars of general devastation.

But, meanwhile, a new country has opened its boundless fields to those great ideas, for the realization of which the old world seems no longer to be wide enough. It is as though the earth herself had taken part in the general revolution, and had thrown up from her sea-covered womb a new battle-ground for the spirit of the new era. That is America. Not only the invention of gunpowder and of the printing-press, but also the discovery of America, inaugurates the modern age.

There is the new and immense continent. The most restless and enterprising elements of European society direct their looks towards it. First, the greediness of the gold-hunting adventurer pounces upon the new conquest; but, his inordinate appetites being disappointed, he gradually abandons the field to men in whose hearts the future of the new world is sleeping, unborn.

While the coast of Virginia is settled by a motley immigration, led and ruled by men of ideas and enterprise, the sturdiest champions of principle descend upon the stony shores of New England. [Applause.] While the southern colonies are settled under the auspices of lordly merchants and proprietaries, original democracy plants its stern banner upon Plymouth Rock. [Applause.] Mercantile speculation, aristocratic ambition, and stern virtue that seeks freedom and nothing but freedom, lead the most different classes of people, different in origin, habits and persuasion, upon the virgin soil, and entrust to them the task of realizing the great principles of the age. Nor is this privilege confined to one nationality alone. While the Anglo-Saxon takes possession of New England, Virginia and Pennsylvania, the Frenchman plants his colonies on the soil of French Florida and the interior of the continent; the Hollander locates New Netherlands on the banks of the Hudson; the Swede, led there by the great mind of Oxenstiern, occupies the banks of the Delaware; the Spaniard maintains himself in peninsular Florida, and a numerous immigration of Germans, who follow the call of religious freedom, and of Irishmen, gradually flowing in, scatters itself all over this vast extent of country. Soon all the social and national elements of the civilized world are represented in the new land. Every people, every creed, every class of society has contributed its share to that wonderful mixture out of which is to grow the great nation of the new world. It is true, the Anglo-Saxon establishes and maintains his ascendancy, but without absolutely absorbing the other national elements. They modify each other, and their peculiar characteristics are to be blended together by the all-assimilating power of freedom. This is the origin of the American nationality, which did not spring from one family, one tribe, one country, but incorporates the vigorous elements of all civilized nations on earth. [Applause.]

This fact is not without great importance. It is an essential link in the chain of historical development. The student of history cannot fail to notice that when new periods of civilization break upon humanity, the people of the earth cannot maintain their national relations. New ideas are to be carried out by young nations. From time to time, violent, irresistible hurricanes sweep over the world, blowing the most different elements of the human family together, which by mingling reinvigorate each other, and the general confusion then becomes the starting-point of a new period of progress. Nations which have long subsisted exclusively on their own resources, will gradually lose their original vigor, and die the death of decrepitude. But mankind becomes young again by its different elements being shaken together, by race crossing race, and mind penetrating mind. [Applause.]

The oldest traditions of history speak of such great revulsions and general migrations, and if we could but lift the veil, which covers the remotest history of Asiatic tribes, we should discover the first scenes and acts of the drama, of which the downfall of the Roman Empire is a portion. When that empire had exhausted its natural vitality, the dark forests of the North poured forth a barbarous but vigorous multitude, who trampled into ruins the decrepit civilization of the Roman world, but infused new blood into the veins of old Europe, grasping the great ideas of Christianity with a bloody but firm hand—and a new period of original progress sprang out of the seeming devastation. The German element took the helm of history. But, in the course of time, the development of things arrived at a new turning-point. The spirit of individualism took possession of the heart of civilized humanity, and the reformatory movement of the sixteenth century was its expression. But continental Europe appeared unable to incorporate the new and progressive ideas growing out of that spirit, in organic political institutions. While the heart of Europe was ravaged by a series of religious wars, the Anglo-Saxons of England attempted what other nations seemed unable to accomplish. But they also clung too fast to the traditions of past centuries; they failed in separating the Church from the State, and did not realize the cosmopolitan tendency of the new principle. Then the time of a new migration was at hand, and that migration rolled its waves towards America. [Applause.] The old process repeated itself under new forms, milder and more congenial to the humane ideas it represented. It is now not a barbarous multitude pouncing upon old and decrepit empires; not a violent concussion of tribes accompanied by all the horrors of general destruction; but we see the vigorous elements of all nations, we see the Anglo-Saxon, the leader in the practical movement, with his spirit of independence, of daring enterprise and of indomitable perseverance; the German, the original leader in the movement of ideas, with his spirit of inquiry and his quiet and thoughtful application; the Celt, with the impulsive vivacity of his race; the Frenchman, the Scandinavian, the Scot, the Hollander, the Spaniard, and Italian—all these peaceably congregating and mingling together on virgin soil, where the backwoodsman's hatchet is the only battle-axe of civilization; led together by the irresistible attraction of free and broad principles; undertaking to commence a new era in the history of the world, without first destroying the results of the progress of past periods; undertaking to found a new cosmopolitan nation without marching over the dead bodies of slain millions. Thus was founded the *great colony of free humanity*, which has not old England alone, but the *world*, for its mother-country. [Cheers.]

This idea is, perhaps, not palatable to those who pride themselves on their unadulterated Anglo-Saxondom. To them I have to say, that the destinies of men are often greater than men themselves, and that a good many are swerving from the path of glory by not obeying the true instincts of their nature, and by sacrificing their mission to one-sided pride. [Applause.]

The Anglo-Saxon may justly be proud of the growth and development of this country, and if he ascribes most of it to the undaunted spirit of his race, we may not accuse him of overweening self-glorification. He possesses, in an eminent degree, the enviable talent of acting when others only think; of promptly executing his own ideas, and of appropriating the ideas of other people to his own use. [Applause.] There is, perhaps, no other race that, at so early a day, would have founded the stern democracy of the Plymouth settlement, no other race that would have defied the trials and hardships of the original settler's life so victoriously. No other race, perhaps, possesses in so high a degree not only the daring spirit of independent enterprise, but at the same time the stubborn steadfastness necessary to the final execution of great designs. The Anglo-Saxon spirit has been the locomotive of progress [applause]; but do not forget, that this locomotive would be of little use to the world, if it refused to draw its train over the iron highway, and carry its valuable freight towards its destination; that train consists of the vigorous elements of all nations; that freight is the vital ideas of our age; that destination is universal freedom and the ideal development of man. [Cheers.] That is the true greatness of the Anglo-Saxon race; that ought to be the source of Anglo-Saxon pride. I esteem the son who is proud of his father, if, at the same time, he is worthy of him.

Thus, I say, was founded the colony of free humanity on virgin soil. The youthful elements which constitute people of the new world, cannot submit to rules which are not of their own making; they must throw off the fetters which bind them to an old decrepit order of things. They resolve to enter the great family of nations as an independent member. And in the colony of free humanity, whose mother-country is the world, they establish *the Republic of equal rights, where the title of manhood is the title to citizenship.* [Applause.] My friends, if I had a thousand tongues, and a voice strong as the thunder of heaven, they would not be sufficient to impress upon your minds forcibly enough the greatness of this idea, the overshadowing glory of this result. This was the dream of the truest friends of man from the beginning; for this the noblest blood of martyrs has been shed; for this has mankind waded through seas of blood and tears. There it is now; there it stands, the noble fabric in all the splendor of reality.

They speak of the greatness of the Roman Republic! Oh, sir, if I could call the proudest of Romans from his grave, I would take him by the hand and say to him, Look at this picture, and at this! The greatness of thy Roman Republic consisted in its despotic rule over the world; the greatness of the American Republic consists in the secured right of man to govern himself. [Applause.] The dignity of the Roman citizen consisted in his exclusive privileges; the dignity of the American citizen consists in his holding the natural rights of his neighbor just as sacred as his own. [Continued applause.] The Roman Republic recognized and protected the *rights of the citizen*, at the same time disregarding and leaving unprotected the *rights of man*; Roman citizenship was founded upon monopoly, not upon the claims of human nature. What the citizen of Rome claimed for himself, he did not respect in others; his own greatness was his only object; his own liberty, as he regarded it, gave him the privilege to oppress his fellow-beings. His democracy, instead of elevating mankind to his own level, trampled the rights of man into the dust. The security of the Roman Republic, therefore, consisted in the power of the sword; the security of the American Republic rests in the equality of human rights! [Loud applause.] The Roman Republic perished by the sword; the American Republic will stand as long as the equality of human rights remains inviolate. [Cheers.] Which of the two Republics is the greater—the Republic of the Roman, or the Republic of *man*?

Sir, I wish the words of the Declaration of Independence "that all men are created free and equal, and are endowed with certain inalienable rights," were inscribed upon every gate-post within the limits of this Republic. From this principle the Revolutionary Fathers derived their claim to independence; upon this they founded the institutions of this country, and the whole structure was to be the living incarnation of this idea. This principle contains the programme of our political existence. It is the most progressive, and at the same time the most conservative one; the most progressive, for it takes even the lowliest members of the human family out of their degradation, and inspires them with the elevating consciousness of equal human dignity; the most conservative, for it makes a common cause of individual rights. [Tumultuous applause.] From the equality of rights springs identity of our highest interests; you cannot subvert your neighbor's rights without striking a dangerous blow at your own. And when the rights of one cannot be infringed without finding a ready defense in all others who defend their own rights in defending his, then, and only then, are the rights of all safe against the usurpations of governmental authority.

This general identity of interests is the only thing that can guarantee the stability of democratic institutions. Equality of rights, embodied in general self-government, is the great moral element of true democracy; it is the only reliable safety-valve in the machinery of modern society. There is the solid foundation of our system of government; there is our mission; there is our greatness; there is our safety; there, and nowhere else! This is true Americanism, and to this I pay the tribute of my devotion. [Long and loud applause.]

Shall I point out to you the consequences of a deviation from this principle? Look at the Slave States. There is a class of men who are deprived of their natural rights. But this is not the only deplorable feature of that peculiar organization of society. Equally deplorable is it, that there is another class of men who keep the former in subjection. That there are slaves is bad; but almost worse is it, that there are masters. Are not the masters freemen? No, sir! Where is their liberty of the press? Where is their liberty of speech? Where is the man among them who dares to advocate openly principles not in strict accordance with the ruling system? They speak of a republican form of government—they speak of democracy, but the despotic spirit of slavery and mastership combined pervades their whole political life like a liquid poison. They do not dare to be free, lest the spirit of liberty become contagious. The system of slavery has enslaved them all, master as well as slave. [Applause; "true!"] What is the cause of all this? It is that you cannot deny one class of society the full measure of their natural rights without imposing restraints upon your own liberty. If you want to be free, there is but one way; it is to guarantee an equally full measure of liberty to all your neighbors. There is no other.

True, there are difficulties connected with an organization of society founded upon the basis of equal rights. Nobody denies it. A large number of those who come to you from foreign lands are not as capable of taking part in the administration of government as the man who was fortunate enough to drink the milk of liberty in his cradle. And certain religious denominations do, perhaps, nourish principles which are hardly in accordance with the doctrines of true democracy. There is a conglomeration on this continent of heterogeneous elements; there is a warfare of clashing interest and unruly aspirations; and with all this, our democratic system gives rights to the ignorant and power to the inexperienced. And the billows of passion will lash the sides of the ship, and the storm of party warfare will bend its masts, and the pusillanimous will cry out—"Master, master, we perish!" But the genius of true democracy will arise from his slumber, and rebuke the winds and the raging of the water, and say unto them—"Where is your faith?" Aye, where is the faith that led the fathers of this republic to invite the weary and burdened of all nations to the enjoyment of equal rights? Where is that broad and generous confidence in the efficiency of true democratic institutions? Has the present generation forgotten that true democracy bears in itself the remedy for all the difficulties that may grow out of it?

It is an old dodge of the advocates of despotism throughout the world, that the people who are not experienced in self-government are not fit for the exercise of self-government, and must first be educated under the rule of a superior authority. But at the same time the advocates of despotism will never offer them an opportunity to acquire experience in self-government, lest they suddenly become fit for its independent exercise. To this treacherous sophistry the fathers of this republic opposed the noble doctrine, that liberty is the best school for liberty, and that self-government cannot be learned but by practicing it. [Loud applause.] This, sir, is a truly American idea; this is true Americanism, and to this I pay the tribute of my devotion.

You object that some people do not understand their own interests? There is nothing that, in the course of time, will make a man better understand his interests than the independent management of his own affairs on his own responsibility. You object that people are ignorant? There is no better schoolmaster in the world than self-government, independently exercised. You object that people have no just idea of their duties as citizens? There is no other source from which they can derive a just notion of their duties, than the enjoyment of the rights from which they arise. You object that people are misled by their religious prejudices, and by the intrigues of the Roman hierarchy? Since when have the enlightened citizens of this Republic lost their faith in the final invincibility of truth? Since when have they forgotten that if the Roman or any other church plants the seed of superstition, liberty sows broadcast the seed of enlightenment? [Applause.] Do they no longer believe in the invincible spirit of inquiry, which characterizes the reformatory age? If the struggle be fair, can the victory be doubtful? As to religious fanaticism, it will prosper under oppression; it will feed on persecution; it will grow strong by proscription; but it is powerless against genuine democracy. [Applause.] It may indulge in short-lived freaks of passion, or in wily intrigues, but it will die of itself, for its lungs are not adapted to breathe the atmosphere of liberty. [Prolonged applause.] It is like the shark of the sea: drag him into the air, and the monster will perhaps struggle fearfully and frighten timid people with the powerful blows of his tail, and the terrible array of his teeth, but leave him quietly to die and he will die. [Hearty applause.] But engage with him in a hand to hand struggle even then, and the last of his convulsions may fatally punish your rash attempt. Against fanaticism genuine democracy wields an irresistible weapon—it is *Toleration*. Toleration will not strike down the fanatic, but it will quietly and gently disarm him. But fight fanaticism *with* fanaticism, and you will restore it to its own congenial element. It is like Antæus, who gained strength when touching his native earth.

Whoever reads the history of this country calmly and thoroughly, cannot but discover that religious liberty is slowly but steadily rooting out the elements of superstition, and even of prejudice. It has dissolved the war of sects, of which persecution was characteristic, into a contest of abstract opinions, which creates convictions without oppressing men. By recognizing perfect freedom of inquiry, it will engender among men of different belief that mutual respect of true convictions which makes inquiry earnest, and discussion fair. It will recognize as supremely inviolable, what Roger Williams, one of the most luminous stars of the American sky, called the sanctity of conscience. Read your history, and add the thousands and thousands of Romanists and their offspring together, who, from the first establishment of the colonies, gradually came to this country, and the sum will amount to many millions; compare that number with the number of Romanists who are now here, and you will find that millions are missing. Where are they? You did not kill them; you did not drive them away; they did not perish as the victims of persecution. But where are they? The peaceable working of the great principles which called this Republic into existence, has gradually and silently absorbed them. True Americanism, toleration, the equality of rights, has absorbed their prejudices, and will peaceably absorb everything that is not consistent with the victorious spirit of our institutions. [Cheers.]

Oh, sir, there is a wonderful vitality in true democracy, founded upon the equality of rights. There is an inexhaustible power of resistance in that system of government, which makes the protection of individual rights a matter of common interest. If preserved in its purity, there is no warfare of opinions which can endanger it—there is no conspiracy of despotic aspirations that can destroy it. But if not preserved in its purity! There are dangers which only blindness can not see, and which only stubborn party prejudice will not see.

I have already called your attention to the despotic tendency of the slaveholding system. I need not enlarge upon it; I need not describe how the existence of slavery in the South affected and demoralized even the political life of the Free

States; how they attempted to press us, you and me, into the posse of the slave-catcher by that abominable act, which, worse than the "alien and sedition laws," still disgraces our statute-book; how the ruling party, which has devoted itself to the service of that despotic interest, shrinks from no violation of good faith, from no adulteration of the constitutional compact, from no encroachment upon natural right, from no treacherous abandonment of fundamental principles. And I do not hesitate to prophesy, that if the theories engendered by the institution of slavery be suffered to outgrow the equalizing tendency of true democracy, the American Republic will, at no distant day, crumble down under the burden of the laws and measures which the ruling interest will demand for its protection, and its name will be added to the sad catalogue of the broken hopes of humanity.

But the mischief does not come from that side alone; it is in things of small beginning, but fearful in their growth. One of these is the propensity of men *to lose sight of fundamental principles, when passing abuses are to be corrected.*

Is it not wonderful how nations who have won their liberty by the severest struggles, become so easily impatient of the small inconveniences and passing difficulties, which are almost inseparably connected with the practical working of general self-government? How they so easily forget that rights may be abused, and yet remain inalienable rights? Europe has witnessed many an attempt for the establishment of democratic institutions; some of them were at first successful, and the people were free, but the abuses and inconveniences connected with liberty became at once apparent. Then the ruling classes of society, in order to get rid of the abuses, restricted liberty; they did, indeed, get rid of the abuses, but they got rid of liberty at the same time. You heard liberal governments there speak of protecting and regulating the liberty of the press; and, in order to prevent that liberty from being abused, they adopted measures, apparently harmless at first, which ultimately resulted in an absolute censorship. Would it be much better if we, recognizing the right of man to the exercise of self-government, should, in order to protect the purity of the ballot-box, restrict the right of suffrage?

Liberty, sir, is like a spirited housewife; she will have her whims, she will be somewhat unruly sometimes, and, like so many husbands, you cannot always have it all your own way. She may spoil your favorite dish sometimes; but will you, therefore, at once smash her china, break her kettles, and shut her out from the kitchen? Let her practise, let her try again and again, and even when she makes a mistake, encourage her with a benignant smile, and your broth will be right after a while. [Laughter.] But meddle with her concerns, tease her, bore her, and your little squabbles, spirited as she is, will ultimately result in a divorce. What then? It is one of Jefferson's wisest words that "he would much rather be exposed to the inconveniences arising from too much liberty, than to those arising from too small a degree of it." [Immense applause.] It is a matter of historical experience, that nothing that is wrong in principle can be right in practice. [Sensation.] People are apt to delude themselves on that point; but the ultimate result will always prove the truth of the maxim. A violation of equal rights can never serve to maintain institutions which are founded upon equal rights. [Loud applause.] A contrary policy is not only pusillanimous and small, but it is senseless. It reminds me of the soldier who, for fear of being shot in battle, committed suicide on the march; or of the man who would cut off his foot, because he had a corn on his toe. [Laughter.] It is that ridiculous policy of premature despair, which commences to throw the freight overboard when there is a suspicious cloud in the sky.

Another danger for the safety of our institutions, and perhaps the most formidable one, arises from the general propensity of political parties and public men to act on a policy of mere expediency, and to sacrifice principle to local and temporary success. [Great sensation.] And here, sir, let me address a solemn appeal to the consciences of those with whom I am proud to struggle side by side against human thraldom.

You hate kingcraft, and you would sacrifice your fortunes and your lives in order to prevent its establishment on the soil of this Republic. But let me tell you that the rule of political parties which sacrifice principle to expediency, is no less dangerous, no less disastrous, no less aggressive, of no less despotic a nature, than the rule of monarchs. Do not indulge in the delusion, that in order to make a government fair and liberal, the only thing necessary is to make it elective. When a political party in power, however liberal their principles may be, have once adopted the policy of knocking down their opponents instead of voting them down, there is an end of justice and equal rights. [Applause.] The history of the world shows no example of a more arbitrary despotism, than that exercised by the party which ruled the National Assembly of France in the bloodiest days of the great French Revolution. I will not discuss here what might have been done, and what not, in those times of a fearful crisis; but I will say that they tried to establish liberty by means of despotism, and that in her gigantic struggle against the united monarchs of Europe, revolutionary France won the victory, but lost her liberty.

Remember the shout of indignation that went all over the Northern States when we heard that the border ruffians of Kansas had crowded the free-state men away from the polls and had not allowed them to vote. That indignation was just, not only because the men thus terrorized were free-state men and friends of liberty, but because they were deprived of their right of suffrage, and because the government of that territory was placed on the basis of force, instead of equal rights. Sir, if ever the party of liberty should use their local predominance for the purpose of disarming their opponents instead of convincing them, they will but follow the example set by the ruffians of Kansas, although legislative enactments may be a genteeler weapon than the revolver and bowie knife. [Cheering.] They may perhaps achieve some petty local success, they may gain some small temporary advantage, but they will help to introduce a system of action into our politics which will gradually undermine the very foundations upon which our republican edifice rests. Of all the dangers and difficulties that beset us, there is none more horrible than the hideous monster, whose name is "Proscription for opinion's sake." [Cheers, and cries of "good."] I am an anti-slavery man, and I have a right to my opinion in South Carolina just as well as in Massachusetts. [Prolonged cheering.] My neighbor is a pro-slavery man; I may be sorry for it, but I solemnly acknowledge his right to his opinion in Massachusetts as well as in South Carolina. You tell me, that for my opinion they would mob me in South Carolina? Sir, there is the difference between South Carolina and Massachusetts. [Prolonged cheering.] There is the difference between an anti-slavery man, who is a freeman, and a slaveholder, who is himself a slave. [Continued applause.]

Our present issues will pass away. The slavery question will be settled, liberty will be triumphant, and other matters of difference will divide the political parties of this country. What if we, in our struggle against slavery, had removed the solid basis of equal rights, on which such new matters of difference may be peaceably settled? What if we had based the institutions of this country upon a difference of rights between different classes of people? What if, in destroying the generality of natural rights, we had resolved them into privileges? There is a thing which stands above the command of the most ingenious of politicians: *it is the logic of things and events.* It cannot be turned and twisted by artificial arrangements and delusive settlements; it will go its own way with the steady step of fate. It will force you, with uncompromising severity, to choose between two social organizations, one of which is founded upon privilege, and the other upon the doctrine of equal rights.

Force instead of right, privilege instead of equality, expediency instead of principle, being once the leading motives of your policy, you will have no power to stem the current. There will be new abuses to be corrected, new inconveniences to be remedied, new supposed dangers to be obviated, new equally exacting ends to be subserved, and your encroachments upon the natural rights of your opponents now, will be used as welcome precedents for the mutual oppression of parties then. Having once knowingly disregarded the doctrine of equal rights, the ruling parties will soon accustom themselves to consult only their interests where fundamental principles are at stake. Those who lead us into this channel will be like the sorcerer who knew the art of making a giant snake. And when he had made it, he forgot the charm-word that would destroy it again. And the giant snake threw its horrid coils around him, and the unfortunate man was choked to death by the monster of his own creation.

On the evening of the 2d day of November, 1855, there stood on this very platform a man, known and loved by every true son of Massachusetts, who, unmoved by the whirlwind of proscriptive movement howling around him, spoke the following words:—

"It is proposed to attaint men for their religion, and also for their birth. If this object can prevail, vain are the triumphs of civil freedom in its many hard-fought fields; vain is that religious toleration which we all profess. The fires of Smithfield, the tortures of the inquisition, the proscription of the Non-conformists, may all be revived. Slowly among the struggling sects was evolved the great idea of the equality of all men before the law, without regard to religious belief; nor can any party now organize a proscription merely for religious (and I may add political) belief, without calling in question this unquestionable principle."

The man who said so was Charles Sumner. [Long continued applause, and three hearty cheers "for Charles Sumner."] Then the day was not far off when suddenly the whole country was startled by the incredible news, that his noble head had drooped under the murderous blows of a Southern fanatic, and that his warm blood had covered the floor of the Senate Chamber, the noblest sprinkling that ever fertilized a barren soil. [Laughter and applause.] And now I tell you, when he lay on the lounge of the ante-chamber, his anxious friends busy around him, and his cowardly murderers slinking away like Cain—if at that solemn moment the first question addressed to his slowly returning senses had been: Shall those who support your dastardly assailants with their votes be deprived of their suffrage? he would have raised his bleeding head, and with the fire of indignation kindling in his dim eye, he would have answered: "No! In the name of my country, no! For the honor of Massachusetts, no! For the sake of the principles for which my blood is flowing, no! Let them kill me, but let the rights of man be safe!" [Tremendous applause.]

Sir, if you want to bestow a high praise upon a man, you are apt to say he is an old Roman. But I know a higher epithet of praise; it is—He is a true American! Aye, Charles Sumner is a true American; he is a representative of the truest Americanism, and to him I pay the tribute of my enthusiastic admiration. [Enthusiastic cheering.]

Sir, I am coming to the close of my remarks. But I cannot refrain from alluding to a circumstance which concerns myself. I understand it has been said, that in speaking a few words on the principles of Jeffersonian democracy a few evenings since, I had attempted to interfere with the home affairs of this State, and to dictate to the Republicans their policy. Ah, sir, is there a man in Massachusetts, except he be a servant of the slave-power, who cannot hear me advocate the equal rights of man, without feeling serious pangs of conscience? [Laughter.] Is there a son of this glorious old Commonwealth who cannot hear me draw logical conclusions from the Declaration of Independence—who cannot hear me speak of the natural right of man to the exercise of self-government, without feeling a blush fluttering upon his cheeks? If so, sir, I am sorry for him; it is his fault, not mine. [Loud applause.]

Interfere with your local matters! How could I? What influence could I, an humble stranger among you, exercise on the action of Massachusetts? But one thing I must tell you. It ought never to be forgotten that this old Commonwealth occupies a representative position. Her history is familiar to the nation; even South Carolina knows it. [Laughter and applause.] The nation is so accustomed to admire her glorious deed for freedom, that with this expectation their eyes are turned upon her. Massachusetts can do nothing in secret; Massachusetts can do nothing for herself alone; every one of her acts involves a hundred-fold responsibility. What Massachusetts does is felt from the Atlantic to the Pacific. But Massachusetts need only be herself, in order to be great. This is her position among the Free States, recognised by all. Can there be a more honorable one? Sons of Massachusetts, you may be proud of it. Do not forget that from her greatness you cannot separate your responsibility.

No, I will not meddle with your home concerns. I will, however, say a word for the West. Strenuous advocate of individual rights and of local self-government as I am, if you ever hear of any movement in the West against the integrity of the fundamental principles underlying our system of government, I invite you, I entreat you, I conjure you, come one and all, and make our prairies resound and our forests shake, and our ears ring and tingle, with your appeals for the equal rights of man. [Loud and continued cheering.]

Sir, I was to speak on Republicanism at the West, and so I did. This *is* Western Republicanism. These are its principles, and I am proud to say its principles are its policy. These are the ideas which have rallied around the banner of liberty not only the natives of the soil, but an innumerable host of Germans, Scandinavians, Scotchmen, Frenchmen and a goodly number of Irishmen, also. And here I tell you, those are mistaken who believe that the Irish heart is devoid of those noble impulses which will lead him to the side of justice, where he sees his own rights respected and unendangered. [Applause.] Under this banner, all the languages of civilized mankind are spoken, every creed is protected, every right is sacred. There stands every element of Western society, with enthusiasm for a great cause, with confidence in each other, with honor to themselves. This is the banner floating over the glorious valley which stretches from the Western slope of the Alleghanies to the Rocky Mountains—that Valley of Jehoshaphat, where the nations of the world assemble to celebrate the resurrection of human freedom. [Tremendous applause.] The inscription on that banner is not "Opposition to the Democratic party for the sake of placing a new set of men into office"; for this battle-cry of speculators our hearts have no response. Nor is it "Restriction of slavery and restriction of the right of suffrage," for this—believe my words, I entreat you— this would be the signal of deserved, inevitable and disgraceful defeat. But the inscription is "Liberty and equal rights, common to all as the air of Heaven— Liberty and equal rights, one and inseparable!" [Enthusiastic cheers.]

With this banner we stand before the world. In this sign—in this sign alone, and no other—there is victory. And thus sir, we mean to realize the great cosmopolitan idea, upon which the existence of the American nation rests. Thus we mean to fulfill the great mission of true Americanism—thus we mean to answer the anxious question of down-trodden humanity—"Has *man* the faculty to be free and to govern himself?" The answer is a triumphant "Aye," thundering into the ears of the despots of the old world that "a man is a man for all that"; proclaiming to the oppressed that they are held in subjection on false pretences; cheering the hearts of the despondent friends of man with consolation and renewed confidence.

This is true Americanism, clasping mankind to its great heart. Under its banner we march; let the world follow. [Loud applause, and three cheers for the champion of freedom in the West.]

The Burial of John Brown

(Delivered at the grave of John Brown, North Elba, New York, December 8, 1859)

How feeble words seem here! How can I hope to utter what your hearts are full of? I fear to disturb the harmony which his life breathes round this home. One and another of you, his neighbors, say, "I have known him five years," "I have known him ten years." It seems to me as if we had none of us known him. How our admiring, loving wonder has grown, day by day, as he has unfolded trait after trait of earnest, brave, tender, Christian life! We see him walking with radiant, serene face to the scaffold, and think what an iron heart, what devoted faith! We take up his letters, beginning "My dear wife and children, every one,"—see him stoop on his way to the scaffold and kiss that negro child,—and this iron heart seems all tenderness. Marvellous old man! We have hardly said it when the loved forms of his sons, in the bloom of young devotion, encircle him, and we remember he is not alone, only the majestic centre of a group. Your neighbor farmer went, surrounded by his household, to tell the slaves there were still hearts and right arms ready and nerved for their service. From this roof four, from a neighboring roof two, to make up that score of heroes. How resolute each looked into the face of Virginia, how loyally each stood at his forlorn post, meeting death cheerfully, till that master-voice said, "It is enough." And these weeping children and widow seem so lifted up and consecrated by long, single-hearted devotion to his great purpose, that we dare, even at this moment, to remind them how blessed they are in the privilege of thinking that in the last throbs of those brave young hearts, which lie buried on the banks of the Shenandoah, thoughts of them mingled with love to God and hope for the slave.

He has abolished slavery in Virginia. You may say this is too much. Our neighbors are the last men we know. The hours that pass us are the ones we appreciate the least. Men walked Boston streets, when night fell on Bunker's Hill, and pitied Warren, saying, "Foolish man! Thrown away his life! Why didn't he measure his means better?" Now we see him standing colossal on that blood-stained sod, and severing that day the tie which bound Boston to Great Britain. That night

George III ceased to rule in New England. History will date Virginia Emancipation from Harper's Ferry. True, the slave is still there. So, when the tempest uproots a pine on your hills, it looks green for months,—a year or two. Still, it is timber, not a tree. John Brown has loosened the roots of the slave system; it only breathes,—it does not live,—hereafter.

Men say, "How coolly brave!" But matchless courage seems the least of his merits. How gentleness graced it! When the frightened town wished to bear off the body of the Mayor, a man said, "I will go, Miss Fowke, under their rifles, if you will stand between them and me." He knew he could trust their gentle respect for woman. He was right. He went in the thick of the fight and bore off the body in safety. That same girl flung herself between Virginia rifles and your brave young Thompson. They had no pity. The pitiless bullet reached him, spite of woman's prayers, though the fight had long been over. How God has blessed him! How truly he may say, "I have fought a good fight, I have *finished* my course." Truly he has *finished*,—done his work. God granted him the privilege to look on his work accomplished. He said, "I will show the South that twenty men can take possession of a town, hold it twenty-four hours, and carry away all the slaves who wish to escape." Did he not do it? On Monday night he stood master of Harper's Ferry,— could have left unchecked with a score or a hundred slaves. The wide sympathy and secret approval are shown by the eager, quivering lips of lovers of slavery, asking, "O, why did he not take his victory and go away?" Who checked him at last? Not startled Virginia. Her he had conquered. The Union crushed,—seemed to crush him. In reality God said, "That work is done; you have proved that a Slave State is only fear in the mask of despotism; come up higher, and baptize by your martyrdom a million hearts into holier life." Surely such a life is no failure. How vast the change in men's hearts! Insurrection was a harsh, horrid word to millions a month ago. John Brown went a whole generation beyond it, claiming the right for white men to help the slave to freedom by arms. And now men run up and down, not disputing his principle, but trying to frame excuses for Virginia's hanging of so pure, honest, high-hearted, and heroic a man. Virginia stands at the bar of the civilized world on trial. Round her victim crowd the apostles and martyrs, all the brave, high souls who have said, "God is God," and trodden wicked laws under their feet. As I stood looking at his grandfather's gravestone, brought here from Connecticut, telling, as it does, of his death in the Revolution, I thought I could hear our hero-saint saying, "My fathers gave their swords to the oppressor,—the slave still sinks before the pledged force of this nation. I give my sword to the slave my fathers forgot." If any swords ever reflected the smile of Heaven, surely it was those drawn at Harper's Ferry. If our God is ever the Lord of Hosts, making one man chase a thousand, surely that little band might claim him for their captain. Harper's Ferry was no single hour, standing alone,—taken out from a common life,—it was the flowering out of fifty years of single-hearted devotion. He must have lived wholly for one great idea, when these who owe their being to him, and these whom love has joined to the circle, group so harmoniously around him, each accepting serenely his and her part.

I feel honored to stand under such a roof. Hereafter you will tell children standing at your knees, "I saw John Brown buried,—I sat under his roof." Thank God for such a master. Could we have asked a nobler representative of the Christian North putting her foot on the accursed system of slavery? As time passes, and these hours float back into history, men will see against the clear December sky that gallows, and round it thousands of armed men guarding Virginia from her slaves. On the other side, the serene brow of that calm old man, as he stoops to kiss the child of a forlorn race. Thank God for our emblem. May he soon bring Virginia to blot out hers in repentant shame, and cover that hateful gallows and soldiery with thousands of broken fetters.

What lesson shall those lips teach us? Before that still, calm brow let us take a new baptism. How can we stand here without a fresh and utter consecration? These tears! how shall we dare even to offer consolation? Only lips fresh from such a vow have the right to mingle their words with your tears. We envy you your nearer place to these martyred children of God. I do not believe slavery will go down in blood. Ours is the age of thought. Hearts are stronger than swords. That last fortnight! How sublime its lesson! the Christian one of conscience,—of truth. Virginia is weak, because each man's heart said amen to John Brown. His words,—they are stronger even than his rifles. These crushed a State. Those have changed the thoughts of millions, and will yet crush slavery. Men said, "Would he had died in arms!" God ordered better, and granted to him and the slave those noble prison hours,—that single hour of death; granted him a higher than the soldier's place, that of teacher; the echoes of his rifles have died away in the hills,—a million hearts guard his words. God bless this roof,—make it bless us. We dare not say bless you, children of this home! you stand nearer to one whose lips God touched, and we rather bend for your blessing. God make us all worthier of him whose dust we lay among these hills he loved. Here he girded himself and went forth to battle. Fuller success than his heart ever dreamed God granted him. He sleeps in the blessings of the crushed and the poor, and men believe more firmly in virtue, now that such a man has lived. Standing here, let us thank God for a firmer faith and fuller hope.

Abraham Lincoln

First Inaugural Address

(Delivered in Washington, D.C., March 4, 1861)

In compliance with a custom as old as the government itself, I appear before you to address you briefly, and to take, in your presence, the oath prescribed by the Constitution of the United States, to be taken by the President "before he enters on the execution of his office."

I do not consider it necessary, at present, for me to discuss those matters of administration about which there is no special anxiety, or excitement.

Apprehension seems to exist among the people of the Southern States, that by the accession of a Republican Administration, their property, and their peace, and personal security, are to be endangered. There has never been any reasonable cause for such apprehension. Indeed, the most ample evidence to the contrary has all the while existed, and been open to their inspection. It is found in nearly all the published speeches of him who now addresses you.

I do but quote from one of those speeches when I declare that "I have no purpose, directly or indirectly, to interfere with the institution of slavery in the States where it exists. I believe I have no lawful right to do so, and I have no inclination to do so." Those who nominated and elected me did so with full knowledge that I had made this, and many similar declarations, and had never recanted them. And more than this, they placed in the platform, for my acceptance, and as a law to themselves, and to me, the clear and emphatic resolution which I now read:

"*Resolved*, That the maintenance inviolate of the rights of the States, and especially the right of each State to order and control its own domestic institutions according to its own judgment exclusively, is essential to that balance of power on which the perfection and endurance of our political fabric depend; and we denounce the lawless invasion by armed force of the soil of any State or Territory, no matter under what pretext, as among the gravest of crimes."

I now reiterate these sentiments: and in doing so, I only press upon the public attention the most conclusive evidence of which the case is susceptible, that the property, peace and security of no section are to be in anywise endangered by the now incoming Administration. I add too, that all the protection which, consistently with the Constitution and the laws, can be given, will be cheerfully given to all the States when lawfully demanded, for whatever cause—as cheerfully to one section, as to another.

There is much controversy about the delivering up of fugitives from service or labor. The clause I now read is as plainly written in the Constitution as any other of its provisions:

"No person held to service or labor in one State, under the laws thereof, escaping into another, shall, in consequence of any law or regulation therein, be discharged from such service or labor, but shall be delivered up on claim of the party to whom such service or labor may be due."

It is scarcely questioned that this provision was intended by those who made it, for the reclaiming of what we call fugitive slaves; and the intention of the law-giver is the law. All members of Congress swear their support to the whole Constitution—to this provision as much as to any other. To the proposition, then, that slaves whose cases come within the terms of this clause, "shall be delivered up," their oaths are unanimous. Now, if they would make the effort in good temper, could they not, with nearly equal unanimity, frame and pass a law, by means of which to keep good that unanimous oath?

There is some difference of opinion whether this clause should be enforced by national or by state authority; but surely that difference is not a very material one. If the slave is to be surrendered, it can be of but little consequence to him, or to others, by which authority it is done. And should any one, in any case, be content that his oath shall go unkept, on a merely unsubstantial controversy as to *how* it shall be kept?

Again, in any law upon this subject, ought not all the safeguards of liberty known in civilized and humane jurisprudence to be introduced, so that a free man be not, in any case, surrendered as a slave? And might it not be well, at the same time, to provide by law for the enforcement of that clause in the Constitution which guarranties that "The citizens of each State shall be entitled to all previleges and immunities of citizens in the several States?"

I take the official oath to-day, with no mental reservations, and with no purpose to construe the Constitution or laws, by any hypercritical rules. And while I do not choose now to specify particular acts of Congress as proper to be enforced, I do suggest, that it will be much safer for all, both in official and private stations, to conform to, and abide by, all those acts which stand unrepealed, than to violate any of them, trusting to find impunity in having them held to be unconstitutional.

It is seventy-two years since the first inauguration of a President under our national Constitution. During that period fifteen different and greatly distinguished citizens, have, in succession, administered the executive branch of the government. They have conducted it through many perils; and, generally, with great success. Yet, with all this scope for precedent, I now enter upon the same task for the brief constitutional term of four years, under great and peculiar difficulty. A disruption of the Federal Union heretofore only menaced, is now formidably attempted.

I hold, that in contemplation of universal law, and of the Constitution, the Union of these States is perpetual. Perpetuity is implied, if not expressed, in the fundamental law of all national governments. It is safe to assert that no government proper, ever had a provision in its organic law for its own termination. Continue to execute all the express provisions of our national Constitution, and the Union will endure forever—it being impossible to destroy it, except by some action not provided for in the instrument itself.

Again, if the United States be not a government proper, but an association of States in the nature of contract merely, can it, as a contract, be peaceably unmade, by less than all the parties who made it? One party to a contract may violate it—break it, so to speak; but does it not require all to lawfully rescind it?

Descending from these general principles, we find the proposition that, in legal contemplation, the Union is perpetual, confirmed by the history of the Union itself. The Union is much older than the Constitution. It was formed in fact, by the Articles of Association in 1774. It was matured and continued by the Declaration of Independence in 1776. It was further matured and the faith of all the then thirteen States expressly plighted and engaged that it should be perpetual, by the Articles of Confederation in 1778. And finally, in 1787, one of the declared objects for ordaining and establishing the Constitution, was "*to form a more perfect union.*"

But if destruction of the Union, by one, or by a part only, of the States, be lawfully possible, the Union is *less* perfect than before the Constitution, having lost the vital element of perpetuity.

It follows from these views that no State, upon its own mere motion, can lawfully get out of the Union,—that *resolves* and *ordinances* to that effect are legally void; and that acts of violence, within any State or States, against the authority of the United States, are insurrectionary or revolutionary, according to circumstances.

I therefore consider that, in view of the Constitution and the laws, the Union is unbroken; and, to the extent of my ability, I shall take care, as the Constitution itself expressly enjoins upon me, that the laws of the Union be faithfully executed in all the States. Doing this I deem to be only a simple duty on my part; and I shall perform it, so far as practicable, unless my rightful masters, the American people, shall withhold the requisite means, or, in some authoritative manner, direct the contrary. I trust this will not be regarded as a menace, but only as the declared purpose of the Union that it *will* constitutionally defend, and maintain itself.

In doing this there needs to be no bloodshed or violence; and there shall be none, unless it be forced upon the national authority. The power the confided to me, will be used to hold, occupy, and possess the property, and places belonging to the government, and to collect the duties and imposts; but beyond what may be necessary for these objects, there will be no invasion—no using of force against, or among the people anywhere. Where hostility to the United States, in any interior locality, shall be so great and so universal, as to prevent competent resident citizens from holding the Federal offices, there will be no attempt to force obnoxious strangers among the people for that object. While the strict legal right may exist in the government to enforce the exercise of these offices, the attempt to do so would be so irritating, and so nearly impracticable with all, that I deem it better to forego, for the time, the uses of such offices.

The mails, unless repelled, will continue to be furnished in all parts of the Union. So far as possible, the people everywhere shall have that sense of perfect security which is most favorable to calm thought and reflection. The course here indicated will be followed, unless current events, and experience, shall show a modification, or change, to be proper; and in every case and exigency, my best discretion will be exercised, according to circumstances actually existing, and with a view and a hope of a peaceful solution of the national troubles, and the restoration of fraternal sympathies and affections.

That there are persons in one section, or another who seek to destroy the Union at all events, and are glad of any pretext to do it, I will neither affirm or deny; but if there be such, I need address no word to them. To those, however, who really love the Union, may I not speak?

Before entering upon so grave a matter as the destruction of our national fabric, with all its benefits, its memories, and its hopes, would it not be wise to ascertain precisely why we do it? Will you hazard so desperate a step, while there is any possibility that any portion of the ills you fly from, have no real existence? Will you, while the certain ills you fly to, are greater than all the real ones you fly from? Will you risk the commission of so fearful a mistake?

All profess to be content in the Union, if all constitutional rights can be maintained. Is it true, then, that any right, plainly written in the Constitution, has been denied? I think not. Happily the human mind is so constituted, that no party can reach to the audacity of doing this. Think, if you can, of a single instance in which a plainly written provision of the Constitution has ever been denied. If, by the mere force of numbers, a majority should deprive a minority of any clearly written constitutional right, it might, in a moral point of view, justify revolution—certainly would, if such right were a vital one. But such is not our case. All the vital rights of minorities, and of individuals, are so plainly assured to them, by affirmations and negations, guarranties and prohibitions, in the Constitution, that controversies never arise concerning them. But no organic law can ever be framed with a provision specifically applicable to every question which may occur in practical administration. No foresight can anticipate, nor any document of reasonable length contain express provisions for all possible questions. Shall fugitives from labor be surrendered by national or by State authority? The Constitution does not expressly say. *May* Congress prohibit slavery in the territories? The Constitution does not expressly say. *Must* Congress protect slavery in the territories? The Constitution does not expressly say.

From questions of this class spring all our constitutional controversies, and we divide upon them into majorities and minorities. If the minority will not acquiesce, the majority must, or the government must cease. There is no other alternative; for continuing the government, is acquiescence on one side or the other. If a minority, in such case, will secede rather than acquiesce, they make a precedent which, in turn, will divide and ruin them; for a minority of their own will secede from them, whenever a majority refuses to be controlled by such minority. For instance, why may not any portion of a new confederacy, a year or two hence, arbitrarily secede again, precisely as portions of the present Union now claim to secede from it. All who cherish disunion sentiments, are now being educated to the exact temper of doing this. Is there such perfect identity of interests among the States to compose a new Union, as to produce harmony only, and prevent renewed secession?

Plainly, the central idea of secession, is the essence of anarchy. A majority, held in restraint by constitutional checks, and limitations, and always changing easily, with deliberate changes of popular opinions and sentiments, is the only true sovereign of a free people. Whoever rejects it, does, of necessity, fly to anarchy or to despotism. Unanimity is impossible; the rule of a minority, as a permanent arrangement, is wholly inadmissable; so that, rejecting the majority principle, anarchy, or despotism in some form, is all that is left.

I do not forget the position assumed by some, that constitutional questions are to be decided by the Supreme Court; nor do I deny that such decisions must be binding in any case, upon the parties to a suit, as to the object of that suit, while they are also entitled to very high respect and consideration, in all paralel cases, by all other departments of the government. And while it is obviously possible that such decision may be erroneous in any given case, still the evil effect following it, being limited to that particular case, with the chance that it may be over-ruled, and never become a precedent for other cases, can better be borne than could the evils of a different practice. At the same time the candid citizen must confess that if the policy of the government, upon vital questions, affecting the whole people, is to be irrevocably fixed by decisions of the Supreme Court, the instant they are made, in ordinary litigation between parties, in personal actions, the people will have ceased, to be their own rulers, having, to that extent, practically resigned their government, into the hands of that eminent tribunal. Nor is there, in this view, any assault upon the court, or the judges. It is a duty, from which they may not shrink, to decide cases properly brought before them; and it is no fault of theirs, if others seek to turn their decisions to political purposes.

One section of our country believes slavery is *right*, and ought to be extended, while the other believes it is *wrong*, and ought not to be extended. This is the only substantial dispute. The fugitive slave clause of the Constitution, and the law for the suppression of the foreign slave trade, are each as well enforced, perhaps, as any law can ever be in a community where the moral sense of the people imperfectly supports the law itself. The great body of the people abide by the dry legal obligation in both cases, and a few break over in each. This, I think, cannot be perfectly cured; and it would be worse in both cases *after* the separation of the sections, than before. The foreign slave trade, now imperfectly suppressed, would be ultimately revived without restriction, in one section; while fugitive slaves, now only partially surrendered, would not be surrendered at all, by the other.

Physically speaking, we cannot separate. We cannot remove our respective sections from each other, nor build an impassable wall between them. A husband and wife may be divorced, and go out of the presence, and beyond the reach of each other; but the different parts of our country cannot do this. They cannot but remain face to face; and intercourse, either amicable or hostile, must continue between them. Is it possible then to make that intercourse more advantageous, or more satisfactory, *after* separation than *before*? Can aliens make treaties easier than friends can make laws? Can treaties be more faithfully enforced between aliens, than laws can among friends? Suppose you go to war, you cannot fight always; and when, after much loss on both sides, and no gain on either, you cease fighting, the identical old questions, as to terms of intercourse, are again upon you.

This country, with its institutions, belongs to the people who inhabit it. Whenever they shall grow weary of the existing government, they can exercise their *constitutional* right of amending it, or their *revolutionary* right to dismember, or overthrow it. I can not be ignorant of the fact that many worthy, and patriotic citizens are desirous of having the national constitution amended. While I make no recommendation of amendments, I fully recognize the rightful authority of the people over the whole subject, to be exercised in either of the modes prescribed in the instrument itself; and I should, under existing circumstances, favor, rather than oppose, a fair oppertunity being afforded the people to act upon it.

I will venture to add that, to me, the convention mode seems preferable, in that it allows amendments to originate with the people themselves, instead of only permitting them to take, or reject, propositions, originated by others, not especially chosen for the purpose, and which might not be precisely such, as they would wish to either accept or refuse. I understand a proposed amendment to the Constitution—which amendment, however, I have not seen, has passed Congress, to the effect that the federal government, shall never interfere with the domestic institutions of the States, including that of persons held to service. To avoid misconstruction of what I have said, I depart from my purpose not to speak of particular amendments, so far as to say that, holding such a provision to now be implied constitutional law, I have no objection to its being made express, and irrevocable.

The Chief Magistrate derives all his authority from the people, and they have conferred none upon him to fix terms for the separation of the States. The people themselves can do this also if they choose; but the executive, as such, has nothing to do with it. His duty is to administer the present government, as it came to his hands, and to transmit it, unimpaired by him, to his successor.

Why should there not be a patient confidence in the ultimate justice of the people? Is there any better, or equal hope, in the world? In our present differences, is either party without faith of being in the right? If the Almighty Ruler of nations, with his eternal truth and justice, be on your side of the North, or on yours of the South, that truth, and that justice, will surely prevail, by the judgment of this great tribunal, the American people.

By the frame of the government under which we live, this same people have wisely given their public servants but little power for mischief; and have, with equal wisdom, provided for the return of that little to their own hands at very short intervals.

While the people retain their virtue, and vigilence, no administration, by any extreme of wickedness or folly, can very seriously injure the government, in the short space of four years.

My countrymen, one and all, think calmly and *well*, upon this whole subject. Nothing valuable can be lost by taking time. If there be an object to *hurry* any of you, in hot haste, to a step which you would never take *deliberately*, that object will be frustrated by taking time; but no good object can be frustrated by it. Such of you as are now dissatisfied, still have the old Constitution unimpaired, and, on the sensitive point, the laws of your own framing under it; while the new administration will have no immediate power, if it would, to change either. If it were admitted that you who are dissatisfied, hold the right side in the dispute, there still is no single good reason for precipitate action. Intelligence, patriotism, Christianity, and a firm reliance on Him, who has never yet forsaken this favored land, are still competent to adjust, in the best way, all our present difficulty.

In *your* hands, my dissatisfied fellow countrymen, and not in *mine*, is the momentous issue of civil war. The government will not *assail* you. *You* can have no conflict, without being yourselves the aggressors. You have no oath registered in Heaven to destroy the government, while *I* shall have the most solemn one to "preserve, protect and defend" it.

I am loth to close. We are not enemies, but friends. We must not be enemies. Though passion may have strained, it must not break our bonds of affection. The mystic chords of memory, streching from every battle-field, and patriot grave, to every living heart and hearthstone, all over this broad land, will yet swell the chorus of the Union, when again touched, as surely they will be, by the better angels of our nature.

The Gettysburg Address

(Delivered at the dedication of the Cemetery at Gettysburg, Pennsylvania, November 19, 1863)

Four score and seven years ago our fathers brought forth upon this continent, a new nation, conceived in Liberty, and dedicated to the proposition that all men are created equal.

Now we are engaged in a great civil war, testing whether that nation, or any nation so conceived and so dedicated, can long endure. We are met on a great battle-field of that war. We have come to dedicate a portion of that field, as a final resting place for those who here gave their lives that this nation might live. It is altogether fitting and proper that we should do this.

But, in a larger sense, we can not dedicate—we can not consecrate—we cannot hallow—this ground. The brave men, living and dead, who struggled here, have consecrated it, far above our poor power to add or detract. The world will little note, nor long remember what we say here, but it can never forget what they did here. It is for us the living, rather, to be dedicated here to the unfinished work which they who fought here have thus far so nobly advanced. It is rather for us to be here dedicated to the great task remaining before us—that from these honored dead we take increased devotion to that cause for which they gave the last full measure of devotion—that we here highly resolve that these dead shall not have died in vain—that this nation, under God, shall have a new birth of freedom— and that government of the people, by the people, for the people, shall not perish from the earth.

Abraham Lincoln

Second Inaugural Address

(Delivered in Washington, D.C., March 4, 1865)

At this second appearing to take the oath of the presidential office, there is less occasion for an extended address than there was at the first. Then a statement, somewhat in detail, of a course to be pursued, seemed fitting and proper. Now, at the expiration of four years, during which public declarations have been constantly called forth on every point and phase of the great contest, which still absorbs the attention, and engrosses the energies of the nation, little that is new could be presented. The progress of our arms, upon which all else chiefly depends, is as well known to the public as to myself; and it is, I trust, reasonably satisfactory and encouraging to all. With high hope for the future, no prediction in regard to it is ventured.

On the occasion corresponding to this four years ago, all thoughts were anxiously directed to an impending civil war. All dreaded it—all sought to avert it. While the inaugural address was being delivered from this place, devoted altogether to *saving* the Union without war, insurgent agents were in the city seeking to *destroy* it without war—seeking to dissolve the Union, and divide effects, by negotiation. Both parties deprecated war; but one of them would *make* war rather than let the nation survive; and the other would *accept* war rather than let it perish. And the war came.

One eighth of the whole population were colored slaves, not distributed generally over the Union, but localized in the Southern part of it. These slaves constituted a peculiar and powerful interest. All knew that this interest was, somehow, the cause of the war. To strengthen, perpetuate, and extend this interest was the object for which the insurgents would rend the Union, even by war; while the government claimed no right to do more than to restrict the territorial enlargement of it. Neither party expected for the war, the magnitude, or the duration, which it has already attained. Neither anticipated that the *cause* of the conflict might cease with, or even before, the conflict itself should cease. Each looked for an easier triumph, and a result less fundamental and astounding. Both read the same Bible, and pray to the same God; and each invokes His aid against the other.

It may seem strange that any men should dare to ask a just God's assistance in wringing their bread from the sweat of other men's faces; but let us judge not that we be not judged. The prayers of both could not be answered; that of neither has been answered fully. The Almighty has His own purposes. "Woe unto the world because of offences! for it must needs be that offences come; but woe to that man by whom the offence cometh!" If we shall suppose that American Slavery is one of those offences which, in the providence of God, must needs come, but which, having continued through His appointed time, He now wills to remove, and that He gives to both North and South, this terrible war, as the woe due to those by whom the offence came, shall we discern therein any departure from those divine attributes which the believers in a Living God always ascribe to Him? Fondly do we hope—fervently do we pray—that this mighty scourge of war may speedily pass away. Yet, if God wills that it continue, until all the wealth piled by the bond-man's two hundred and fifty years of unrequited toil shall be sunk, and until every drop of blood drawn by the lash, shall be paid by another drawn with the sword, as was said three thousand years ago, so still it must be said, "the judgments of the Lord, are true and righteous altogether."

With malice toward none; with charity for all; with firmness in the right, as God gives us to see the right, let us strive on to finish the work we are in; to bind up the nation's wounds; to care for him who shall have borne the battle, and for his widow, and his orphan—to do all which may achieve and cherish a just, and lasting peace, among ourselves, and with all nations.

SUSAN B. ANTHONY

Constitutional Argument

(Delivered in Monroe and Ontario counties in New York, between January and June 1873, on the occasion of Anthony's arrest for voting)

I stand before you under indictment for the alleged crime of having voted at the last presidential election, without having a lawful right to vote. It shall be my work this evening to prove to you that in thus doing, I not only committed no crime, but instead simply exercised my citizen's right, guaranteed to me and all United States citizens by the National Constitution beyond the power of any State to deny.

Our democratic-republican government is based on the idea of the natural right of every individual member thereof to a voice and a vote in making and executing the laws. We assert the province of government to be to secure the people in the enjoyment of their inalienable rights. We throw to the winds the old dogma that government can give rights. No one denies that before governments were organized each individual possessed the right to protect his own life, liberty and property. When 100 or 1,000,000 people enter into a free government, they do not barter away their natural rights; they simply pledge themselves to protect each other in the enjoyment of them through prescribed judicial and legislative tribunals. They agree to abandon the methods of brute force in the adjustment of their differences and adopt those of civilization. Nor can you find a word in any of the grand documents left us by the fathers which assumes for government the power to create or to confer rights. The Declaration of Independence, the United States Constitution, the constitutions of the several States and the organic laws of the Territories, all alike propose to *protect* the people in the exercise of their God-given rights. Not one of them pretends to bestow rights.

> All men are created equal, and endowed by their Creator with certain inalienable rights. Among these are life, liberty and the pursuit of happiness. To secure these, governments are instituted among men, deriving their just powers from the consent of the governed.

Here is no shadow of government authority over rights, or exclusion of any class from their full and equal enjoyment. Here is pronounced the right of all men, and "consequently," as the Quaker preacher said, "of all women," to a voice in the government. And here, in this first paragraph of the Declaration, is the assertion of the natural right of all to the ballot; for how can "the consent of the governed" be given, if the right to vote be denied? Again:

> Whenever any form of government becomes destructive of these ends, it is the right of the people to alter or abolish it, and to institute a new government, laying its foundations on such principles, and organizing its powers in such form, as to them shall seem most likely to effect their safety and happiness.

Surely the right of the whole people to vote is here clearly implied; for however destructive to their happiness this government might become, a disfranchised class could neither alter nor abolish it, nor institute a new one, except by the old brute force method of insurrection and rebellion. One-half of the people of this nation today are utterly powerless to blot from the statute books an unjust law, or to write there a new and a just one. The women, dissatisfied as they are with this form of government, that enforces taxation without representation—that compels them to obey laws to which they never have given their consent— that imprisons and hangs them without a trial by a jury of their peers—that robs them, in marriage, of the custody of their own persons, wages and children— are this half of the people who are left wholly at the mercy of the other half, in direct violation of the spirit and letter of the declarations of the framers of this government, every one of which was based on the immutable principle of equal rights to all. By these declarations, kings, popes, priests, aristocrats, all were alike dethroned and placed on a common level, politically, with the lowliest born subject or serf. By them, too, men, as such, were deprived of their divine right to rule and placed on a political level with women. By the practice of these declarations all class and caste distinctions would be abolished, and slave, serf, plebeian, wife, woman, all alike rise from their subject position to the broader platform of equality.

The preamble of the Federal Constitution says:

> We, the people of the United States, in order to form a more perfect union, establish justice, insure domestic tranquillity, provide for the common defence, promote the general welfare and secure the blessings of liberty to ourselves and our posterity,

do ordain and establish this Constitution for the United States
of America.

It was we, the people, not we, the white male citizens, nor we, the male citizens; but we, the whole people, who formed this Union. We formed it not to give the blessings of liberty but to secure them; not to the half of ourselves and the half of our posterity, but to the whole people—women as well as men. It is downright mockery to talk to women of their enjoyment of the blessings of liberty while they are denied the only means of securing them provided by this democratic-republican government—the ballot.

The early journals of Congress show that, when the committee reported to that body the original articles of confederation, the very first one which became the subject of discussion was that respecting equality of suffrage. Article IV said:

> The better to secure and perpetuate mutual friendship and intercourse between the people of the different States of this Union, the free inhabitants of each of the States (paupers, vagabonds and fugitives from justice excepted) shall be entitled to all the privileges and immunities of the free citizens of the several States.

Thus, at the very beginning, did the fathers see the necessity of the universal application of the great principle of equal rights to all, in order to produce the desired result—a harmonious union and a homogeneous people.

Luther Martin, attorney-general of Maryland, in his report to the legislature of that State of the convention which framed the United States Constitution, said:

> Those who advocated the equality of suffrage took the matter up on the original principles of government: that the reason why each individual man in forming a State government should have an equal vote, is because each individual, before he enters into government, is equally free and equally independent.

James Madison said:

> Under every view of the subject, it seems indispensable that the mass of the citizens should not be without a voice in making the laws which they are to obey, and in choosing the magistrates

who are to administer them. . . . Let it be remembered, finally, that it has ever been the pride and the boast of America that the rights for which she contended were the rights of human nature.

These assertions by the framers of the United States Constitution of the equal and natural right of all the people to a voice in the government, have been affirmed and reaffirmed by the leading statesmen of the nation throughout the entire history of our government. Thaddeus Stevens, of Pennsylvania, said in 1866: "I have made up my mind that the elective franchise is one of the inalienable rights meant to be secured by the Declaration of Independence." B. Gratz Brown, of Missouri, in the three days' discussion in the United States Senate in 1866, on Senator Cowan's motion to strike "male" from the District of Columbia suffrage bill, said:

Mr. President, I say here on the floor of the American Senate, I stand for universal suffrage; and as a matter of fundamental principle, do not recognize the right of society to limit it on any ground of race or sex. I will go farther and say that I recognize the right of franchise as being intrinsically a natural right. I do not believe that society is authorized to impose any limitations upon it that do not spring out of the necessities of the social state itself. Sir, I have been shocked, in the course of this debate, to hear senators declare this right only a conventional and political arrangement, a privilege yielded to you and me and others; not a right in any sense, only a concession! Mr. President, I do not hold my liberties by any such tenure. On the contrary, I believe that whenever you establish that doctrine, whenever you crystallize that idea in the public mind of this country, you ring the death-knell of American liberties.

Charles Sumner, in his brave protests against the Fourteenth and Fifteenth Amendments, insisted that so soon as by the Thirteenth Amendment the slaves became free men, the original powers of the United States Constitution guaranteed to them equal rights—the right to vote and to be voted for. In closing one of his great speeches he said:

I do not hesitate to say that when the slaves of our country became "citizens" they took their place in the body politic as a component part of the "people," entitled to equal rights and under the protection of these two guardian principles: First, that all just governments stand on the consent of the governed; and second, that taxation without representation is tyranny; and these rights it is the duty of Congress to guarantee as essential to the idea of a republic.

The preamble of the constitution of the State of New York declares the same purpose. It says: "We, the people of the State of New York, grateful to Almighty God for our freedom, in order to secure its blessings, do establish this constitution." Here is not the slightest intimation either of receiving freedom from the United States Constitution, or of the State's conferring the blessings of liberty upon the people; and the same is true of every other State constitution. Each and all declare rights God-given, and that to secure the people in the enjoyment of their inalienable rights is their one and only object in ordaining and establishing government. All of the State constitutions are equally emphatic in their recognition of the ballot as the means of securing the people in the enjoyment of these rights. Article I of the New York State constitution says:

> No member of this State shall be disfranchised or deprived of the rights or privileges secured to any citizen thereof, unless by the law of the land, or the judgment of his peers.

So carefully guarded is the citizen's right to vote, that the constitution makes special mention of all who may be excluded. It says: "Laws may be passed excluding from the right of suffrage all persons who have been or may be convicted of bribery, larceny or any infamous crime."

In naming the various employments which shall not affect the residence of voters, Section 3, Article II, says "that neither being kept in any almshouse, or other asylum, at public expense, nor being confined in any public prison, shall deprive a person of his residence," and hence of his vote. Thus is the right of voting most sacredly hedged about. The only seeming permission in the New York State constitution for the disfranchisement of women is in Section 1, Article II, which says: "Every male citizen of the age of twenty-one years, etc., shall be entitled to vote."

But I submit that in view of the explicit assertions of the equal right of the whole people, both in the preamble and previous article of the constitution, this omission of the adjective "female" should not be construed into a denial; but instead should be considered as of no effect. Mark the direct prohibition, "No member of this State shall be disfranchised, unless by the law of the land, or the judgment of his peers." "The law of the land" is the United States Constitution; and there is no provision in that document which can be fairly construed into a permission to the States to deprive any class of citizens of their right to vote. Hence New York can get no power from that source to disfranchise one entire half of her members. Nor has "the judgment of their peers" been pronounced against women exercising their right to vote; no disfranchised person is allowed to be judge or juror—and none but disfranchised persons can be women's peers. Nor has the legislature passed laws excluding women as a class on account of idiocy or lunacy; nor have the courts convicted them of bribery, larceny or any infamous crime. Clearly, then, there is no constitutional ground for the exclusion of women from the ballot-box in the State of New York. No barriers whatever stand today between women and the exercise of their right to vote save those of precedent and prejudice, which refuse to expunge the word "male" from the constitution.

The clauses of the United States Constitution cited by our opponents as giving power to the States to disfranchise any classes of citizens they please, are contained in Sections 2 and 4, Article I. The second says:

> The House of Representatives shall be composed of members chosen every second year by the people of the several States; and the electors in each State shall have the qualifications requisite for electors of the most numerous branch of the State legislature.

This can not be construed into a concession to the States of the power to destroy the right to become an elector, but simply to prescribe what shall be the qualifications, such as competency of intellect, maturity of age, length of residence, that shall be deemed necessary to enable them to make an intelligent choice of candidates. If, as our opponents assert, it is the duty of the United States to protect citizens in the several States against higher or different qualifications for electors for representatives in Congress than for members of the Assembly, then it must be equally imperative for the national government to interfere with the States, and forbid them from arbitrarily cutting off the right of one-half the people to become electors altogether. Section 4 says:

> The times, places and manner of holding elections for senators and representatives shall be prescribed in each State by the legislature thereof; but Congress may at any time, by law, make or alter such regulations, except as to the places of choosing senators.

Here is conceded to the States only the power to prescribe times, places and manner of holding the elections; and even with these Congress may interfere in all excepting the mere place of choosing senators. Thus, you see, there is not the slightest permission for the States to discriminate against the right of any class of citizens to vote. Surely, to regulate can not be to annihilate; to qualify can not be wholly to deprive. To this principle every true Democrat and Republican said amen, when applied to black men by Senator Sumner in his great speeches from 1865 to 1869 for equal rights to all; and when, in 1871, I asked that senator to declare the power of the United States Constitution to protect women in their right to vote—as he had done for black men—he handed me a copy of all his speeches during that reconstruction period, and said:

> Put "sex" where I have "race" or "color," and you have here the best and strongest argument I can make for woman. There is not a doubt but women have the constitutional right to vote, and I will never vote for a Sixteenth Amendment to guarantee it to them. I voted for both the Fourteenth and Fifteenth under protest; would never have done it but for the pressing emergency of that hour; would have insisted that the power of the original Constitution to protect all citizens in the equal enjoyment of their rights should have been vindicated through the courts. But the newly-made freedmen had neither the intelligence, wealth nor time to await that slow process. Women do possess all these in an eminent degree, and I insist that they shall appeal to the courts, and through them establish the powers of our American magna charta to protect every citizen of the republic.

But, friends, when in accordance with Senator Sumner's counsel I went to the ballot-box, last November, and exercised my citizen's right to vote, the courts did not wait for me to appeal to them—they appealed to me, and indicted me on the charge of having voted illegally. Putting sex where he did color, Senator Sumner would have said:

> Qualifications can not be in their nature permanent or insurmountable. Sex can not be a qualification any more than size, race, color or previous condition of servitude. A permanent or insurmountable qualification is equivalent to a deprivation of the suffrage. In other words, it is the tyranny of taxation without

representation, against which our Revolutionary mothers, as well as fathers, rebelled.

For any State to make sex a qualification, which must ever result in the disfranchisement of one entire half of the people, is to pass a bill of attainder, an ex post facto law, and is therefore a violation of the supreme law of the land. By it the blessings of liberty are forever withheld from women and their female posterity. For them, this government has no just powers derived from the consent of the governed. For them this government is not a democracy; it is not a republic. It is the most odious aristocracy ever established on the face of the globe. An oligarchy of wealth, where the rich govern the poor; an oligarchy of learning, where the educated govern the ignorant; or even an oligarchy of race, where the Saxon rules the African, might be endured; but this oligarchy of sex which makes father, brothers, husband, sons, the oligarchs over the mother and sisters, the wife and daughters of every household; which ordains all men sovereigns, all women subjects—carries discord and rebellion into every home of the nation. This most odious aristocracy exists, too, in the face of Section 4, Article IV, which says: "The United States shall guarantee to every State in the Union a republican form of government."

What, I ask you, is the distinctive difference between the inhabitants of a monarchical and those of a republican form of government, save that in the monarchical the people are subjects, helpless, powerless, bound to obey laws made by political superiors; while in the republican the people are citizens, individual sovereigns, all clothed with equal power to make and unmake both their laws and law-makers? The moment you deprive a person of his right to a voice in the government, you degrade him from the status of a citizen of the republic to that of a subject. It matters very little to him whether his monarch be an individual tyrant, as is the Czar of Russia, or a 15,000,000 headed monster, as here in the United States; he is a powerless subject, serf or slave; not in any sense a free and independent citizen.

It is urged that the use of the masculine pronouns *he, his* and *him* in all the constitutions and laws, is proof that only men were meant to be included in their provisions. If you insist on this version of the letter of the law, we shall insist that you be consistent and accept the other horn of the dilemma, which would compel you to exempt women from taxation for the support of the government and from penalties for the violation of laws. There is no *she* or *her* or *hers* in the tax laws, and this is equally true of all the criminal laws.

Take for example the civil rights law which I am charged with having violated; not only are all the pronouns in it masculine, but everybody knows that it was intended expressly to hinder the rebel men from voting. It reads, "If any person shall knowingly vote without *his* having a lawful right." It was precisely so with all the papers served on me—the United States marshal's warrant, the bail-bond, the petition for habeas corpus, the bill of indictment—not one of them had a feminine pronoun; but to make them applicable to me, the clerk of the court prefixed an "s" to the "he" and made "her" out of "his" and "him"; and I insist if government officials may thus manipulate the pronouns to tax, fine, imprison and hang women, it is their duty to thus change them in order to protect us in our right to vote.

So long as any classes of men were denied this right, the government made a show of consistency by exempting them from taxation. When a property qualification of $250 was required of black men in New York, they were not compelled to pay taxes so long as they were content to report themselves worth less than that sum; but the moment the black man died and his property fell to his widow or daughter, the black woman's name was put on the assessor's list and she was compelled to pay taxes on this same property. This also is true of ministers in New York. So long as the minister lives, he is exempted from taxation on $1,500 of property, but the moment the breath leaves his body, his widow's name goes on the assessor's list and she has to pay taxes on the $1,500. So much for special legislation in favor of women!

In all the penalties and burdens of government (except the military) women are reckoned as citizens, equally with men. Also, in all the privileges and immunities, save those of the jury and the ballot-box, the foundation on which rest all the others. The United States government not only taxes, fines, imprisons and hangs women, but it allows them to pre-empt lands, register ships and take out passports and naturalization papers. Not only does the law permit single women and widows the right of naturalization, but Section 2 says, "A married woman may be naturalized without the concurrence of her husband"; (I wonder the fathers were not afraid of creating discord in the families of foreigners;) and again:

> When an alien, having complied with the law and declared his intention to become a citizen, dies before he is actually naturalized, his widow and children shall be considered citizens, entitled to all rights and privileges as such, on taking the required oath.

If a foreign born woman by becoming a naturalized citizen is entitled to all the rights and privileges of citizenship, do not these include the ballot which would have belonged to her husband? If this is true of a naturalized woman, is it not equally true of one who is native born?

The question of the masculine pronouns—yes, and nouns too—was settled by the United States Supreme Court, in the case of Silver *versus* Ladd, December, 1868. The court said:

> In construing a benevolent statute of the government, made for the benefit of its own citizens, inviting and encouraging them to settle on its distant public lands, the words "single man" and "unmarried man" may, especially if aided by the context and other parts of the statute, be taken in a generic sense. Held, accordingly, that the Fourth Section of the Act of Congress, of September 27, 1850, granting by way of donation lands in Oregon Territory to every white settler or occupant, American half-breed Indians included, embraced within the term single man an unmarried woman.

Though the words persons, people, inhabitants, electors, citizens, are all used indiscriminately in the national and State constitutions, there was always a conflict of opinion, prior to the war, as to whether they were synonymous terms, but whatever room there was for doubt, under the old regime, the adoption of the Fourteenth Amendment settled that question forever in its first sentence:

> All persons born or naturalized in the United States, and subject to the jurisdiction thereof, are citizens of the United States, and of the State wherein they reside.

The second settles the equal status of all citizens:

> No State shall make or enforce any law which shall abridge the privileges or immunities of citizens of the United States; nor shall any State deprive any person of life, liberty or property without due process of law, or deny to any person within its jurisdiction the equal protection of the laws.

The only question left to be settled now is: Are women persons? I scarcely believe any of our opponents will have the hardihood to say they are not. Being persons, then, women are citizens, and no State has a right to make any new law, or to enforce any old law, which shall abridge their privileges or immunities. Hence, every discrimination against women in the constitutions and laws of the several States is today null and void, precisely as is every one against negroes.

Is the right to vote one of the privileges or immunities of citizens? I think the disfranchised ex-rebels and ex-State prisoners all will agree that it is not only one of them, but the one without which all the others are nothing. Seek first the kingdom of the ballot and all things else shall be added, is the political injunction.

Webster, Worcester and Bouvier all define citizen to be a person, in the United States, entitled to vote and hold office. Prior to the adoption of the Thirteenth Amendment, by which slavery was forever abolished and black men transformed from property to persons, the judicial opinions of the country had always been in harmony with this definition: In order to be a citizen one must be a voter. Associate-Justice Washington, in defining the privileges and immunities of the citizen, more than fifty years ago, said: "They include all such privileges as are fundamental in their nature; and among them is the right to exercise the elective franchise, and to hold office." Even the Dred Scott decision, pronounced by the Abolitionists and Republicans infamous because it virtually declared "black men had no rights white men were bound to respect," gave this true and logical conclusion, that to be one of the people was to be a citizen and a voter.

Chief-Justice Daniels said:

> There is not, it is believed, to be found in the theories of writers on government, or in any actual experiment heretofore made, an exposition of the term citizen which has not been considered as conferring the actual possession and enjoyment of an entire equality of privileges, civil and political.

Associate-Justice Taney said:

> The words "people of the United States" and "citizens" are synonymous terms, and mean the same thing. They both describe the political body, who, according to our republican institutions, form the sovereignty, and who hold the power and conduct the government through their representatives. They are what we familiarly call "the sovereign people," and every citizen is one of this people, and a constituent member of this sovereignty.

Thus does Judge Taney's decision, which was so terrible a ban to the black man while he was a slave, now that he is a person and no longer property, pronounce him a citizen, possessed of entire equality of privileges, civil and political;

and not only the black man, but the black woman, and all women. It was not until after the abolition of slavery, by which the negroes became free men and hence citizens, that any contrary opinion was rendered. U.S. Attorney-General Bates then said:

> The Constitution uses the word "citizen" only to express the political quality, [not equality, mark,] of the individual in his relation to the nation; to declare that he is a member of the body politic, and bound to it by the reciprocal obligations of allegiance on the one side and protection on the other. The phrase, "a citizen of the United States," without addition or qualification, means neither more nor less than a member of the nation.

Then, to be a citizen of this republic is no more than to be a subject of an empire. You and I, and all true and patriotic citizens, must repudiate this base conclusion. We all know that American citizenship, without addition or qualification, means the possession of equal rights, civil and political. We all know that the crowning glory of every citizen of the United States is that he can either give or withhold his vote from every law and every legislator under the government.

Did "I am a Roman citizen" mean nothing more than that I am a "member" of the body politic of the republic of Rome, bound to it by the reciprocal obligations of allegiance on the one side and protection on the other? When you, young man, shall travel abroad, among the monarchies of the old world, and there proudly boast yourself an "American citizen," will you thereby declare yourself neither more nor less than a "member" of the American nation?

This opinion of Attorney-General Bates, that a black citizen was not a voter, given merely to suit the political exigency of the Republican party in that transition hour between emancipation and enfranchisement, was no less infamous, in spirit or purpose, than was the decision of Judge Taney, that a black man was not one of the people, rendered in the interest and at the behest of the old Democratic party in its darkest hour of subjection to the slave power. Nevertheless, all of the adverse arguments, congressional reports and judicial opinions, thus far, have been based on this purely partisan, timeserving decision of General Bates, that the normal condition of the citizen of the United States is that of disfranchisement; that only such classes of citizens as have had special legislative guarantee have a legal right to vote.

If this decision of Attorney-General Bates was infamous, as against black men, but yesterday plantation slaves, what shall we pronounce upon Judge Bingham, in the House of Representatives, and Carpenter, in the Senate of the United States, for citing it against the women of the entire nation, vast numbers of whom are the peers of those honorable gentlemen themselves in morals, intellect, culture, wealth, family, paying taxes on large estates, and contributing equally with them and their sex, in every direction, to the growth, prosperity and well-being of the republic? And what shall be said of the judicial opinions of Judges Cartter, Jameson, McKay and Sharswood, all based upon this aristocratic, monarchial idea of the right of one class to govern another?

I am proud to mention the names of the two United States judges who have given opinions honorable to our republican idea, and honorable to themselves—Judge Howe, of Wyoming Territory, and Judge Underwood, of Virginia. The former gave it as his opinion a year ago, when the legislature seemed likely to revoke the law enfranchising the women of that Territory that, in case they succeeded, the women would still possess the right to vote under the Fourteenth Amendment. The latter, in noticing the recent decision of Judge Cartter, of the Supreme Court of the District of Columbia, denying to women the right to vote under the Fourteenth and Fifteenth Amendments, says:

> If the people of the United States, by amendment of their Constitution, could expunge, without any explanatory or assisting legislation, an adjective of five letters from all State and local constitutions, and thereby raise millions of our most ignorant fellow-citizens to all of the rights and privileges of electors, why should not the same people, by the same amendment, expunge an adjective of four letters from the same State and local constitutions, and thereby raise other millions of more educated and better informed citizens to equal rights and privileges, without explanatory or assisting legislation?

If the Fourteenth Amendment does not secure to all citizens the right to vote, for what purpose was that grand old charter of the fathers lumbered with its unwieldy proportions? The Republican party, and Judges Howard and Bingham, who drafted the document, pretended it was to do something for black men; and if that something were not to secure them in their right to vote and hold office, what could it have been? For by the Thirteenth Amendment black men had become people, and hence were entitled to all the privileges and immunities of the government, precisely as were the women of the country and foreign men not naturalized. According to Associate-Justice Washington, they already had:

> Protection of the government, the enjoyment of life and liberty, with the right to acquire and possess property of every kind, and to pursue and obtain happiness and safety, subject to such restraints as the government may justly prescribe for the general welfare of the whole; the right of a citizen of one State to pass through or to reside in any other State for the purpose of trade, agriculture, professional pursuit, or otherwise; to claim the benefit of the writ of habeas corpus, to institute and maintain actions of any kind in the courts of the State; to take, hold, and dispose of property, either real or personal, and an exemption from higher taxes or impositions than are paid by the other citizens of the State.

Thus, you see, those newly-freed men were in possession of every possible right, privilege and immunity of the government, except that of suffrage, and hence needed no constitutional amendment for any other purpose. What right in this country has the Irishman the day after he receives his naturalization papers that he did not possess the day before, save the right to vote and hold office? The Chinamen now crowding our Pacific coast are in precisely the same position. What privilege or immunity has California or Oregon the right to deny them, save that of the ballot? Clearly, then, if the Fourteenth Amendment was not to secure to black men their right to vote it did nothing for them, since they possessed everything else before. But if it was intended to prohibit the States from denying or abridging their right to vote, then it did the same for all persons, white women included, born or naturalized in the United States; for the amendment does not say that all male persons of African descent, but that all persons are citizens.

> The second section is simply a threat to punish the States by reducing their representation on the floor of Congress, should they disfranchise any of their male citizens, and can not be construed into a sanction to disfranchise female citizens, nor does it in any wise weaken or invalidate the universal guarantee of the first section.

However much the doctors of the law may disagree as to whether people and citizens, in the original Constitution, were one and the same, or whether the privileges and immunities in the Fourteenth Amendment include the right of suffrage, the question of the citizen's right to vote is forever settled by the Fifteenth Amendment. "The right of citizens of the United States to vote shall not be denied or abridged by the United States, or by any State, on account of race, color or previous condition of servitude." How can the State deny or abridge the right of the citizen, if the citizen does not possess it? There is no escape from the conclusion that to vote is the citizen's right, and the specifications of race, color or previous condition of servitude can in no way impair the force of that emphatic assertion that the citizen's right to vote shall not be denied or abridged.

The political strategy of the second section of the Fourteenth Amendment failing to coerce the rebel States into enfranchising their negroes, and the necessities of the Republican party demanding their votes throughout the South to ensure the re-election of Grant in 1872, that party was compelled to place this positive prohibition of the Fifteenth Amendment upon the United States and all the States thereof.

If once we establish the false principle that United States citizenship does not carry with it the right to vote in every State in this Union, there is no end to the petty tricks and cunning devices which will be attempted to exclude one and another class of citizens from the right of suffrage. It will not always be the men combining to disfranchise all women; native born men combining to abridge the rights of all naturalized citizens, as in Rhode Island. It will not always be the rich and educated who may combine to cut off the poor and ignorant; but we may live to see the hard-working, uncultivated day laborers, foreign and native born, learning the power of the ballot and their vast majority of numbers, combine and amend State constitutions so as to disfranchise the Vanderbilts, the Stewarts, the Conklings and the Fentons. It is a poor rule that won't work more ways than one. Establish this precedent, admit the State's right to deny suffrage, and there is no limit to the confusion, discord and disruption that may await us. There is and can be but one safe principle of government—equal rights to all. Discrimination against any class on account of color, race, nativity, sex, property, culture, can but embitter and disaffect that class, and thereby endanger the safety of the whole people. Clearly, then, the national government not only must define the rights of citizens, but must stretch out its powerful hand and protect them in every State in this Union.

If, however, you will insist that the Fifteenth Amendment's emphatic interdiction against robbing United States citizens of their suffrage "on account of race, color or previous condition of servitude," is a recognition of the right of either the United States or any State to deprive them of the ballot for any or all other reasons, I will prove to you that the class of citizens for whom I now plead are, by all the principles of our government and many of the laws of the States, included under the term "previous condition of servitude."

Consider first married women and their legal status. What is servitude? "The condition of a slave." What is a slave? "A person who is robbed of the proceeds of his labor; a person who is subject to the will of another." By the laws of Georgia, South Carolina and all the States of the South, the negro had no right to the custody and control of his person. He belonged to his master. If he were disobedient, the master had the right to use correction. If the negro did not like the correction and ran away, the master had the right to use coercion to bring him back. By the laws of almost every State in this Union today, North as well as South, the married woman has no right to the custody and control of her person. The wife belongs to the husband; and if she refuse obedience he may use moderate correction, and if she do not like his moderate correction and leave his "bed and board," the husband may use moderate coercion to bring her back. The little word "moderate," you see, is the saving clause for the wife, and would doubtless be overstepped should her offended husband administer his correction with the "cat-o'-nine-tails," or accomplish his coercion with blood-hounds.

Again the slave had no right to the earnings of his hands, they belonged to his master; no right to the custody of his children, they belonged to his master; no right to sue or be sued, or to testify in the courts. If he committed a crime, it was the master who must sue or be sued. In many of the States there has been special legislation, giving married women the right to property inherited or received by bequest, or earned by the pursuit of any avocation outside the home; also giving them the right to sue and be sued in matters pertaining to such separate property; but not a single State of this Union has ever secured the wife in the enjoyment of her right to equal ownership of the joint earnings of the marriage copartnership. And since, in the nature of things, the vast majority of married women never earn a dollar by work outside their families, or inherit a dollar from their fathers, it follows that from the day of their marriage to the day of the death of their husbands not one of them ever has a dollar, except it shall please her husband to let her have it.

In some of the States, also, laws have been passed giving to the mother a joint right with the father in the guardianship of the children. Twenty-five years ago, when our woman's rights movement commenced, by the laws of all the States the father had the sole custody and control of the children. No matter if he were a brutal, drunken libertine, he had the legal right, without the mother's consent, to apprentice her sons to rumsellers or her daughters to brothel-keepers. He even could will away an unborn child from the mother. In most of the States this law still prevails, and the mothers are utterly powerless.

I doubt if there is, today, a State in this Union where a married woman can sue or be sued for slander of character, and until recently there was not one where she could sue or be sued for injury of person. However damaging to the wife's reputation any slander may be, she is wholly powerless to institute legal proceedings against her accuser unless her husband shall join with her; and how often have we heard of the husband conspiring with some outside barbarian to blast the good name of his wife? A married woman can not testify in courts in cases of joint interest with her husband.

A good farmer's wife in Illinois, who had all the rights she wanted, had had made for herself a full set of false teeth. The dentist pronounced them an admirable fit, and the wife declared it gave her fits to wear them. The dentist sued the husband for his bill; his counsel brought the wife as witness; the judge ruled her off the stand, saying, "A married woman can not be a witness in matters of joint interest between herself and her husband." Think of it, ye good wives, the false teeth in your mouths are a joint interest with your husbands, about which you are legally incompetent to speak! If a married woman is injured by accident, in nearly all of the States it is her husband who must sue, and it is to him that the damages will be awarded. In Massachusetts a married woman was severely injured by a defective sidewalk. Her husband sued the corporation and recovered $13,000 damages, which belong to him absolutely, and whenever that unfortunate wife wishes a dollar of that money she must ask her husband for it; and if he be of a niggardly nature, she will hear him say, every time, "What have you done with the twenty-five cents I gave you yesterday?" Isn't such a position humiliating enough to be called "servitude"? That husband sued and obtained damages for the loss of the services of his wife, precisely as he would have done had it been his ox, cow or horse; and exactly as the master, under the old regime, would have recovered for the services of his slave.

I submit the question, if the deprivation by law of the ownership of one's own person, wages, property, children, the denial of the right as an individual to sue and be sued and testify in the courts, is not a condition of servitude most bitter and absolute, even though under the sacred name of marriage? Does any lawyer doubt my statement of the legal status of married women? I will remind him of the fact that the common law of England prevails in every State but two in this Union, except where the legislature has enacted special laws annulling it. I am ashamed that not one of the States yet has blotted from its statute books the old law of marriage, which, summed up in the fewest words possible, is in effect "husband and wife are one, and that one the husband."

Thus may all married women and widows, by the laws of the several States, be technically included in the Fifteenth Amendment's specification of "condition of servitude," present or previous. The facts also prove that, by all the great fundamental principles of our free government, not only married women but the entire womanhood of the nation are in a "condition of servitude" as surely as were our Revolutionary fathers when they rebelled against King George. Women are taxed without representation, governed without their consent, tried, convicted and punished without a jury of their peers. Is all this tyranny any less humiliating and degrading to women under our democratic-republican government today than it was to men under their aristocratic, monarchial government one hundred years ago? There is not an utterance of John Adams, John Hancock or Patrick Henry, but finds a living response in the soul of every intelligent, patriotic woman of the nation. Show me a justice-loving woman property-holder, and I will show you one whose soul is fired with all the indignation of 1776 every time the tax-collector presents himself at her door. You will not find one such but feels her condition of servitude as galling as did James Otis when he said:

> The very act of taxing exercised over those who are not repre-
> sented appears to me to be depriving them of one of their most
> essential rights, and if continued seems to be in effect an entire
> disfranchisement of every civil right. For what one civil right is
> worth a rush after a man's property is subject to be taken from
> him at pleasure without his consent? If a man is not his own
> assessor in person, or by deputy, his liberty is gone, for he is
> wholly at the mercy of others.

What was the three-penny tax on tea or the paltry tax on paper and sugar to which our Revolutionary fathers were subjected, when compared with the taxation of the women of this republic? And again, to show that disfranchisement was precisely the slavery of which the fathers complained, allow me to cite Benjamin Franklin, who in those olden times was admitted to be good authority, not merely in domestic but also in political economy:

> Every man of the commonalty, except infants, insane persons
> and criminals, is, of common right and the law of God, a free-
> man and entitled to the free enjoyment of liberty. That liberty or
> freedom consists in having an actual share in the appointment of
> those who are to frame the laws, and who are to be the guardians

of every man's life, property and peace. For the all of one man is as dear to him as the all of another; and the poor man has an equal right, but more need, to have representatives in the legislature than the rich one. They who have no voice or vote in the electing of representatives do not enjoy liberty, but are absolutely enslaved to those who have votes and to their representatives; for to be enslaved is to have governors whom other men have set over us, and to be subject to laws made by the representatives of others, without having had representatives of our own to give consent in our behalf.

Suppose I read it with the feminine gender:

Women who have no voice or vote in the electing of representatives do not enjoy liberty, but are absolutely enslaved to men who have votes and to their representatives; for to be enslaved is to have governors whom men have set over us, and to be subject to the laws made by the representatives of men, without having representatives of our own to give consent in our behalf.

And yet one more authority, that of Thomas Paine, than whom not one of the Revolutionary patriots more ably vindicated the principles upon which our government is founded:

The right of voting for representatives is the primary right by which other rights are protected. To take away this right is to reduce man to a state of slavery; for slavery consists in being subject to the will of another; and he that has not a vote in the election of representatives is in this case. The proposal, therefore, to disfranchise any class of men is as criminal as the proposal to take away property.

Is anything further needed to prove woman's condition of servitude sufficient to entitle her to the guarantees of the Fifteenth Amendment? Is there a man who will not agree with me that to talk of freedom without the ballot is mockery to the women of this republic, precisely as New England's orator, Wendell Phillips, at the close of the late war declared it to be to the newly emancipated black man? I admit that, prior to the rebellion, by common consent, the right to enslave, as well as to disfranchise both native and foreign born persons, was conceded to the States. But the one grand principle settled by the war and the reconstruction legislation, is the supremacy of the national government to protect the citizens of the United States in their right to freedom and the elective franchise, against any and every interference on the part of the several States; and again and again have the American people asserted the triumph of this principle by their overwhelming majorities for Lincoln and Grant.

The one issue of the last two presidential elections was whether the Fourteenth and Fifteenth Amendments should be considered the irrevocable will of the people; and the decision was that they should be, and that it is not only the right, but the duty of the national government to protect all United States citizens in the full enjoyment and free exercise of their privileges and immunities against the attempt of any State to deny or abridge. In this conclusion Republicans and Democrats alike agree. Senator Frelinghuysen said: "The heresy of State rights has been completely buried in these amendments, and as amended, the Constitution confers not only National but State citizenship upon all persons born or naturalized within our limits."

The call for the National Republican Convention of 1872 said: "Equal suffrage has been engrafted on the National Constitution; the privileges and immunities of American citizenship have become a part of the organic law." The National Republican platform said: "Complete liberty and exact equality in the enjoyment of all civil, political and public rights, should be established and maintained throughout the Union by efficient and appropriate State and Federal legislation."

If that means anything it is that Congress should pass a law to protect women in their equal political rights, and that the States should enact laws making it the duty of inspectors of elections to receive the votes of women on precisely the same conditions as they do those of men.

Judge Stanley Matthews, a substantial Ohio Democrat, in his preliminary speech at the Cincinnati Liberal Convention, said most emphatically: "The constitutional amendments have established the political equality of all citizens before the law."

President Grant, in his message to Congress, March 30, 1870, on the adoption of the Fifteenth Amendment, said, "A measure which makes at once four millions of people voters, is indeed a measure of greater importance than any act of the kind from the foundation of the government to the present time."

How could *four* million negroes be made voters if two million out of the four were women?

The California Republican platform of 1872 said:

> Among the many practical and substantial triumphs of the prin-
> ciples achieved by the Republican party during the past twelve
> years, it enumerates with pride and pleasure the prohibiting
> of any State from abridging the privileges of any citizen of the
> republic, the declaring the civil and political equality of every
> citizen, and the establishing all these principles in the Federal
> Constitution, by amendments thereto, as the permanent law.

Benjamin F. Butler, in a recent letter to me, said: "I do not believe anybody in Congress doubts that the Constitution authorizes the right of women to vote, precisely as it authorizes trial by jury and many other like rights guaranteed to citizens."

It is upon this just interpretation of the United States Constitution that our National Woman Suffrage Association, which celebrates the twenty-fifth anniversary of the woman's rights movement next May in New York City, has based all its arguments and action since the passage of these amendments. We no longer petition legislature or Congress to give us the right to vote, but appeal to women everywhere to exercise their too long neglected "citizen's right." We appeal to the inspectors of election to receive the votes of all United States citizens, as it is their duty to do. We appeal to United States commissioners and marshals to arrest, as is their duty, the inspectors who reject the votes of United States citizens, and leave alone those who perform their duties and accept these votes. We ask the juries to return *verdicts* of "not guilty" in the cases of law-abiding United States citizens who cast their votes, and inspectors of election who receive and count them.

We ask the judges to render unprejudiced opinions of the law, and wherever there is room for doubt to give the benefit to the side of liberty and equal rights for women, remembering that, as Sumner says, "The true rule of interpretation under our National Constitution, especially since its amendments, is that anything *for* human rights is constitutional, everything *against* human rights unconstitutional." It is on this line that we propose to fight our battle for the ballot—peaceably but nevertheless persistently—until we achieve complete triumph and all United States citizens, men and women alike, are recognized as equals in the government.

Oliver Wendell Holmes, Jr.

Memorial Day Address

(Delivered in Keene, New Hampshire, May 30, 1884)

Not long ago I heard a young man ask why people still kept up Memorial Day, and it set me thinking of the answer. Not the answer that you and I should give to each other—not the expression of those feelings that, so long as you live, will make this day sacred to memories of love and grief and heroic youth—but an answer which should command the assent of those who do not share our memories, and in which we of the North and our brethren of the South could join in perfect accord.

So far as this last is concerned, to be sure, there is no trouble. The soldiers who were doing their best to kill one another felt less of personal hostility, I am very certain, than some who were not imperiled by their mutual endeavors. I have heard more than one of those who had been gallant and distinguished officers on the Confederate side say that they had had no such feeling. I know that I and those whom I knew best had not. We believed that it was most desirable that the North should win; we believed in the principle that the Union is indissoluable; we, or many of us at least, also believed that the conflict was inevitable, and that slavery had lasted long enough. But we equally believed that those who stood against us held just as sacred conviction that were the opposite of ours, and we respected them as every men with a heart must respect those who give all for their belief. The experience of battle soon taught its lesson even to those who came into the field more bitterly disposed. You could not stand up day after day in those indecisive contests where overwhelming victory was impossible because neither side would run as they ought when beaten, without getting at least something of the same brotherhood for the enemy that the north pole of a magnet has for the south—each working in an opposite sense to the other, but each unable to get along without the other. As it was then, it is now. The soldiers of the war need no explanations; they can join in commemorating a soldier's death with feelings not different in kind, whether he fell toward them or by their side.

But Memorial Day may and ought to have a meaning also for those who do not share our memories. When men have instinctively agreed to celebrate an anniversary, it will be found that there is some thought of feeling behind it which is too large to be dependent upon associations alone. The Fourth of July, for instance, has still its serious aspect, although we no longer should think of rejoicing like children that we have escaped from an outgrown control, although we have achieved not only our national but our moral independence and know it far too profoundly to make a talk about it, and although an Englishman can join in the celebration without a scruple. For, stripped of the temporary associations which gives rise to it, it is now the moment when by common consent we pause to become conscious of our national life and to rejoice in it, to recall what our country has done for each of us, and to ask ourselves what we can do for the country in return.

So to the indifferent inquirer who asks why Memorial Day is still kept up we may answer, It celebrates and solemnly reaffirms from year to year a national act of enthusiasm and faith. It embodies in the most impressive form our belief that to act with enthusiasm and faith is the condition of acting greatly. To fight out a war you must believe something and want something with all your might. So must you do to carry anything else to an end worth reaching. More than that, you must be willing to commit yourself to a course, perhaps a long and hard one, without being able to foresee exactly where you will come out. All that is required of you is that you should go somewhither as hard as ever you can. The rest belongs to fate. One may fall—at the beginning of the charge or at the top of the earthworks—but in no other way can he reach the rewards of victory.

When it was felt so deeply as it was on both sides that a man ought to take his part in the war unless some conscientious scruple or strong practical reason made it impossible, was that feeling simply the requirement of a local majority that their neighbors should agree with them? I think not: I think the feeling was right—in the South as in the North. I think that as life is action and passion, it is required of a man that he should share the passion and action of his time at peril of being judged not to have lived.

If this be so, the use of this day is obvious. It is true that I cannot argue a man into a desire. If he says to me, Why should I seek to know the secrets of philosophy? Why seek to decipher the hidden laws of creation that are graven upon the tablets of the rocks, or to unravel the history of civilization that is woven in the tissue of our jurisprudence, or to do any great work, either of speculation or of practical affairs? I cannot answer him; or, at least my answer is as little worth making for any effect it will have upon his wishes as if he asked, why I should eat this or drink that? You must begin by wanting to. But, although desire cannot be imparted by argument, it can be by contagion. Feeling begets feeling, and great feeling begets great feeling. We can hardly share the emotions that make this day to us the most sacred day of the year and embody them in ceremonial pomp without in some degree imparting them to those who come after us. I believe from the bottom of my heart that our memorial halls and statues and tablets, the tattered flags of our regiments gathered in the Statehouses, are worth more to our young men by way of chastening and inspiration than the monuments of another hundred years of peaceful life could be.

But even if I am wrong, even if those, who come after us are to forget all that we hold dear, and the future is to teach and kindle its children in ways as yet unrevealed, it is enough for us that to us this day is dear and sacred.

Accidents may call up the events of the war. You see a battery of guns go by at a trot, and for a moment you are back at White Oak Swamp, or Antietam or on the Jerusalem Road. You hear a few shots fired in the distance, and for an instant your heart stops as you say to yourself, The skirmishers are at it, and listen for the long roll of fire from the main line. You meet an old comrade after many years of absence; he recalls the moment when you were nearly surrounded by the enemy, and again there comes up to you that swift and cunning thinking on which once hung life and freedom—Shall I stand the best chance if I try the pistol or the saber on that man who means to stop me? Will he get his carbine free before I reach him, or can I kill him first? These and the thousand other events we have known are called up, I say, by accident, and, apart from accident, they lie forgotten.

But as surely as this day comes round we are in the presence of the dead. For one hour, twice a year at least—at the regimental dinner, where the ghosts sit at table more numerous than the living, and on this day when we decorate their graves—the dead come back and live with us.

I see them now, more than I can number, as once I saw them on this earth. They are the same bright figures, or their counterparts, that come also before your eyes; and when I speak of those who were my brothers the same words describe yours.

I see a fair-haired lad, a lieutenant, and a captain on whom life had begun somewhat to tell, but still young, sitting by the long mess-table in camp before the regiment left the State and wondering how many of those who gathered in our tent could hope to see the end of what was then beginning. For neither of them was that destiny reserved. I remember, as I awoke from my first long stupor in the hospital after the battle of Ball's Bluff, I heard the doctor say, "He was a beautiful boy," and I knew that one of those two speakers was no more. The other, after passing harmless through all the previous battles, went into Fredericksburg with strange premonition of the end and there met his fate.

I see another youthful lieutenant as I saw him in the Seven Days, when I looked down the line at Glendale. The officers were at the head of their companies.

The advance was beginning. We caught each other's eye and saluted. When next I looked, he was gone.

I see the brother of the last—the flame of genius and daring in his face—as he rode before us into the wood of Antietam, out of which came only dead and deadly wounded men. So, a little later, he rode to his death at the head of his cavalry in the Valley.

In the portraits of some of those who fell in the civil wars of England, Vandyke has fixed on canvas the type of those who stand before my memory. Young and gracious figures, somewhat remote and proud, but with a melancholy and sweet kindness. There is upon their faces the shadow of approaching fate and the glory of generous acceptance of it. I may say of them, as I once heard it said of two Frenchmen, relics of the *ancien régime,* "They were very gentle. They cared nothing for their lives." High breeding, romantic chivalry—we who have seen these men can never believe that the power of money or the enervation of pleasure has put an end to them. We know that life may still be lifted into poetry and lit with spiritual charm.

But the men, not less, perhaps even more, characteristic of New England, were the Puritans of our day—for the Puritan still lives in New England, thank God! and will live there so long as New England lives and keeps her old renown. New England is not dead yet. She still is mother of a race of conquerors. Stern men, little given to the expression of their feelings, sometimes careless of the graces, but fertile, tenacious, and knowing only duty. Each of you, as I do, thinks of a hundred such that he has known. I see one—grandson of a hard rider of the Revolution and bearer of his historic name—who was with us at Fair Oaks, and afterwards for five days and nights in front of the enemy the only sleep that he would take was what he could snatch sitting erect in his uniform and resting his back against a hut. He fell at Gettysburg.

His brother, a surgeon, who rode, as our surgeons so often did, wherever the troops would go, I saw kneeling in ministration to a wounded man just in rear of our line at Antietam, his horse's bridle round his arm—the next moment his ministrations were ended. His senior associate survived all the wounds and perils of the war, but, not yet through with duty as he understood it, fell in helping the helpless poor who were dying of cholera in a Western city.

I see another quiet figure of virtuous life and silent ways, not much heard of until our left was turned at Petersburg. He was in command of the regiment as he saw our comrades driven in. He threw back our left wing and the advancing tide of defeat was shattered against his iron wall. He saved an army corps from disaster, and then a round shot ended all for him.

There is one who on this day is always present to my mind. He entered the army at nineteen, a second lieutenant. In the Wilderness, already at the head of his regiment, he fell, using the moment that was left him of life to give all of his little fortune to his soldiers. I saw him in camp, on the march, in action. I crossed debatable land with him when we were rejoining the army together. I observed him in every kind of duty, and never in all the time I knew him did I see him fail to choose that alternative of conduct which was most disagreeable to himself. He was indeed a Puritan in all his virtues without the Puritan austerity; for, when duty was at an end, he who had been the master and leader became the chosen companion in every pleasure that a man might honestly enjoy. In action he was sublime. His few surviving companions will never forget the awful spectacle of his advance alone with his company in the streets of Fredericksburg. In less than sixty seconds he would become the focus of a hidden and annihilating fire from a semicircle of houses. His first platoon had vanished under it in an instant, ten men falling dead by his side. He had quietly turned back to where the other half of his company was waiting, had given the order, "Second Platoon, forward!" and was again moving on, in obedience to superior command, to certain and useless death, when the order he was obeying was countermanded. The end was distant only a few seconds; but if you had seen him with his indifferent carriage, and sword swinging from his finger like a cane, you would never have suspected that he was doing more than conducting a company drill on the camp parade ground. He was little more than a boy, but the grizzled corps commanders knew and admired him; and for us, who not only admired, but loved, his death seemed to end a portion of our life also.

There is one grave and commanding presence that you all would recognize, for his life has become a part of our common history. Who does not remember the leader of the assault at the mine of Petersburg? the solitary horseman in front of Port Hudson, whom a foeman worthy of him bade his soldiers spare, from love and admiration of such gallant bearing? Who does not still hear the echo of those eloquent lips after the war teaching reconciliation and peace? I may not do more than allude to his death, fit ending of his life. All that the world has a right to know has been told by a beloved friend in a book wherein friendship has found no need to exaggerate facts that speak for themselves. I knew him; and I may even say I knew him well; yet, until that book appeared, I had not known the governing motive of his soul. I had admired him as a hero. When I read, I learned to revere him as a saint. His strength was not in honor alone but in religion; and those who do not share his creed must see that it was on the wings of religious faith that he mounted above even valiant deeds into an empyrean of ideal life.

I have spoken of some of the men who were near to me among others very near and dear, not because their lives have become historic, but because their lives are the type of what every soldier has known and seen in his own company. In the great democracy of self-devotion private and general stand side by side. Unmarshaled save by their own deeds, the army of the dead sweep before us, "wearing their wounds like stars." It is not because the men I have mentioned were my friends that I have spoken of them, but, I repeat, because they are types. I speak of those whom I have seen. But you all have known such; you, too, remember!

It is not of the dead alone that we think on this day. There are those still living whose sex forbade them to offer their lives, but who gave instead their happiness. Which of us has not been lifted above himself by the sight of one of those lovely, lonely women, around whom the wand of sorrow has traced its excluding circle— et apart, even when surrounded by loving friends who would fain bring back joy to their lives? I think of one whom the poor of a great city know as their benefactress and friend. I think of one who has lived not less greatly in the midst of her children, to whom she has taught such lessons as may not be heard elsewhere from mortal lips. The story of these and her sisters we must pass in reverent silence. All that may be said has been said by one of their own sex:

> But when the days of golden dreams had perished,
> And even despair was powerless to destroy;
> Then did I learn how existence could be cherished,
> Strengthened, and fed without the aid of joy.
>
> Then did I check the tears of useless passion,
> Weaned my young soul from yearning after thine;
> Sternly denied its burning wish to hasten
> Down to that tomb already more than mine.

Comrades, some of the associations of this day are not only triumphant but joyful. Not all of those with whom we once stood shoulder to shoulder—not all of those whom we once loved and revered—are gone. On this day we still meet our companions in the freezing winter bivouacs and in those dreadful summer marches where every faculty of the soul seemed to depart one after another, leaving only a dumb animal power to set the teeth and to persist—a blind belief that somewhere and at last there was bread and water. On this day, at least, we still meet and rejoice in the closest tie which is possible between men—a tie which suffering has made indissoluble for better, for worse.

When we meet thus, when we do honor to the dead in terms that must sometimes embrace the living, we do not deceive ourselves. We attribute no special merit to a man for having served when all were serving. We know that if the armies of our war did anything worth remembering, the credit belongs not mainly to the individuals who did it, but to average human nature. We also know very well that we cannot live in associations with the past alone, and we admit that if we would be worthy of the past we must find new fields for action or thought and make for ourselves new careers.

But, nevertheless, the generation that carried on the war has been set apart by its experience. Through our great good fortune, in our youth our hearts were touched with fire. It was given to us to learn at the outset that life is a profound and passionate thing. While we are permitted to scorn nothing but indifference, and do not pretend to undervalue the worldly rewards of ambition, we have seen with our own eyes beyond and above the gold fields the snowy heights of honor, and it is for us to bear the report to those who come after us. But above all, we have learned that whether a man accepts from Fortune her spade, and will look downward and dig, or from Aspiration her axe and cord, and will scale the ice, the one and only success which it is his to command is to bring to his work a mighty heart.

Such hearts—ah me, how many!—were stilled twenty years ago; and to us who remain behind is left this day of memories. Every year—in the full tide of spring—at the height of the symphony of flowers and love and life—there comes a pause, and through the silence we hear the lonely pipe of death. Year after year lovers wandering under the apple boughs and through the clover and deep grass are surprised with sudden tears as they see black veiled figures stealing through the morning to a soldier's grave. Year after year the comrades of the dead follow with public honor, procession and commemorative flags and funeral march—honor and grief from us who stand almost alone, and have seen the best and noblest of our generation pass away.

But grief is not the end of all. I seem to hear the funeral march become a pæan. I see beyond the forest the moving banners of a hidden column. Our dead brothers still live for us, and bid us think of life, not death—of life to which in their youth they lent the passion and joy of the spring. As I listen, the great chorus of life and joy begins again, and amid the awful orchestra of seen and unseen powers and destinies of good and evil our trumpets sound once more a note of daring, hope, and will.

The Atlanta Cotton States and International Exposition Speech

(Delivered in Atlanta, Georgia, September 18, 1895)

One-third of the population of the South is of the Negro race. No enterprise seeking the material, civil, or moral welfare of this section can disregard this element of our population and reach the highest success. I but convey to you, Mr. President and Directors, the sentiment of the masses of my race when I say that in no way have the value and manhood of the American Negro been more fittingly and generously recognized than by the managers of this magnificent Exposition at every stage of its progress. It is a recognition that will do more to cement the friendship of the two races than any occurrence since the dawn of our freedom.

Not only this, but the opportunity here afforded will awaken among us a new era of industrial progress. Ignorant and inexperienced, it is not strange that in the first years of our new life we began at the top instead of at the bottom; that a seat in Congress or the state legislature was more sought than real estate or industrial skill; that the political convention or stump speaking had more attractions than starting a dairy farm or truck garden.

A ship lost at sea for many days suddenly sighted a friendly vessel. From the mast of the unfortunate vessel was seen a signal, "Water, water; we die of thirst!" The answer from the friendly vessel at once came back, "Cast down your bucket where you are." A second time the signal, "Water, water; send us water!" ran up from the distressed vessel, and was answered, "Cast down your bucket where you are." And a third and fourth signal for water was answered, "Cast down your bucket where you are." The captain of the distressed vessel, at last heeding the injunction, cast down his bucket, and it came up full of fresh, sparkling water from the mouth of the Amazon River. To those of my race who depend on bettering their condition in a foreign land or who underestimate the importance of cultivating friendly relations with the Southern white man, who is their next-door neighbor, I would say: "Cast down your bucket where you are"—cast it down in making friends in every manly way of the people of all races by whom we are surrounded.

Cast it down in agriculture, mechanics, in commerce, in domestic service, and in the professions. And in this connection it is well to bear in mind that whatever other sins the South may be called to bear, when it comes to business, pure and simple, it is in the South that the Negro is given a man's chance in the commercial world, and in nothing is this Exposition more eloquent than in emphasizing this chance. Our greatest danger is that in the great leap from slavery to freedom we may overlook the fact that the masses of us are to live by the productions of our hands, and fail to keep in mind that we shall prosper in proportion as we learn to dignify and glorify common labour, and put brains and skill into the common occupations of life; shall prosper in proportion as we learn to draw the line between the superficial and the substantial, the ornamental gew-gaws of life and the useful. No race can prosper till it learns that there is as much dignity in tilling a field as in writing a poem. It is at the bottom of life we must begin, and not at the top. Nor should we permit our grievances to overshadow our opportunities.

To those of the white race who look to the incoming of those of foreign birth and strange tongue and habits for the prosperity of the South, were I permitted I would repeat what I say to my own race, "Cast down your bucket where you are." Cast it down among the eight millions of Negroes whose habits you know, whose fidelity and love you have tested in days when to have proved treacherous meant the ruin of your firesides. Cast down your bucket among these people who have, without strikes and labour wars, tilled your fields, cleared your forests, builded your railroads and cities, and brought forth treasures from the bowels of the earth, and helped make possible this magnificent representation of the progress of the South. Casting down your bucket among my people, helping and encouraging them as you are doing on these grounds, and to education of head, hand, and heart, you will find that they will buy your surplus land, make blossom the waste places in your fields, and run your factories. While doing this, you can be sure in the future, as in the past, that you and your families will be surrounded by the most patient, faithful, law-abiding, and unresentful people that the world has seen. As we have proved our loyalty to you in the past, in nursing your children, watching by the sick-bed of your mothers and fathers, and often following them with tear-dimmed eyes to their graves, so in the future, in our humble way, we shall stand by you with a devotion that no foreigner can approach, ready to lay down our lives, if need be, in defense of yours, interlacing our industrial, com-mercial, civil, and religious life with yours in a way that shall make the interests of both races one. In all things that are purely social we can be as separate as the fingers, yet one as the hand in all things essential to mutual progress.

There is no defense or security for any of us except in the highest intelligence and development of all. If anywhere there are efforts tending to curtail the fullest growth of the Negro, let these efforts be turned into stimulating, encouraging, and making him the most useful and intelligent citizen. Effort or means so invested will pay a thousand per cent interest. These efforts will be twice blessed— "blessing him that gives and him that takes. "

There is no escape through law of man or God from the inevitable:—

> The laws of changeless justice bind
> Oppressor with oppressed;
> And close as sin and suffering joined
> We march to fate abreast.

Nearly sixteen millions of hands will aid you in pulling the load upward, or they will pull against you the load downward. We shall constitute one-third and more of the ignorance and crime of the South, or one-third its intelligence and progress; we shall contribute one-third to the business and industrial prosperity of the South, or we shall prove a veritable body of death, stagnating, depressing, retarding every effort to advance the body politic.

Gentlemen of the Exposition, as we present to you our humble effort at an exhibition of our progress, you must not expect overmuch. Starting thirty years ago with ownership here and there in a few quilts and pumpkins and chickens (gathered from miscellaneous sources), remember the path that has led from these to the inventions and production of agricultural implements, buggies, steam-engines, newspapers, books, statuary, carving, paintings, the management of drug stores and banks, has not been trodden without contact with thorns and thistles. While we take pride in what we exhibit as a result of our independent efforts, we do not for a moment forget that our part in this exhibition would fall far short of your expectations but for the constant help that has come to our educational life, not only from the Southern states, but especially from Northern philanthropists, who have made their gifts a constant stream of blessing and encouragement.

The wisest among my race understand that the agitation of questions of social equality is the extremest folly, and that progress in the enjoyment of all the privileges that will come to us must be the result of severe and constant struggle rather than of artificial forcing. No race that has anything to contribute to the markets of the world is long in any degree ostracized. It is important and right that all privileges of the law be ours, but it is vastly more important that we be prepared for the exercise of these privileges. The opportunity to earn a dollar in a factory just now is worth infinitely more than the opportunity to spend a dollar in an opera-house.

In conclusion, may I repeat that nothing in thirty years has given us more hope and encouragement, and drawn us so near to you of the white race, as this opportunity offered by the Exposition; and here bending, as it were, over the altar that represents the results of the struggles of your race and mine, both starting practically empty-handed three decades ago, I pledge that in your effort to work out the great and intricate problem which God has laid at the doors of the South, you shall have at all times the patient, sympathetic help of my race; only let this be constantly in mind, that, while from representations in these buildings of the product of field, of forest, of mine, of factory, letters, and art, much good will come, yet far above and beyond material benefits will be that higher good, that, let us pray God, will come, in a blotting out of sectional differences and racial animosities and suspicions, in a determination to administer absolute justice, in a willing obedience among all classes to the mandates of law. This, coupled with our material prosperity, will bring into our beloved South a new heaven and a new earth.

EUGENE V. DEBS

Liberty

(Delivered on Debs's release from Woodstock Jail,
Chicago, Illinois, November 22, 1895)

Manifestly the spirit of '76 still survives. The fires of liberty and noble aspirations are not yet extinguished. I greet you tonight as lovers of liberty and as despisers of despotism. I comprehend the significance of this demonstration and appreciate the honor that makes it possible for me to be your guest on such an occasion. The vindication and glorification of American principles of government, as proclaimed to the world in the Declaration of Independence, is the high purpose of this convocation.

Speaking for myself personally, I am not certain whether this is an occasion for rejoicing or lamentation. I confess to a serious doubt as to whether this day marks my deliverance from bondage to freedom or my doom from freedom to bondage. Certain it is, in the light of recent judicial proceedings, that I stand in your presence stripped of my constitutional rights as a freeman and shorn of the most sacred prerogatives of American citizenship, and what is true of myself is true of every other citizen who has the temerity to protest against corporation rule or question the absolute sway of the money power. It is not law nor the administration of law of which I complain. It is the flagrant violation of the constitution, the total abrogation of law and the usurpation of judicial and despotic power, by virtue of which my colleagues and myself were committed to jail, against which I enter my solemn protest; and any honest analysis of the proceedings must sustain the haggard truth of the indictment.

In a letter recently written by the venerable Judge Trumbull that eminent jurist says: "The doctrine announced by the supreme court in the Debs case, carried to its logical conclusion, places every citizen at the mercy of any prejudiced or malicious federal judge who may think proper to imprison him." This is the deliberate conclusion of one of the purest, ablest and most distinguished judges the Republic has produced. The authority of Judge Trumbull upon this question will not be impeached by anyone whose opinions are not deformed or debauched.

At this juncture I deem it proper to voice my demands for a trial by a jury of my peers. At the instigation of the railroad corporations centering here in Chicago I was indicted for conspiracy and I insist upon being tried as to my innocence or guilt. It will be remembered that the trial last winter terminated very abruptly on account of a sick juror. It was currently reported at the time that this was merely a pretext to abandon the trial and thus defeat the vindication of a favorable verdict, which seemed inevitable, and which would have been in painfully embarrassing contrast with the sentence previously pronounced by Judge Woods in substantially the same case. Whether this be true or not, I do not know. I do know, however, that I have been denied a trial, and here and now I demand a hearing of my case. I am charged with conspiracy to commit a crime, and if guilty I should go to the penitentiary. All I ask is a fair trial and no favor. If the counsel for the government, alias the railroads, have been correctly quoted in the press, the case against me is "not to be pressed," as they "do not wish to appear in the light of persecuting the defendants." I repel with scorn their professed mercy. Simple justice is the demand. I am not disposed to shrink from the fullest responsibility for my acts. I have had time for meditation and reflection and I have no hesitancy in declaring that under the same circumstances I would pursue precisely the same policy. So far as my acts are concerned, I have neither apology nor regrets.

Dismissing this branch of the subject, permit me to assure you that I am not here to bemoan my lot. In my vocabulary there are no wails of despondency or despair. However gloomy the future may appear to others, I have an abiding faith in the ultimate triumph of the right. My heart responds to the sentiments of the poet who says:

Swing back today, O prison gate,
    O winds, stream out the stripes and stars,
O men, once more in high debate
    Denounce injunction rule and czars.
By Freedom's travail pangs we swear
That slavery's chains we will not wear.

Ring joyously, O prison bell,
    O iron tongue, the truth proclaim;
O winds and lightnings, speed to tell
    That ours is not a czar's domain.
By all the oracles divine
We pledge defense of Freedom's shrine.

O freemen true! O sons of sires!
    O sons of men who dared to die!
O fan to life old Freedom's fires
    And light with glory Freedom's sky.
Then swear by God's eternal throne,
America shall be Freedom's home.

O workingmen! O Labor's hosts!
    O men of courage, heart and will;
O far and wide send Labor's toasts
    Till every heart feels Freedom's thrill,
And freemen's shouts like billows roar
O'er all the land from shore to shore.

Liberty is not a word of modern coinage. Liberty and slavery are primal words, like good and evil, right and wrong; they are opposites and coexistent.

There has been no liberty in the world since the gift, like sunshine and rain, came down from heaven, for the maintenance of which man has not been required to fight, and man's complete degradation is secured only when subjugation and slavery have sapped him of the last spark of the noble attributes of his nature and reduced him to the unresisting inertness of a clod.

The theme tonight is personal liberty; or giving it its full height, depth and breadth, American liberty, something that Americans have been accustomed to eulogize since the foundation of the Republic, and multiplied thousands of them continue in the habit to this day because they do not recognize the truth that in the imprisonment of one man in defiance of all constitutional guarantees, the liberties of all are invaded and placed in peril. In saying this, I conjecture I have struck the keynote of alarm that has convoked this vast audience.

For the first time in the records of all the ages, the inalienable rights of man, "life, liberty and the pursuit of happiness," were proclaimed July 4, 1776.

It was then that crowns, sceptres, thrones and the divine right of kings to rule sunk together and man expanded to glorious liberty and sovereignty. It was then that the genius of Liberty, speaking to all men in the commanding voice of Eternal Truth, bade them assert their heaven-decreed prerogatives and emancipate themselves from bondage. It was a proclamation countersigned by the Infinite—and man stood forth the coronated sovereign of the world, free as the tides that flow, free as the winds that blow, and on that primal morning when creation was complete, the morning stars and the sons of God, in anthem chorus, sang the song of Liberty.

It may be a fancy, but within the limitless boundaries of the imagination I can conceive of no other theme more appropriate to weave into the harmonies of Freedom. The Creator had surveyed his work and pronounced it good, but nothing can be called good in human affairs with liberty eliminated. As well talk of air without nitrogen, or water without oxygen, as of goodness without liberty.

It does not matter that the Creator has sown with stars the fields of ether and decked the earth with countless beauties for man's enjoyment. It does not matter that air and ocean teem with the wonders of innumerable forms of life to challenge man's admiration and investigation. It does not matter that nature spreads forth all her scenes of beauty and gladness and pours forth the melodies of her myriad-tongued voices for man's delectation. If liberty is ostracised and exiled, man is a slave, and the world rolls in space and whirls around the sun a gilded prison, a doomed dungeon, and though painted in all the enchanting hues that infinite art could command, it must still stand forth a blotch amidst the shining spheres of the sidereal heavens, and those who cull from the vocabularies of nations, living or dead, their flashing phrases with which to apostrophize Liberty, are engaged in perpetuating the most stupendous delusion the ages have known. Strike down liberty, no matter by what subtle and infernal art the deed is done, the spinal cord of humanity is sundered and the world is paralyzed by the indescribable crime.

Strike the fetters from the slave, give him liberty and he becomes an inhabitant of a new world. He looks abroad and beholds life and joy in all things around him. His soul expands beyond all boundaries. Emancipated by the genius of Liberty, he aspires to communion with all that is noble and beautiful, feels himself allied to all the higher order of intelligences, and walks abroad, redeemed from animalism, ignorance and superstition, a new being throbbing with glorious life.

What pen or tongue from primeval man to the loftiest intellect of the present generation has been able to fittingly anathematize the more than satanic crime of stealing the jewel of liberty from the crown of manhood and reducing the victim of the burglary to slavery or to prison, to gratify those monsters of iniquity who for some inscrutable reason are given breath to contaminate the atmosphere and poison every fountain and stream designed to bless the world!

It may be questioned if such interrogatories are worth the time required to state them, and I turn from their consideration to the actualities of my theme. As Americans, we have boasted of our liberties and continue to boast of them. They were once the nation's glory, and, if some have vanished, it may be well to remember that a remnant still remains. Out of prison, beyond the limits of Russian injunctions, out of reach of a deputy marshal's club, above the throttling clutch of corporations and the enslaving power of plutocracy, out of range of the government's machine guns and knowing the location of judicial traps and deadfalls, Americans may still indulge in the exaltation of liberty, though pursued through every lane and avenue of life by the baying hounds of usurped and unconstitutional power, glad if when night lets down her sable curtains, they are out of prison, though still the wage-slaves of a plutocracy which, were it in the celestial city, would wreck every avenue leading up to the throne of the Infinite by stealing the gold with which they are paved, and debauch Heaven's supreme court to obtain a decision that the command "thou shall not steal" is unconstitutional.

Liberty, be it known, is for those only who dare strike the blow to secure and retain the priceless boon. It has been written that the "love of liberty with life is given" and that life itself is an inferior gift; that with liberty exiled life is a continuous curse and that "an hour of liberty is worth an eternity of bondage." It would be an easy task to link together gilded periods extolling liberty until the mind, weary with delight, becomes oblivious of the fact that while dreaming of security, the blessings we magnified had, one by one, and little by little, disappeared, emphasizing the truth of the maxim that "eternal vigilance is the price of liberty."

Is it worth while to iterate that all men are created free and that slavery and bondage are in controvention of the Creator's decree and have their origin in man's depravity?

If liberty is a birthright which has been wrested from the weak by the strong, or has been placed in peril by those who were commissioned to guard it as Gheber priests watch the sacred fires they worship, what is to be done? Leaving all other nations, kindred and tongues out of the question, what is the duty of Americans? Above all, what is the duty of American workingmen whose liberties have been placed in peril? They are not hereditary bondsmen. Their fathers were free born—their sovereignty none denied and their children yet have the ballot. It has been called "a weapon that executes a free man's will as lighting does the will of God." It is a metaphor pregnant with life and truth. There is nothing in our government it can not remove or amend. It can make and unmake presidents and congresses and courts. It can abolish unjust laws and consign to eternal odium and oblivion unjust judges, strip from them their robes and gowns and send them forth unclean as lepers to bear the burden of merited obloquy as Cain with the mark of a murderer. It can sweep away trusts, syndicates, corporations, monopolies, and every other abnormal development of the money power designed to abridge the liberties of workingmen and enslave them by the degradation incident to poverty and enforced idleness, as cyclones scatter the leaves of the forest. The ballot can do all this and more. It can give our civilization its crowning glory—the co-operative commonwealth.

To the unified hosts of American workingmen fate has committed the charge of rescuing American liberties from the grasp of the vandal horde that have placed them in peril, by seizing the ballot and wielding it to regain the priceless heritage and to preserve and transmit it without scar or blemish to the generations yet to come.

> Snatch from the ashes of their sires
> The embers of their former fires,
> And he who in the strife expires
> Will add to theirs a name of fear
> That Tyranny shall quake to hear.

Standing before you tonight re-clothed in theory at least with the prerogatives of a free man, in the midst of free men, what more natural, what more in consonance with the proprieties of the occasion, than to refer to the incarceration of myself and associate officials of the American Railway Union in the county jail at Woodstock?

I have no ambition to avail myself of this occasion to be sensational, or to thrust my fellow prisoners and myself into prominence. My theme expands to proportions which obscure the victims of judicial tyranny, and yet, regardless of reluctance, it so happens by the decree of circumstances, that personal references are unavoidable. To wish it otherwise would be to deplore the organization of the American Railway Union and every effort that great organization has made to extend a helping hand to oppressed, robbed, suffering and starving men, women and children, the victims of corporate greed and rapacity. It would be to bewail every lofty attribute of human nature, lament the existence of the golden rule and wish the world were a jungle, inhabited by beasts of prey, that the seas were peopled with sharks and devil-fish and that between the earth and the stars only vultures held winged sway.

The American Railway Union was born with a sympathetic soul. Its ears were attuned to the melodies of mercy, to catch the whispered wailings of the oppressed. It had eyes to scan the fields of labor, a tongue to denounce the wrong, hands to grasp the oppressed and a will to lift them out of the sloughs of despondency to highlands of security and prosperity.

Here and now I challenge the records, and if in all the land the American Railway Union has an enemy, one or a million, I challenge them all to stand up before the labor world and give a reason why they have maligned and persecuted the order. I am not here to assert the infallibility of the organization or its officials, or to claim exemption from error. But I am here to declare to every friend of American toilers, regardless of banner, name or craft, that if the American Railway Union has erred, it has been on the side of sympathy, mercy and humanity—zeal in a great cause, devotion to the spirit of brotherhood which knows no artificial boundaries, whose zones are mapped by lines of truth as vivid as lightning, and whose horizon is measured only by the eye of faith in man's redemption from slavery.

I hold it to have been inconceivable that an organization of workingmen, animated by such inspirations and aspirations, should have become the target for the shafts of judicial and governmental malice.

But the fact that such was the case brings into haggard prominence a condition of affairs that appeals to all thoughtful men in the ranks of organized labor and all patriotic citizens, regardless of vocation, who note the subtle invasions of the liberties of the American people by the courts, sustained by an administration that is equally dead to the guarantees of the constitution.

It is in no spirit of laudation that I aver here tonight that it has fallen to the lot of the American Railway Union to arouse workingmen to a sense of the perils that environ their liberties.

In the great Pullman strike the American Railway Union challenged the power of corporations in a way that had not previously been done, and the analyzation of this fact serves to expand it to proportions that the most conservative men of the nation regard with alarm.

It must be borne in mind that the American Railway Union did not challenge the government. It threw down no gauntlet to courts or armies—it simply resisted the invasion of the rights of workingmen by corporations. It challenged and defied the power of corporations. Thrice armed with a just cause, the organization believed that justice would win for labor a notable victory, and the records proclaim that its confidence was not misplaced.

The corporations, left to their own resources of money, mendacity and malice, of thugs and ex-convicts, leeches and lawyers, would have been overwhelmed with defeat and the banners of organized labor would have floated triumphant in the breeze.

This the corporations saw and believed—hence the crowning act of infamy in which the federal courts and the federal armies participated, and which culminated in the defeat of labor.

Had this been all, the simple defeat of a labor organization, however disrupted and despoiled, this grand convocation of the lovers of liberty would never have been heard of. The robbed, idle and blacklisted victims of defeat would have suffered in silence in their darkened homes amidst the sobbings and wailings of wives and children. It would have been the oft repeated old, old story, heard along the track of progress and poverty for three-quarters of a century in the United States, where brave men, loyal to law and duty, have struck to better their condition or to resist degradation, and have gone down in defeat. But the defeat of the American Railway Union involved questions of law, constitution and government which, all things considered, are without a parallel in court and governmental proceedings under the constitution of the Republic. And it is this judicial and administrative usurpation of power to override the rights of states and strike down the liberties of the people that has conferred upon the incidents connected with the Pullman strike such commanding importance as to attract the attention of men of the highest attainments in constitutional law and of statesmen who, like Jefferson, view with alarm the processes by which the Republic is being wrecked and a despotism reared upon its ruins.

I have said that in the great battle of labor fought in 1894 between the American Railway Union and the Corporations banded together under the name of the "General Managers' Association," victory would have perched upon the standards of labor if the battle had been left to these contending forces—and this statement, which has been verified and established beyond truthful contradiction, suggests the inquiry, what other resources had the corporations aside from their money and the strength which their federation conferred?

In replying to the question, I am far within the limits of accepted facts when I say the country stood amazed as the corporations put forth their latent powers to debauch such departments of the government as were required to defeat labor in the greatest struggle for the right that was ever chronicled in the United States.

Defeated at every point, their plans all frustrated, out generated in tactics and strategy, while the hopes of labor were brightening and victory was in sight, the corporations, goaded to desperation, played their last card in the game of oppression by an appeal to the federal judiciary and to the federal administration. To this appeal the response came quick as lightning from a storm cloud. It was an exhibition of the debauching power of money which the country had never before beheld.

The people had long been familiar with such expressions as "money talks," "money rules," and they had seen the effects of its power in legislatures and in congress. They were conversant with Jay Gould's methods of gaining his legal victories by "buying a judge" in critical cases. They had tracked this money power, this behemoth beast of prey, into every corporate enterprise evolved by our modern civilization, as hunters track tigers in India jungles, but never before in the history of the country had they seen it grasp with paws and jaws the government of the United States and bend it to its will and make it a mere travesty of its pristine grandeur.

The people had seen this money power enter the church, touch the robed priest at the altar, blotch his soul, freeze his heart and make him a traitor to his consecrated vows and send him forth a Judas with a bag containing the price of his treason; or, if true to his conviction, ideas and ideals, to suffer the penalty of ostracism, to be blacklisted and to seek in vain for a sanctuary in which to expound Christ's doctrine of the brotherhood of man.

The people had seen this money power enter a university and grasp a professor and hurl him headlong into the street because every faculty of mind, redeemed by education and consecrated to truth, pointed out and illumined new pathways to the goal of human happiness and national glory.

The people had seen this money power practicing every art of duplicity, growing more arrogant and despotic as it robbed one and crushed another, building its fortifications of the bones of its victims, and its palaces out of the profits of its piracies, until purple and fine linen on the one side and rags upon the other side, defined conditions as mountain ranges and rivers define the boundaries of nations—palaces on the hills, with music and dancing and the luxuries of all climes, earth, air and sea-huts in the valley, dark and dismal, where the music is the dolorous "song of the shirt" and the luxuries rags and crusts.

These things had been seen by the people, but it was reserved for them in the progress of the Pullman strike to see this money power, by the fiat of corporations, grasp one by one the departments of the government and compel them to do its bidding as in old plantation days the master commanded the obedience of his chattel slaves.

The corporations first attacked the judicial department of the government, a department which, according to Thomas Jefferson, has menaced the integrity of the Republic from the beginning.

They did not attack the supreme bench. A chain is no stronger than its weakest link, and the corporations knew where that was and the amount of strain it would bear. How did they attack this weakling in the judicial chain?

I am aware that innuendoes, dark intimations of venality are not regarded as courageous forms of arraignment, and yet the judicial despotism which marked every step of the proceedings by which my official associates and myself were doomed to imprisonment, was marked by infamies, supported by falsehoods and perjuries as destitute of truth as are the Arctic regions of orange blossoms.

Two men quarrelled because one had killed the other's dog with an ax. The owner of the dog inquired, "when my dog attacked you, why did you not use some less deadly weapon?" The other replied, "why did not your dog come at me with the end that had no teeth in it?"

There is an adage which says, "fight the devil with fire." In this connection why may it not be intimated that a judge who pollutes his high office at the behest of the money power has the hinges of his knees lubricated with oil from the tank of the corporation that thrift may follow humiliating obedience to its commands?

If not this, I challenge the world to assign a reason why a judge, under the solemn obligation of an oath to obey the, constitution, should in a temple dedicated to justice, stab the Magna Charta of American liberty to death in the interest of corporations, that labor might be disrobed of its inalienable rights and those who advocated its claim to justice imprisoned as if they were felons?

You may subject such acts of despotism to the severest analysis, you may probe for the motive, you may dissect the brain and lay bare the quivering heart, and, when you have completed the task, you will find a tongue in every gash of your dissecting knife uttering the one word "pelf."

Once upon a time a corporation dog of good reputation was charged with killing sheep, though he had never been caught in the act. The corporation had always found him to be an obedient dog, willing to lick the hand of his master, and declared that he was a peaceable and law-abiding dog; but one day upon investigation the dog was found to have wool in his teeth and thenceforward, though the corporation stood manfully by him, he was believed to be a sheep-killing dog. The world has no means of knowing what methods corporations employ to obtain despotic decrees in their interest, but it is generally believed that if an examination could be made, there would be found wool in the teeth of the judge.

I do not profess to be a student of heredity, and yet I am persuaded that men inherit the peculiarities of the primal molecules from which they have been evolved. If the modern man, in spite of our civilizing influences, books, stage and rostrum, has more devil than divinity in his nature, where rests the blame?

Leaving the interrogatory unanswered, as it has been in all the past, it is only required to say that men with the ballot make a fatal mistake when they select mental and moral deformities and clothe them with despotic power. When such creatures are arrayed in the insignia of authority, right, justice and liberty are forever in peril.

What reasons exist today for rhetorical apostrophes to the constitution of the Republic? Those who are familiar by experience, or by reading, with the pathways of the storms on the ocean will recall recollections of ships with their sails rent and torn by the fury of the winds, rolling upon the yeasty billows and flying signals of distress. Clouds had for days obscured sun and stars and only the eye of omnipotence could tell whither the hulk was drifting—and today the constitution of our ship of state, the chart by which she had been steered for a century, has encountered a judicial tornado and only the gods of our fathers can tell whither she is drifting. True, Longfellow, inspired by the genius of hope, sang of the good old ship:

> We know what master laid thy keel,
> What workmen wrought thy ribs of steel,
>   Who made each mast and sail and rope,
> What anvils rang, what hammers beat,
> In what a forge and what a heat
>   Were shaped the anchors of thy hope.

But the poet wrote before the chart by which the good old ship sailed had been mutilated and torn and flung aside as a thing of contempt; before Shiras "flopped" and before corporations knew the price of judges, legislators and public officials as certainly as Armour knows the price of pork and mutton.

Longfellow wrote before men with heads as small as chipmunks and pockets as big as balloons were elevated to public office, and before the corporation ruled in courts and legislative halls as the fabled bull ruled in a china shop.

No afflatus, however divine, no genius, though saturated with the inspiring waters of Hippocrene, could now write in a spirit of patriotic fire of the old constitution, nor ever again until the people by the all pervading power of the ballot have repaired the old chart, closed the rents and obscured the judicial dagger holes made for the accommodation of millionaires and corporations, through which they drive their four-in-hands as if they were Cumberland gaps.

Here, this evening, I am inclined to indulge in eulogistic phrase of Liberty because once more I am permitted to mingle with my fellow-citizens outside of prison locks and bars.

Shakespeare said:

> Sweet are the uses of adversity,
> Which, like the toad, ugly and venomous,
> Wears yet a precious jewel in his head.

I know something of adversity, and with such philosophy as I could summon have extracted what little sweetness it contained. I know little of toads, except that of the genus judicial, and if they have a precious jewel in their heads or hearts it has not fallen to my lot to find it, though the corporations seem to have been more successful.

The immortal bard also wrote that

> This our life, exempt from public haunt,
> Finds tongues in trees, books in running brooks,
> Sermons in stones, and good in everything.

If to be behind prison bars is to be "exempt from public haunt," then for the past six months I may claim such exemption, with all the rapture to be found in listening to the tongues of trees, to the charming lessons taught by the books of the running brooks and to the profound sermons of the stones. There is not a tree on the Woodstock prison campus, or near by, to whose tongued melodies or maledictions I have not in fancy listened when liberty, despotism or justice was the theme.

The bard of Avon, the one Shakespeare of all the ages, was up to high-water mark of divine inspiration when he said there were those who could find tongues in trees, and never since trees were planted in the garden of Eden has the tongue of a tree voiced a sentiment hostile to liberty.

Thus, when in prison and exempt from judicial persecution, the tongues of trees as well as the tongues of friends taught me that sweets could be extracted from adversity.

Nor was I less fortunate when I permitted my fancy to see a book in a running brook as it laughed and sang and danced its way to the sea, and find that on every page was written a diviner song to liberty and love and sympathy than was ever sung by human voice.

And as for the stones in Woodstock prison, they were forever preaching sermons and their themes were all things good and evil among men.

In prison my life was a busy one, and the time for meditation and to give the imagination free rein was when the daily task was over and night's sable curtains enveloped the world in darkness, relieved only by the sentinel stars and the earth's silver satellite "walking in lovely beauty to her midnight throne."

It was at such times that the "Reverend Stones" preached their sermons, sometimes rising in grandeur to the Sermon on the Mount.

It might be a question in the minds of some if this occasion warrants the indulgence of the fancy. It will be remembered that Aesop taught the world by fables and Christ by parables, but my recollection is that the old "stone preachers" were as epigrammatic as an unabridged dictionary.

I remember one old divine who, one night, selected for his text George M. Pullman, and said: "George is a bad egg—handle him with care. Should you crack his shell the odor would depopulate Chicago in an hour." All said "Amen" and the services closed. Another old sermonizer who said he had been preaching since man was a molecule, declared he had of late years studied corporations, and that they were warts on the nose of our national industries,—that they were vultures whose beaks and claws were tearing and mangling the vitals of labor and transforming workingmen's homes into caves. Another old stone said he knew more about strikes than Carroll D. Wright, and that he was present when the slaves built the pyramids; that God Himself had taught His lightning, thunderbolts, winds, waves and earthquakes to strike, and that strikes would proceed, with bullets or ballots, until workingmen, no longer deceived and cajoled by their enemies, would unify, proclaims their sovereignty and walk the earth free men.

O, yes, Shakespeare was right when he said there were sermons in stones. I recall one rugged-visaged old stone preacher who claimed to have been a pavement bowlder in a street of heaven before the gold standard was adopted, and who discussed courts. He said they had been antagonizing the decrees of heaven since the day when Lucifer was cast into the bottomless pit. Referring to our Supreme Court he said it was a nest of rodents forever gnawing at the stately pillars supporting the temple of our liberties. I recall how his eyes, as he lifted their stony lids, flashed indignation like orbs of fire, and how his stony lips quivered as he uttered his maledictions of judicial treason to constitutional liberty.

But occasionally some old bald-headed ashler, with a heart beating responsive to every human joy or sorrow, would preach a sermon on love or sympathy or some other noble trait that in spite of heredity still lived even in the heart of stones. One old divine, having read some of the plutocratic papers on the Pullman strike and their anathemas of sympathy, when one workingman's heart, throbbing responsive to the divine law of love, prompted him to aid his brother in distress, discussed sympathy. He said sympathy was one of the perennial flowers of the Celestial City, and that angels had transplanted it in Eden for the happiness of Adam and Eve, and that the winds had scattered the seed throughout the earth. He said there was no humanity, no elevating, refining, ennobling influences in operation where there was no sympathy. Sympathy, he said, warmed in every ray of the sun, freshened in every breeze that scattered over the earth the perfume of flowers and glowed with the divine scintillation of the stars in all the expanse of the heavens.

Referring to the men and women of other labor organizations who had sympathized with the American Railway Union in its efforts to rescue Pullman's slaves from death by starvation, the old preacher placed a crown of jeweled eulogies

upon their heads and said that in all the mutations of life, in adversity or prosperity, in the vigor of youth or the infirmities of age, there would never come a
time to them when like the Peri grasping a penitent's tear as a passport to heaven,
they would not cherish as a valued souvenir of all their weary years that one act
of sympathy of the victims of the Pullman piracy, and that when presented at the
pearly gate of paradise, it would swing wide open and let them in amidst the joyous acclaims of angels.

From such reflections I turn to the practical lessons taught by this "Liberation
Day" demonstration. It means that American lovers of liberty are setting in operation forces to rescue their constitutional liberties from the grasp of monopoly and
its mercenary hirelings. It means that the people are aroused in view of impending
perils and that agitation, organization, and unification are to be the future battle
cries of men who will not part with their birthrights and, like Patrick Henry, will
have the courage to exclaim: "Give me liberty or give me death!"

I have borne with such composure as I could command the imprisonment
which deprived me of my liberty. Were I a criminal; were I guilty of crimes merit-
ing a prison cell; had I ever lifted my hand against the life or the liberty of my
fellowmen; had I ever sought to filch their good name, I would not be here. I
would have fled from the haunts of civilization and taken up my residence in
some cave where the voice of my kindred is never heard. But I am standing here
without a self-accusation of crime or criminal intent festering in my conscience,
in the sunlight once more, among my fellowmen, contributing as best I can to
make this "Liberation Day" from Woodstock prison a memorial day, realizing
that, as Lowell sang:

> He's true to God who's true to man; wherever wrong is done,
> To the humblest and the weakest, 'neath the all-beholding sun.
> That wrong is also done to us, and they are slaves most base,
> Whose love of right is for themselves and not for all their race.

WILLIAM JENNINGS BRYAN

"Cross of Gold" Speech

*(Delivered at the Democratic National Convention in
Chicago, Illinois, July 9, 1896)*

I would be presumptuous, indeed, to present myself against the distinguished gentleman to whom you have listened if this were but a measuring of ability, but this is not a contest among persons. The humblest citizen in all the land, when clad in the armor of a righteous cause, is stronger than all the whole hosts of error that they can bring. I come to speak to you in defense of a cause as holy as the cause of liberty— the cause of humanity. When this debate is concluded a motion will be made to lay upon the table the resolution offered in commendation of the administration and also the resolution in condemnation of the administration. I shall object to bringing this question down to a level of persons. The individual is but an atom; he is born, he acts, he dies, but principles are eternal, and this has been a contest of principle.

Never before in the history of this country has there been witnessed such a contest as that through which we have passed. Never before in the history of American politics has a great issue been fought out, as this issue has been, by the voters themselves.

On the 4th of March, 1895, a few Democrats, most of them members of Congress, issued an address to the Democrats of the nation asserting that the money question was the paramount issue of the hour, asserting also the right of a majority of the Democratic party to control the position of the party on this paramount issue; concluding with the request that all believers in free coinage of silver in the Democratic party should organize and take charge of and control the policy of the Democratic party. Three months later, at Memphis, an organization was perfected, and the silver Democrats went forth openly and boldly and courageously proclaiming their belief, and declaring that if successful they would crystallize in a platform the declaration which they had made; and then began the conflict with a zeal approaching the zeal which inspired the crusaders who followed Peter the Hermit. Our silver Democrats went forth from victory unto victory until they are assembled now not to discuss, not to debate, but to enter up the judgment rendered by the plain people of this country.

In this contest brother has been arrayed against brother and father against son. The warmest ties of love and acquaintance and association have been disregarded. Old leaders have been cast aside when they refused to give expression to the sentiments of those whom they would lead, and new leaders have sprung up to give direction to this cause of truth. Thus has the contest been waged, and we have assembled here under as binding and solemn instructions as were ever fastened upon the representatives of a people.

We do not come as individuals. Why, as individuals we might have been glad to compliment the gentleman from New York, but we knew that the people for whom we speak would never be willing to put him in a position where he could thwart the will of the Democratic party. I say it was not a question of persons; it was a question of principle, and it is not with gladness, my friends, that we find ourselves brought into conflict with those who are now arrayed on the other side. The gentleman who just preceded spoke of the old state of Massachusetts. Let me assure him that not one person in all this convention entertains the least hostility to the people of the state of Massachusetts.

But we stand here representing people who are the equals before the law of the largest citizens in the state of Massachusetts. When you come before us and tell us that we shall disturb your business interests, we reply that you have disturbed our business interests by your course. We say to you that you have made too limited in its application the definition of business man. The man who is employed for wages is as much a business man as his employer. The attorney in a country town is as much a business man as the corporation counsel in a great metropolis. The merchant at the crossroads store is as much a business man as the merchant of New York. The farmer who goes forth in the morning and toils all day, begins in the spring and toils all summer, and by the application of brain and muscle to the natural resources of this country creates wealth, is as much a business man as the man who goes upon the Board of Trade and bets upon the price of grain.

The miners who go a thousand feet into the earth or climb two thousand feet upon the cliffs and bring forth from their hiding places the precious metals to be poured in the channels of trade are as much business men as the few financial magnates who in a back room corner the money of the world.

We come to speak for this broader class of business men. Ah, my friends, we say not one word against those who live upon the Atlantic coast; but those hardy pioneers who have braved all the dangers of the wilderness, who have made the desert to blossom as the rose—those pioneers away out there, rearing their children near to nature's heart, where they can mingle their voices with the voices of the birds—out there where they have erected schoolhouses for the education of their young, and churches where they praise their Creator, and cemeteries where sleep the ashes of their dead—are as deserving of the consideration of this party as any people in this country.

It is for these that we speak. We do not come as aggressors. Our war is not a war of conquest. We are fighting in the defense of our homes, our families and posterity. We have petitioned, and our petitions have been scorned. We have entreated, and our entreaties have been disregarded. We have begged, and they have mocked, and our calamity came.

We beg no longer; we entreat no more; we petition no more. We defy them!

The gentleman from Wisconsin has said he fears a Robespierre. My friend, in this land of the free you need fear no tyrant who will spring up from among the people. What we need is an Andrew Jackson to stand as Jackson stood, against the encroachments of aggrandized wealth.

They tell us that this platform was made to catch votes. We reply to them that changing conditions make new issues; that the principles upon which rest democracy are as everlasting as the hills, but that they must be applied to new conditions as they arise. Conditions have arisen and we are attempting to meet those conditions. They tell us that the income tax ought not to be brought in here; that is a new idea. They criticise us for our criticisms of the Supreme Court of the United States. My friends, we have not criticised. We have simply called attention to what you know. If you want criticisms read the dissenting opinions of the court. That will give you criticisms.

They say we passed an unconstitutional law. I deny it. The income tax was not unconstitutional when it was passed. It was not unconstitutional when it went before the Supreme Court for the first time. It did not become unconstitutional until one judge changed his mind, and we cannot be expected to know when a judge will change his mind.

The income tax is a just law. It simply intends to put the burdens of government justly upon the backs of the people. I am in favor of an income tax.

When I find a man who is not willing to pay his share of the burden of the government which protects him I find a man who is unworthy to enjoy the blessings of a government like ours.

He says that we are opposing the national bank currency. It is true. If you will read what Thomas Benton said you will find that he said that in searching history he could find but one parallel to Andrew Jackson. That was Cicero, who destroyed the conspiracies of Cataline and saved Rome. He did for Rome what Jackson did when he destroyed the bank conspiracy and saved America. We say in our platform that we believe that the right to coin money and issue money is a function of government. We believe it. We believe it is a part of sovereignty, and can no more with safety be delegated to private individuals than we could afford to delegate to private individuals the power to make penal statutes or levy laws for taxation.

Mr. Jefferson, who was once regarded as good Democratic authority, seems to have a different opinion from the gentleman who has addressed us on the part of the minority. Those who are opposed to this proposition tell us that the issue of paper money is a function of the bank, and that the government ought to go out of the banking business. I stand with Jefferson, rather than with them, and tell them, as he did, that the issue of money is a function of the government and that the banks ought to go out of the government business.

They complain about the plank which declares against the life tenure in office. They have tried to strain it to mean that which it does not mean. What we oppose in that plank is the life tenure that is being built up in Washington, which excludes from participation in the benefits the humbler members of our society. I cannot dwell longer in my limited time. Let me call attention to two or three great things. The gentleman from New York says that he will propose an amendment providing that this change in our law shall not affect contracts already made. Let me remind you that there is no intention of affecting those contracts, which, according to the present laws, are made payable in gold. But if he means to say that we cannot change our monetary system without protecting those who have loaned money before the change was made I want to ask him where, in law or in morals, he can find authority for not protecting the debtors when the act of 1873 was passed, but now insists that we must protect the creditor. He says he also wants to amend this law and provide that if we fail to maintain a parity within a year that we will then suspend the coinage of silver. We reply that when we advocate a thing which we believe will be successful we are not compelled to raise a doubt as to our own sincerity by trying to show what we will do if we can. I ask him, if he would apply his logic to us, why he does not apply it to himself? He says that he wants this country to try to secure an international agreement. Why doesn't he tell us what he is going to do if they fail to secure an international agreement.

There is more reason for him to do that than for us to fail to maintain the parity. They have tried for thirty years—for thirty years—to secure an international agreement, and those are waiting for it most patiently who don't want it at all.

Now, my friends, let me come to the great paramount issue. If they ask us here why it is that we say more on the money question than we say upon the tariff question, I reply that if protection has slain its thousands the gold standard has slain its tens of thousands. If they ask us why we did not embody all these things in our platform which we believe, we reply to them that when we have restored the money of the Constitution all other necessary reforms will be possible, and that until that is done there is no reform that can be accomplished.

Why is it that within three months such a change has come over the sentiments of this country? Three months ago, when it was confidently asserted that those who believed in the gold standard would frame our platform and nominate our candidates, even the advocates of the gold standard did not think that we could elect a President; but they had good reason for the suspicion, because there is scarcely a state here to-day asking for the gold standard that is not within the absolute control of the Republican party. But note the change. Mr. McKinley was nominated at St. Louis upon a platform that declared for the maintenance of the gold standard until it should be changed into bimetallism by an international agreement. Mr. McKinley was the most popular man among the Republicans, and everybody three months ago in the Republican party prophesied his election. How is it to-day? Why, that man who used to boast that he looked like Napoleon—that man shudders to-day when he thinks that he was nominated on the anniversary of the battle of Waterloo.

Not only that, but as he listens he can hear with ever-increasing distinctness the sound of the waves as they beat upon the lonely shores of St. Helena.

Why this change? Ah, my friends, is not the change evident to any one who will look at the matter? It is no private character, however pure, no personal popularity, however great, that can protect from the avenging wrath of an indignant people the man who will either declare that he is in favor of fastening the gold standard upon this people, or who is willing to surrender the right of self-government and place legislative control in the hands of foreign potentates and powers.

We go forth confident that we shall win. Why? Because upon the paramount issue in this campaign there is not a spot of ground upon which the enemy will dare to challenge battle. Why, if they tell us that the gold standard is a good thing we point to their platform and tell them that their platform pledges the party to get rid of a gold standard and substitute bimetallism. If the gold standard is a good thing why try to get rid of it? If the gold standard—and I might call your attention to the fact that some of the very people who are in this convention to-day and who tell you that you ought to declare in favor of bimetallism, and thereby declare that the gold standard is wrong, and that the principle of bimetallism is better—these very people four months ago were open and avowed advocates of the gold standard and telling us that we could not legislate two metals together even with all the world.

I want to suggest this truth, that if the gold standard is a good thing we ought to declare in favor of its retention and not in favor of abandoning it; and if the gold standard is a bad thing why should we wait until some other nations are willing to help us to let go?

Here is the line of battle. We care not upon which issue they force the fight. We are prepared to meet them on either issue or on both. If they tell us that the gold standard is the standard of civilization we reply to them that this, the most enlightened of all the nations of the earth, has never declared for a gold standard, and both the parties this year are declaring against it. If the gold standard is the standard of civilization, why, my friends, should we not have it? So if they come to meet us on that we can present the history of our nation. More than that. We can tell them this, that they will search the pages of history in vain to find a single instance in which the common people of any land have ever declared themselves in favor of a gold standard. They can find where the holders of fixed investments have.

Mr. Carlisle said in 1878 that this was a struggle between the idle holders of idle capital and the struggling masses, who produce the wealth and pay the taxes of the country, and, my friends, it is simply a question that we shall decide, upon which side shall the Democratic party fight?

Upon the side of the idle holders of idle capital, or upon the side of the struggling masses? That is the question that the party must answer first, and then it must be answered by each individual here after. The sympathies of the Democratic party, as described by the platform, are on the side of the struggling masses, who have ever been the foundation of the Democratic party.

There are two ideas of government. There are those who believe that if you just legislate to make the well-to-do prosperous that their prosperity will leak through on those below. The Democratic idea has been that if you legislate to make the masses prosperous their prosperity will find its way up and through every class and rest upon it.

You come to us and tell us that the great cities are in favor of the gold standard. I tell you that the great cities rest upon these broad and fertile prairies. Burn down your cities and leave our farms and your cities will spring up again as if by magic. But destroy our farms and the grass will grow in the streets of every city in this country.

My friends, we shall declare that this nation is able to legislate for its own people on every question, without waiting for the aid or consent of any other nation on earth—and upon that issue we expect to carry every single state in this Union.

I shall not slander the fair state of Massachusetts nor the state of New York by saying that when its citizens are confronted with the proposition, Is this nation able to attend to its own business?—I will not slander either one by saying that the people of those states will declare our helpless impotency as a nation to attend to our own business. It is the issue of 1776 over again. Our ancestors, when but three millions, had the courage to declare their political independence of every other nation upon earth. Shall we, their descendants, when we have grown to seventy millions, declare that we are less independent than our forefathers? No, my friends, it will never be the judgment of this people. Therefore, we care not upon what lines the battle is fought. If they say bimetallism is good, but we cannot have it till some nation helps us, we reply that, instead of having a gold standard because England has, we shall restore bimetallism, and then let England have bimetallism because the United States has.

If they dare to come out and in the open defend the gold standard as a good thing, we shall fight them to the uttermost, having behind us the producing masses of this nation and the world. Having behind us the commercial interests and the laboring interests and all the toiling masses, we shall answer their demands for a gold standard by saying to them, you shall not press down upon the brow of labor this crown of thorns. You shall not crucify mankind upon a cross of gold.

Theodore Roosevelt

The Strenuous Life

(Delivered at the Hamilton Club in Chicago, Illinois, April 10, 1899)

In speaking to you, men of the greatest city of the West, men of the State which gave to the country Lincoln and Grant, men who preëminently and distinctly embody all that is most American in the American character, I wish to preach, not the doctrine of ignoble ease, but the doctrine of the strenuous life, the life of toil and effort, of labor and strife; to preach that highest form of success which comes, not to the man who desires mere easy peace, but to the man who does not shrink from danger, from hardship, or from bitter toil, and who out of these wins the splendid ultimate triumph.

A life of slothful ease, a life of that peace which springs merely from lack either of desire or of power to strive after great things, is as little worthy of a nation as of an individual. I ask only that what every self-respecting American demands from himself and from his sons shall be demanded of the American nation as a whole. Who among you would teach your boys that ease, that peace, is to be the first consideration in their eyes—to be the ultimate goal after which they strive? You men of Chicago have made this city great, you men of Illinois have done your share, and more than your share, in making America great, because you neither preach nor practice such a doctrine. You work yourselves, and you bring up your sons to work. If you are rich and are worth your salt, you will teach your sons that though they may have leisure, it is not to be spent in idleness; for wisely used leisure merely means that those who possess it, being free from the necessity of working for their livelihood, are all the more bound to carry on some kind of non-remunerative work in science, in letters, in art, in exploration, in historical research—work of the type we most need in this country, the successful carrying out of which reflects most honor upon the nation. We do not admire the man of timid peace. We admire the man who embodies victorious effort; the man who never wrongs his neighbor, who is prompt to help a friend, but who has those virile qualities necessary to win in the stern strife of actual life. It is hard to fail, but it is worse never to have tried to succeed. In this life we get nothing save by effort. Freedom from effort in the present merely means that there has been stored up effort in the past. A man can be freed from the necessity of work only by the fact that he or his fathers before him have worked to good purpose. If the freedom thus purchased is used aright, and the man still does actual work, though of a different kind, whether as a writer or a general, whether in the field of politics or in the field of exploration and adventure, he shows he deserves his good fortune. But if he treats this period of freedom from the need of actual labor as a period, not of preparation, but of mere enjoyment, even though perhaps not of vicious enjoyment, he shows that he is simply a cumberer of the earth's surface, and he surely unfits himself to hold his own with his fellows if the need to do so should again arise. A mere life of ease is not in the end a very satisfactory life, and, above all, it is a life which ultimately unfits those who follow it for serious work in the world.

In the last analysis a healthy state can exist only when the men and women who make it up lead clean, vigorous, healthy lives; when the children are so trained that they shall endeavor, not to shirk difficulties, but to overcome them; not to seek ease, but to know how to wrest triumph from toil and risk. The man must be glad to do a man's work, to dare and endure and to labor; to keep himself, and to keep those dependent upon him. The woman must be the housewife, the helpmeet of the homemaker, the wise and fearless mother of many healthy children. In one of Daudet's powerful and melancholy books he speaks of "the fear of maternity, the haunting terror of the young wife of the present day." When such words can be truthfully written of a nation, that nation is rotten to the heart's core. When men fear work or fear righteous war, when women fear motherhood, they tremble on the brink of doom; and well it is that they should vanish from the earth, where they are fit subjects for the scorn of all men and women who are themselves strong and brave and high-minded.

As it is with the individual, so it is with the nation. It is a base untruth to say that happy is the nation that has no history. Thrice happy is the nation that has a glorious history. Far better it is to dare mighty things, to win glorious triumphs, even though checkered by failure, than to take rank with those poor spirits who neither enjoy much nor suffer much, because they live in the gray twilight that knows not victory nor defeat. If in 1861 the men who loved the Union had believed that peace was the end of all things, and war and strife the worst of all things, and had acted up to their belief, we would have saved hundreds of thousands of lives, we would have saved hundreds of millions of dollars. Moreover, besides saving all the blood and treasure we then lavished, we would have prevented the heartbreak of many women, the dissolution of many homes, and we would have spared the country those months of gloom and shame when it seemed as if our armies marched only to defeat. We could have avoided all this suffering simply by shrinking from strife. And if we had thus avoided it, we would have shown that we were weaklings, and that we were unfit to stand among the great nations of the earth. Thank God for the iron in the blood of our fathers, the men who upheld the wisdom of Lincoln, and bore sword or rifle in the armies of Grant! Let us, the children of the men who proved themselves equal to the mighty days, let us, the children of the men who carried the great Civil War to a triumphant conclusion, praise the God of our fathers that the ignoble counsels of peace were rejected; that the suffering and loss, the blackness of sorrow and despair, were unflinchingly faced, and the years of strife endured; for in the end the slave was freed, the Union restored, and the mighty American republic placed once more as a helmeted queen among nations.

We of this generation do not have to face a task such as that our fathers faced, but we have our tasks, and woe to us if we fail to perform them! We cannot, if we would, play the part of China, and be content to rot by inches in ignoble ease within our borders, taking no interest in what goes on beyond them, sunk in a scrambling commercialism; heedless of the higher life, the life of aspiration, of toil and risk, busying ourselves only with the wants of our bodies for the day, until suddenly we should find, beyond a shadow of question, what China has already found, that in this world the nation that has trained itself to a career of unwarlike and isolated ease is bound, in the end, to go down before other nations which have not lost the manly and adventurous qualities. If we are to be a really great people, we must strive in good faith to play a great part in the world. We cannot avoid meeting great issues. All that we can determine for ourselves is whether we shall meet them well or ill. In 1898 we could not help being brought face to face with the problem of war with Spain. All we could decide was whether we should shrink like cowards from the contest, or enter into it as beseemed a brave and high-spirited people; and, once in, whether failure or success should crown our banners. So it is now. We cannot avoid the responsibilities that confront us in Hawaii, Cuba, Porto Rico, and the Philippines. All we can decide is whether we shall meet them in a way that will redound to the national credit, or whether we shall make of our dealings with these new problems a dark and shameful page in our history. To refuse to deal with them at all merely amounts to dealing with them badly. We have a given problem to solve. If we undertake the solution, there is, of course, always danger that we may not solve it aright; but to refuse to undertake the solution simply renders it certain that we cannot possibly solve it aright. The timid man, the lazy man, the man who distrusts his country, the over-civilized man, who has lost the great fighting, masterful virtues, the ignorant man, and the man of dull mind, whose soul is incapable of feeling the mighty lift that thrills "stern men with empires in their brains"—all these, of course, shrink from seeing the nation undertake its new duties; shrink from seeing us build a navy and an army adequate to our needs; shrink from seeing us do our share of the world's work, by bringing order out of chaos in the great, fair tropic islands from which the valor of our soldiers and sailors has driven the Spanish flag. These are the men who fear the strenuous life, who fear the only national life which is really worth leading. They believe in that cloistered life which saps the hardy virtues in a nation, as it saps them in the individual; or else they are wedded to that base spirit of gain and greed which recognizes in commercialism the be-all and end-all of national life, instead of realizing that, though an indispensable element, it is, after all, but one of the many elements that go to make up true national greatness. No country can long endure if its foundations are not laid deep in the material prosperity which comes from thrift, from business energy and enterprise, from hard, unsparing effort in the fields of industrial activity; but neither was any nation ever yet truly great if it relied upon material prosperity alone. All honor must be paid to the architects of our material prosperity, to the great captains of industry who have built our factories and our railroads, to the strong men who toil for wealth with brain or hand; for great is the debt of the nation to these and their kind. But our debt is yet greater to the men whose highest type is to be found in a statesman like Lincoln, a soldier like Grant. They showed by their lives that they recognized the law of work, the law of strife; they toiled to win a competence for themselves and those dependent upon them; but they recognized that there were yet other and even loftier duties—duties to the nation and duties to the race.

We cannot sit huddled within our own borders and avow ourselves merely an assemblage of well-to-do hucksters who care nothing for what happens beyond. Such a policy would defeat even its own end; for as the nations grow to have ever wider and wider interests, and are brought into closer and closer contact, if we are to hold our own in the struggle for naval and commercial supremacy, we must build up our powers without our own borders. We must build the isthmian canal, and we must grasp the points of vantage which will enable us to have our say in deciding the destiny of the oceans of the East and the West.

So much for the commercial side. From the standpoint of international honor the argument is even stronger. The guns that thundered off Manila and Santiago left us echoes of glory, but they also left us a legacy of duty. If we drove out a medieval tyranny only to make room for savage anarchy, we had better not have begun the task at all. It is worse than idle to say that we have no duty to perform, and can leave to their fates the islands we have conquered. Such a course would be the course of infamy. It would be followed at once by utter chaos in the wretched islands themselves. Some stronger, manlier power would have to step in and do the work, and we would have shown ourselves weaklings, unable to carry to successful completion the labors that great and high-spirited nations are eager to undertake.

The work must be done; we cannot escape our responsibility; and if we are worth our salt, we shall be glad of the chance to do the work—glad of the chance to show ourselves equal to one of the great tasks set modern civilization. But let us not deceive ourselves as to the importance of the task. Let us not be misled by vainglory into underestimating the strain it will put on our powers. Above all, let us, as we value our own self-respect, face the responsibilities with proper seriousness, courage, and high resolve. We must demand the highest order of integrity and ability in our public men who are to grapple with these new problems. We must hold to a rigid accountability those public servants who show unfaithfulness to the interests of the nation or inability to rise to the high level of the new demands upon our strength and our resources.

Of course we must remember not to judge any public servant by any one act, and especially should we beware of attacking the men who are merely the occasions and not the causes of disaster. Let me illustrate what I mean by the army and the navy. If twenty years ago we had gone to war, we should have found the navy as absolutely unprepared as the army. At that time our ships could not have encountered with success the fleets of Spain any more than nowadays we can put untrained soldiers, no matter how brave, who are armed with archaic black-powder weapons, against well-drilled regulars armed with the highest type of modern repeating rifle. But in the early eighties the attention of the nation became directed to our naval needs. Congress most wisely made a series of appropriations to build up a new navy, and under a succession of able and patriotic secretaries, of both political parties, the navy was gradually built up, until its material became equal to its splendid personnel, with the result that in the summer of 1898 it leaped to its proper place as one of the most brilliant and formidable fighting navies in the entire world. We rightly pay all honor to the men controlling the navy at the time it won these great deeds, honor to Secretary Long and Admiral Dewey, to the captains who handled the ships in action, to the daring lieutenants who braved death in the smaller craft, and to the heads of bureaus at Washington who saw that the ships were so commanded, so armed, so equipped, so well engined, as to insure the best results. But let us also keep ever in mind that all of this would not have availed if it had not been for the wisdom of the men who during the preceding fifteen years had built up the navy. Keep in mind the secretaries of the navy during those years; keep in mind the senators and congressmen who by their votes gave the money necessary to build and to armor the ships, to construct the great guns, and to train the crews; remember also those who actually did build the ships, the armor, and the guns; and remember the admirals and captains who handled battle-ship, cruiser, and torpedo-boat on the high seas, alone and in squadrons, developing the seamanship, the gunnery, and the power of acting together, which their successors utilized so gloriously at Manila and off Santiago. And, gentlemen, remember the converse, too. Remember that justice has two sides. Be just to those who built up the navy, and, for the sake of the future of the country, keep in mind those who opposed its building up. Read the "Congressional Record." Find out the senators and congressmen who opposed the grants for building the new ships; who opposed the purchase of armor without which the ships were worthless, who opposed any adequate maintenance for the Navy Department, and strove to cut down the number of men necessary to man our fleets. The men who did these things were one and all working to bring disaster on the country. They have no share in the glory of Manila, in the honor of Santiago. They have no cause to feel proud of the valor of our sea-captains, of the renown of our flag. Their motives may or may not have been good, but their acts were heavily fraught with evil. They did ill for the national honor, and we won in spite of their sinister opposition.

Now, apply all this to our public men of to-day. Our army has never been built up as it should be built up. I shall not discuss with an audience like this the puerile suggestion that a nation of seventy millions of freemen is in danger of losing its liberties from the existence of an army of one hundred thousand men, three fourths of whom will be employed in certain foreign islands, in certain coast fortresses, and on Indian reservations. No man of good sense and stout heart can take such a proposition seriously. If we are such weaklings as the proposition implies, then we are unworthy of freedom in any event. To no body of men in the United States is the country so much indebted as to the splendid officers and enlisted men of the regular army and navy. There is no body from which the country has less to fear, and none of which it should be prouder, none which it should be more anxious to upbuild.

Our army needs complete reorganization,—not merely enlarging,—and the reorganization can only come as the result of legislation. A proper general staff should be established, and the positions of ordnance, commissary, and quartermaster officers should be filled by detail from the line. Above all, the army must be given the chance to exercise in large bodies. Never again should we see, as we saw in the Spanish war, major-generals in command of divisions who had never before commanded three companies together in the field. Yet, incredible to relate, Congress has shown a queer inability to learn some of the lessons of the war. There were large bodies of men in both branches who opposed the declaration of war, who opposed the ratification of peace, who opposed the upbuilding of the army, and who even opposed the purchase of armor at a reasonable price for the battle-ships and cruisers, thereby putting an absolute stop to the building of any new fighting-ships for the navy. If, during the years to come, any disaster should befall our arms, afloat or ashore, and thereby any shame come to the United States, remember that the blame will lie upon the men whose names appear upon the roll-calls of Congress on the wrong side of these great questions. On them will lie the burden of any loss of our soldiers and sailors, of any dishonor to the flag; and upon you and the people of this country will lie the blame if you do not repudi-ate, in no unmistakable way, what these men have done. The blame will not rest upon the untrained commander of untried troops, upon the civil officers of a department the organization of which has been left utterly inadequate, or upon the admiral with an insufficient number of ships; but upon the public men who have so lamentably failed in forethought as to refuse to remedy these evils long in advance, and upon the nation that stands behind those public men.

So, at the present hour, no small share of the responsibility for the blood shed in the Philippines, the blood of our brothers, and the blood of their wild and ignorant foes, lies at the thresholds of those who so long delayed the adoption of the treaty of peace, and of those who by their worse than foolish words deliberately invited a savage people to plunge into a war fraught with sure disaster for them— a war, too, in which our own brave men who follow the flag must pay with their blood for the silly, mock humanitarianism of the prattlers who sit at home in peace.

The army and the navy are the sword and the shield which this nation must carry if she is to do her duty among the nations of the earth—if she is not to stand merely as the China of the western hemisphere. Our proper conduct toward the tropic islands we have wrested from Spain is merely the form which our duty has taken at the moment. Of course we are bound to handle the affairs of our own household well. We must see that there is civic honesty, civic cleanliness, civic good sense in our home administration of city, State, and nation. We must strive for honesty in office, for honesty toward the creditors of the nation and of the individual; for the widest freedom of individual initiative where possible, and for the wisest control of individual initiative where it is hostile to the welfare of the many. But because we set our own household in order we are not thereby excused from playing our part in the great affairs of the world. A man's first duty is to his own home, but he is not thereby excused from doing his duty to the State; for if he fails in this second duty it is under the penalty of ceasing to be a freeman. In the same way, while a nation's first duty is within its own borders, it is not thereby absolved from facing its duties in the world as a whole; and if it refuses to do so, it merely forfeits its right to struggle for a place among the peoples that shape the destiny of mankind.

In the West Indies and the Philippines alike we are confronted by most difficult problems. It is cowardly to shrink from solving them in the proper way; for solved they must be, if not by us, then by some stronger and more manful race. If we are too weak, too selfish, or too foolish to solve them, some bolder and abler people must undertake the solution. Personally, I am far too firm a believer in the greatness of my country and the power of my countrymen to admit for one moment that we shall ever be driven to the ignoble alternative.

The problems are different for the different islands. Porto Rico is not large enough to stand alone. We must govern it wisely and well, primarily in the interest of its own people. Cuba is, in my judgment, entitled ultimately to settle for itself whether it shall be an independent state or an integral portion of the mightiest of republics. But until order and stable liberty are secured, we must remain in the island to insure them, and infinite tact, judgment, moderation, and courage must be shown by our military and civil representatives in keeping the island pacified, in relentlessly stamping out brigandage, in protecting all alike, and yet in showing proper recognition to the men who have fought for Cuban liberty. The Philippines offer a yet graver problem. Their population includes half-caste and native Christians, warlike Moslems, and wild pagans. Many of their people are utterly unfit for self-government, and show no signs of becoming fit. Others may in time become fit but at present can only take part in self-government under a wise supervision, at once firm and beneficent. We have driven Spanish tyranny from the islands. If we now let it be replaced by savage anarchy, our work has been for harm and not for good. I have scant patience with those who fear to undertake the task of governing the Philippines, and who openly avow that they do fear to undertake it, or that they shrink from it because of the expense and trouble; but I have even scanter patience with those who make a pretense of humanitarianism to hide and cover their timidity and who cant about "liberty" and the "consent of the governed," in order to excuse themselves for their unwillingness to play the part of men. Their doctrines, if carried out, would make it incumbent upon us to leave the Apaches of Arizona to work out their own salvation, and to decline to interfere in a single Indian reservation. Their doctrines condemn your forefathers and mine for ever having settled in these United States.

England's rule in India and Egypt has been of great benefit to England, for it has trained up generations of men accustomed to look at the larger and loftier side of public life. It has been of even greater benefit to India and Egypt. And finally, and most of all, it has advanced the cause of civilization. So, if we do our duty aright in the Philippines, we will add to that national renown which is the highest and finest part of national life, will greatly benefit the people of the Philippine Islands, and, above all, we will play our part well in the great work of uplifting mankind. But to do this work, keep ever in mind that we must show in a very high degree the qualities of courage, of honesty, and of good judgment. Resistance must be stamped out. The first and all-important work to be done is to establish the supremacy of our flag. We must put down armed resistance before we can accomplish anything else, and there should be no parleying, no faltering, in dealing with our foe. As for those in our own country who encourage the foe, we can afford contemptuously to disregard them; but it must be remembered that their utterances are not saved from being treasonable merely by the fact that they are despicable.

When once we have put down armed resistance, when once our rule is acknowledged, then an even more difficult task will begin, for then we must see to it that the islands are administered with absolute honesty and with good judgment. If we let the public service of the islands be turned into the prey of the spoils politician, we shall have begun to tread the path which Spain trod to her own destruction. We must send out there only good and able men, chosen for their fitness, and not because of their partisan service, and those men must not only administer impartial justice to the natives and serve their own government with honesty and fidelity, but must show the utmost tact and firmness, remembering that, with such people as those with whom we are to deal, weakness is the greatest of crimes, and that next to weakness comes lack of consideration for their principles and prejudices.

I preach to you, then, my countrymen, that our country calls not for the life of ease but for the life of strenuous endeavor. The twentieth century looms before us big with the fate of many nations. If we stand idly by, if we seek merely swollen, slothful ease and ignoble peace, if we shrink from the hard contests where men must win at hazard of their lives and at the risk of all they hold dear, then the bolder and stronger peoples will pass us by, and will win for themselves the domination of the world. Let us therefore boldly face the life of strife, resolute to do our duty well and manfully; resolute to uphold righteousness by deed and by word; resolute to be both honest and brave, to serve high ideals, yet to use practical methods. Above all, let us shrink from no strife, moral or physical, within or without the nation, provided we are certain that the strife is justified, for it is only through strife, through hard and dangerous endeavor, that we shall ultimately win the goal of true national greatness.

Theodore Roosevelt

National Duties

(Delivered at the Minnesota State Fair in St. Paul, September 2, 1901)

In his admirable series of studies of twentieth-century problems, Dr. Lyman Abbott has pointed out that we are a nation of pioneers; that the first colonists to our shores were pioneers, and that pioneers selected out from among the descendants of these early pioneers, mingled with others selected afresh from the Old World, pushed westward into the wilderness and laid the foundations for new commonwealths. They were men of hope and expectation, of enterprise and energy; for the men of dull content or more dull despair had no part in the great movement into and across the New World. Our country has been populated by pioneers, and therefore it has in it more energy, more enterprise, more expansive power than any other in the wide world.

You whom I am now addressing stand for the most part but one generation removed from these pioneers. You are typical Americans, for you have done the great, the characteristic, the typical work of our American life. In making homes and carving out careers for yourselves and your children, you have built up this State. Throughout our history the success of the home-maker has been but another name for the upbuilding of the nation. The men who with ax in the forests and pick in the mountains and plow on the prairies pushed to completion the dominion of our people over the American wilderness have given the definite shape to our nation. They have shown the qualities of daring, endurance, and far-sightedness, of eager desire for victory and stubborn refusal to accept defeat, which go to make up the essential manliness of the American character. Above all, they have recognized in practical form the fundamental law of success in American life—the law of worthy work, the law of high, resolute endeavor. We have but little room among our people for the timid, the irresolute, and the idle; and it is no less true that there is scant room in the world at large for the nation with mighty thews that dares not to be great.

Surely in speaking to the sons of the men who actually did the rough and hard and infinitely glorious work of making the great Northwest what it now is, I need hardly insist upon the righteousness of this doctrine. In your own vigorous lives you show by every act how scant is your patience with those who do not see in the life of effort the life supremely worth living. Sometimes we hear those who do not work spoken of with envy. Surely the willfully idle need arouse in the breast of a healthy man no emotion stronger than that of contempt—at the outside no emotion stronger than angry contempt. The feeling of envy would have in it an admission of inferiority on our part, to which the men who know not the sterner joys of life are not entitled. Poverty is a bitter thing; but it is not as bitter as the existence of restless vacuity and physical, moral, and intellectual flabbiness, to which those doom themselves who elect to spend all their years in that vainest of all vain pursuits—the pursuit of mere pleasure as a sufficient end in itself. The wilfully idle man, like the wilfully barren woman, has no place in a sane, healthy, and vigorous community. Moreover, the gross and hideous selfishness for which each stands defeats even its own miserable aims. Exactly as infinitely the happiest woman is she who has borne and brought up many healthy children, so infinitely the happiest man is he who has toiled hard and successfully in his life-work. The work may be done in a thousand different ways— with the brain or the hands, in the study, the field, or the workshop—if it is honest work, honestly done and well worth doing, that is all we have a right to ask. Every father and mother here, if they are wise, will bring up their children not to shirk difficulties, but to meet them and overcome them; not to strive after a life of ignoble ease, but to strive to do their duty, first to themselves and their families, and then to the whole State; and this duty must inevitably take the shape of work in some form or other. You, the sons of the pioneers, if you are true to your ancestry, must make your lives as worthy as they made theirs. They sought for true success, and therefore they did not seek ease. They knew that success comes only to those who lead the life of endeavor.

It seems to me that the simple acceptance of this fundamental fact of American life, this acknowledgment that the law of work is the fundamental law of our being, will help us to start aright in facing not a few of the problems that confront us from without and from within. As regards internal affairs, it should teach us the prime need of remembering that, after all has been said and done, the chief factor in any man's success or failure must be his own character—that is, the sum of his common sense, his courage, his virile energy and capacity. Nothing can take the place of this individual factor.

I do not for a moment mean that much cannot be done to supplement it. Besides each one of us working individually, all of us have got to work together. We cannot possibly do our best work as a nation unless all of us know how to act in combination as well as how to act each individually for himself. The acting in combination can take many forms, but of course its most effective form must be when it comes in the shape of law—that is, of action by the community as a whole through the lawmaking body.

But it is not possible ever to insure prosperity merely by law. Something for good can be done by law, and a bad law can do an infinity of mischief; but, after all, the best law can only prevent wrong and injustice, and give to the thrifty, the far-seeing, and the hard-working a chance to exercise to best advantage their special and peculiar abilities. No hard-and-fast rule can be laid down as to where our legislation shall stop in interfering between man and man, between interest and interest. All that can be said is that it is highly undesirable, on the one hand, to weaken individual initiative, and, on the other hand, that in a constantly increasing number of cases we shall find it necessary in the future to shackle cunning as in the past we have shackled force. It is not only highly desirable but necessary that there should be legislation which shall carefully shield the interests of wage-workers, and which shall discriminate in favor of the honest and humane employer by removing the disadvantage under which he stands when compared with unscrupulous competitors who have no conscience and will do right only under fear of punishment.

Nor can legislation stop only with what are termed labor questions. The vast individual and corporate fortunes, the vast combinations of capital, which have marked the development of our industrial system create new conditions, and necessitate a change from the old attitude of the State and the nation toward property. It is probably true that the large majority of the fortunes that now exist in this country have been amassed not by injuring our people, but as an incident to the conferring of great benefits upon the community; and this, no matter what may have been the conscious purpose of those amassing them. There is but the scantiest justification for most of the outcry against the men of wealth *as such*; and it ought to be unnecessary to state that any appeal which directly or indirectly leads to suspicion and hatred among ourselves, which tends to limit opportunity, and therefore to shut the door of success against poor men of talent, and, finally, which entails the possibility of lawlessness and violence, is an attack upon the fundamental properties of American citizenship. Our interests are at bottom common; in the long run we go up or go down together. Yet more and more it is evident that the State, and if necessary the nation, has got to possess the right of supervision and control as regards the great corporations which are its creatures; particularly as regards the great business combinations which derive a portion of their importance from the existence of some monopolistic tendency. The right should be exercised with caution and self-restraint; but it should exist, so that it may be invoked if the need arises.

So much for our duties, each to himself and each to his neighbor, within the limits of our own country. But our country, as it strides forward with ever-increasing rapidity to a foremost place among the world powers, must necessarily find, more and more, that it has world duties also. There are excellent people who believe that we can shirk these duties and yet retain our self-respect; but these good people are in error. Other good people seek to deter us from treading the path of hard but lofty duty by bidding us remember that all nations that have achieved greatness, that have expanded and played their part as world powers, have in the end passed away. So they have; and so have all others. The weak and the stationary have vanished as surely as, and more rapidly than, those whose citizens felt within them the lift that impels generous souls to great and noble effort. This is only another way of stating the universal law of death, which is itself part of the universal law of life. The man who works, the man who does great deeds, in the end dies as surely as the veriest idler who cumbers the earth's surface; but he leaves behind him the great fact that he has done his work well. So it is with nations. While the nation that has dared to be great, that has had the will and the power to change the destiny of the ages, in the end must die, yet no less surely the nation that has played the part of the weakling must also die; and whereas the nation that has done nothing leaves nothing behind it, the nation that has done a great work really continues, though in changed form, to live forevermore. The Roman has passed away exactly as all the nations of antiquity which did not expand when he expanded have passed away; but their very memory has vanished, while he himself is still a living force throughout the wide world in our entire civilization of to-day, and will so continue through countless generations, through untold ages.

It is because we believe with all our heart and soul in the greatness of this country, because we feel the thrill of hardy life in our veins, and are confident that to us is given the privilege of playing a leading part in the century that has just opened, that we hail with eager delight the opportunity to do whatever task Providence may allot us. We admit with all sincerity that our first duty is within our own household; that we must not merely talk, but act, in favor of cleanliness and decency and righteousness, in all political, social, and civic matters. No prosperity and no glory can save a nation that is rotten at heart. We must ever keep the core of our national being sound, and see to it that not only our citizens in private life, but, above all, our statesmen in public life, practice the old commonplace virtues which from time immemorial have lain at the root of all true national well-being. Yet while this is our first duty, it is not our whole duty. Exactly as each man, while doing first his duty to his wife and the children within his home, must yet, if he hopes to amount to much, strive mightily in the world outside his home, so our nation, while first of all seeing to its own domestic well-being, must not shrink from playing its part among the great nations without. Our duty may take many forms in the future as it has taken many forms in the past. Nor is it possible to lay down a hard-and-fast rule for all cases. We must ever face the fact of our shifting national needs, of the always-changing opportunities that present themselves. But we may be certain of one thing: whether we wish it or not, we cannot avoid hereafter having duties to do in the face of other nations. All that we can do is to settle whether we shall perform these duties well or ill.

Right here let me make as vigorous a plea as I know how in favor of saying nothing that we do not mean, and of acting without hesitation up to whatever we say. A good many of you are probably acquainted with the old proverb: "Speak softly and carry a big stick—you will go far." If a man continually blusters, if he lacks civility, a big stick will not save him from trouble; and neither will speaking softly avail, if back of the softness there does not lie strength, power. In private life there are few beings more obnoxious than the man who is always loudly boasting; and if the boaster is not prepared to back up his words his position becomes absolutely contemptible. So it is with the nation. It is both foolish and undignified to indulge in undue self-glorification, and, above all, in loose-tongued denunciation of other peoples. Whenever on any point we come in contact with a foreign power, I hope that we shall always strive to speak courteously and respectfully of that foreign power. Let us make it evident that we intend to do justice. Then let us make it equally evident that we will not tolerate injustice being done to us in return. Let us further make it evident that we use no words which we are not prepared to back up with deeds, and that while our speech is always moderate, we are ready and willing to make it good. Such an attitude will be the surest possible guarantee of that self-respecting peace, the attainment of which is and must ever be the prime aim of a self-governing people.

This is the attitude we should take as regards the Monroe Doctrine. There is not the least need of blustering about it. Still less should it be used as a pretext for our own aggrandizement at the expense of any other American state. But, most emphatically, we must make it evident that we intend on this point ever to maintain the old American position. Indeed, it is hard to understand how any man can take any other position, now that we are all looking forward to the building of the Isthmian Canal. The Monroe Doctrine is not international law; but there is no necessity that it should be. All that is needful is that it should continue to be a cardinal feature of American policy on this continent; and the Spanish-American states should, in their own interests, champion it as strongly as we do. We do not by this doctrine intend to sanction any policy of aggression by one American commonwealth at the expense of any other, nor any policy of commercial discrimination against any foreign power whatsoever. Commercially, as far as this doctrine is concerned, all we wish is a fair field and no favor; but if we are wise we shall strenuously insist that under no pretext whatsoever shall there be any territorial aggrandizement on American soil by any European power, and this, no matter what form the territorial aggrandizement may take.

We most earnestly hope and believe that the chance of our having any hostile military complication with any foreign power is very small. But that there will come a strain, a jar, here and there, from commercial and agricultural—that is, from industrial—competition, is almost inevitable. Here again we have got to remember that our first duty is to our own people, and yet that we can best get justice by doing justice. We must continue the policy that has been so brilliantly successful in the past, and so shape our economic system as to give every advantage to the skill, energy, and intelligence of our farmers, merchants, manufacturers, and wage-workers; and yet we must also remember, in dealing with other nations, that benefits must be given where benefits are sought. It is not possible to dogmatize as to the exact way of attaining this end, for the exact conditions cannot be foretold. In the long run, one of our prime needs is stability and continuity of economic policy; and yet, through treaty or by direct legislation, it may, at least in certain cases, become advantageous to supplement our present policy by a system of reciprocal benefit and obligation.

Throughout a large part of our national career our history has been one of expansion, the expansion being of different kinds at different times. This expansion is not a matter of regret, but of pride. It is vain to tell a people as masterful as ours that the spirit of enterprise is not safe. The true American has never feared to run risks when the prize to be won was of sufficient value. No nation capable of self-government, and of developing by its own efforts a sane and orderly civilization, no matter how small it may be, has anything to fear from us. Our dealings with Cuba illustrate this, and should be forever a subject of just national pride. We speak in no spirit of arrogance when we state as a simple historic fact that never in recent times has any great nation acted with such disinterestedness as we have shown in Cuba. We freed the island from the Spanish yoke. We then earnestly did our best to help the Cubans in the establishment of free education, of law and order, of material prosperity, of the cleanliness necessary to sanitary well-being in their great cities. We did all this at great expense of treasure, at some expense of life; and now we are establishing them in a free and independent commonwealth, and have asked in return nothing whatever save that at no time shall their independence be prostituted to the advantage of some foreign rival of ours, or so as to menace our well-being. To have failed to ask this would have amounted to national stultification on our part.

In the Philippines we have brought peace, and we are at this moment giving them such freedom and self-government as they could never under any conceivable conditions have obtained had we turned them loose to sink into a welter of blood and confusion, or to become the prey of some strong tyranny without or within. The bare recital of the facts is sufficient to show that we did our duty; and what prouder title to honor can a nation have than to have done its duty? We have done our duty to ourselves, and we have done the higher duty of promoting the civilization of mankind. The first essential of civilization is law. Anarchy is simply the handmaiden and forerunner of tyranny and despotism. Law and order enforced with justice and by strength lie at the foundations of civilization. Law must be based upon justice, else it cannot stand, and it must be enforced with resolute firmness, because weakness in enforcing it means in the end that there is no justice and no law, nothing but the rule of disorderly and unscrupulous strength. Without the habit of orderly obedience to the law, without the stern enforcement of the laws at the expense of those who defiantly resist them, there can be no possible progress, moral or material, in civilization. There can be no weakening of the law-abiding spirit here at home, if we are permanently to succeed; and just as little can we afford to show weakness abroad. Lawlessness and anarchy were put down in the Philippines as a prerequisite to introducing the reign of justice.

Barbarism has, and can have, no place in a civilized world. It is our duty toward the people living in barbarism to see that they are freed from their chains, and we can free them only by destroying barbarism itself. The missionary, the merchant, and the soldier may each have to play a part in this destruction, and in the consequent uplifting of the people. Exactly as it is the duty of a civilized power scrupulously to respect the rights of all weaker civilized powers and gladly to help those who are struggling toward civilization, so it is its duty to put down savagery and barbarism. As in such a work human instruments must be used, and as human instruments are imperfect, this means that at times there will be injustice; that at times merchant or soldier, or even missionary, may do wrong. Let us instantly condemn and rectify such wrong when it occurs, and if possible punish the wrongdoer. But shame, thrice shame to us, if we are so foolish as to make such occasional wrongdoing an excuse for failing to perform a great and righteous task. Not only in our own land, but throughout the world, throughout all history, the advance of civilization has been of incalculable benefit to mankind, and those through whom it has advanced deserve the highest honor. All honor to the missionary, all honor to the soldier, all honor to the merchant who now in our own day have done so much to bring light into the world's dark places.

Let me insist again, for fear of possible misconstruction, upon the fact that our duty is twofold, and that we must raise others while we are benefiting ourselves. In bringing order to the Philippines, our soldiers added a new page to the honor roll of

American history, and they incalculably benefited the islanders themselves. Under the wise administration of Governor Taft the islands now enjoy a peace and liberty of which they have hitherto never even dreamed. But this peace and liberty under the law must be supplemented by material, by industrial development. Every encouragement should be given to their commercial development, to the introduction of American industries and products; not merely because this will be a good thing for our people, but infinitely more because it will be of incalculable benefit to the people in the Philippines.

We shall make mistakes; and if we let these mistakes frighten us from our work we shall show ourselves weaklings. Half a century ago Minnesota and the two Dakotas were Indian hunting-grounds. We committed plenty of blunders, and now and then worse than blunders, in our dealings with the Indians. But who does not admit at the present day that we were right in wresting from barbarism and adding to civilization the territory out of which we have made these beautiful States? And now we are civilizing the Indian and putting him on a level to which he could never have attained under the old conditions.

In the Philippines let us remember that the spirit and not the mere form of government is the essential matter. The Tagalogs have a hundredfold the freedom under us that they would have if we had abandoned the islands. We are not trying to subjugate a people; we are trying to develop them and make them a law-abiding, industrious, and educated people, and we hope ultimately a self-governing people. In short, in the work we have done we are but carrying out the true principles of our democracy. We work in a spirit of self-respect for ourselves and of good will toward others, in a spirit of love for and of infinite faith in mankind. We do not blindly refuse to face the evils that exist, or the shortcomings inherent in humanity; but across blundering and shirking, across selfishness and meanness of motive, across short-sightedness and cowardice, we gaze steadfastly toward the far horizon of golden triumph. If you will study our past history as a nation you will see we have made many blunders and have been guilty of many shortcomings, and yet that we have always in the end come out victorious because we have refused to be daunted by blunders and defeats, have recognized them, but have persevered in spite of them. So it must be in the future. We gird up our loins as a nation, with the stern purpose to play our part manfully in winning the ultimate triumph; and therefore we turn scornfully aside from the paths of mere ease and idleness, and with unfaltering steps tread the rough road of endeavor, smiting down the wrong and battling for the right, as Greatheart smote and battled in Bunyan's immortal story.

W. E. B. Du Bois

Address of the Niagara Movement, to the Country

(Delivered at the Second Annual Convention of the "Niagara Movement" at Harper's Ferry, West Virginia, August 16, 1906)

The men of the Niagara Movement coming from the toil of the year's hard work and pausing a moment from the earning of their daily bread turn toward the nation and again ask in the name of ten million the privilege of a hearing. In the past year the work of the Negro-hater has flourished in the land. Step by step the defenders of the rights of American citizens have retreated. The work of stealing the black man's ballot has progressed and the fifty and more representatives of stolen votes still sit in the nation's capital. Discrimination in travel and public accommodation has so spread that some of our weaker brethren are actually afraid to thunder against color discrimination as such and are simply whispering for ordinary decencies.

Against this the Niagara Movement eternally protests. We will not be satisfied to take one jot or tittle less than our full manhood rights. We claim for ourselves every single right that belongs to a freeborn American, political, civil and social; and until we get these rights we will never cease to protest and assail the ears of America. The battle we wage is not for ourselves alone but for all true Americans. It is a fight for ideals, lest this, our common fatherland, false to its founding, become in truth the land of the thief and the home of the Slave—a by-word and a hissing among the nations for its sounding pretensions and pitiful accomplishment.

Never before in the modern age has a great and civilized folk threatened to adopt so cowardly a creed in the treatment of its fellow-citizens born and bred on its soil. Stripped of verbiage and subterfuge and in its naked nastiness the new American creed says: Fear to let black men even try to rise lest they become the equals of the white. And this is the land that professes to follow Jesus Christ. The blasphemy of such a course is only matched by its cowardice.

In detail our demands are clear and unequivocal. First, we would vote; with the right to vote goes everything: Freedom, manhood, the honor of your wives, the chastity of your daughters, the right to work, and the chance to rise. And let no man listen to those who deny this.

We want full manhood suffrage, and we want it now, henceforth and forever.

Second. We want discrimination in public accommodation to cease. Separation in railway and street cars, based simply on race and color, is un-American, un-democratic, and silly. We protest against all such discrimination.

Third. We claim the right of freemen to walk, talk, and be with them that wish to be with us. No man has a right to choose another man's friends, and to attempt to do so is an impudent interference with the most fundamental human privilege.

Fourth. We want the laws enforced against rich as well as poor, against Capitalist as well as Laborer, against white as well as black. We are not more lawless than the white race, we are more often arrested, convicted, and mobbed. We want justice even for criminals and outlaws. We want the Constitution of the country enforced. We want Congress to take charge of Congressional elections. We want the Fourteenth amendment carried out to the letter and every State disfranchised in Congress which attempts to disfranchise its rightful voters. We want the Fifteenth amendment enforced and no State allowed to base its franchise simply on color.

The failure of the Republican party in Congress at the session just closed to redeem its pledge of 1904 with reference to suffrage conditions at the South seems a plain, deliberate, and premeditated breach of promise, and stamps that party as guilty of obtaining votes under false pretense.

Fifth. We want our children educated. The school system in the country districts of the South is a disgrace and in few towns and cities are Negro schools what they ought to be. We want the national government to step in and wipe out illiteracy in the South. Either the United States will destroy ignorance or ignorance will destroy the United States.

And when we call for education we mean real education. We believe in work. We ourselves are workers, but work is not necessarily education. Education is the development of power and ideal. We want our children trained as intelligent human beings should be, and we will fight for all time against any proposal to educate black boys and girls simply as servants and underlings, or simply for the use of other people. They have a right to know, to think, to aspire.

These are some of the chief things which we want. How shall we get them? By voting where we may vote, by persistent, unceasing agitation; by hammering at the truth; by sacrifice and work.

We do not believe in violence, neither in the despised violence of the raid, nor the lauded violence of the soldier, nor the barbarous violence of the mob; but we do believe in John Brown, in that incarnate spirit of justice, that hatred of a lie, that willingness to sacrifice money, reputation, and life itself on the altar of right.

And here on the scene of John Brown's martyrdom we reconsecrate ourselves, our honor, our property to the final emancipation of the race which John Brown died to make free.

Our enemies, triumphant for the present, are fighting the stars in their courses. Justice and humanity must prevail. We live to tell these dark brothers of ours—scattered in counsel, wavering and weak—that no bribe of money or notoriety, no promise of wealth or fame, is worth the surrender of a people's manhood or the loss of a man's self-respect. We refuse to surrender the leadership of this race to cowards and trucklers. We are men; we will be treated as men. On this rock we have planted our banners. We will never give up, though the trump of doom find us still fighting.

And we shall win. The past promised it, the present foretells it. Thank God for John Brown! Thank God for Garrison and Douglass! Sumner and Phillips, Nat Turner and Robert Gould Shaw, and all the hallowed dead who died for freedom! Thank God for all those to-day, few though their voices be, who have not forgotten the divine brotherhood of all men white and black, rich and poor, fortunate and unfortunate.

We appeal to the young men and women of this nation, to those whose nostrils are not yet befouled by greed and snobbery and racial narrowness: Stand up for the right, prove yourselves worthy of your heritage, and whether born North or south dare to treat men as men. Cannot the nation that has absorbed ten million foreigners into its political life without catastrophe, absorb ten million Negro Americans into that same political life at less cost than their unjust and illegal exclusion will involve?

Courage brothers! The battle for humanity is not lost or losing. All across the skies sit signs of promise. The Slav is raising in his might, the yellow millions are tasting liberty, the black Africans are writhing toward the light, and everywhere the laborer, with ballot in his hand, is voting open the gates of Opportunity and Peace. The morning breaks over blood-stained hills. We must not falter, we may not shrink. Above are the everlasting stars.

WOODROW WILSON

Why We Went to War

(Delivered in Washington, D.C., April 2, 1917)

I have called the Congress into extraordinary session because there are serious, very serious, choices of policy to be made, and made immediately, which it was neither right nor constitutionally permissible that I should assume the responsibility of making.

On the third of February last I officially laid before you the extraordinary announcement of the Imperial German Government that on and after the first day of February it was its purpose to put aside all restraints of law or of humanity and use its submarines to sink every vessel that sought to approach either the ports of Great Britain and Ireland or the western coasts of Europe or any of the ports controlled by the enemies of Germany within the Mediterranean. That had seemed to be the object of the German submarine warfare earlier in the war, but since April of last year the Imperial Government had somewhat restrained the commanders of its undersea craft in conformity with its promise then given to us that passenger boats should not be sunk and that due warning would be given to all other vessels which its submarines might seek to destroy, when no resistance was offered or escape attempted, and care taken that their crews were given at least a fair chance to save their lives in their open boats. The precautions taken were meagre and haphazard enough, as was proved in distressing instance after instance in the progress of the cruel and unmanly business, but a certain degree of restraint was observed. The new policy has swept every restriction aside. Vessels of every kind, whatever their flag, their character, their cargo, their destination, their errand, have been ruthlessly sent to the bottom without warning and without thought of help or mercy for those on board, the vessels of friendly neutrals along with those of belligerents. Even hospital ships and ships carrying relief to the sorely bereaved and stricken people of Belgium, though the latter were provided with safe conduct through the proscribed areas by the German Government itself and were distinguished by unmistakable marks of identity, have been sunk with the same reckless lack of compassion or of principle.

I was for a little while unable to believe that such things would in fact be done by any government that had hitherto subscribed to the humane practices of civilized nations. International law had its origin in the attempt to set up some law which would be respected and observed upon the seas, where no nation had right of dominion and where lay the free highways of the world. This minimum of right the German Government has swept aside under the plea of retaliation and necessity and because it had no weapons which it could use at sea except these which it is impossible to employ as it is employing them without throwing to the winds all scruples of humanity or of respect for the understandings that were supposed to underlie the intercourse of the world. I am not now thinking of the loss of property involved, immense and serious as that is, but only of the wanton and wholesale destruction of the lives of non-combatants, men, women, and children, engaged in pursuits which have always, even in the darkest periods of modern history, been deemed innocent and legitimate. Property can be paid for; the lives of peaceful and innocent people cannot be. The present German submarine warfare against commerce is a warfare against mankind.

It is a war against all nations. American ships have been sunk, American lives taken, in ways which it has stirred us very deeply to learn of, but the ships and people of other neutral and friendly nations have been sunk and overwhelmed in the waters in the same way. There has been no discrimination. The challenge is to all mankind. Each nation must decide for itself how it will meet it. The choice we make for ourselves must be made with a moderation of counsel and a temperateness for judgment befitting our character and our motives as a nation. We must put excited feeling away. Our motive will not be revenge or the victorious assertion of the physical might of the nation, but only the vindication of right, of human right, of which we are only a single champion.

When I addressed the Congress on the twenty-sixth of February last I thought that it would suffice to assert our neutral rights with arms, our right to use the seas against unlawful interference, our right to keep our people safe against unlawful violence. But armed neutrality, it now appears, is impracticable. Because submarines are in effect outlaws when used as the German submarines have been used against merchant shipping, it is impossible to defend ships against their attacks as the law of nations has assumed that merchantmen would defend themselves against privateers or cruisers, visible craft giving chase upon the open sea. It is common prudence in such circumstances, grim necessity indeed, to endeavor to destroy them before they have shown their own intention. They must be dealt with upon sight, if dealt with at all. The German Government denies the right of neutrals to use arms at all within the areas of the sea which it has proscribed, even in the defense of rights which no modern publicist has ever before questioned their right to defend. The intimation is conveyed that the armed guards which we have placed on our merchant ships will be treated as beyond the pale of law and subject to be dealt with as pirates would be. Armed neutrality is ineffectual enough at best; in such circumstances and in the face of such pretensions it is worse than ineffectual: it is likely only to produce what it was meant to prevent; it is practically certain to draw us into the war without either the rights or the effectiveness of belligerents. There is one choice we cannot make, we are incapable of making: we will not choose the path of submission and suffer the most sacred rights of our nation and our people to be ignored or violated. The wrongs against which we now array ourselves are no common wrongs; they cut to the very roots of human life.

With a profound sense of the solemn and even tragical character of the step I am taking and of the grave responsibilities which it involves, but in unhesitating obedience to what I deem my constitutional duty, I advise that the Congress declare the recent course of the Imperial German Government to be in fact nothing less than war against the government and people of the United States; that it formally accept the status of belligerent which has thus been thrust upon it; and that it take immediate steps not only to put the country in a more thorough state of defense but also to exert all its power and employ all its resources to bring the Government of the German Empire to terms and end the war.

What this will involve is clear. It will involve the utmost practicable cooperation in counsel and action with the governments now at war with Germany, and, as incident to that, the extension to those governments of the most liberal financial credits, in order that our resources may so far as possible be added to theirs. It will involve the organization and mobilization of all the material resources of the country to supply the materials of war and serve the incidental needs of the nation in the most abundant and yet the most economical and efficient way possible. It will involve the immediate full equipment of the navy in all respects, but particularly in supplying it with the best means of dealing with the enemy's submarines. It will involve the immediate addition to the armed forces of the United States already provided for by law in case of war at least five hundred thousand men, who should, in my opinion, be chosen upon the principle of universal liability to service, and also the authorization of subsequent additional increments of equal force so soon as they may be needed and can be handled in training. It will involve also, of course, the granting of adequate credits to the Government, sustained, I hope, so far as they can equitably be sustained by the present generation, by well conceived taxation.

I say sustained so far as may be equitable by taxation because it seems to me that it would be most unwise to base the credits which will now be necessary entirely on money borrowed. It is our duty, I most respectfully urge, to protect our people so far as we may against the very serious hardships and evils which would be likely to arise out of the inflation which would be produced by vast loans.

In carrying out the measures by which these things are to be accomplished we should keep constantly in mind the wisdom of interfering as little as possible in our own preparation and in the equipment of our own military forces with the duty—for it will be a very practical duty—of supplying the nations already at war with Germany with the materials which they can obtain only from us or by our assistance. They are in the field and we should help them in every way to be effective there.

I shall take the liberty of suggesting, through the several executive departments of the Government, for the consideration of your committees, measures for the accomplishment of the several objects I have mentioned. I hope that it will be your pleasure to deal with them as having been framed after very careful thought by the branch of the Government upon which the responsibility of conducting the war and safeguarding the nation will most directly fall.

While we do these things, these deeply momentous things, let us be very clear, and make very clear to all the world what our motives and our objectives are. My own thought has not been driven from its habitual and normal course by the unhappy events of the last two months, and I do not believe that the thought of the nation has been altered or clouded by them. I have exactly the same things in mind now that I had in mind when I addressed the Senate on the twenty-second of January last; the same that I had in mind when I addressed the Congress on the third of February and on the twenty-sixth of February. Our object now, as then, is to vindicate the principles of peace and justice in the life of the world as against selfish and autocratic power and to set up amongst the really free and self-governed peoples of the world such a concert of purpose and of action as will henceforth insure the observance of those principles. Neutrality is no longer feasible or desirable where the peace of the world is involved and the freedom of its people, and the menace to that peace and freedom lies in the existence of autocratic governments backed by organized force which is controlled wholly by their will, not by the will of their people. We have seen the last of neutrality in such circumstances. We are at the beginning of an age in which it will be insisted that the same standards of conduct and of responsibility for wrong done shall be observed among nations and their governments that are observed among the individual citizens of civilized states.

We have no quarrel with the German people. We have no feeling toward them but one of sympathy and friendship. It was not upon their impulse that their

Government acted in entering this war. It was not with their previous knowledge or approval. It was a war determined upon as wars used to be determined upon in the old, unhappy days when peoples were nowhere consulted by their rulers and wars were provoked and waged in the interest of dynasties or of little groups of ambitious men who were accustomed to use their fellow men as pawns and tools. Self-governed nations do not fill their neighbor states with spies or set the course of intrigue to bring about some critical posture of affairs which will give them an opportunity to strike and make conquest. Such designs can be successfully worked out only under cover and where no one has the right to ask questions. Cunningly contrived plans of deception or aggression, carried, it may be, from generation to generation, can be worked out and kept from the light only within the privacy of courts or behind the carefully guarded confidences of a narrow and privileged class. They are happily impossible where public opinion commands and insists upon full information concerning all the nation's affairs.

A steadfast concert for peace can never be maintained except by a partnership of democratic nations. No autocratic government could be trusted to keep faith within it or observe its covenants. It must be a league of honor, a partnership of opinion. Intrigue would eat its vitals away; the plottings of inner circles who could plan what they would and render account to no one would be a corruption seated at its very heart. Only free peoples can hold their purpose and their honor steady to a common end and prefer the interests of mankind to any narrow interest of their own.

Does not every American feel that assurance has been added to our hope for the future peace of the world by the wonderful and heartening things that have been happening within the last few weeks in Russia? Russia was known by those who knew it best to have been always in fact democratic at heart, in all the vital habits of her thought, in all the intimate relationships of her people that spoke their natural instinct, their habitual attitude towards life. The autocracy that crowned the summit of her political structure, long as it had stood and terrible as was the reality of its power, was not in fact Russian in origin, character, or purpose; and now it has been shaken off and the great, generous Russian people have been added in all their native majesty and might to the forces that are fighting for freedom in the world, for justice, and for peace. Here is a fit partner for a League of Honor.

One of the things that has served to convince us that the Prussian autocracy was not and could never be our friend is that from the very outset of the present war it has filled our unsuspecting communities and even our offices of government with spies and set criminal intrigues everywhere afoot against our national unity of counsel, our peace within and without, our industries and our commerce. Indeed, it is now evident that its spies were here even before the war began; and it is unhappily not a matter of conjecture, but a fact proved in our courts of justice that the intrigues which have more than once come perilously near to disturbing the peace and dislocating the industries of the country have been carried on at the instigation, with the support, and even under the personal direction of official agents of the Imperial Government accredited to the Government of the United States. Even in checking these things and trying to extirpate them we have sought to put the most generous interpretation possible upon them because we knew that their source lay, not in any hostile feeling or purpose of the German people toward us (who were, no doubt, as ignorant of them as we ourselves were), but only in the selfish designs of a Government that did what it pleased and told its people nothing. But they have played their part in serving to convince us at last that that Government entertains no real friendship for us and means to act against our peace and security at its convenience. That it means to stir up enemies against us at our very doors the intercepted note to the German Minister at Mexico City is eloquent evidence.

We are accepting this challenge of hostile purpose because we know that in such a government, following such methods, we can never have a friend; and that in the presence of its organized power, always lying in wait to accomplish we know not what purpose, there can be no assured security for the democratic governments of the world. We are now about to accept gage of battle with this natural foe to liberty and shall, if necessary, spend the whole force of the nation to check and nullify its pretensions and its power. We are glad, now that we see the facts with no veil of false pretense about them, to fight thus for the ultimate peace of the world and for the liberation of its peoples, the German peoples included: for the rights of nations great and small and the privilege of men everywhere to choose their way of life and of obedience. The world must be made safe for democracy. Its peace must be planted upon the tested foundations of political liberty. We have no selfish ends to serve. We desire no conquest, no dominion. We seek no indemnities for ourselves, no material compensation for the sacrifices we shall freely make. We are but one of the champions of the rights of mankind. We shall be satisfied when those rights have been made as secure as the faith and the freedom of nations can make them.

Just because we fight without rancour and without selfish object, seeking nothing for ourselves but what we shall wish to share with all free peoples, we shall, I feel confident, conduct our operations as belligerents without passion and ourselves observe with proud punctilio the principles of right and of fair play we profess to be fighting for.

I have said nothing of the governments allied with the Imperial Government of Germany because they have not made war upon us or challenged us to defend our right and our honor. The Austro-Hungarian Government has, indeed, avowed its unqualified endorsement and acceptance of the reckless and lawless submarine warfare adopted now without disguise by the Imperial German Government, and it has therefore not been possible for this Government to receive Count Tarnowski, the Ambassador recently accredited to this Government by the Imperial and Royal Government of Austria-Hungary; but that Government has not actually engaged in warfare against citizens of the United States on the seas, and I take the liberty, for the present at least, of postponing a discussion of our relations with the authorities at Vienna. We enter this war only where we are clearly forced into it because there are no other means of defending our rights.

It will be all the easier for us to conduct ourselves as belligerents in a high spirit of right and fairness because we act without animus, not in enmity towards a people or with the desire to bring any injury or disadvantage upon them, but only in armed opposition to an irresponsible government which has thrown aside all considerations of humanity and of right and is running amuck. We are, let me say again, the sincere friends of the German people, and shall desire nothing so much as the early re-establishment of intimate relations of mutual advantage between us—however hard it may be for them, for the time being, to believe that this is spoken from our hearts. We have borne with their present government through all these bitter months because of that friendship—exercising a patience and forbearance which would otherwise have been impossible. We shall, happily, still have an opportunity to prove that friendship in our daily attitude and actions towards the millions of men and women of German birth and native sympathy who live amongst us and share our life, and we shall be proud to prove it towards all who are in fact loyal to their neighbors and to the Government in the hour of test. They are, most of them, as true and loyal Americans as if they had never known any other fealty or allegiance. They will be prompt to stand with us in rebuking and restraining the few who may be of a different mind and purpose. If there should be disloyalty, it will be dealt with with a firm hand of stern repression; but, if it lifts its head at all, it will lift it only here and there and without countenance except from a lawless and malignant few.

It is a distressing and oppressive duty, Gentlemen of the Congress, which I have performed in thus addressing you. There are, it may be, many months of fiery trial and sacrifice ahead of us. It is a fearful thing to lead this great peaceful people into war, into the most terrible and disastrous of all wars, civilization itself seeming to be in the balance. But the right is more precious than peace, and we shall fight for the things which we have always carried nearest our hearts—for democracy, for the right of those who submit to authority to have voice in their own governments, for the rights and liberties of small nations, for a universal dominion of right by such a concert of free peoples as shall bring peace and safety to all nations and make the world itself at last free. To such a task we can dedicate our lives and our fortunes, everything that we are and everything that we have, with the pride of those who know that the day has come when America is privileged to spend her blood and her might for the principles that gave her birth and happiness and the peace which she has treasured. God helping her, she can do not other.

FRANKLIN D. ROOSEVELT

First Inaugural Address

(Delivered in Washington, D.C., March 4, 1933)

I am certain that my fellow Americans expect that on my induction into the Presidency I will address them with a candor and a decision which the present situation of our people impel. This is preeminently the time to speak the truth, the whole truth, frankly and boldly. Nor need we shrink from honestly facing conditions in our country today. This great Nation will endure as it has endured, will revive and will prosper. So, first of all, let me assert my firm belief that the only thing we have to fear is fear itself—nameless, unreasoning, unjustified terror which paralyzes needed efforts to convert retreat into advance. In every dark hour of our national life a leadership of frankness and vigor has met with that under- standing and support of the people themselves which is essential to victory. I am convinced that you will again give that support to leadership in these critical days.

In such a spirit on my part and on yours we face our common difficulties. They concern, thank God, only material things. Values have shrunken to fantastic levels; taxes have risen; our ability to pay has fallen; government of all kinds is faced by seri- ous curtailment of income; the means of exchange are frozen in the currents of trade; the withered leaves of industrial enterprise lie on every side; farmers find no markets for their produce; the savings of many years in thousands of families are gone.

More important, a host of unemployed citizens face the grim problem of exis- tence, and an equally great number toil with little return. Only a foolish optimist can deny the dark realities of the moment.

Yet our distress comes from no failure of substance. We are stricken by no plague of locusts. Compared with the perils which our forefathers conquered because they believed and were not afraid, we have still much to be thankful for. Nature still offers her bounty and human efforts have multiplied it. Plenty is at our doorstep, but a generous use of it languishes in the very sight of the supply. Primarily this is because the rulers of the exchange of mankind's goods have failed, through their own stubbornness and their own incompetence, have admitted their failure, and abdicated. Practices of the unscrupulous money changers stand indicted in the court of public opinion, rejected by the hearts and minds of men.

True they have tried, but their efforts have been cast in the pattern of an outworn tradition. Faced by failure of credit they have proposed only the lending of more money. Stripped of the lure of profit by which to induce our people to follow their false leadership, they have resorted to exhortations, pleading tearfully for restored confidence. They know only the rules of a generation of self-seekers. They have no vision, and when there is no vision the people perish.

The money changers have fled from their high seats in the temple of our civilization. We may now restore that temple to the ancient truths. The measure of the restoration lies in the extent to which we apply social values more noble than mere monetary profit.

Happiness lies not in the mere possession of money; it lies in the joy of achievement, in the thrill of creative effort. The joy and moral stimulation of work no longer must be forgotten in the mad chase of evanescent profits. These dark days will be worth all they cost us if they teach us that our true destiny is not to be ministered unto but to minister to ourselves and to our fellow men.

Recognition of the falsity of material wealth as the standard of success goes hand in hand with the abandonment of the false belief that public office and high political position are to be valued only by the standards of pride of place and personal profit; and there must be an end to a conduct in banking and in business which too often has given to a sacred trust the likeness of callous and selfish wrongdoing. Small wonder that confidence languishes, for it thrives only on honesty, on honor, on the sacredness of obligations, on faithful protection, on unselfish performance; without them it cannot live.

Restoration calls, however, not for changes in ethics alone. This Nation asks for action, and action now.

Our greatest primary task is to put people to work. This is no unsolvable problem if we face it wisely and courageously. It can be accomplished in part by direct recruiting by the Government itself, treating the task as we would treat the emergency of a war, but at the same time, through this employment, accomplishing greatly needed projects to stimulate and reorganize the use of our natural resources.

Hand in hand with this we must frankly recognize the overbalance of population in our industrial centers and, by engaging on a national scale in a redistribution, endeavor to provide a better use of the land for those best fitted for the land. The task can be helped by definite efforts to raise the values of agricultural products and with this the power to purchase the output of our cities. It can be helped by preventing realistically the tragedy of the growing loss through foreclosure of our small homes and our farms. It can be helped by insistence that the Federal, State, and local governments act forthwith on the demand that their cost be drastically reduced. It can be helped by the unifying of relief activities which today are often scattered, uneconomical, and unequal. It can be helped by national planning for and supervision of all forms of transportation and of communications and other utilities which have a definitely public character. There are many ways in which it can be helped, but it can never be helped merely by talking about it. We must act and act quickly.

Finally, in our progress toward a resumption of work we require two safeguards against a return of the evils of the old order; there must be a strict supervision of all banking and credits and investments; there must be an end to speculation with other people's money, and there must be provision for an adequate but sound currency.

These are the lines of attack. I shall presently urge upon a new Congress, in special session, detailed measures for their fulfillment, and I shall seek the immediate assistance of the several States.

Through this program of action we address ourselves to putting our own national house in order and making income balance outgo. Our international trade relations, though vastly important, are in point of time and necessity secondary to the establishment of a sound national economy. I favor as a practical policy the putting of first things first. I shall spare no effort to restore world trade by international economic readjustment, but the emergency at home cannot wait on that accomplishment.

The basic thought that guides these specific means of national recovery is not narrowly nationalistic. It is the insistence, as a first consideration, upon the interdependence of the various elements in all parts of the United States—a recognition of the old and permanently important manifestation of the American spirit of the pioneer. It is the way to recovery. It is the immediate way. It is the strongest assurance that the recovery will endure.

In the field of world policy I would dedicate this Nation to the policy of the good neighbor—the neighbor who resolutely respects himself and, because he does so, respects the rights of others—the neighbor who respects his obligations and respects the sanctity of his agreements in and with a world of neighbors.

If I read the temper of our people correctly, we now realize as we have never realized before our interdependence on each other; that we can not merely take but we must give as well; that if we are to go forward, we must move as a trained and loyal army willing to sacrifice for the good of a common discipline, because without such discipline no progress is made, no leadership becomes effective. We are, I know, ready and willing to submit our lives and property to such discipline, because it makes possible a leadership which aims at a larger good. This I propose to offer, pledging that the larger purposes will bind upon us all as a sacred obligation with a unity of duty hitherto evoked only in time of armed strife.

With this pledge taken, I assume unhesitatingly the leadership of this great army of our people dedicated to a disciplined attack upon our common problems.

Action in this image and to this end is feasible under the form of government which we have inherited from our ancestors. Our Constitution is so simple and practical that it is possible always to meet extraordinary needs by changes in emphasis and arrangement without loss of essential form. That is why our constitutional system has proved itself the most superbly enduring political mechanism the modern world has produced. It has met every stress of vast expansion of territory, of foreign wars, of bitter internal strife, of world relations.

It is to be hoped that the normal balance of Executive and legislative authority may be wholly adequate to meet the unprecedented task before us. But it may be that an unprecedented demand and need for undelayed action may call for temporary departure from that normal balance of public procedure.

I am prepared under my constitutional duty to recommend the measures that a stricken Nation in the midst of a stricken world may require. These measures, or such other measures as the Congress may build out of its experience and wisdom, I shall seek, within my constitutional authority, to bring to speedy adoption.

But in the event that the Congress shall fail to take one of these two courses, and in the event that the national emergency is still critical, I shall not evade the clear course of duty that will then confront me. I shall ask the Congress for the one remaining instrument to meet the crisis—broad Executive power to wage a war against the emergency, as great as the power that would be given to me if we were in fact invaded by a foreign foe.

For the trust reposed in me I will return the courage and the devotion that befit the time. I can do no less.

We face the arduous days that lie before us in the warm courage of the national unity; with the clear consciousness of seeking old and precious moral values; with the clean satisfaction that comes from the stern performance of duty by old and young alike. We aim at the assurance of a rounded and permanent national life.

We do not distrust the future of essential democracy. The people of the United States have not failed. In their need they have registered a mandate that they want direct, vigorous action. They have asked for discipline and direction under leadership. They have made me the present instrument of their wishes. In the spirit of the gift I take it.

In this dedication of a Nation we humbly ask the blessing of God. May He protect each and every one of us. May He guide me in the days to come.

Franklin D. Roosevelt

Fireside Chat on the War in Europe

(Delivered in Washington, D.C., September 3, 1939)

Tonight my single duty is to speak to the whole of America.

Until four-thirty this morning I had hoped against hope that some miracle would prevent a devastating war in Europe and bring to an end the invasion of Poland by Germany.

For four long years a succession of actual wars and constant crises have shaken the entire world and have threatened in each case to bring on the gigantic conflict which is today unhappily a fact.

It is right that I should recall to your minds the consistent and at time successful efforts of your government in these crises to throw the full weight of the United States into the cause of peace. In spite of spreading wars I think that we have every right and every reason to maintain as a national policy the fundamental moralities, the teachings of religion and the continuation of efforts to restore peace—for some day, though the time may be distant, we can be of even greater help to a crippled humanity.

It is right, too, to point out that the unfortunate events of these recent years have, without question, been based on the use of force and the threat of force. And it seems to me clear, even at the outbreak of this great war, that the influence of America should be consistent in seeking for humanity a final peace which will eliminate, as far as it is possible to do so, the continued use of force between nations.

It is, of course, impossible to predict the future. I have my constant stream of information from American representatives and other sources throughout the world. You, the people of this country, are receiving news through your radios and your newspapers at every hour of the day.

You are, I believe, the most enlightened and the best informed people in all the world at this moment. You are subjected to no censorship of news, and I want to add that your government has no information which it withholds or which it has any thought of withholding from you.

At the same time, as I told my press conference on Friday, it is of the highest importance that the press and the radio use the utmost caution to discriminate between actual verified fact on the one hand, and mere rumor on the other.

I can add to that by saying that I hope the people of this country will also discriminate most carefully between news and rumor. Do not believe of necessity everything you hear or read. Check up on it first.

You must master at the outset a simple but unalterable fact in modern foreign relations between nations. When peace has been broken anywhere, the peace of all countries everywhere is in danger.

It is easy for you and for me to shrug our shoulders and to say that conflicts taking place thousands of miles from the continental United States, and, indeed, thousands of miles from the whole American Hemisphere, do not seriously affect the Americas—and that all the United States has to do is to ignore them and go about its own business. Passionately though we may desire detachment, we are forced to realize that every word that comes through the air, every ship that sails the sea, every battle that is fought, does affect the American future.

Let no man or woman thoughtlessly or falsely talk of America sending its armies to European fields. At this moment there is being prepared a proclamation of American neutrality. This would have been done even if there had been no neutrality statute on the books, for this proclamation is in accordance with international law and in accordance with American policy.

This will be followed by a Proclamation required by the existing Neutrality Act. And I trust that in the days to come our neutrality can be made a true neutrality.

It is of the utmost importance that the people of this country, with the best information in the world, think things through. The most dangerous enemies of American peace are those who, without well-rounded information on the whole broad subject of the past, the present and the future, undertake to speak with assumed authority, to talk in terms of glittering generalities, to give to the nation assurances or prophecies which are of little present or future value.

I myself cannot and do not prophesy the course of events abroad—and the reason is that, because I have of necessity such a complete picture of what is going on in every part of the world, that I do not dare to do so. And the other reason is that I think it is honest for me to be honest with the people of the United States.

I cannot prophesy the immediate economic effect of this new war on our nation, but I do say that no American has the moral right to profiteer at the expense either of his fellow citizens or of the men, the women and the children who are living and dying in the midst of war in Europe.

Some things we do know. Most of us in the United States believe in spiritual values. Most of us, regardless of what church we belong to, believe in the spirit of the New Testament—a great teaching which opposes itself to the use of force, of armed force, of marching armies and falling bombs. The overwhelming masses of our people seek peace—peace at home, and the kind of peace in other lands which will not jeopardize our peace at home.

We have certain ideas and certain ideals of national safety and we must act to preserve that safety today and to preserve the safety of our children in future years.

That safety is and will be bound up with the safety of the Western Hemisphere and of the seas adjacent thereto. We seek to keep war from our own firesides by keeping war from coming to the Americas. For that we have historic precedent that goes back to the days of the administration of President George Washington. It is serious enough and tragic enough to every American family in every State in the Union to live in a world that is torn by wars on other continents. Those wars today affect every American home. It is our national duty to use every effort to keep them out of the Americas.

And at this time let me make the simple plea that partisanship and selfishness be adjourned; and that national unity be the thought that underlies all others.

This nation will remain a neutral nation, but I cannot ask that every American remain neutral in thought as well. Even a neutral has a right to take account of facts. Even a neutral cannot be asked to close his mind or his conscience.

I have said not once, but many times, that I have seen war and that I hate war. I say that again and again.

I hope the United States will keep out of this war. I believe that it will. And I give you assurance and reassurance that every effort of your government will be directed toward that end.

As long as it remains within my power to prevent, there will be no black-out of peace in the United States.

FRANKLIN D. ROOSEVELT

Joint Address in Congress Leading to a Declaration of War Against Japan

(Delivered in Washington, D.C., December 8, 1941)

Yesterday, December 7, 1941—a date which will live in infamy—the United States of America was suddenly and deliberately attacked by naval and air forces of the Empire of Japan.

The United States was at peace with that Nation and, at the solicitation of Japan, was still in conversation with its Government and its Emperor looking toward the maintenance of peace in the Pacific. Indeed, one hour after Japanese air squadrons had commenced bombing in the American Island of Oahu, the Japanese Ambassador to the United States and his colleague delivered to our Secretary of State a formal reply to a recent American message. And while this reply stated that it seemed useless to continue the existing diplomatic negotiations, it contained no threat or hint of war or of armed attack.

It will be recorded that the distance of Hawaii from Japan makes it obvious that the attack was deliberately planned many days or even weeks ago. During the intervening time the Japanese Government has deliberately sought to deceive the United States by false statements and expressions of hope for continued peace.

The attack yesterday on the Hawaiian Islands has caused severe damage to American naval and military forces. I regret to tell you that very many American lives have been lost. In addition American ships have been reported torpedoed on the high seas between San Francisco and Honolulu.

Yesterday the Japanese Government also launched an attack against Malaya.

Last night Japanese forces attacked Hong Kong.

Last night Japanese forces attacked Guam.

Last night Japanese forces attacked the Philippine Islands.

Last night the Japanese attacked Wake Island.

And this morning the Japanese attacked Midway Island.

Japan has, therefore, undertaken a surprise offensive extending throughout the Pacific area. The facts of yesterday and today speak for themselves. The people of the United States have already formed their opinions and well understand the implications to the very life and safety of our Nation.

As Commander in Chief of the Army and Navy I have directed that all measures be taken for our defense.

But always will our whole Nation remember the character of the onslaught against us.

No matter how long it may take us to overcome this premeditated invasion, the American people in their righteous might will win through to absolute victory.

I believe that I interpret the will of the Congress and of the people when I assert that we will not only defend ourselves to the uttermost but will make it very certain that this form of treachery shall never again endanger us.

Hostilities exist. There is no blinking at the fact that our people, our territory, and our interests are in grave danger.

With confidence in our armed forces—with the unbounding determination of our people—we will gain the inevitable triumph—so help us God.

I ask that the Congress declare that since the unprovoked and dastardly attack by Japan on Sunday, December 7, 1941, a state of war has existed between the United States and the Japanese Empire.

Franklin D. Roosevelt

Fireside Chat on the Progress of the War

(Delivered in Washington, D.C., February 23, 1942)

Washington's Birthday is a most appropriate occasion for us to talk with each other about things as they are today and things as we know they shall be in the future.

For eight years, General Washington and his Continental Army were faced continually with formidable odds and recurring defeats. Supplies and equipment were lacking. In a sense, every winter was a Valley Forge. Throughout the thirteen states there existed fifth columnists—and selfish men, jealous men, fearful men, who proclaimed that Washington's cause was hopeless, and that he should ask for a negotiated peace.

Washington's conduct in those hard times has provided the model for all Americans ever since—a model of moral stamina. He held to his course, as it had been charted in the Declaration of Independence. He and the brave men who served with him knew that no man's life or fortune was secure without freedom and free institutions.

The present great struggle has taught us increasingly that freedom of person and security of property anywhere in the world depend upon the security of the rights and obligations of liberty and justice everywhere in the world.

This war is a new kind of war. It is different from all other wars of the past, not only in its methods and weapons but also in its geography. It is warfare in terms of every continent, every island, every sea, every air lane in the world.

That is the reason why I have asked you to take out and spread before you a map of the whole earth, and to follow with me in the references which I shall make to the world-encircling battle lines of this war. Many questions will, I fear, remain unanswered tonight; but I know you will realize that I cannot cover everything in any one short report to the people.

The broad oceans which have been heralded in the past as our protection from attack have become endless battlefields on which we are constantly being challenged by our enemies.

We must all understand and face the hard fact that our job now is to fight at distances which extend all the way around the globe.

We fight at these vast distances because that is where our enemies are. Until our flow of supplies gives us clear superiority we must keep on striking our enemies wherever and whenever we can meet them, even if, for a while, we have to yield ground. Actually, though, we are taking a heavy toll of the enemy every day that goes by.

We must fight at these vast distances to protect our supply lines and our lines of communication with our allies—protect these lines from the enemies who are bending every ounce of their strength, striving against time, to cut them. The object of the Nazis and the Japanese is to separate the United States, Britain, China, and Russia, and to isolate them one from another, so that each will be surrounded and cut off from sources of supplies and reinforcements. It is the old familiar Axis policy of "divide and conquer."

There are those who still think in terms of the days of sailing ships. They advise us to pull our warships and our planes and our merchant ships into our own home waters and concentrate solely on last-ditch defense. But let me illustrate what would happen if we followed such foolish advice.

Look at your map. Look at the vast area of China, with its millions of fighting men. Look at the vast area of Russia, with its powerful armies and proven military might. Look at the British Isles, Australia, New Zealand, the Dutch Indies, India, the Near East, and the continent of Africa, with their resources of raw materials, and of peoples determined to resist Axis domination. Look too at North America, Central America, and South America.

It is obvious what would happen if all of these great reservoirs of power were cut off from each other either by enemy action or by self-imposed isolation:

First, in such a case, we could no longer send aid of any kind to China—to the brave people who, for nearly five years, have withstood Japanese assault, destroyed hundreds of thousands of Japanese soldiers and vast quantities of Japanese war munitions. It is essential that we help China in her magnificent defense and in her inevitable counteroffensive—for that is one important element in the ultimate defeat of Japan.

Second, if we lost communication with the southwest Pacific, all of that area, including Australia and New Zealand and the Dutch Indies, would fall under Japanese domination. Japan in such a case could release great numbers of ships and men to launch attacks on a large scale against the coasts of the Western Hemisphere—South America and Central America, and North America—including Alaska. At the same time, she could immediately extend her conquests in the other direction toward India, and through the Indian Ocean to Africa, to the Near East, and try to join forces with Germany and Italy.

Third, if we were to stop sending munitions to the British and the Russians in the Mediterranean, in the Persian Gulf and the Red Sea, we would be helping the Nazis to overrun Turkey, Syria, Iraq, Persia, Egypt and the Suez Canal, the whole coast of North Africa itself, and with that inevitably the whole coast of West Africa—putting Germany within easy striking distance of South America—fifteen hundred miles away.

Fourth, if by such a fatuous policy we ceased to protect the North Atlantic supply line to Britain and to Russia, we would help to cripple the splendid counter-offensive by Russia against the Nazis, and we would help to deprive Britain of essential food supplies and munitions.

Those Americans who believed that we could live under the illusion of isolationism wanted the American eagle to imitate the tactics of the ostrich. Now, many of those same people, afraid that we may be sticking our necks out, want our national bird to be turned into a turtle. But we prefer to retain the eagle as it is—flying high and striking hard.

I know that I speak for the mass of the American people when I say that we reject the turtle policy and will continue increasingly the policy of carrying the war to the enemy in distant lands and distant waters—as far away as possible from our own home grounds.

There are four main lines of communication now being traveled by our ships: the North Atlantic, the South Atlantic, the Indian Ocean, and the South Pacific. These routes are not one-way streets—for the ships that carry our troops and munitions outbound bring back essential raw materials which we require for our own use.

The maintenance of these vital lines is a very tough job. It is a job which requires tremendous daring, tremendous resourcefulness, and, above all, tremendous production of planes and tanks and guns and also of the ships to carry them. And I speak again for the American people when I say that we can and will do that job.

The defense of the world-wide lines of communication demands relatively safe use by us of the sea and of the air along the various routes; and this, in turn, depends upon control by the United Nations of many strategic bases along those routes.

Control of the air involves the simultaneous use of two types of planes—first, the long-range heavy bomber; and, second, the light bombers, dive bombers, torpedo planes, and short-range pursuit planes, all of which are essential to the protection of the bases and of the bombers themselves.

Heavy bombers can fly under their own power from here to the Southwest Pacific; but the smaller planes cannot. Therefore, these lighter planes have to be packed in crates and sent on board cargo ships. Look at your map again; and you will see that the route is long—and at many places perilous—either across the South Atlantic all the way around South Africa and the Cape of Good Hope, or from California to the East Indies direct. A vessel can make a round trip by either route in about four months, or only three round trips in a whole year.

In spite of the length, and in spite of the difficulties of this transportation, I can tell you that in two and a half months we already have a large number of bombers and pursuit planes, manned by American pilots and crews, which are now in daily contact with the enemy in the Southwest Pacific. And thousands of American troops are today in that area engaged in operations not only in the air but on the ground as well.

In this battle area, Japan has had an obvious initial advantage. For she could fly even her short-range planes to the points of attack by using many stepping stones open to her—bases in a multitude of Pacific islands and also bases on the China coast, Indo-China coast, and in Thailand and Malaya coasts. Japanese troop transports could go south from Japan and from China through the narrow China Sea which can be protected by Japanese planes throughout its whole length.

I ask you to look at your maps again, particularly at that portion of the Pacific Ocean lying west of Hawaii. Before this war even started, the Philippine Islands were already surrounded on three sides by Japanese power. On the west, the China side, the Japanese were in possession of the coast of China and the coast of Indo-China which had been yielded to them by the Vichy French. On the north are the islands of Japan themselves, reaching down almost to northern Luzon. On the east are the Mandated Islands—which Japan had occupied exclusively, and had fortified in absolute violation of her written word.

The islands that lie between Hawaii and the Philippines—these islands, hundreds of them, appear only as small dots on most maps. But they cover a large strategic area. Guam lies in the middle of them—a lone outpost which we have never fortified.

Under the Washington Treaty of 1921 we had solemnly agreed not to add to the fortification of the Philippines. We had no safe naval bases there, so we could not use the islands for extensive naval operations.

Immediately after this war started, the Japanese forces moved down on either side of the Philippines to numerous points south of them—thereby completely encircling the Philippines from north, south, east, and west.

It is that complete encirclement, with control of the air by Japanese land-based aircraft, which has prevented us from sending substantial reinforcements of men and material to the gallant defenders of the Philippines. For forty years it has always been our strategy—a strategy born of necessity—that in the event of a full-scale attack on the Islands by Japan, we should fight a delaying action, attempting to retire slowly into Bataan Peninsula and Corregidor.

We knew that the war as a whole would have to be fought and won by a process of attrition against Japan itself. We knew all along that, with our greater resources, we could ultimately outbuild Japan and ultimately overwhelm her on sea, and on land, and in the air. We knew that, to attain our objective, many varieties of operations would be necessary in areas other than the Philippines.

Now nothing that has occurred in the past two months has caused us to revise this basic strategy of necessity—except that the defense put up by General MacArthur has magnificently exceeded the previous estimates of endurance; and he and his men are gaining eternal glory therefore.

MacArthur's army of Filipinos and Americans, and the forces of the United Nations in China, in Burma, and the Netherlands East Indies, are all together fulfilling the same essential task. They are making Japan pay an increasingly terrible price for her ambitious attempts to seize control of the whole Asiatic world. Every Japanese transport sunk off Java is one less transport that they can use to carry reinforcements to their army opposing General MacArthur in Luzon.

It has been said that Japanese gains in the Philippines were made possible only by the success of their surprise attack on Pearl Harbor. I tell you that this is not so.

Even if the attack had not been made your map will show that it would have been a hopeless operation for us to send the fleet to the Philippines through thousands of miles of ocean, while all those island bases were under the sole control of the Japanese.

The consequences of the attack on Pearl Harbor—serious as they were—have been wildly exaggerated in other ways. And these exaggerations come originally from Axis propagandists; but they have been repeated, I regret to say, by Americans in and out of public life.

You and I have the utmost contempt for Americans who, since Pearl Harbor, have whispered or announced "off the record" that there was no longer any Pacific Fleet—that the fleet was all sunk or destroyed on December 7—that more than a thousand of our planes were destroyed on the ground. They have suggested slyly that the Government has withheld the truth about casualties—that eleven or twelve thousand men were killed at Pearl Harbor instead of the figures as officially announced. They have even served the enemy propagandists by spreading the incredible story that shiploads of bodies of our honored American dead were about to arrive in New York harbor to be put into a common grave.

Almost every Axis broadcast—Berlin, Rome, Tokyo—directly quotes Americans who, by speech or in the press, make damnable misstatements such as these.

The American people realize that in many cases details of military operations cannot be disclosed until we are absolutely certain that the announcement will not give to the enemy military information which he does not already possess.

Your Government has unmistakable confidence in your ability to hear the worst, without flinching or losing heart. You must, in turn, have complete confidence that your Government is keeping nothing from you except information that will help the enemy in his attempt to destroy us. In a democracy there is always a solemn pact of truth between Government and the people; but there must also always be a full use of discretion—and that word "discretion" applies to the critics of Government as well.

This is war. The American people want to know, and will be told, the general trend of how the war is going. But they do not wish to help the enemy any more than our fighting forces do, and they will pay little attention to the rumor-mongers and the poison peddlers in our midst.

To pass from the realm of rumor and poison to the field of facts: the number of our officers and men killed in the attack on Pearl Harbor on December 7 was 2,340, and the number wounded was 946. Of all of the combatant ships based at Pearl Harbor—battleships, heavy cruisers, light cruisers, aircraft carriers, destroyers and submarines—only three are permanently put out of commission.

Very many of the ships of the Pacific Fleet were not even in Pearl Harbor. Some of those that were there were hit very slightly; and others that were damaged have either rejoined the fleet by now or are still undergoing repairs. And when those repairs are completed, the ships will be more efficient fighting machines than they were before.

The report that we lost more than a thousand planes at Pearl Harbor is as baseless as the other weird rumors. The Japanese do not know just how many planes they destroyed that day, and I am not going to tell them. But I can say that to date—and including Pearl Harbor—we have destroyed considerably more Japanese planes than they have destroyed of ours.

We have most certainly suffered losses—from Hitler's U-boats in the Atlantic as well as from the Japanese in the Pacific—and we shall suffer more of them before the turn of the tide. But, speaking for the United States of America, let me say once and for all to the people of the world: We Americans have been compelled to yield ground, but we will regain it. We and the other United Nations are committed to the destruction of the militarism of Japan and Germany. We are daily increasing our strength. Soon, we and not our enemies will have the offensive; we, not they, will win the final battles; and we, not they, will make the final peace.

Conquered Nations in Europe know what the yoke of the Nazis is like. And the people of Korea and of Manchuria know in their flesh the harsh despotism of Japan. All of the people of Asia know that if there is to be an honorable and decent future for any of them or any of us, that future depends on victory by the United Nations over the forces of Axis enslavement.

If a just and durable peace is to be attained, or even if all of us are merely to save our own skins, there is one thought for us here at home to keep uppermost—the fulfillment of our special task of production.

Germany, Italy, and Japan are very close to their maximum output of planes, guns, tanks, and ships. The United Nations are not—especially the United States of America.

Our first job then is to build up production—uninterrupted production—so that the United Nations can maintain control of the seas and attain control of the air—not merely a slight superiority, but an overwhelming superiority.

On January 6 of this year, I set certain definite goals of production for airplanes, tanks, guns, and ships. The Axis propagandists called them fantastic. Tonight, nearly two months later, and after a careful survey of progress by Donald Nelson and others charged with responsibility for our production, I can tell you that those goals will be attained.

In every part of the country, experts in production and the men and women at work in the plants are giving loyal service. With few exceptions, labor, capital and farming realize that this is no time either to make undue profits or to gain special advantages, one over the other.

We are calling for new plants and additions to old plants. We are calling for plant conversion to war needs. We are seeking more men and more women to run them. We are working longer hours. We are coming to realize that one extra plane or extra tank or extra gun or extra ship completed tomorrow may, in a few months, turn the tide on some distant battlefield; it may make the difference between life and death for some of our own fighting men. We know now that if we lose this war it will be generations or even centuries before our conception of democracy can live again. And we can lose this war only if use slow up our effort or if we waste our ammunition sniping at each other.

Here are three high purposes for every American:

1. We shall not stop work for a single day. If any dispute arises we shall keep on working while the dispute is solved by mediation, conciliation, or arbitration—until the war is won.

2. We shall not demand special gains or special privileges or special advantages for any one group or occupation.

3. We shall give up conveniences and modify the routine of our lives if our country asks us to do so. We will do it cheerfully, remembering that the common enemy seeks to destroy every home and every freedom in every part of our land.

This generation of Americans has come to realize, with a present and personal realization, that there is something larger and more important than the life of any individual or of any individual group—something for which a man will sacrifice, and gladly sacrifice, not only his pleasures, not only his goods, not only his associations with those he loves, but his life itself. In time of crisis when the future is in the balance, we come to understand, with full recognition and devotion, what this Nation is and what we owe to it.

The Axis propagandists have tried in various evil ways to destroy our determination and our morale. Failing in that, they are now trying to destroy our confidence in our own allies. They say that the British are finished—that the Russians and the Chinese are about to quit. Patriotic and sensible Americans will reject these absurdities. And instead of listening to any of this crude propaganda, they will recall some of the things that Nazis and Japanese have said and are still saying about us.

Ever since this Nation became the arsenal of democracy—ever since enactment of lend-lease—there has been one persistent theme through all Axis propaganda.

This theme has been that Americans are admittedly rich, that Americans have considerable industrial power—but that Americans are soft and decadent, that they cannot and will not unite and work and fight.

From Berlin, Rome, and Tokyo we have been described as a Nation of weaklings—"playboys"—who would hire British soldiers, or Russian soldiers, or Chinese soldiers to do our fighting for us.

Let them repeat that now!

Let them tell that to General MacArthur and his men.

Let them tell that to the sailors who today are hitting hard in the far waters of the Pacific.

Let them tell that to the boys in the Flying Fortresses.

Let them tell that to the Marines!

The United Nations constitute an association of independent peoples of equal dignity and equal importance. The United Nations are dedicated to a common cause. We share equally and with equal zeal the anguish and the awful sacrifices of war. In the partnership of our common enterprise, we must share in a unified plan in which all of us must play our several parts, each of us being equally indispensable and dependent one on the other.

We have unified command and cooperation and comradeship.

We Americans will contribute unified production and unified acceptance of sacrifice and of effort. That means a national unity that can know no limitations of race or creed or selfish politics. The American people expect that much from themselves. And the American people will find ways and means of expressing their determination to their enemies, including the Japanese Admiral who has said that he will dictate the terms of peace here in the White House.

We of the United Nations are agreed on certain broad principles in the kind of peace we seek. The Atlantic Charter applies not only to the parts of the world that border the Atlantic but to the whole world; disarmament of aggressors, self-determination of nations and peoples, and the four freedoms—freedom of speech, freedom of religion, freedom from want, and freedom from fear.

The British and the Russian people have known the full fury of Nazi onslaught. There have been times when the fate of London and Moscow was in serious doubt. But there was never the slightest question that either the British or the Russians would yield. And today all the United Nations salute the superb Russian Army as it celebrates the twenty-fourth anniversary of its first assembly.

Though their homeland was overrun, the Dutch people are still fighting stubbornly and powerfully overseas.

The great Chinese people have suffered grievous losses; Chungking has been almost wiped out of existence—yet it remains the Capital of an unbeatable China.

That is the conquering spirit which prevails throughout the United Nations in this war.

The task that we Americans now face will test us to the uttermost. Never before have we been called upon for such a prodigious effort. Never before have we had so little time in which to do so much.

"These are the times that try men's souls." Tom Paine wrote those words on a drumhead, by the light of a campfire. That was when Washington's little army of ragged, rugged men was retreating across New Jersey, having tasted nothing but defeat.

And General Washington ordered that these great words written by Tom Paine be read to the men of every regiment in the Continental Army, and this was the assurance given to the first American armed forces:

"The summer soldier and the sunshine patriot will, in this crisis, shrink from the service of their country; but he that stands it now, deserves the love and thanks of man and woman. Tyranny, like hell, is not easily conquered, yet we have this consolation with us, that the harder the sacrifice, the more glorious the triumph."

So spoke Americans in the year 1776.

So speak Americans today!

Harry S. Truman

Statement by the President Announcing the Dropping of the Atomic Bomb on Hiroshima

(Delivered in Washington, D.C., August 6, 1945)

Sixteen hours ago an American airplane dropped one bomb on Hiroshima, an important Japanese Army base. That bomb had more power than 20,000 tons of T.N.T. It had more than two thousand times the blast power of the British "Grand Slam" which is the largest bomb ever yet used in the history of warfare.

The Japanese began the war from the air at Pearl Harbor. They have been repaid many fold. And the end is not yet. With this bomb we have now added a new and revolutionary increase in destruction to supplement the growing power of our armed forces. In their present form these bombs are now in production and even more powerful forms are in development.

It is an atomic bomb. It is a harnessing of the basic power of the universe. The force from which the sun draws its power has been loosed against those who brought war to the Far East.

Before 1939, it was the accepted belief of scientists that it was theoretically possible to release atomic energy. But no one knew any practical method of doing it. By 1942, however, we knew that the Germans were working feverishly to find a way to add atomic energy to the other engines of war with which they hoped to enslave the world. But they failed. We may be grateful to Providence that the Germans got the V-1's and V-2's late and in limited quantities and even more grateful that they did not get the atomic bomb at all.

The battle of the laboratories held fateful risks for us as well as the battles of the air, land and sea, and we have now won the battle of the laboratories as we have won the other battles.

Beginning in 1940, before Pearl Harbor, scientific knowledge useful in war was pooled between the United States and Great Britain, and many priceless helps to our victories have come from that arrangement. Under that general policy the research on the atomic bomb was begun. With American and British scientists working together we entered the race of discovery against the Germans.

The United States had available the large number of scientists of distinction in the many needed areas of knowledge. It had the tremendous industrial and financial resources necessary for the project and they could be devoted to it without undue impairment of other vital war work. In the United States the laboratory work and the production plants, on which a substantial start had already been made, would be out of reach of enemy bombing, while at that time Britain was exposed to constant air attack and was still threatened with the possibility of invasion. For these reasons Prime Minister Churchill and President Roosevelt agreed that it was wise to carry on the project here. We now have two great plants and many lesser works devoted to the production of atomic power. Employment during peak construction numbered 125,000 and over 65,000 individuals are even now engaged in operating the plants. Many have worked there for two and a half years. Few know what they have been producing. They see great quantities of material going in and they see nothing coming out of these plants, for the physical size of the explosive charge is exceedingly small. We have spent two billion dollars on the greatest scientific gamble in history—and won.

But the greatest marvel is not the size of the enterprise, its secrecy, nor its cost, but the achievement of scientific brains in putting together infinitely complex pieces of knowledge held by many men in different fields of science into a workable plan. And hardly less marvelous has been the capacity of industry to design, and of labor to operate, the machines and methods to do things never done before so that the brain child of many minds came forth in physical shape and performed as it was supposed to do. Both science and industry worked under the direction of the United States Army, which achieved a unique success in managing so diverse a problem in the advancement of knowledge in an amazingly short time. It is doubtful if such another combination could be got together in the world. What has been done is the greatest achievement of organized science in history. It was done under pressure and without failure.

We are now prepared to obliterate more rapidly and completely every productive enterprise the Japanese have above ground in any city. We shall destroy their docks, their factories, and their communications. Let there be no mistake; we shall completely destroy Japan's power to make war.

It was to spare the Japanese people from utter destruction that the ultimatum of July 26 was issued at Potsdam. Their leaders promptly rejected that ultimatum. If they do not now accept our terms they may expect a rain of ruin from the air, the like of which has never been seen on this earth. Behind this air attack will follow sea and land forces in such numbers and power as they have not yet seen and with the fighting skill of which they are already well aware.

The Secretary of War, who has kept in personal touch with all phases of the project, will immediately make public a statement giving further details.

His statement will give facts concerning the sites at Oak Ridge near Knoxville, Tennessee, and at Richland, near Pasco, Washington, and an installation near Santa Fe, New Mexico. Although the workers at the sites have been making materials to be used in producing the greatest destructive force in history they have not themselves been in danger beyond that of many other occupations, for the utmost care has been taken of their safety.

The fact that we can release atomic energy ushers in a new era in man's understanding of nature's forces. Atomic energy may in the future supplement the power that now comes from coal, oil, and falling water, but at present it cannot be produced on a basis to compete with them commercially. Before that comes there must be a long period of intensive research.

It has never been the habit of the scientists of this country or the policy of this Government to withhold from the world scientific knowledge. Normally, therefore, everything about the work with atomic energy would be made public.

But under the present circumstances it is not intended to divulge the technical processes of production or all the military applications, pending further examination of possible methods of protecting us and the rest of the world from the danger of sudden destruction.

I shall recommend that the Congress of the United States consider promptly the establishment of an appropriate commission to control the production and use of atomic power within the United States. I shall give further consideration and make further recommendations to the Congress as to how atomic power can become a powerful and forceful influence towards the maintenance of world peace.

Dwight D. Eisenhower

Second Inaugural Address

(Delivered in Washington, D.C., January 21, 1957)

We meet again, as upon a like moment four years ago, and again you have witnessed my solemn oath of service to you.

I, too, am a witness, today testifying in your name to the principles and purposes to which we, as a people, are pledged.

Before all else, we seek, upon our common labor as a nation, the blessings of Almighty God. And the hopes in our hearts fashion the deepest prayers of our whole people.

May we pursue the right—without self-righteousness.

May we know unity—without conformity.

May we grow in strength—without pride in self.

May we, in our dealings with all peoples of the earth, ever speak truth and serve justice.

And so shall America—in the sight of all men of good will—prove true to the honorable purposes that bind and rule us as a people in all this time of trial through which we pass.

We live in a land of plenty, but rarely has this earth known such peril as today.

In our nation work and wealth abound. Our population grows. Commerce crowds our rivers and rails, our skies, harbors, and highways. Our soil is fertile, our agriculture productive. The air rings with the song of our industry—rolling mills and blast furnaces, dynamos, dams and assembly lines—the chorus of America the bountiful.

Now this is our home—yet this is not the whole of our world. For our world is where our full destiny lies—with men, of all peoples, and all nations, who are or would be free. And for them—and so for us—this is no time of ease or of rest.

In too much of the earth there is want, discord, danger. New forces and new nations stir and strive across the earth, with power to bring, by their fate, great good or great evil to the free world's future. From the deserts of North Africa to the islands of the South Pacific one third of all mankind has entered upon an historic struggle for a new freedom: freedom from grinding poverty. Across all continents, nearly a billion people seek, sometimes almost in desperation, for the skills and knowledge and assistance by which they may satisfy from their own resources, the material wants common to all mankind.

No nation, however old or great, escapes this tempest of change and turmoil. Some, impoverished by the recent World War, seek to restore their means of livelihood. In the heart of Europe, Germany still stands tragically divided. So is the whole continent divided. And so, too, is all the world.

The divisive force is International Communism and the power that it controls.

The designs of that power, dark in purpose, are clear in practice. It strives to seal forever the fate of those it has enslaved. It strives to break the ties that unite the free. And it strives to capture—to exploit for its own greater power—all forces of change in the world, especially the needs of the hungry and the hopes of the oppressed.

Yet the world of International Communism has itself been shaken by a fierce and mighty force: the readiness of men who love freedom to pledge their lives to that love. Through the night of their bondage, the unconquerable will of heroes has struck with the swift, sharp thrust of lightning. Budapest is no longer merely the name of a city; henceforth it is a new and shining symbol of man's yearning to be free.

Thus across all the globe there harshly blow the winds of change. And, we—though fortunate be our lot—know that we can never turn our backs to them.

We look upon this shaken earth, and we declare our firm and fixed purpose—the building of a peace with justice in a world where moral law prevails.

The building of such a peace is a bold and solemn purpose. To proclaim it is easy. To serve it will be hard. And to attain it, we must be aware of its full meaning—and ready to pay its full price.

We know clearly what we seek, and why.

We seek peace, knowing that peace is the climate of freedom. And now, as in no other age, we seek it because we have been warned, by the power of modern weapons, that peace may be the only climate possible for human life itself.

Yet this peace we seek cannot be born of fear alone: it must be rooted in the lives of nations. There must be justice, sensed and shared by all peoples, for, without justice the world can know only a tense and unstable truce. There must be law, steadily invoked and respected by all nations, for without law, the world promises only such meager justice as the pity of the strong upon the weak. But the law of which we speak, comprehending the values of freedom, affirms the equality of all nations, great and small.

Splendid as can be the blessings of such a peace, high will be its cost: in toil patiently sustained, in help honorably given, in sacrifice calmly borne.

We are called to meet the price of this peace.

To counter the threat of those who seek to rule by force, we must pay the costs of our own needed military strength, and help to build the security of others.

We must use our skills and knowledge and, at times, our substance, to help others rise from misery, however far the scene of suffering may be from our shores. For wherever in the world a people knows desperate want, there must appear at least the spark of hope, the hope of progress—or there will surely rise at last the flames of conflict.

We recognize and accept our own deep involvement in the destiny of men everywhere. We are accordingly pledged to honor, and to strive to fortify, the authority of the United Nations. For in that body rests the best hope of our age for the assertion of that law by which all nations may live in dignity.

And, beyond this general resolve, we are called to act a responsible role in the world's great concerns or conflicts—whether they touch upon the affairs of a vast region, the fate of an island in the Pacific, or the use of a canal in the Middle East. Only in respecting the hopes and cultures of others will we practice the equality of all nations. Only as we show willingness and wisdom in giving counsel— in receiving counsel—and in sharing burdens, will we wisely perform the work of peace.

For one truth must rule all we think and all we do. No people can live to itself alone. The unity of all who dwell in freedom is their only sure defense. The economic need of all nations—in mutual dependence—makes isolation an impossibility: not even America's prosperity could long survive if other nations did not also prosper. No nation can longer be a fortress, lone and strong and safe. And any people, seeking such shelter for themselves, can now build only their own prison.

Our pledge to these principles is constant, because we believe in their rightness.

We do not fear this world of change. America is no stranger to much of its spirit. Everywhere we see the seeds of the same growth that America itself has known. The American experiment has, for generations, fired the passion and the courage of millions elsewhere seeking freedom, equality, opportunity. And the American story of material progress has helped excite the longing of all needy peoples for some satisfaction of their human wants. These hopes that we have helped to inspire, we can help to fulfill.

In this confidence, we speak plainly to all peoples.

We cherish our friendship with all nations that are or would be free. We respect, no less, their independence. And when, in time of want or peril, they ask our help, they may honorably receive it; for we no more seek to buy their sovereignty than we would sell our own. Sovereignty is never bartered among freemen.

We honor the aspirations of those nations which, now captive, long for freedom. We seek neither their military alliance nor any artificial imitation of our society. And they can know the warmth of the welcome that awaits them when, as must be, they join again the ranks of freedom.

We honor, no less in this divided world than in a less tormented time, the people of Russia. We do not dread, rather do we welcome, their progress in education and industry. We wish them success in their demands for more intellectual freedom, greater security before their own laws, fuller enjoyment of the rewards of their own toil. For as such things come to pass, the more certain will be the coming of that day when our peoples may freely meet in friendship.

So we voice our hope and our belief that we can help to heal this divided world. Thus may the nations cease to live in trembling before the menace of force. Thus may the weight of fear and the weight of arms be taken from the burdened shoulders of mankind.

This, nothing less, is the labor to which we are called and our strength dedicated.

And so the prayer of our people carries far beyond our own frontiers, to the wide world of our duty and our destiny.

May the light of freedom, coming to all darkened lands, flame brightly—until at last the darkness is no more.

May the turbulence of our age yield to a true time of peace, when men and nations shall share a life that honors the dignity of each, the brotherhood of all.

Thank you very much.

Dwight D. Eisenhower

Farewell Address

(Delivered in Washington, D.C., January 17, 1961)

Three days from now, after half a century in the service of our country, I shall lay down the responsibilities of office as, in traditional and solemn ceremony, the authority of the Presidency is vested in my successor.

This evening I come to you with a message of leave-taking and farewell, and to share a few final thoughts with you, my countrymen.

Like every other citizen, I wish the new President, and all who will labor with him, Godspeed. I pray that the coming years will be blessed with peace and prosperity for all.

Our people expect their President and the Congress to find essential agreement on issues of great moment, the wise resolution of which will better shape the future of the Nation.

My own relations with the Congress, which began on a remote and tenuous basis when, long ago, a member of the Senate appointed me to West Point, have since ranged to the intimate during the war and immediate post-war period, and, finally, to the mutually interdependent during these past eight years.

In this final relationship, the Congress and the Administration have, on most vital issues, cooperated well, to serve the national good rather than mere partisanship, and so have assured that the business of the Nation should go forward. So, my official relationship with the Congress ends in a feeling, on my part, of gratitude that we have been able to do so much together.

II.

We now stand ten years past the midpoint of a century that has witnessed four major wars among great nations. Three of these involved our own country. Despite these holocausts America is today the strongest, the most influential and most productive nation in the world. Understandably proud of this pre-eminence, we yet realize that America's leadership and prestige depend, not merely upon our unmatched material progress, riches and military strength, but on how we use our power in the interests of world peace and human betterment.

III.

Throughout America's adventure in free government, our basic purposes have been to keep the peace; to foster progress in human achievement, and to enhance liberty, dignity and integrity among people and among nations. To strive for less would be unworthy of a free and religious people. Any failure traceable to arrogance, or our lack of comprehension or readiness to sacrifice would inflict upon us grievous hurt both at home and abroad.

Progress toward these noble goals is persistently threatened by the conflict now engulfing the world. It commands our whole attention, absorbs our very beings. We face a hostile ideology—global in scope, atheistic in character, ruthless in purpose, and insidious in method. Unhappily the danger it poses promises to be of indefinite duration. To meet it successfully, there is called for, not so much the emotional and transitory sacrifices of crisis, but rather those which enable us to carry forward steadily, surely, and without complaint the burdens of a prolonged and complex struggle—with liberty the stake. Only thus shall we remain, despite every provocation, on our charted course toward permanent peace and human betterment.

Crises there will continue to be. In meeting them, whether foreign or domestic, great or small, there is a recurring temptation to feel that some spectacular and costly action could become the miraculous solution to all current difficulties. A huge increase in newer elements of our defense; development of unrealistic programs to cure every ill in agriculture; a dramatic expansion in basic and applied research—these and many other possibilities, each possibly promising in itself, may be suggested as the only way to the road we wish to travel.

But each proposal must be weighed in the light of a broader consideration: the need to maintain balance in and among national programs—balance between the private and the public economy, balance between cost and hoped for advantage—balance between the clearly necessary and the comfortably desirable; balance between our essential requirements as a nation and the duties imposed by the nation upon the individual; balance between actions of the moment and the national welfare of the future. Good judgment seeks balance and progress; lack of it eventually finds imbalance and frustration.

The record of many decades stands as proof that our people and their government have, in the main, understood these truths and have responded to them well, in the face of stress and threat. But threats, new in kind or degree, constantly arise. I mention two only.

IV.

A vital element in keeping the peace is our military establishment. Our arms must be mighty, ready for instant action, so that no potential aggressor may be tempted to risk his own destruction.

Our military organization today bears little relation to that known by any of my predecessors in peacetime, or indeed by the fighting men of World War II or Korea.

Until the latest of our world conflicts, the United States had no armaments industry. American makers of plowshares could, with time and as required, make swords as well. But now we can no longer risk emergency improvisation of national defense; we have been compelled to create a permanent armaments industry of vast proportions. Added to this, three and a half million men and women are directly engaged in the defense establishment. We annually spend on military security more than the net income of all United States corporations.

This conjunction of an immense military establishment and a large arms industry is new in the American experience. The total influence—economic, political, even spiritual—is felt in every city, every State house, every office of the Federal government. We recognize the imperative need for this development. Yet we must not fail to comprehend its grave implications. Our toil, resources and livelihood are all involved; so is the very structure of our society.

In the councils of government, we must guard against the acquisition of unwarranted influence, whether sought or unsought, by the military-industrial complex. The potential for the disastrous rise of misplaced power exists and will persist.

We must never let the weight of this combination endanger our liberties or democratic processes. We should take nothing for granted. Only an alert and knowledgeable citizenry can compel the proper meshing of the huge industrial and military machinery of defense with our peaceful methods and goals, so that security and liberty may prosper together.

Akin to, and largely responsible for the sweeping changes in our industrial-military posture, has been the technological revolution during recent decades.

In this revolution, research has become central; it also becomes more formalized, complex, and costly. A steadily increasing share is conducted for, by, or at the direction of, the Federal government.

Today, the solitary inventor, tinkering in his shop, has been overshadowed by task forces of scientists in laboratories and testing fields. In the same fashion, the free university, historically the fountainhead of free ideas and scientific discovery, has experienced a revolution in the conduct of research. Partly because of the huge costs involved, a government contract becomes virtually a substitute for intellectual curiosity. For every old blackboard there are now hundreds of new electronic computers.

The prospect of domination of the nation's scholars by Federal employment, project allocations, and the power of money is ever present—and is gravely to be regarded.

Yet, in holding scientific research and discovery in respect, as we should, we must also be alert to the equal and opposite danger that public policy could itself become the captive of a scientific-technological elite.

It is the task of statesmanship to mold, to balance, and to integrate these and other forces, new and old, within the principles of our democratic system—ever aiming toward the supreme goals of our free society.

V.

Another factor in maintaining balance involves the element of time. As we peer into society's future, we—you and I, and our government—must avoid the impulse to live only for today, plundering, for our own ease and convenience, the precious resources of tomorrow. We cannot mortgage the material assets of our grandchildren without risking the loss also of their political and spiritual heritage. We want democracy to survive for all generations to come, not to become the insolvent phantom of tomorrow.

VI.

Down the long lane of the history yet to be written America knows that this world of ours, ever growing smaller, must avoid becoming a community of dreadful fear and hate, and be instead, a proud confederation of mutual trust and respect.

Such a confederation must be one of equals. The weakest must come to the conference table with the same confidence as do we, protected as we are by our moral, economic, and military strength. That table, though scarred by many past frustrations, cannot be abandoned for the certain agony of the battlefield.

Disarmament, with mutual honor and confidence, is a continuing imperative. Together we must learn how to compose differences, not with arms, but with intellect and decent purpose. Because this need is so sharp and apparent I confess that I lay down my official responsibilities in this field with a definite sense of disappointment. As one who has witnessed the horror and the lingering sadness of war—as one who knows that another war could utterly destroy this civilization which has been so slowly and painfully built over thousands of years—I wish I could say tonight that a lasting peace is in sight.

Happily, I can say that war has been avoided. Steady progress toward our ultimate goal has been made. But, so much remains to be done. As a private citizen, I shall never cease to do what little I can to help the world advance along that road.

VII.

So—in this my last good night to you as your President—I thank you for the many opportunities you have given me for public service in war and peace. I trust that in that service you find some things worthy; as for the rest of it, I know you will find ways to improve performance in the future.

You and I—my fellow citizens—need to be strong in our faith that all nations, under God, will reach the goal of peace with justice. May we be ever unswerving in devotion to principle, confident but humble with power, diligent in pursuit of the Nation's great goals.

To all the peoples of the world, I once more give expression to America's prayerful and continuing aspiration:

We pray that peoples of all faiths, all races, all nations, may have their great human needs satisfied; that those now denied opportunity shall come to enjoy it to the full; that all who yearn for freedom may experience its spiritual blessings; that those who have freedom will understand, also, its heavy responsibilities; that all who are insensitive to the needs of others will learn charity; that the scourges of poverty, disease and ignorance will be made to disappear from the earth, and that, in the goodness of time, all peoples will come to live together in a peace guaranteed by the binding force of mutual respect and love.

Inaugural Address

(Delivered in Washington, D.C., January 20, 1961)

We observe today not a victory of party but a celebration of freedom—symbolizing an end as well as a beginning—signifying renewal as well as change. For I have sworn before you and Almighty God the same solemn oath our forbears prescribed nearly a century and three-quarters ago.

The world is very different now. For man holds in his mortal hands the power to abolish all forms of human poverty and all forms of human life. And yet the same revolutionary beliefs for which our forebears fought are still at issue around the globe—the belief that the rights of man come not from the generosity of the state but from the hand of God.

We dare not forget today that we are the heirs of that first revolution. Let the word go forth from this time and place, to friend and foe alike, that the torch has been passed to a new generation of Americans—born in this century, tempered by war, disciplined by a hard and bitter peace, proud of our ancient heritage—and unwilling to witness or permit the slow undoing of those human rights to which this nation has always been committed, and to which we are committed today at home and around the world.

Let every nation know, whether it wishes us well or ill, that we shall pay any price, bear any burden, meet any hardship, support any friend, oppose any foe to assure the survival and the success of liberty.

This much we pledge—and more.

To those old allies whose cultural and spiritual origins we share, we pledge the loyalty of faithful friends. United, there is little we cannot do in a host of cooperative ventures. Divided, there is little we can do—for we dare not meet a powerful challenge at odds and split asunder.

To those new states whom we welcome to the ranks of the free, we pledge our word that one form of colonial control shall not have passed away merely to be replaced by a far more iron tyranny. We shall not always expect to find them supporting our view. But we shall always hope to find them strongly supporting their own freedom—and to remember that, in the past, those who foolishly sought power by riding the back of the tiger ended up inside.

To those people in the huts and villages of half the globe struggling to break the bonds of mass misery, we pledge our best efforts to help them help themselves, for whatever period is required—not because the communists may be doing it, not because we seek their votes, but because it is right. If a free society cannot help the many who are poor, it cannot save the few who are rich.

To our sister republics south of our border, we offer a special pledge—to convert our good words into good deeds—in a new alliance for progress—to assist free men and free governments in casting off the chains of poverty. But this peaceful revolution of hope cannot become the prey of hostile powers. Let all our neighbors know that we shall join with them to oppose aggression or subversion anywhere in the Americas. And let every other power know that this Hemisphere intends to remain the master of its own house.

To that world assembly of sovereign states, the United Nations, our last best hope in an age where the instruments of war have far outpaced the instruments of peace, we renew our pledge of support—to prevent it from becoming merely a forum for invective—to strengthen its shield of the new and the weak—and to enlarge the area in which its writ may run.

Finally, to those nations who would make themselves our adversary, we offer not a pledge but a request: that both sides begin anew the quest for peace, before the dark powers of destruction unleashed by science engulf all humanity in planned or accidental self-destruction.

We dare not tempt them with weakness. For only when our arms are sufficient beyond doubt can we be certain beyond doubt that they will never be employed.

But neither can two great and powerful groups of nations take comfort from our present course—both sides overburdened by the cost of modern weapons, both rightly alarmed by the steady spread of the deadly atom, yet both racing to alter that uncertain balance of terror that stays the hand of mankind's final war.

So let us begin anew—remembering on both sides that civility is not a sign of weakness, and sincerity is always subject to proof. Let us never negotiate out of fear. But let us never fear to negotiate.

Let both sides explore what problems unite us instead of belaboring those problems which divide us.

Let both sides, for the first time, formulate serious and precise proposals for the inspection and control of arms—and bring the absolute power to destroy other nations under the absolute control of all nations.

Let both sides seek to invoke the wonders of science instead of its terrors. Together let us explore the stars, conquer the deserts, eradicate disease, tap the ocean depths and encourage the arts and commerce.

Let both sides unite to heed in all corners of the earth the command of Isaiah—to "undo the heavy burdens . . . (and) let the oppressed go free."

And if a beach-head of cooperation may push back the jungle of suspicion, let both sides join in creating a new endeavor, not a new balance of power, but a new world of law, where the strong are just and the weak secure and the peace preserved.

All this will not be finished in the first one hundred days. Nor will it be finished in the first one thousand days, nor in the life of this Administration, nor even perhaps in our lifetime on this planet. But let us begin.

In your hands, my fellow citizens, more than mine, will rest the final success or failure of our course. Since this country was founded, each generation of Americans has been summoned to give testimony to its national loyalty. The graves of young Americans who answered the call to service surround the globe.

Now the trumpet summons us again—not as a call to bear arms, though arms we need—not as a call to battle, though embattled we are—but a call to bear the burden of a long twilight struggle, year in and year out, "rejoicing in hope, patient in tribulation"—a struggle against the common enemies of man: tyranny, poverty, disease and war itself.

Can we forge against these enemies a grand and global alliance, North and South, East and West, that can assure a more fruitful life for all mankind? Will you join in that historic effort?

In the long history of the world, only a few generations have been granted the role of defending freedom in its hour of maximum danger. I do not shrink from this responsibility—I welcome it. I do not believe that any of us would exchange places with any other people or any other generation. The energy, the faith, the devotion which we bring to this endeavor will light our country and all who serve it—and the glow from that fire can truly light the world.

And so, my fellow Americans: ask not what your country can do for you—ask what you can do for your country.

My fellow citizens of the world: ask not what America will do for you, but what together we can do for the freedom of man.

Finally, whether you are citizens of America or citizens of the world, ask of us here the same high standards of strength and sacrifice which we ask of you. With a good conscience our only sure reward, with history the final judge of our deeds, let us go forth to lead the land we love, asking His blessing and His help, but knowing that here on earth God's work must truly be our own.

Remarks in the Rudolph Wilde Platz, Berlin

(Delivered in Berlin, West Germany, June 26, 1963)

I am proud to come to this city as the guest of your distinguished Mayor, who has symbolized throughout the world the fighting spirit of West Berlin. And I am proud to visit the Federal Republic with your distinguished Chancellor who for so many years has committed Germany to democracy and freedom and progress, and to come here in the company of my fellow American, General Clay, who has been in this city during its great moments of crisis and will come again if ever needed.

Two thousand years ago the proudest boast was *"civis Romanus sum."* Today, in the world of freedom, the proudest boast is *"Ich bin ein Berliner."*

I appreciate my interpreter translating my German!

There are many people in the world who really don't understand, or say they don't, what is the great issue between the free world and the Communist world. Let them come to Berlin. There are some who say that communism is the wave of the future. Let them come to Berlin. And there are some who say in Europe and elsewhere we can work with the Communists. Let them come to Berlin. And there are even a few who say that it is true that communism is an evil system, but it permits us to make economic progress. *Lass' sie nach Berlin kommen.* Let them come to Berlin.

Freedom has many difficulties and democracy is not perfect, but we have never had to put a wall up to keep our people in, to prevent them from leaving us. I want to say, on behalf of my countrymen, who live many miles away on the other side of the Atlantic, who are far distant from you, that they take the greatest pride that they have been able to share with you, even from a distance, the story of the last eighteen years. I know of no town, no city, that has been besieged for eighteen years that still lives with the vitality and the force, and the hope and the determination of the city of West Berlin. While the wall is the most obvious and vivid demonstration of the failures of the Communist system, for all the world to see, we take no satisfaction in it, for it is, as your Mayor has said, an offense not only against history but an offense against humanity, separating families, dividing husbands and wives and brothers and sisters, and dividing a people who wish to be joined together.

What is true of this city is true of Germany—real, lasting peace in Europe can never be assured as long as one German out of four is denied the elementary right of free men, and that is to make a free choice. In eighteen years of peace and good faith, this generation of Germans has earned the right to be free, including the right to unite their families and their nation in lasting peace, with good will to all people. You live in a defended island of freedom, but your life is part of the main. So let me ask you, as I close, to lift your eyes beyond the dangers of today, to the hopes of tomorrow, beyond the freedom merely of this city of Berlin, or your country of Germany, to the advance of freedom everywhere, beyond the wall to the day of peace with justice, beyond yourselves and ourselves to all mankind.

Freedom is indivisible, and when one man is enslaved, all are not free. When all are free, then we can look forward to that day when this city will be joined as one and this country and this great Continent of Europe in a peaceful and hopeful globe. When that day finally comes, as it will, the people of West Berlin can take sober satisfaction in the fact that they were in the front lines for almost two decades.

All free men, wherever they may live, are citizens of Berlin, and, therefore, as a free man, I take pride in the words *"Ich bin ein Berliner."*

Report to the American People on Civil Rights

(Delivered in Washington, D.C., June 11, 1963)

This afternoon, following a series of threats and defiant statements, the presence of Alabama National Guardsmen was required on the University of Alabama to carry out the final and unequivocal order of the United States District Court of the Northern District of Alabama. That order called for the admission of two clearly qualified young Alabama residents who happened to have been born Negro.

That they were admitted peacefully on the campus is due in good measure to the conduct of the students of the University of Alabama, who met their responsibilities in a constructive way.

I hope that every American, regardless of where he lives, will stop and examine his conscience about this and other related incidents. This Nation was founded by men of many nations and backgrounds. It was founded on the principle that all men are created equal, and that the rights of every man are diminished when the rights of one man are threatened.

Today we are committed to a worldwide struggle to promote and protect the rights of all who wish to be free. And when Americans are sent to Viet-Nam or West Berlin, we do not ask for whites only. It ought to be possible, therefore, for American students of any color to attend any public institution they select without having to be backed up by troops.

It ought to be possible for American consumers of any color to receive equal service in places of public accommodation, such as hotels and restaurants and theaters and retail stores, without being forced to resort to demonstrations in the street, and it ought to be possible for American citizens of any color to register and to vote in a free election without interference or fear of reprisal.

It ought to be possible, in short, for every American to enjoy the privileges of being American without regard to his race or his color. In short, every American ought to have the right to be treated as he would wish to be treated, as one would wish his children to be treated. But this is not the case.

The Negro baby born in America today, regardless of the section of the Nation in which he is born, has about one-half as much chance of completing a high school as a white baby born in the same place on the same day, one-third as much chance of completing college, one-third as much chance of becoming a professional man, twice as much chance of becoming unemployed, about one-seventh as much chance of earning $10,000 a year, a life expectancy which is seven years shorter, and the prospects of earning only half as much.

This is not a sectional issue. Difficulties over segregation and discrimination exist in every city, in every State of the Union, producing in many cities a rising tide of discontent that threatens the public safety. Nor is this a partisan issue. In a time of domestic crisis men of good will and generosity should be able to unite regardless of party or politics. This is not even a legal or legislative issue alone. It is better to settle these matters in the courts than on the streets, and new laws are needed at every level, but law alone cannot make men see right.

We are confronted primarily with a moral issue. It is as old as the scriptures and is as clear as the American Constitution.

The heart of the question is whether all Americans are to be afforded equal rights and equal opportunities, whether we are going to treat our fellow Americans as we want to be treated. If an American, because his skin is dark, cannot eat lunch in a restaurant open to the public, if he cannot send his children to the best public school available, if he cannot vote for the public officials who represent him, if, in short, he cannot enjoy the full and free life which all of us want, then who among us would be content to have the color of his skin changed and stand in his place? Who among us would then be content with the counsels of patience and delay?

One hundred years of delay have passed since President Lincoln freed the slaves, yet their heirs, their grandsons, are not fully free. They are not yet freed from the bonds of injustice. They are not yet freed from social and economic oppression. And this Nation, for all its hopes and all its boasts, will not be fully free until all its citizens are free.

We preach freedom around the world, and we mean it, and we cherish our freedom here at home, but are we to say to the world, and much more importantly, to each other that this is a land of the free except for the Negroes; that we have no second-class citizens except Negroes; that we have no class or cast system, no ghettoes, no master race except with respect to Negroes?

Now the time has come for this Nation to fulfill its promise. The events in Birmingham and elsewhere have so increased the cries for equality that no city or State or legislative body can prudently choose to ignore them.

The fires of frustration and discord are burning in every city, North and South, where legal remedies are not at hand. Redress is sought in the streets, in demonstrations, parades, and protests which create tensions and threaten violence and threaten lives.

We face, therefore, a moral crisis as a country and as a people. It cannot be met by repressive police action. It cannot be left to increased demonstrations in the streets. It cannot be quieted by token moves or talk. It is a time to act in the Congress, in your State and local legislative body and, above all, in all of our daily lives.

It is not enough to pin the blame on others, to say this is a problem of one section of the country or another, or deplore the fact that we face. A great change is at hand, and our task, our obligation, is to make that revolution, that change, peaceful and constructive for all.

Those who do nothing are inviting shame as well as violence. Those who act boldly are recognizing right as well as reality.

Next week I shall ask the Congress of the United States to act, to make a commitment it has not fully made in this century to the proposition that race has no place in American life or law. The Federal judiciary has upheld that proposition in a series of forthright cases. The executive branch has adopted that proposition in the conduct of its affairs, including the employment of Federal personnel, the use of Federal facilities, and the sale of federally financed housing.

But there are other necessary measures which only the Congress can provide, and they must be provided at this session. The old code of equity law under which we live commands for every wrong a remedy, but in too many communities, in too many parts of the country, wrongs are inflicted on Negro citizens and there are no remedies at law. Unless the Congress acts, their only remedy is in the street.

I am, therefore, asking the Congress to enact legislation giving all Americans the right to be served in facilities which are open to the public—hotels, restaurants, theaters, retail stores, and similar establishments.

This seems to me to be an elementary right. Its denial is an arbitrary indignity that no American in 1963 should have to endure, but many do.

I have recently met with scores of business leaders urging them to take voluntary action to end this discrimination and I have been encouraged by their response, and in the last two weeks over seventy-five cities have seen progress made in desegregating these kinds of facilities. But many are unwilling to act alone, and for this reason, nationwide legislation is needed if we are to move this problem from the streets to the courts.

I am also asking Congress to authorize the Federal Government to participate more fully in lawsuits designed to end segregation in public education. We have succeeded in persuading many districts to de-segregate voluntarily. Dozens have admitted Negroes without violence. Today a Negro is attending a State-supported institution in every one of our fifty States, but the pace is very slow.

Too many Negro children entering segregated grade schools at the time of the Supreme Court's decision nine years ago will enter segregated high schools this fall, having suffered a loss which can never be restored. The lack of an adequate education denies the Negro a chance to get a decent job.

The orderly implementation of the Supreme Court decision, therefore, cannot be left solely to those who may not have the economic resources to carry the legal action or who may be subject to harassment.

Other features will be also requested, including greater protection for the right to vote. But legislation, I repeat, cannot solve this problem alone. It must be solved in the homes of every American in every community across our country.

In this respect, I want to pay tribute to those citizens North and South who have been working in their communities to make life better for all. They are acting not out of a sense of legal duty but out of a sense of human decency.

Like our soldiers and sailors in all parts of the world they are meeting freedom's challenge on the firing line, and I salute them for their honor and their courage.

My fellow Americans, this is a problem which faces us all—in every city of the North as well as the South. Today there are Negroes unemployed, two or three times as many compared to whites, inadequate in education, moving into the large cities, unable to find work, young people particularly out of work without hope, denied equal rights, denied the opportunity to eat at a restaurant or lunch counter or go to a movie theater, denied the right to a decent education, denied almost today the right to attend a State university even though qualified. It seems to me that these are matters which concern us all, not merely Presidents or Congressmen or Governors, but every citizen of the United States.

This is one country. It has become one country because all of us and all the people who came here had an equal chance to develop their talents.

We cannot say to ten percent of the population that you can't have that right; that your children can't have the chance to develop whatever talents they have; that the only way that they are going to get their rights is to go into the streets and demonstrate. I think we owe them and we owe ourselves a better country than that.

Therefore, I am asking for your help in making it easier for us to move ahead and to provide the kind of equality of treatment which we would want ourselves; to give a chance for every child to be educated to the limit of his talents.

As I have said before, not every child has an equal talent or an equal ability or an equal motivation, but they should have the equal right to develop their talent and their ability and their motivation, to make something of themselves.

We have a right to expect that the Negro community will be responsible, will uphold the law, but they have a right to expect that the law will be fair, that the Constitution will be color blind, as Justice Harlan said at the turn of the century.

This is what we are talking about and this is a matter which concerns this country and what it stands for, and in meeting it I ask the support of all our citizens.

Thank you very much.

Lyndon B. Johnson

"The Great Society" Speech

(Delivered at the University of Michigan in Ann Arbor, May 22, 1964)

It is a great pleasure to be here today. This university has been coeducational since 1870, but I do not believe it was on the basis of your accomplishments that a Detroit high school girl said, "In choosing a college, you first have to decide whether you want a coeducational school or an educational school."

Well, we can find both here at Michigan, although perhaps at different hours.

I came out here today very anxious to meet the Michigan student whose father told a friend of mine that his son's education had been a real value. It stopped his mother from bragging about him.

I have come today from the turmoil of your Capital to the tranquility of your campus to speak about the future of your country.

The purpose of protecting the life of our Nation and preserving the liberty of our citizens is to pursue the happiness of our people. Our success in that pursuit is the test of our success as a Nation.

For a century we labored to settle and to subdue a continent. For half a century we called upon unbounded invention and untiring industry to create an order of plenty for all of our people.

The challenge of the next half century is whether we have the wisdom to use that wealth to enrich and elevate our national life, and to advance the quality of our American civilization.

Your imagination, your initiative, and your indignation will determine whether we build a society where progress is the servant of our needs, or a society where old values and new visions are buried under unbridled growth. For in your time we have the opportunity to move not only toward the rich society and the powerful society, but upward to the Great Society.

The Great Society rests on abundance and liberty for all. It demands an end to poverty and racial injustice, to which we are totally committed in our time. But that is just the beginning.

The Great Society is a place where every child can find knowledge to enrich his mind and to enlarge his talents. It is a place where leisure is a welcome chance to build and reflect, not a feared cause of boredom and restlessness. It is a place where the city of man serves not only the needs of the body and the demands of commerce but the desire for beauty and the hunger for community.

It is a place where man can renew contact with nature. It is a place which honors creation for its own sake and for what it adds to the understanding of the race. It is a place where men are more concerned with the quality of their goals than the quantity of their goods.

But most of all, the Great Society is not a safe harbor, a resting place, a final objective, a finished work. It is a challenge constantly renewed, beckoning us toward a destiny where the meaning of our lives matches the marvelous products of our labor.

So I want to talk to you today about three places where we begin to build the Great Society—in our cities, in our countryside, and in our classrooms.

Many of you will live to see the day, perhaps fifty years from now, when there will be 400 million Americans—four-fifths of them in urban areas. In the remainder of this century urban population will double, city land will double, and we will have to build homes, highways, and facilities equal to all those built since this country was first settled. So in the next forty years we must rebuild the entire urban United States.

Aristotle said: "Men come together in cities in order to live, but they remain together in order to live the good life." It is harder and harder to live the good life in American cities today.

The catalog of ills is long: there is the decay of the centers and the despoiling of the suburbs. There is not enough housing for our people or transportation for our traffic. Open land is vanishing and old landmarks are violated.

Worst of all expansion is eroding the precious and time honored values of community with neighbors and communion with nature. The loss of these values breeds loneliness and boredom and indifference.

Our society will never be great until our cities are great. Today the frontier of imagination and innovation is inside those cities and not beyond their borders.

New experiments are already going on. It will be the task of your generation to make the American city a place where future generations will come, not only to live but to live the good life.

I understand that if I stayed here tonight I would see that Michigan students are really doing their best to live the good life.

This is the place where the Peace Corps was started. It is inspiring to see how all of you, while you are in this country, are trying so hard to live at the level of the people.

A second place where we begin to build the Great Society is in our countryside. We have always prided ourselves on being not only America the strong and America the free, but America the beautiful. Today that beauty is in danger. The water we drink, the food we eat, the very air that we breathe, are threatened with pollution. Our parks are overcrowded, our seashores overburdened. Green fields and dense forests are disappearing.

A few years ago we were greatly concerned about the "Ugly American." Today we must act to prevent an ugly America.

For once the battle is lost, once our natural splendor is destroyed, it can never be recaptured. And once man can no longer walk with beauty or wonder at nature his spirit will wither and his sustenance be wasted.

A third place to build the Great Society is in the classrooms of America. There your children's lives will be shaped. Our society will not be great until every young mind is set free to scan the farthest reaches of thought and imagination. We are still far from that goal.

Today, eight million adult Americans, more than the entire population of Michigan, have not finished five years of school. Nearly twenty million have not finished eight years of school. Nearly fifty-four million—more than one-quarter of all America—have not even finished high school.

Each year more than 100,000 high school graduates, with proved ability, do not enter college because they cannot afford it. And if we cannot educate today's youth, what will we do in 1970 when elementary school enrollment will be five million greater than 1960? And high school enrollment will rise by five million. College enrollment will increase by more than three million.

In many places, classrooms are overcrowded and curricula are outdated. Most of our qualified teachers are underpaid, and many of our paid teachers are unqualified. So we must give every child a place to sit and a teacher to learn from. Poverty must not be a bar to learning, and learning must offer an escape from poverty.

But more classrooms and more teachers are not enough. We must seek an educational system which grows in excellence as it grows in size. This means better training for our teachers. It means preparing youth to enjoy their hours of leisure as well as their hours of labor. It means exploring new techniques of teaching, to find new ways to stimulate the love of learning and the capacity for creation.

These are three of the central issues of the Great Society. While our Government has many programs directed at those issues, I do not pretend that we have the full answer to those problems.

But I do promise this: We are going to assemble the best thought and the broadest knowledge from all over the world to find those answers for America. I intend to establish working groups to prepare a series of White House conferences and meetings—on the cities, on natural beauty, on the quality of education, and on other emerging challenges. And from these meetings and from this inspiration and from these studies we will begin to set our course toward the Great Society.

The solution to these problems does not rest on a massive program in Washington, nor can it rely solely on the strained resources of local authority. They require us to create new concepts of cooperation, a creative federalism, between the National Capital and the leaders of local communities.

Woodrow Wilson once wrote: "Every man sent out from his university should be a man of his Nation as well as a man of his time."

Within your lifetime powerful forces, already loosed, will take us toward a way of life beyond the realm of our experience, almost beyond the bounds of our imagination.

For better or for worse, your generation has been appointed by history to deal with those problems and to lead America toward a new age. You have the chance never before afforded to any people in any age. You can help build a society where the demands of morality, and the needs of the spirit, can be realized in the life of the Nation.

So, will you join in the battle to give every citizen the full equality which God enjoins and the law requires, whatever his belief, or race, or the color of his skin?

Will you join in the battle to give every citizen an escape from the crushing weight of poverty?

Will you join in the battle to make it possible for all nations to live in enduring peace—as neighbors and not as mortal enemies?

Will you join in the battle to build the Great Society, to prove that our material progress is only the foundation on which we will build a richer life of mind and spirit?

There are those timid souls who say this battle cannot be won; that we are condemned to a soulless wealth. I do not agree. We have the power to shape the civilization that we want. But we need your will, your labor, your hearts, if we are to build that kind of society.

Those who came to this land sought to build more than just a new country. They sought a new world. So I have come here today to your campus to say that you can make their vision our reality. So let us from this moment begin our work so that in the future men will look back and say: It was then, after a long and weary way, that man turned the exploits of his genius to the full enrichment of his life.

Thank you. Goodby.

The American Promise

(Delivered in Washington, D.C., March 15, 1965)

I speak tonight for the dignity of man and the destiny of democracy.

I urge every member of both parties, Americans of all religions and of all colors, from every section of this country, to join me in that cause.

At times history and fate meet at a single time in a single place to shape a turning point in man's unending search for freedom. So it was at Lexington and Concord. So it was a century ago at Appomattox. So it was last week in Selma, Alabama.

There, long-suffering men and women peacefully protested the denial of their rights as Americans. Many were brutally assaulted. One good man, a man of God, was killed.

There is no cause for pride in what has happened in Selma. There is no cause for self-satisfaction in the long denial of equal rights of millions of Americans. But there is cause for hope and for faith in our democracy in what is happening here tonight.

For the cries of pain and the hymns and protests of oppressed people have summoned into convocation all the majesty of this great Government—the Government of the greatest Nation on earth.

Our mission is at once the oldest and the most basic of this country: to right wrong, to do justice, to serve man.

In our time we have come to live with moments of great crisis. Our lives have been marked with debate about great issues; issues of war and peace, issues of prosperity and depression. But rarely in any time does an issue lay bare the secret heart of America itself. Rarely are we met with a challenge, not to our growth or abundance, our welfare or our security, but rather to the values and the purposes and the meaning of our beloved Nation.

The issue of equal rights for American Negroes is such an issue. And should we defeat every enemy, should we double our wealth and conquer the stars, and still be unequal to this issue, then we will have failed as a people and as a nation.

For with a country as with a person, "What is a man profited, if he shall gain the whole world, and lose his own soul?"

There is no Negro problem. There is no Southern problem. There is no Northern problem. There is only an American problem. And we are met here tonight as Americans—not as Democrats or Republicans—we are met here as Americans to solve that problem.

This was the first nation in the history of the world to be founded with a purpose. The great phrases of that purpose still sound in every American heart, North and South: "All men are created equal"—"government by consent of the governed"—"give me liberty or give me death." Well, those are not just clever words, or those are not just empty theories. In their name Americans have fought and died for two centuries, and tonight around the world they stand there as guardians of our liberty, risking their lives.

Those words are a promise to every citizen that he shall share in the dignity of man. This dignity cannot be found in a man's possessions; it cannot be found in his power, or in his position. It really rests on his right to be treated as a man equal in opportunity to all others. It says that he shall share in freedom, he shall choose his leaders, educate his children, and provide for his family according to his ability and his merits as a human being.

To apply any other test—to deny a man his hopes because of his color or race, his religion or the place of his birth—is not only to do injustice, it is to deny America and to dishonor the dead who gave their lives for American freedom.

THE RIGHT TO VOTE

Our fathers believed that if this noble view of the rights of man was to flourish, it must be rooted in democracy. The most basic right of all was the right to choose your own leaders. The history of this country, in large measure, is the history of the expansion of that right to all of our people.

Many of the issues of civil rights are very complex and most difficult. But about this there can and should be no argument. Every American citizen must have an equal right to vote. There is no reason which can excuse the denial of that right. There is no duty which weighs more heavily on us than the duty we have to ensure that right.

Yet the harsh fact is that in many places in this country men and women are kept from voting simply because they are Negroes.

Every device of which human ingenuity is capable has been used to deny this right. The Negro citizen may go to register only to be told that the day is wrong, or the hour is late, or the official in charge is absent. And if he persists, and if he manages to present himself to the registrar, he may be disqualified because he did not spell out his middle name or because he abbreviated a word on the application.

And if he manages to fill out an application he is given a test. The registrar is the sole judge of whether he passes this test. He may be asked to recite the entire Constitution, or explain the most complex provisions of State law. And even a college degree cannot be used to prove that he can read and write.

For the fact is that the only way to pass these barriers is to show a white skin.

Experience has clearly shown that the existing process of law cannot overcome systematic and ingenious discrimination. No law that we now have on the books—and I have helped to put three of them there—can ensure the right to vote when local officials are determined to deny it.

In such a case our duty must be clear to all of us. The Constitution says that no person shall be kept from voting because of his race or his color. We have all sworn an oath before God to support and to defend that Constitution. We must now act in obedience to that oath.

GUARANTEEING THE RIGHT TO VOTE

Wednesday I will send to Congress a law designed to eliminate illegal barriers to the right to vote.

The broad principles of that bill will be in the hands of the Democratic and Republican leaders tomorrow. After they have reviewed it, it will come here formally as a bill. I am grateful for this opportunity to come here tonight at the invitation of the leadership to reason with my friends, to give them my views, and to visit with my former colleagues.

I have had prepared a more comprehensive analysis of the legislation which I had intended to transmit to the clerk tomorrow but which I will submit to the clerks tonight. But I want to really discuss with you now briefly the main proposals of this legislation.

This bill will strike down restrictions to voting in all elections—Federal, State, and local—which have been used to deny Negroes the right to vote.

This bill will establish a simple, uniform standard which cannot be used, however ingenious the effort, to flout our Constitution.

It will provide for citizens to be registered by officials of the United States Government if the State officials refuse to register them.

It will eliminate tedious, unnecessary lawsuits which delay the right to vote.

Finally, this legislation will ensure that properly registered individuals are not prohibited from voting.

I will welcome the suggestions from all of the Members of Congress—I have no doubt that I will get some—on ways and means to strengthen this law and to make it effective. But experience has plainly shown that this is the only path to carry out the command of the Constitution.

To those who seek to avoid action by their National Government in their own communities; who want to and who seek to maintain purely local control over elections, the answer is simple:

Open your polling places to all your people.

Allow men and women to register and vote whatever the color of their skin.

Extend the rights of citizenship to every citizen of this land.

THE NEED FOR ACTION

There is no constitutional issue here. The command of the Constitution is plain.

There is no moral issue. It is wrong—deadly wrong—to deny any of your fellow Americans the right to vote in this country.

There is no issue of States rights or national rights. There is only the struggle for human rights.

I have not the slightest doubt what will be your answer.

The last time a President sent a civil rights bill to the Congress it contained a provision to protect voting rights in Federal elections. That civil rights bill was passed after eight long months of debate. And when that bill came to my desk from the Congress for my signature, the heart of the voting provision had been eliminated.

This time, on this issue, there must be no delay, no hesitation and no compromise with our purpose.

We cannot, we must not, refuse to protect the right of every American to vote in every election that he may desire to participate in. And we ought not and we cannot and we must not wait another eight months before we get a bill. We have already waited a hundred years and more, and the time for waiting is gone.

So I ask you to join me in working long hours—nights and weekends, if necessary—to pass this bill. And I don't make that request lightly. For from the window where I sit with the problems of our country I recognize that outside this chamber is the outraged conscience of a nation, the grave concern of many nations, and the harsh judgment of history on our acts.

WE SHALL OVERCOME

But even if we pass this bill, the battle will not be over. What happened in Selma is part of a far larger movement which reaches into every section and State of

America. It is the effort of American Negroes to secure for themselves the full blessings of American life.

Their cause must be our cause too. Because it is not just Negroes, but really it is all of us, who must overcome the crippling legacy of bigotry and injustice.

And we shall overcome.

As a man whose roots go deeply into Southern soil I know how agonizing racial feelings are. I know how difficult it is to reshape the attitudes and the structure of our society.

But a century has passed, more than a hundred years, since the Negro was freed. And he is not fully free tonight.

It was more than a hundred years ago that Abraham Lincoln, a great President of another party, signed the Emancipation Proclamation, but emancipation is a proclamation and not a fact.

A century has passed, more than a hundred years, since equality was promised. And yet the Negro is not equal.

A century has passed since the day of promise. And the promise is unkept.

The time of justice has now come. I tell you that I believe sincerely that no force can hold it back. It is right in the eyes of man and God that it should come. And when it does, I think that day will brighten the lives of every American.

For Negroes are not the only victims. How many white children have gone uneducated, how many white families have lived in stark poverty, how many white lives have been scarred by fear, because we have wasted our energy and our substance to maintain the barriers of hatred and terror?

So I say to all of you here, and to all in the Nation tonight, that those who appeal to you to hold on to the past do so at the cost of denying you your future.

This great, rich, restless country can offer opportunity and education and hope to all: black and white, North and South, sharecropper and city dweller. These are the enemies: poverty, ignorance, disease. They are the enemies and not our fellow man, not our neighbor. And these enemies too, poverty, disease and ignorance, we shall overcome.

An American Problem

Now let none of us in any sections look with prideful righteousness on the troubles in another section, or on the problems of our neighbors. There is really no part of America where the promise of equality has been fully kept. In Buffalo as well as in Birmingham, in Philadelphia as well as in Selma, Americans are struggling for the fruits of freedom.

This is one Nation. What happens in Selma or in Cincinnati is a matter of legitimate concern to every American. But let each of us look within our own hearts and our own communities, and let each of us put our shoulder to the wheel to root out injustice wherever it exists.

As we meet here in this peaceful, historic chamber tonight, men from the South, some of whom were at Iwo Jima, men from the North who have carried Old Glory to far corners of the world and brought it back without a stain on it, men from the East and from the West, are all fighting together without regard to religion, or color, or region, in Viet-Nam. Men from every region fought for us across the world twenty years ago.

And in these common dangers and these common sacrifices the South made its contribution of honor and gallantry no less than any other region of the great Republic—and in some instances, a great many of them, more.

And I have not the slightest doubt that good men from everywhere in this country, from the Great Lakes to the Gulf of Mexico, from the Golden Gate to the harbors along the Atlantic, will rally together now in this cause to vindicate the freedom of all Americans. For all of us owe this duty; and I believe that all of us will respond to it.

Your President makes that request of every American.

Progress Through the Democratic Process

The real hero of this struggle is the American Negro. His actions and protests, his courage to risk safety and even to risk his life, have awakened the conscience of this Nation. His demonstrations have been designed to call attention to injustice, designed to provoke change, designed to stir reform.

He has called upon us to make good the promise of America. And who among us can say that we would have made the same progress were it not for his persistent bravery, and his faith in American democracy.

For at the real heart of battle for equality is a deep-seated belief in the democratic process. Equality depends not on the force of arms or tear gas but upon the force of moral right; not on recourse to violence but on respect for law and order.

There have been many pressures upon your President and there will be others as the days come and go. But I pledge you tonight that we intend to fight this battle where it should be fought: in the courts, and in the Congress, and in the hearts of men.

We must preserve the right of free speech and the right of free assembly. But the right of free speech does not carry with it, as has been said, the right to holler fire in a crowded theater. We must preserve the right to free assembly, but free assembly does not carry with it the right to block public thoroughfares to traffic.

We do have a right to protest, and a right to march under conditions that do not infringe the constitutional rights of our neighbors. And I intend to protect all those rights as long as I am permitted to serve in this office.

We will guard against violence, knowing it strikes from our hands the very weapons which we seek—progress, obedience to law, and belief in American values.

In Selma as elsewhere we seek and pray for peace. We seek order. We seek unity. But we will not accept the peace of stifled rights, or the order imposed by fear, or the unity that stifles protest. For peace cannot be purchased at the cost of liberty.

In Selma tonight, as in every—and we had a good day there—as in every city, we are working for just and peaceful settlement. We must all remember that after this speech I am making tonight, after the police and the FBI and the Marshals have all gone, and after you have promptly passed this bill, the people of Selma and the other cities of the Nation must still live and work together. And when the attention of the Nation has gone elsewhere they must try to heal the wounds and to build a new community.

This cannot be easily done on a battleground of violence, as the history of the South itself shows. It is in recognition of this that men of both races have shown such an outstandingly impressive responsibility in recent days—last Tuesday, again today.

RIGHTS MUST BE OPPORTUNITIES

The bill that I am presenting to you will be known as a civil rights bill. But, in a larger sense, most of the program I am recommending is a civil rights program. Its object is to open the city of hope to all people of all races.

Because all Americans just must have the right to vote. And we are going to give them that right.

All Americans must have the privileges of citizenship regardless of race. And they are going to have those privileges of citizenship regardless of race.

But I would like to caution you and remind you that to exercise these privileges takes much more than just legal right. It requires a trained mind and a healthy body. It requires a decent home, and the chance to find a job, and the opportunity to escape from the clutches of poverty.

Of course, people cannot contribute to the Nation if they are never taught to read or write, if their bodies are stunted from hunger, if their sickness goes untended, if their life is spent in hopeless poverty just drawing a welfare check.

So we want to open the gates to opportunity. But we are also going to give all our people, black and white, the help that they need to walk through those gates.

THE PURPOSE OF THIS GOVERNMENT

My first job after college was as a teacher in Cotulla, Texas, in a small Mexican-American school. Few of them could speak English, and I couldn't speak much Spanish. My students were poor and they often came to class without breakfast, hungry. They knew even in their youth the pain of prejudice. They never seemed to know why people disliked them. But they knew it was so, because I saw it in their eyes. I often walked home late in the afternoon, after the classes were finished, wishing there was more that I could do. But all I knew was to teach them the little that I knew, hoping that it might help them against the hardships that lay ahead.

Somehow you never forget what poverty and hatred can do when you see its scars on the hopeful face of a young child.

I never thought then, in 1928, that I would be standing here in 1965. It never even occurred to me in my fondest dreams that I might have the chance to help the sons and daughters of those students and to help people like them all over this country.

But now I do have that chance—and I'll let you in on a secret—I mean to use it. And I hope that you will use it with me.

This is the richest and most powerful country which ever occupied the globe. The might of past empires is little compared to ours. But I do not want to be the President who built empires, or sought grandeur, or extended dominion.

I want to be the President who educated young children to the wonders of their world. I want to be the President who helped to feed the hungry and to prepare them to be taxpayers instead of taxeaters.

I want to be the President who helped the poor to find their own way and who protected the right of every citizen to vote in every election.

I want to be the President who helped to end hatred among his fellow men and who promoted love among the people of all races and all regions and all parties.

I want to be the President who helped to end war among the brothers of this earth.

And so at the request of your beloved Speaker and the Senator from Montana; the majority leader, the Senator from Illinois; the minority leader, Mr. McCulloch, and other Members of both parties, I came here tonight—not as President Roosevelt came down one time in person to veto a bonus bill, not as President Truman came down one time to urge the passage of a railroad bill—but I came down here to ask you to share this task with me and to share it with the people that we both work for. I want this to be the Congress, Republicans and Democrats alike, which did all these things for all these people.

Beyond this great chamber, out yonder in fifty States, are the people that we serve. Who can tell what deep and unspoken hopes are in their hearts tonight as they sit there and listen. We all can guess, from our own lives, how difficult they often find their own pursuit of happiness, how many problems each little family has. They look most of all to themselves for their futures. But I think that they also look to each of us.

Above the pyramid on the great seal of the United States it says—in Latin— "God has favored our undertaking."

God will not favor everything that we do. It is rather our duty to divine His will. But I cannot help believing that He truly understands and that He really favors the undertaking that we begin here tonight.

Lyndon B. Johnson

Special Message to Congress on the Right to Vote

(Delivered in Washington, D.C., March 15, 1965)

In this same month ninety-five years ago—on March 30, 1870—the Constitution of the United States was amended for the fifteenth time to guarantee that no citizen of our land should be denied the right to vote because of race or color.

The command of the Fifteenth Amendment is unequivocal and its equal force upon State Government and the Federal Government is unarguable.

Section 1 of this Amendment provides: "The right of citizens of the United States to vote shall not be denied or abridged by the United States or by any State on account or race, color, or previous condition of servitude.

By the oath I have taken "to preserve, protect and defend the Constitution of the United States," duty directs—and strong personal conviction impels—that I advise the Congress that action is necessary, and necessary now, if the Constitution is to be upheld and the rights of all citizens are not to be mocked, abused and denied.

I must regretfully report to the Congress the following facts:

1. That the Fifteenth Amendment of our Constitution is today being systematically and willfully circumvented in certain State and local jurisdictions of our Nation.

2. That representatives of such State and local governments acting "under the color of law," are denying American citizens the right to vote on the sole basis of race or color.

3. That, as a result of these practices, in some areas of our country today no significant number of American citizens of the Negro race can be registered to vote except upon the intervention and order of the Federal Court.

4. That the remedies available under law to citizens thus denied their Constitutional rights—and the authority presently available to the Federal Government to act in their behalf—are clearly inadequate.

5. That the denial of these rights and the frustration of efforts to obtain meaningful relief from such denial without undue delay is contributing to

the creation of conditions which are both inimical to our domestic order and tranquility and incompatible with the standards of equal justice and individual dignity on which our society stands.

I am, therefore, calling upon the Congress to discharge the duty authorized in Section 2 of the Fifteenth Amendment "to enforce this Article by appropriate legislation."

I.

It could never be a welcome duty for any President to place before Congress such a report of the willful failure and refusal of public officials to honor, respect and abide by any provision of the Constitution of the United States. It is especially repugnant to report such disregard directed against the Fifteenth Amendment by officials at the State and local levels.

The essence of our American tradition of State and local governments is the belief expressed by Thomas Jefferson that Government is best which is closest to the people. Yet that belief is betrayed by those State and local officials who engage in denying the right of citizens to vote. Their actions serve only to assure that their State governments and local governments shall be remote from the people, least representative of the people's will and least responsive to the people's wishes.

If there were no other reasons, the strengthening and protection of the vital role of State and local governments would be reasons enough to act against the denial of the right to vote for any of our citizens.

But there are other reasons to act—clear, compelling and present reasons.

1. The challenge now presented is more than a challenge to our Constitution—it is a blatant affront to the conscience of this generation of Americans. Discrimi-nation based on race or color is reprehensible and intolerable to the great American majority. In every national forum, where they have chosen to test popular sentiment, defenders of discrimination have met resounding rejection. Americans now are not willing that the acid of the few shall be allowed to corrode the souls of the many.

The Congress, the Courts, and the Executive, acting together in clear response to the will of the people and the mandate of the Constitution, have achieved more progress toward equality of rights in recent years than in all the years gone before. This tide will not be turned. The purposeful many need not and will not bow to the willful few.

2. In our system, the first right and most vital of all our rights is the right to vote. Jefferson described the elective franchise as "the ark of our safety." It is from

the exercise of this right that the guarantee of all our other rights flows.

Unless the right to vote be secure and undenied, all other rights are insecure and subject to denial for all our citizens. The challenge to this right is a challenge to America itself. We must meet this challenge as decisively as we would meet a challenge mounted against our land from enemies abroad.

3. In the world, America stands for—and works for—the right of all men to govern themselves through free, uninhibited elections. An ink bottle broken against an American Embassy, a fire set in an American library, an insult committed against our American flag, anywhere in the world, does far less injury to our country and our cause than the discriminatory denial of the right of any American citizen at home to vote on the basis of race or color.

The issue presented by the present challenge to our Constitution and our conscience transcends legalism, although it does not transcend the law itself. We are challenged to demonstrate that there are no sanctuaries within our law for those who flaunt it. We are challenged, also, to demonstrate by our prompt, fitting and adequate response now that the hope of our system is not force, not arms, not the might of militia or marshals—but the law itself.

II.

The problem of discriminatory denial of the right to vote has been with us ever since colonial times.

The test of real property ownership was universal among the colonies and religious qualifications were numerous. Race, color, sex, age, employment and residence were all used as the basis for qualifying voters. Such restrictions continued to flourish among the States even after formation of the Union.

The first literacy tests were legislated in Northern States in an effort to exclude immigrants—especially Irish—from the franchise. When the Fifteenth Amendment was adopted, there were only six States which had never discriminated against voting by Negroes.

If discrimination has been a prevalent practice in our history of voting rights, the struggle against discrimination has been our consistent purpose generation after generation.

Since the adoption of the Bill of Rights, no other right has been strengthened and fortified so often by Constitutional Amendment as the right to vote. As early as 1804—and as recently as 1964—the Constitution of the United States has been amended on at least six occasions to prohibit discrimination against the right to vote, to enlarge the franchise, and to assure the expression of the people's will as registered by them at the polls.

The challenge facing us today is not a challenge of what the Constitution of the United States shall say—but of what it shall mean.

What the Fifteenth Amendment says is unmistakable. What the Fifteenth Amendment actually means for some Americans in some jurisdictions is diametrically opposite to the clear intent of the language.

By the device of equal laws, unequally applied, Negro Americans are being denied the right and opportunity to vote and discrimination is given sanction under color of law. Varieties of techniques are infinite. Three are most commonplace.

1. *The technique of technical "error."*

Negro applicants for registration are disqualified on grounds of technical "errors" in their registration forms. Instances of record show Negroes disqualified for "errors" such as failure to write out middle names, abbreviating the words "street" and "avenue" in addresses, or failing to compute age exactly to the day. Where this techniques is employed, "errors" are found in substantially all applications filed by Negroes but few or none in applications filed by whites.

2. *The techniques of non-cooperation.*

A technique commonly used in conjunction with the "error" technique involves simple non-cooperation by the registrar. Thus, he may be "out" for most of the day during registration periods. Registration may be possible only on certain days each month. Limits may be imposed upon the number of applicants processed each registration day. The variety of circumventions possible by this device is endless.

3. *The technique of subjective tests.*

By far the most common technique by which Negro citizens are prevented from exercising their right to register and to vote is the use of subjective tests, unfairly administered literacy tests, tests of "character." The only standard used is the whim of the registrar. Such devices are used as vehicles for the rejection of untold thousands of voters—solely on the basis of race and color.

Whatever the technique, the intended purpose of such devices is effectively served.

—In one State ten years ago, 59.6 per cent of voting age white persons were registered to vote. Only 4.3 per cent of eligible Negroes were registered to vote. The changes since then are negligible.

—In several States, there are counties with sizeable Negro populations where not a single Negro is registered to vote.

—In scores of other counties where discrimination is not so blatant, it remains far more difficult for Negroes to register than for whites.

Too frequently discrimination is the aim and intent of such devices—and discrimination is the result.

III.

The Congress and the Executive Branch of the Federal Government have recognized—and sought to meet—these challenges to the authority of the Constitution of the United States. I am proud to have been closely associated with the succession of Federal enactments, beginning in 1957 with the first Civil Rights Law in more than eighty years.

The major steps taken have been these:

1. *The Civil Rights Act of 1957*: The approach of this statute was to challenge through litigation the discriminatory use of vote tests.

2. *The Civil Rights Act of 1960*: This statute, pursuing the same approach, sought to simplify such litigation.

3. *The Civil Rights Act of 1964*: Still following the same approach, sought to expedite litigation.

In some areas litigation has been effective. But eight years of litigation has made it clear that the prompt and fair registration of qualified Negro citizens cannot be achieved under present litigation in the face of consistent defiance of the laws of Congress of the command of the Constitution.

IV.

The challenge facing us is clear and immediate—it is also profound.

The Constitution is being flouted.

The intent of Congress expressed three times in the last seven years is being frustrated.

The national will is being denied.

The integrity of our Federal system is in contest.

Unless we act anew, with dispatch and resolution, we shall sanction a sad and sorrowful course for the future. For if the Fifteenth Amendment is successfully flouted today, tomorrow the First Amendment, the Fourth Amendment, the Fifth Amendment—the Sixth, the Eighth, indeed, all the provisions of the Constitution on which our system stands—will be subject to disregard and erosion. Our essential strength as a society governed by the rule of law will be crippled and corrupted and the unity of our system hollowed out and left meaningless.

For these reasons, therefore, I ask the Congress under the power clearly granted by the Fifteenth Amendment to enact legislation which would:

1. Strike down restrictions to voting in all elections—Federal, State, and local—which have been used to deny Negroes the right to vote.

2. Establish in all States and counties where the right to vote has been denied on account of race a simple standard of voter registration which will make it impossible to thwart the Fifteenth Amendment.

3. Prohibit the use of new tests and devices wherever they may be used for discriminatory purposes.

4. Provide adequate power to insure, if necessary, that Federal officials can perform functions essential to the right to vote whenever State officials deny that right.

5. Eliminate the opportunity to delay the right to vote by resort to tedious and unnecessary lawsuits.

6. Provide authority to insure that properly registered individuals will not be prohibited from voting.

Our purpose is not—and shall never be—either the quest for power or the desire to punish. We seek to increase the power of the people over all their governments, not to enhance the power of the Federal Government over any of the people.

For the life of this Republic, our people have zealously guarded their liberty against abuses of power by their governments. The one weapon they have used is the mightiest weapon in the arsenal of democracy—the vote. This has been enough, for as Woodrow Wilson said, "The instrument of all reform in America is the ballot."

Yet today, in areas of America, segments of our populace must live in just that involuntary condition—policed by forces they have no voice in choosing and forced to abide by laws they have no vote in adopting.

A people divided over the right to vote can never build a Nation united.

I am determined that these years shall be devoted to perfecting our unity so that we may pursue more successfully the fulfillment of our high purposes at home and in the world. While I have proposed to you other measures to serve the strengthening of our free society and the happiness of our free people, I regard action on the measure proposed in this Message to be first in priority. We cannot have government for all the people until we first make certain it is government of and by all the people.

Richard M. Nixon

Address to the Nation Announcing the Decision to Resign the Office of President of the United States

(Delivered in Washington, D.C., August 8, 1974)

This is the thirty-seventh time I have spoken to you from this office, where so many decisions have been made that shaped the history of this Nation. Each time I have done so to discuss with you some matter that I believe affected the national interest.

In all the decisions I have made in my public life, I have always tried to do what was best for the Nation. Throughout the long and difficult period of Watergate, I have felt it was my duty to persevere, to make every possible effort to complete the term of office to which you elected me.

In the past few days, however, it has become evident to me that I no longer have a strong enough political base in the Congress to justify continuing that effort. As long as there was such a base, I felt strongly that it was necessary to see the constitutional process through to its conclusion, that to do otherwise would be unfaithful to the spirit of that deliberately difficult process and a dangerously destabilizing precedent for the future.

But with the disappearance of that base, I now believe that the constitutional purpose has been served, and there is no longer a need for the process to be prolonged.

I would have preferred to carry through to the finish, whatever the personal agony it would have involved, and my family unanimously urged me to do so. But the interests of the Nation must always come before any personal considerations.

From the discussions I have had with Congressional and other leaders, I have concluded that because of the Watergate matter, I might not have the support of the Congress that I would consider necessary to back the very difficult decisions and carry out the duties of this office in the way the interests of the Nation will require.

I have never been a quitter. To leave office before my term is completed is abhorrent to every instinct in my body. But as President, I must put the interests of America first. America needs a full-time President and a full-time Congress, particularly at this time with problems we face at home and abroad.

To continue to fight through the months ahead for my personal vindication would almost totally absorb the time and attention of both the President and the Congress in a period when our entire focus should be on the great issues of peace abroad and prosperity without inflation at home.

Therefore, I shall resign the Presidency effective at noon tomorrow. Vice President Ford will be sworn in as President at that hour in this office.

As I recall the high hopes for America with which we began this second term, I feel a great sadness that I will not be here in this office working on your behalf to achieve those hopes in the next two-and-a-half years. But in turning over direction of the Government to Vice President Ford, I know, as I told the Nation when I nominated him for that office ten months ago, that the leadership of America will be in good hands.

In passing this office to the Vice President, I also do so with the profound sense of the weight of responsibility that will fall on his shoulders tomorrow and, therefore, of the understanding, the patience, the cooperation he will need from all Americans.

As he assumes that responsibility, he will deserve the help and the support of all of us. As we look to the future, the first essential is to begin healing the wounds of this Nation, to put the bitterness and divisions of the recent past behind us and to rediscover those shared ideals that lie at the heart of our strength and unity as a great and as a free people.

By taking this action, I hope that I will have hastened the start of that process of healing which is so desperately needed in America.

I regret deeply any injuries that may have been done in the course of the events that led to this decision. I would say only that if some of my judgments were wrong—and some were wrong—they were made in what I believed at the time to be the best interest of the Nation.

To those who have stood with me during these past difficult months—to my family, my friends, to many others who joined in supporting my cause because they believed it was right—I will be eternally grateful for your support.

And to those who have not felt able to give me your support, let me say I leave with no bitterness toward those who have opposed me, because all of us, in the final analysis, have been concerned with the good of the country, however our judgments might differ.

So, let us all now join together in affirming that common commitment and in helping our new President succeed for the benefit of all Americans.

I shall leave this office with regret at not completing my term, but with gratitude for the privilege of serving as your President for the past five-and-a-half years. These years have been a momentous time in the history of our Nation and the world. They have been a time of achievement in which we can all be proud, achievements that represent the shared efforts of the Administration, the Congress, and the people.

But the challenges ahead are equally great, and they, too, will require the support and the efforts of the Congress and the people working in cooperation with the new Administration.

We have ended America's longest war, but in the work of securing a lasting peace in the world, the goals ahead are even more far-reaching and more difficult. We must complete a structure of peace so that it will be said of this generation, our generation of Americans, by the people of all nations, not only that we ended one war but that we prevented future wars.

We have unlocked the doors that for a quarter of a century stood between the United States and the People's Republic of China.

We must now ensure that the one quarter of the world's people who live in the People's Republic of China will be and remain not our enemies, but our friends.

In the Middle East, 100 million people in the Arab countries, many of whom have considered us their enemy for nearly twenty years, now look on us as their friends. We must continue to build on that friendship so that peace can settle at last over the Middle East and so that the cradle of civilization will not become its grave.

Together with the Soviet Union, we have made the crucial breakthroughs that have begun the process of limiting nuclear arms. But we must set as our goal not just limiting but reducing and, finally, destroying these terrible weapons so that they cannot destroy civilization and so that the threat of nuclear war will no longer hang over the world and the people.

We have opened the new relation with the Soviet Union. We must continue to develop and expand that new relationship so that the two strongest nations of the world will live together in cooperation rather than confrontation.

Around the world—in Asia, in Africa, in Latin America, in the Middle East— there are millions of people who live in terrible poverty, even starvation. We must keep as our goal turning away from production for war and expanding production for peace so that people everywhere on this Earth can at last look forward in their children's time, if not in our own time, to having the necessities for a decent life.

Here in America, we are fortunate that most of our people have not only the blessings of liberty but also the means to live full and good and, by the world's standards, even abundant lives. We must press on, however, toward a goal of not only more and better jobs but of full opportunity for every American and of what we are striving so hard right now to achieve, prosperity without inflation.

For more than a quarter of a century in public life, I have shared in the turbulent history of this era. I have fought for what I believed in. I have tried, to the best of my ability, to discharge those duties and meet those responsibilities that were entrusted to me.

Sometimes I have succeeded and sometimes I have failed, but always I have taken heart from what Theodore Roosevelt once said about the man in the arena, "whose face is marred by dust and sweat and blood, who strives valiantly, who errs and comes short again and again because there is not effort without error and shortcoming, but who does actually strive to do the deed, who knows the great enthusiasms, the great devotions, who spends himself in a worthy cause, who at the best knows in the end the triumphs of high achievements and who at the worst, if he fails, at least fails while daring greatly."

I pledge to you tonight that as long as I have a breath of life in my body, I shall continue in that spirit. I shall continue to work for the great causes to which I have been dedicated throughout my years as a Congressman, a Senator, a Vice President, and President, the cause of peace, not just for America but among all nations—prosperity, justice, and opportunity for all of our people.

There is one cause above all to which I have been devoted and to which I shall always be devoted for as long as I live.

When I first took the oath of office as President five-and-a-half years ago, I made this sacred commitment, to "consecrate my office, my energies, and all the wisdom I can summon to the cause of peace among nations."

I have done my very best in all the days since to be true to that pledge. As a result of these efforts, I am confident that the world is a safer place today, not only for the people of America but for the people of all nations, and that all of our children have a better chance than before of living in peace rather than dying in war.

This, more than anything, is what I hoped to achieve when I sought the Presidency. This, more than anything, is what I hope will be my legacy to you, to our country, as I leave the Presidency.

To have served in this office is to have felt a very personal sense of kinship with each and every American. In leaving it, I do so with this prayer: May God's grace be with you in all the days ahead.

"Crisis of Confidence" Speech

(Delivered in Washington, D.C., July 20, 1979)

This is a special night for me. Exactly three years ago, on July 15, 1976, I accepted the nomination of my party to run for President of the United States. I promised you a President who is not isolated from the people, who feels your pain, and who shares your dreams and who draws his strength and his wisdom from you.

During the past three years I've spoken to you on many occasions about national concerns, the energy crisis, reorganizing the Government, our Nation's economy, and issues of war and especially peace. But over those years the subjects of the speeches, the talks, and the press conferences have become increasingly narrow, focused more and more on what the isolated world of Washington thinks is important. Gradually, you've heard more and more about what the Government thinks or what the Government should be doing and less and less about our Nation's hopes, our dreams, and our vision of the future.

Ten days ago I had planned to speak to you again about a very important subject—energy. For the fifth time I would have described the urgency of the problem and laid out a series of legislative recommendations to the Congress. But as I was preparing to speak, I began to ask myself the same question that I now know has been troubling many of you. Why have we not been able to get together as a nation to resolve our serious energy problem?

It's clear that the true problems of our Nation are much deeper—deeper than gasoline lines or energy shortages, deeper even than inflation or recession. And I realize more than ever that as President I need your help. So I decided to reach out and listen to the voices of America.

I invited to Camp David people from almost every segment of our society—business and labor, teachers and preachers, Governors, mayors, and private citizens. And then I left Camp David to listen to other Americans, men and women like you. It has been an extraordinary ten days, and I want to share with you what I've heard.

First of all, I got a lot of personal advice. Let me quote a few of the typical comments that I wrote down.

This from a southern Governor: "Mr. President, you are not leading this Nation—you're just managing the Government."

"You don't see the people enough any more."

"Some of your Cabinet members don't seem loyal. There is not enough discipline among your disciples."

"Don't talk to us about politics or the mechanics of government, but about an understanding of our common good."

"Mr. President, we're in trouble. Talk to us about blood and sweat and tears."

"If you lead, Mr. President, we will follow."

Many people talked about themselves and about the condition of our Nation. This from a young woman in Pennsylvania: "I feel so far from government. I feel like ordinary people are excluded from political power."

And this from a young Chicano: "Some of us have suffered from recession all our lives."

"Some people have wasted energy, but others haven't had anything to waste."

And this from a religious leader: "No material shortage can touch the important things like God's love for us or our love for one another."

And I like this one particularly from a black woman who happens to be the mayor of a small Mississippi town: "The big-shots are not the only ones who are important. Remember, you can't sell anything on Wall Street unless someone digs it up somewhere else first."

This kind of summarized a lot of other statements: "Mr. President, we are confronted with a moral and a spiritual crisis."

Several of our discussions were on energy, and I have a notebook full of comments and advice. I'll read just a few.

"We can't go on consuming forty percent more energy than we produce. When we import oil we are also importing inflation plus unemployment."

"We've got to use what we have. The Middle East has only five percent of the world's energy, but the United States has twenty-four percent."

And this is one of the most vivid statements: "Our neck is stretched over the fence and OPEC has a knife."

"There will be other cartels and other shortages. American wisdom and courage right now can set a path to follow in the future."

This was a good one: "Be bold, Mr. President. We may make mistakes, but we are ready to experiment."

And this one from a labor leader got to the heart of it: "The real issue is freedom. We must deal with the energy problem on a war footing."

And the last that I'll read: "When we enter the moral equivalent of war, Mr. President, don't issue us BB guns."

These ten days confirmed my belief in the decency and the strength and the wisdom of the American people, but it also bore out some of my longstanding concerns about our Nation's underlying problems.

I know, of course, being President, that government actions and legislation can be very important. That's why I've worked hard to put my campaign promises into law—and I have to admit, with just mixed success. But after listening to the American people I have been reminded again that all the legislation in the world can't fix what's wrong with America. So, I want to speak to you first tonight about a subject even more serious than energy or inflation. I want to talk to you right now about a fundamental threat to American democracy.

I do not mean our political and civil liberties. They will endure. And I do not refer to the outward strength of America, a nation that is at peace tonight everywhere in the world, with unmatched economic power and military might.

The threat is nearly invisible in ordinary ways. It is a crisis of confidence. It is a crisis that strikes at the very heart and soul and spirit of our national will. We can see this crisis in the growing doubt about the meaning of our own lives and in the loss of a unity of purpose for our Nation.

The erosion of our confidence in the future is threatening to destroy the social and the political fabric of America.

The confidence that we have always had as a people is not simply some romantic dream or a proverb in a dusty book that we read just on the Fourth of July. It is the idea which founded our Nation and has guided our development as a people. Confidence in the future has supported everything else—public institutions and private enterprise, our own families, and the very Constitution of the United States. Confidence has defined our course and has served as a link between generations. We've always believed in something called progress. We've always had a faith that the days of our children would be better than our own.

Our people are losing that faith, not only in government itself but in the ability as citizens to serve as the ultimate rulers and shapers of our democracy. As a people we know our past and we are proud of it. Our progress has been part of the living history of America, even the world. We always believed that we were part of a great movement of humanity itself called democracy, involved in the search for freedom, and that belief has always strengthened us in our purpose. But just as we are losing our confidence in the future, we are also beginning to close the door on our past.

In a nation that was proud of hard work, strong families, close-knit communities, and our faith in God, too many of us now tend to worship self-indulgence and consumption. Human identity is no longer defined by what one does, but by what one owns. But we've discovered that owning things and consuming things does not satisfy our longing for meaning. We've learned that piling up material goods cannot fill the emptiness of lives which have no confidence or purpose.

The symptoms of this crisis of the American spirit are all around us. For the first time in the history of our country a majority of our people believe that the next five years will be worse than the past five years. Two-thirds of our people do not even vote. The productivity of American workers is actually dropping, and the willingness of Americans to save for the future has fallen below that of all other people in the Western world.

As you know, there is a growing disrespect for government and for churches and for schools, the news media, and other institutions. This is not a message of happiness or reassurance, but it is the truth and it is a warning.

These changes did not happen overnight. They've come upon us gradually over the last generation, years that were filled with shocks and tragedy.

We were sure that ours was a nation of the ballot, not the bullet, until the murders of John Kennedy and Robert Kennedy and Martin Luther King, Jr. We were taught that our armies were always invincible and our causes were always just, only to suffer the agony of Vietnam. We respected the Presidency as a place of honor until the shock of Watergate.

We remember when the phrase "sound as a dollar" was an expression of absolute dependability, until ten years of inflation began to shrink our dollar and our savings. We believed that our Nation's resources were limitless until 1973, when we had to face a growing dependence on foreign oil.

These wounds are still very deep. They have never been healed.

Looking for a way out of this crisis, our people have turned to the Federal Government and found it isolated from the mainstream of our Nation's life. Washington, D.C., has become an island. The gap between our citizens and our Government has never been so wide. The people are looking for honest answers, not easy answers; clear leadership, not false claims and evasiveness and politics as usual.

What you see too often in Washington and elsewhere around the country is a system of government that seems incapable of action. You see a Congress twisted and pulled in every direction by hundreds of well-financed and powerful special interests. You see every extreme position defended to the last vote, almost to the last breath by one unyielding group or another. You often see a balanced and a fair approach that demands sacrifice, a little sacrifice from everyone, abandoned like an orphan without support and without friends.

Often you see paralysis and stagnation and drift. You don't like it, and neither do I. What can we do?

First of all, we must face the truth, and then we can change our course. We simply must have faith in each other, faith in our ability to govern ourselves, and faith in the future of this Nation. Restoring that faith and that confidence to America is now the most important task we face. It is a true challenge of this generation of Americans.

One of the visitors to Camp David last week put it this way: "We've got to stop crying and start sweating, stop talking and start walking, stop cursing and start praying. The strength we need will not come from the White House, but from every house in America."

We know the strength of America. We are strong. We can regain our unity. We can regain our confidence. We are the heirs of generations who survived threats much more powerful and awesome than those that challenge us now. Our fathers and mothers were strong men and women who shaped a new society during the Great Depression, who fought world wars, and who carved out a new charter of peace for the world.

We ourselves are the same Americans who just ten years ago put a man on the Moon. We are the generation that dedicated our society to the pursuit of human rights and equality. And we are the generation that will win the war on the energy problem and in that process rebuild the unity and confidence of America.

We are at a turning point in our history. There are two paths to choose. One is a path I've warned about tonight, the path that leads to fragmentation and self-interest. Down that road lies a mistaken idea of freedom, the right to grasp for ourselves some advantage over others. That path would be one of constant conflict between narrow interests ending in chaos and immobility. It is a certain route to failure.

All the traditions of our past, all the lessons of our heritage, all the promises of our future point to another path, the path of common purpose and the restoration of American values. That path leads to true freedom for our Nation and ourselves. We can take the first steps down that path as we begin to solve our energy problem.

Energy will be the immediate test of our ability to unite this Nation, and it can also be the standard around which we rally. On the battlefield of energy we can win for our Nation a new confidence, and we can seize control again of our common destiny.

In little more than two decades we've gone from a position of energy independence to one in which almost half the oil we use comes from foreign countries, at prices that are going through the roof. Our excessive dependence on OPEC has already taken a tremendous toll on our economy and our people. This is the direct cause of the long lines which have made millions of you spend aggravating hours waiting for gasoline. It's a cause of the increased inflation and unemployment that we now face. This intolerable dependence on foreign oil threatens our economic independence and the very security of our Nation.

The energy crisis is real. It is worldwide. It is a clear and present danger to our Nation. These are facts and we simply must face them.

What I have to say to you now about energy is simple and vitally important.

Point one: I am tonight setting a clear goal for the energy policy of the United States. Beginning this moment, this Nation will never use more foreign oil than we did in 1977—never. From now on, every new addition to our demand for energy will be met from our own production and our own conservation. The generation-long growth in our dependence on foreign oil will be stopped dead in its tracks right now and then reversed as we move through the 1980s, for I am tonight setting the further goal of cutting our dependence on foreign oil by one-half by the end of the next decade—a saving of over four-and-a-half million barrels of imported oil per day.

Point two: To ensure that we meet these targets, I will use my Presidential authority to set import quotas. I'm announcing tonight that for 1979 and 1980, I will forbid the entry into this country of one drop of foreign oil more than these goals allow. These quotas will ensure a reduction in imports even below the ambitious levels we set at the recent Tokyo summit.

Point three: To give us energy security, I am asking for the most massive peacetime commitment of funds and resources in our nation's history to develop America's own alternative sources of fuel—from coal, from oil shale, from plant products for gasohol, from unconventional gas, from the Sun.

I propose the creation of an energy security corporation to lead this effort to replace two-and-a-half million barrels of imported oil per day by 1990. The corporation will issue up to $5 billion in energy bonds, and I especially want them to be in small denominations so that average Americans can invest directly in America's energy security.

Just as a similar synthetic rubber corporation helped us win World War II, so will we mobilize American determination and ability to win the energy war. Moreover, I will soon submit legislation to Congress calling for the creation of this Nation's first solar bank, which will help us achieve the crucial goal of twenty percent of our energy coming from solar power by the year 2000.

These efforts will cost money, a lot of money, and that is why Congress must enact the windfall profits tax without delay. It will be money well spent. Unlike the billions of dollars that we ship to foreign countries to pay for foreign oil, these funds will be paid by Americans to Americans. These funds will go to fight, not to increase, inflation and unemployment.

Point four: I'm asking Congress to mandate, to require as a matter of law, that our nation's utility companies cut their massive use of oil by fifty percent within the next decade and switch to other fuels, especially coal, our most abundant energy source.

Point five: To make absolutely certain that nothing stands in the way of achieving these goals, I will urge Congress to create an energy mobilization board which, like the War Production Board in World War II, will have the responsibility and authority to cut through the redtape, the delays, and the endless roadblocks to completing key energy projects.

We will protect our environment. But when this Nation critically needs a refinery or a pipeline, we will build it.

Point six: I'm proposing a bold conservation program to involve every State, county, and city and every average American in our energy battle. This effort will permit you to build conservation into your homes and your lives at a cost you can afford.

I ask Congress to give me authority for mandatory conservation and for standby gasoline rationing. To further conserve energy, I'm proposing tonight an extra $10 billion over the next decade to strengthen our public transportation systems. And I'm asking you for your good and for your Nation's security to take no unnecessary trips, to use carpools or public transportation whenever you can, to park your car one extra day per week, to obey the speed limit, and to set your thermostats to save fuel. Every act of energy conservation like this is more than just common sense—I tell you it is an act of patriotism.

Our Nation must be fair to the poorest among us, so we will increase aid to needy Americans to cope with rising energy prices. We often think of conservation only in terms of sacrifice. In fact, it is the most painless and immediate way of rebuilding our Nation's strength. Every gallon of oil each one of us saves is a new form of production. It gives us more freedom, more confidence, that much more control over our own lives.

So, the solution of our energy crisis can also help us to conquer the crisis of the spirit in our country. It can rekindle our sense of unity, our confidence in the future, and give our Nation and all of us individually a new sense of purpose.

You know we can do it. We have the natural resources. We have more oil in our shale alone than several Saudi Arabias. We have more coal than any nation on Earth. We have the world's highest level of technology. We have the most skilled work force, with innovative genius, and I firmly believe that we have the national will to win this war.

I do not promise you that this struggle for freedom will be easy. I do not promise a quick way out of our Nation's problems, when the truth is that the only way out is an all-out effort. What I do promise you is that I will lead our fight, and I will enforce fairness in our struggle, and I will ensure honesty. And above all, I will act.

We can manage the short-term shortages more effectively and we will, but there are no short-term solutions to our long-range problems. There is simply no way to avoid sacrifice.

Twelve hours from now I will speak again in Kansas City, to expand and to explain further our energy program. Just as the search for solutions to our energy shortages has now led us to a new awareness of our Nation's deeper problems, so our willingness to work for those solutions in energy can strengthen us to attack those deeper problems.

I will continue to travel this country, to hear the people of America. You can help me to develop a national agenda for the 1980s. I will listen and I will act. We will act together. These were the promises I made three years ago, and I intend to keep them.

Little by little we can and we must rebuild our confidence. We can spend until we empty our treasuries, and we may summon all the wonders of science. But we can succeed only if we tap our greatest resources—America's people, America's values, and America's confidence.

I have seen the strength of America in the inexhaustible resources of our people. In the days to come, let us renew that strength in the struggle for an energy-secure nation.

In closing, let me say this: I will do my best, but I will not do it alone. Let your voice be heard. Whenever you have a chance, say something good about our country. With God's help and for the sake of our Nation, it is time for us to join hands in America. Let us commit ourselves together to a rebirth of the American spirit. Working together with our common faith we cannot fail.

Thank you and good night.

Ronald Reagan

Remarks on East-West Relations at the Brandenburg Gate

(Delivered in West Berlin, Germany, June 12, 1987)

Twenty-four years ago, President John F. Kennedy visited Berlin, speaking to the people of this city and the world at the City Hall. Well, since then two other presidents have come, each in his turn, to Berlin. And today I, myself, make my second visit to your city.

We come to Berlin, we American Presidents, because it's our duty to speak, in this place, of freedom. But I must confess, we're drawn here by other things as well: by the feeling of history in this city, more than 500 years older than our own nation; by the beauty of the Grunewald and the Tiergarten; most of all, by your courage and determination. Perhaps the composer, Paul Lincke, understood something about American Presidents. You see, like so many Presidents before me, I come here today because wherever I go, whatever I do: "*Ich hab noch einen koffer in Berlin.*" [I still have a suitcase in Berlin.]

Our gathering today is being broadcast throughout Western Europe and North America. I understand that it is being seen and heard as well in the East. To those listening throughout Eastern Europe, a special word: Although I cannot be with you, I address my remarks to you just as surely as to those standing here before me. For I join you, as I join your fellow countrymen in the West, in this firm, this unalterable belief: "*Es gibt nur ein Berlin.*" [There is only one Berlin.]

Behind me stands a wall that encircles the free sectors of this city, part of a vast system of barriers that divides the entire continent of Europe. From the Baltic, south, those barriers cut across Germany in a gash of barbed wire, concrete, dog runs, and guard towers. Farther south, there may be no visible, no obvious wall. But there remain armed guards and checkpoints all the same—still a restriction on the right to travel, still an instrument to impose upon ordinary men and women the will of a totalitarian state. Yet it is here in Berlin where the wall emerges most clearly; here, cutting across your city, where the news photo and the television screen have imprinted this brutal division of a continent upon the mind of the world. Standing before the Brandenburg Gate, every man is a

German, separated from his fellow men. Every man is a Berliner, forced to look upon a scar.

President von Weizsäcker has said, "The German question is open as long as the Brandenburg Gate is closed." Today I say: As long as the gate is closed, as long as this scar of a wall is permitted to stand, it is not the German question alone that remains open, but the question of freedom for all mankind. Yet I do not come here to lament. For I find in Berlin a message of hope, even in the shadow of this wall, a message of triumph.

In this season of spring in 1945, the people of Berlin emerged from their air-raid shelters to find devastation. Thousands of miles away, the people of the United States reached out to help. And in 1947 Secretary of State—as you've been told—George Marshall announced the creation of what would become known as the Marshall plan. Speaking precisely forty years ago this month, he said: "Our policy is directed not against any country or doctrine, but against hunger, poverty, desperation, and chaos."

In the Reichstag a few moments ago, I saw a display commemorating this fortieth anniversary of the Marshall plan. I was struck by the sign on a burnt-out, gutted structure that was being rebuilt. I understand that Berliners of my own generation can remember seeing signs like it dotted throughout the western sectors of the city. The sign read simply: "The Marshall plan is helping here to strengthen the free world." A strong, free world in the West, that dream became real. Japan rose from ruin to become an economic giant. Italy, France, Belgium—virtually every nation in Western Europe saw political and economic rebirth; the European Community was founded.

In West Germany and here in Berlin, there took place an economic miracle, the *Wirtschaftswunder*. Adenauer, Erhard, Reuter, and other leaders understood the practical importance of liberty—that just as truth can flourish only when the journalist is given freedom of speech, so prosperity can come about only when the farmer and businessman enjoy economic freedom. The German leaders reduced tariffs, expanded free trade, lowered taxes. From 1950 to 1960 alone, the standard of living in West Germany and Berlin doubled.

Where four decades ago there was rubble, today in West Berlin there is the greatest industrial output of any city in Germany—busy office blocks, fine homes and apartments, proud avenues, and the spreading lawns of park land. Where a city's culture seemed to have been destroyed, today there are two great universities, orchestras and an opera, countless theaters, and museums. Where there was want, today there's abundance—food, clothing, automobiles—the wonderful goods of the Ku'damm. From devastation, from utter ruin, you Berliners have, in freedom, rebuilt a city that once again ranks as one of the greatest on Earth. The Soviets may have had other plans. But, my friends, there were a few things the Soviets didn't count on—*Berliner herz, Berliner humor, ja, und Berliner schnauze.* [Berliner heart, Berliner humor, yes, and a Berliner *schnauze*.] [*Laughter*]

In the 1950s, Khrushchev predicted: "We will bury you." But in the West today, we see a free world that has achieved a level of prosperity and well-being unprecedented in all human history. In the Communist world, we see failure, technological backwardness, declining standards of health, even want of the most basic kind—too little food. Even today, the Soviet Union still cannot feed itself. After these four decades, then, there stands before the entire world one great and inescapable conclusion: Freedom leads to prosperity. Freedom replaces the ancient hatreds among the nations with comity and peace. Freedom is the victor.

And now the Soviets themselves may, in a limited way, be coming to understand the importance of freedom. We hear much from Moscow about a new policy of reform and openness. Some political prisoners have been released. Certain foreign news broadcasts are no longer being jammed. Some economic enterprises have been permitted to operate with greater freedom from state control. Are these the beginnings of profound changes in the Soviet state? Or are they token gestures, intended to raise false hopes in the West, or to strengthen the Soviet system without changing it? We welcome change and openness; for we believe that freedom and security go together, that the advance of human liberty can only strengthen the cause of world peace.

There is one sign the Soviets can make that would be unmistakable, that would advance dramatically the cause of freedom and peace. General Secretary Gorbachev, if you seek peace, if you seek prosperity for the Soviet Union and Eastern Europe, if you seek liberalization: Come here to this gate! Mr. Gorbachev, open this gate! Mr. Gorbachev, tear down this wall!

I understand the fear of war and the pain of division that afflict this continent—and I pledge to you my country's efforts to help overcome these burdens. To be sure, we in the West must resist Soviet expansion. So we must maintain defenses of unassailable strength. Yet we seek peace; so we must strive to reduce arms on both sides. Beginning ten years ago, the Soviets challenged the Western alliance with a grave new threat, hundreds of new and more deadly SS-20 nuclear missiles, capable of striking every capital in Europe. The Western alliance responded by committing itself to a counterdeployment unless the Soviets agreed to negotiate a better solution; namely, the elimination of such weapons on both sides. For many months, the Soviets refused to bargain in earnestness. As the alliance, in turn, prepared to go forward with its counterdeployment, there were difficult days—days of protests like those during my 1982 visit to this city—and the Soviets later walked away from the table.

But through it all, the alliance held firm. And I invite those who protested then—I invite those who protest today—to mark this fact: Because we remained strong, the Soviets came back to the table. And because we remained strong, today we have within reach the possibility, not merely of limiting the growth of arms, but of eliminating, for the first time, an entire class of nuclear weapons from the face of the Earth. As I speak, NATO ministers are meeting in Iceland to review the progress of our proposals for eliminating these weapons. At the talks in Geneva, we have also proposed deep cuts in strategic offensive weapons. And the Western allies have likewise made far-reaching proposals to reduce the danger of conventional war and to place a total ban on chemical weapons.

While we pursue these arms reductions, I pledge to you that we will maintain the capacity to deter Soviet aggression at any level at which it might occur. And in cooperation with many of our allies, the United States is pursuing the Strategic Defense Initiative—research to base deterrence not on the threat of offensive retaliation, but on defenses that truly defend; on systems, in short, that will not target populations, but shield them. By these means we seek to increase the safety of Europe and all the world. But we must remember a crucial fact: East and West do not mistrust each other because we are armed; we are armed because we mistrust each other. And our differences are not about weapons but about liberty. When President Kennedy spoke at the City Hall those twenty-four years ago, freedom was encircled, Berlin was under siege. And today, despite all the pressures upon this city, Berlin stands secure in its liberty. And freedom itself is transforming the globe.

In the Philippines, in South and Central America, democracy has been given a rebirth. Throughout the Pacific, free markets are working miracle after miracle of economic growth. In the industrialized nations, a technological revolution is taking place—a revolution marked by rapid, dramatic advances in computers and telecommunications.

In Europe, only one nation and those it controls refuse to join the community of freedom. Yet in this age of redoubled economic growth, of information and innovation, the Soviet Union faces a choice: It must make fundamental changes, or it will become obsolete. Today thus represents a moment of hope. We in the West stand ready to cooperate with the East to promote true openness, to break down barriers that separate people, to create a safer, freer world.

And surely there is no better place than Berlin, the meeting place of East and West, to make a start. Free people of Berlin: Today, as in the past, the United States stands for the strict observance and full implementation of all parts of the

Four Power Agreement of 1971. Let us use this occasion, the 750th anniversary of this city, to usher in a new era, to seek a still fuller, richer life for the Berlin of the future. Together, let us maintain and develop the ties between the Federal Republic and the Western sectors of Berlin, which is permitted by the 1971 agreement.

And I invite Mr. Gorbachev: Let us work to bring the Eastern and Western parts of the city closer together, so that all the inhabitants of all Berlin can enjoy the benefits that come with life in one of the great cities of the world. To open Berlin still further to all Europe, East and West, let us expand the vital air access to this city, finding ways of making commercial air service to Berlin more convenient, more comfortable, and more economical. We look to the day when West Berlin can become one of the chief aviation hubs in all central Europe.

With our French and British partners, the United States is prepared to help bring international meetings to Berlin. It would be only fitting for Berlin to serve as the site of United Nations meetings, or world conferences on human rights and arms control or other issues that call for international cooperation. There is no better way to establish hope for the future than to enlighten young minds, and we would be honored to sponsor summer youth exchanges, cultural events, and other programs for young Berliners from the East. Our French and British friends, I'm certain, will do the same. And it's my hope that an authority can be found in East Berlin to sponsor visits from young people of the Western sectors.

One final proposal, one close to my heart: Sport represents a source of enjoyment and ennoblement, and you may have noted that the Republic of Korea—South Korea—has offered to permit certain events of the 1988 Olympics to take place in the North. International sports competitions of all kinds could take place in both parts of this city. And what better way to demonstrate to the world the openness of this city than to offer in some future year to hold the Olympic games here in Berlin, East and West?

In these four decades, as I have said, you Berliners have built a great city. You've done so in spite of threats—the Soviet attempts to impose the East-mark, the blockade. Today the city thrives in spite of the challenges implicit in the very presence of this wall. What keeps you here? Certainly there's a great deal to be said for your fortitude, for your defiant courage. But I believe there's something deeper, something that involves Berlin's whole look and feel and way of life—not mere sentiment. No one could live long in Berlin without being completely disabused of illusions. Something instead, that has seen the difficulties of life in Berlin but chose to accept them, that continues to build this good and proud city in contrast to a surrounding totalitarian presence that refuses to release human energies or aspirations. Something that speaks with a powerful voice of affirmation, that says yes to this city, yes to the future, yes to freedom. In a word, I would submit that what keeps you in Berlin is love—love both profound and abiding.

Perhaps this gets to the root of the matter, to the most fundamental distinction of all between East and West. The totalitarian world produces backwardness because it does such violence to the spirit, thwarting the human impulse to create, to enjoy, to worship. The totalitarian world finds even symbols of love and of worship an affront. Years ago, before the East Germans began rebuilding their churches, they erected a secular structure: the television tower at Alexander Platz. Virtually ever since, the authorities have been working to correct what they view as the tower's one major flaw, treating the glass sphere at the top with paints and chemicals of every kind. Yet even today when the sun strikes that sphere—that sphere that towers over all Berlin—the light makes the sign of the cross. There in Berlin, like the city itself, symbols of love, symbols of worship, cannot be suppressed.

As I looked out a moment ago from the Reichstag, that embodiment of German unity, I noticed words crudely spray-painted upon the wall, perhaps by a young Berliner: "This wall will fall. Beliefs become reality." Yes, across Europe, this wall will fall. For it cannot withstand faith; it cannot withstand truth. The wall cannot withstand freedom.

And I would like, before I close, to say one word. I have read, and I have been questioned since I've been here about certain demonstrations against my coming. And I would like to say just one thing, and to those who demonstrate so. I wonder if they have ever asked themselves that if they should have the kind of government they apparently seek, no one would ever be able to do what they're doing again.

Thank you and God bless you all.

William Clinton

Remarks on the Fiftieth Anniversary of D-Day

(Delivered at Pointe du Hoc in Normandy, France, on June 6, 1994)

We stand on sacred soil. Fifty years ago at this place a miracle of liberation began. On that morning, democracy's forces landed to end the enslavement of Europe.

Around 7:00 A.M., Lieutenant Colonel James Earl Rudder, 2d Ranger Battalion, United States Army, led 224 men onto the beaches below and up these unforgiving cliffs. Bullets and grenades came down upon them, but by a few minutes after 7:00, here, exactly here, the first Rangers stood. Today let us ask those American heroes to stand again. [*Applause*]

Corporal Ken Bargmann, who sits here to my right, was one of them. He had just celebrated his twentieth birthday out in the Channel, a young man like all the rest of them, cold and wet, far from home, preparing for the challenge of his life. Ken Bargmann and the other Rangers of Pointe du Hoc and all the other Americans, British, Canadian, and Free French who landed, were the tip of a spear the free world had spent years sharpening, a spear they began on this morning in 1944 to plunge into the heart of the Nazi empire. Most of them were new to war, but all were armed with the ingenuity of free citizens and the confidence that they fought for a good cause under the gaze of a loving God.

The fortunate ones would go home, changed forever. Thousands would never return. And today we mourn their loss. But on that gray dawn, millions, literally millions, of people on this continent awaited their arrival. Young Anne Frank wrote in her diary these words: "It's no exaggeration to say that all Amsterdam, all Holland, yes, the whole west coast of Europe talks about the invasion day and night, debates about it, makes bets on it, and hopes. I have the feeling friends are approaching."

The young men who came fought for the very survival of democracy. Just four years earlier, some thought democracy's day had passed. Hitler was rolling across Europe. In America, factories worked at only half capacity. Our people were badly divided over what to do. The future seemed to belong to the dictators. They sneered at democracy, its mingling of races and religions, its tolerance of dissent. They were sure we didn't have what it took.

Well, they didn't know James Rudder or Ken Bargmann or the other men of D-Day. They didn't understand what happens when the free unite behind a great and worthy cause. For human miracles begin with personal choices, millions of them gathered together as one, like the stars of a majestic galaxy. Here at this place, in Britain, in North America, and among Resistance fighters in France and across Europe, all those numberless choices came together, the choices of lion-hearted leaders to rally their people, the choices of people to mobilize for freedom's fight, the choices of their soldiers to carry on that fight into a world worn weary by devastation and despair.

Every person in the democracies pitched in. Every shipbuilder who built a landing craft, every woman who worked in a factory, every farmer who grew food for the troops, every miner who carved coal out of a cavern, every child who tended a victory garden, all of them did their part. All produced things with their hands and their hearts that went into this battle. And on D-Day, all across the free world, the peoples of democracy prayed that they had done their job right. Well, they had done their job right.

And here, you, the Army Rangers, did yours. Your mission was to scale these cliffs and destroy the howitzers at the top that threatened every Allied soldier and ship within miles. You fired grappling hooks onto the cliff tops. You waded to shore, and you began to climb up on ropes slick with sea and sand, up, as the Germans shot down and tried to cut your lines, up, sometimes holding to the cliffs with nothing but the knives you had and your own bare hands.

As the battle raged at Juno, Sword, and Gold, on Omaha and Utah, you took devastating casualties. But you also took control of these commanding heights. Around 9:00 A.M., two Rangers discovered the big guns hidden inland and disabled them with heat grenades. At the moment, you became the first Americans on D-Day to complete your mission.

We look at this terrain and we marvel at your fight. We look around us and we see what you were fighting for. For here are the daughters of Colonel Rudder. Here are the son and grandson of Corporal Bargmann. Here are the faces for whom you risked your lives. Here are the generations for whom you won a war. We are the children of your sacrifice. We are the sons and daughters you saved from tyranny's reach. We grew up behind the shield of the strong alliances you forged in blood upon these beaches, on the shores of the Pacific, and in the skies above. We flourished in the Nation you came home to build.

The most difficult days of your lives bought us fifty years of freedom. You did your job; now we must do ours. Let us begin by teaching our young people about the villainy that started this war and the valor that ended it. Let us carry on the work you began here. The sparks of freedom you struck on these beaches were never extinguished, even in the darkest days behind the Iron Curtain. Five years ago the miracle of liberation was repeated as the rotting timbers of communism came tumbling down.

Now we stand at the start of a new day. The Soviet empire is gone. So many people who fought as our partners in this war, the Russians, the Poles, and others, now stand again as our partners in peace and democracy. Our work is far from done. Still there are cliffs to scale. We must work to contain the world's most deadly weapons, to expand the reach of democracy. We must keep ready arms and strong alliances. We must have strong families and cohesive societies and educated citizens and vibrant, open, economies that promote cooperation, not conflict.

And if we should ever falter, we need only remember you at this spot fifty years ago and you, again, at this spot today. The flame of your youth became freedom's lamp, and we see its light reflected in your faces still and in the faces of your children and grandchildren.

We commit ourselves, as you did, to keep that lamp burning for those who will follow. You completed your mission here. But the mission of freedom goes on; the battle continues. The "longest day" is not yet over.

God bless you, and God bless America.

Second Inaugural Address

(Delivered in Washington, D.C., January 20, 1997)

At this last Presidential Inauguration of the twentieth century, let us lift our eyes toward the challenges that await us in the next century. It is our great good fortune that time and chance have put us not only at the edge of a new century, in a new millennium, but on the edge of a bright new prospect in human affairs, a moment that will define our course, and our character, for decades to come. We must keep our old democracy forever young. Guided by the ancient vision of a promised land, let us set our sights upon a land of new promise.

The promise of America was born in the 18th century out of the bold conviction that we are all created equal. It was extended and preserved in the 19th century, when our Nation spread across the continent, saved the Union, and abolished the awful scourge of slavery.

Then, in turmoil and triumph, that promise exploded onto the world stage to make this the American Century. And what a century it has been. America became the world's mightiest industrial power; saved the world from tyranny in two World Wars and a long cold war, and time and again reached out across the globe to millions who, like us, longed for the blessings of liberty.

Along the way, Americans produced a great middle class and security in old age, built unrivaled centers of learning and opened public schools to all, split the atom and explored the heavens, invented the computer and the microchip, and deepened the wellspring of justice by making a revolution in civil rights for African-Americans and all minorities and extending the circle of citizenship, opportunity and dignity to women.

Now, for the third time, a new century is upon us and another time to choose. We began the nineteenth century with a choice: to spread our nation from coast to coast. We began the twentieth century with a choice, to harness the industrial revolution to our values of free enterprise, conservation, and human decency. Those choices made all the difference. At the dawn of the twenty-first century, a free people must now choose to shape the forces of the information age and the global society, to unleash the limitless potential of all our people, and, yes, to form a more perfect Union.

When last we gathered, our march to this new future seemed less certain than it does today. We vowed then to set a clear course to renew our Nation. In these four years, we have been touched by tragedy, exhilarated by challenge, strengthened by achievement. America stands alone as the world's indispensable nation. Once again, our economy is the strongest on Earth. Once again, we are building stronger families, thriving communities, better educational opportunities, a cleaner environment. Problems that once seemed destined to deepen, now bend to our efforts. Our streets are safer, and record numbers of our fellow citizens have moved from welfare to work. And once again, we have resolved for our time a great debate over the role of Government. Today we can declare: Government is not the problem, and Government is not the solution. We—the American people—we are the solution. Our Founders understood that well and gave us a democracy strong enough to endure for centuries, flexible enough to face our common challenges and advance our common dreams in each new day.

As times change, so Government must change. We need a new Government for a new century, humble enough not to try to solve all our problems for us but strong enough to give us the tools to solve our problems for ourselves; a Government that is smaller, lives within its means, and does more with less. Yet where it can stand up for our values and interests in the world, and where it can give Americans the power to make a real difference in their everyday lives, Government should do more, not less. The preeminent mission of our new Government is to give all Americans an opportunity, not a guarantee but a real opportunity, to build better lives.

Beyond that, my fellow citizens, the future is up to us. Our Founders taught us that the preservation of our liberty and our Union depends upon responsible citizenship. And we need a new sense of responsibility for a new century. There is work to do, work that Government alone cannot do: teaching children to read, hiring people off welfare rolls, coming out from behind locked doors and shuttered windows to help reclaim our streets from drugs and gangs and crime, taking time out of our own lives to serve others.

Each and every one of us, in our own way, must assume personal responsibility, not only for ourselves and our families, but for our neighbors and our Nation. Our greatest responsibility is to embrace a new spirit of community for a new century. For any one of us to succeed, we must succeed as one America. The challenge of our past remains the challenge of our future: Will we be one Nation, one people, with one common destiny, or not? Will we all come together, or come apart?

The divide of race has been America's constant curse. And each new wave of immigrants gives new targets to old prejudices. Prejudice and contempt cloaked in the pretense of religious or political conviction are no different. These forces have nearly destroyed our Nation in the past. They plague us still. They fuel the fanaticism of terror. And they torment the lives of millions in fractured nations all around the world.

These obsessions cripple both those who hate and of course those who are hated, robbing both of what they might become. We cannot, we will not, succumb to the dark impulses that lurk in the far regions of the soul everywhere. We shall overcome them. And we shall replace them with the generous spirit of a people who feel at home with one another. Our rich texture of racial, religious, and political diversity will be a godsend in the twenty-first century. Great rewards will come to those who can live together, learn together, work together, forge new ties that bind together.

As this new era approaches, we can already see its broad outlines. Ten years ago, the Internet was the mystical province of physicists; today, it is a commonplace encyclopedia for millions of schoolchildren. Scientists now are decoding the blueprint of human life. Cures for our most feared illnesses seem close at hand. The world is no longer divided into two hostile camps. Instead, now we are building bonds with nations that once were our adversaries. Growing connections of commerce and culture give us a chance to lift the fortunes and spirits of people the world over. And for the very first time in all of history, more people on this planet live under democracy than dictatorship.

My fellow Americans, as we look back at this remarkable century, we may ask, can we hope not just to follow but even to surpass the achievements of the twentieth century in America and to avoid the awful bloodshed that stained its legacy? To that question, every American here and every American in our land today must answer a resounding "Yes!" This is the heart of our task. With a new vision of Government, a new sense of responsibility, a new spirit of community, we will sustain America's journey.

The promise we sought in a new land, we will find again in a land of new promise. In this new land, education will be every citizen's most prized possession. Our schools will have the highest standards in the world, igniting the spark of possibility in the eyes of every girl and every boy. And the doors of higher education will be open to all. The knowledge and power of the information age will be within reach not just of the few, but of every classroom, every library, every child. Parents and children will have time not only to work but to read and play together. And the plans they make at their kitchen table will be those of a better home, a better job, the certain chance to go to college.

Our streets will echo again with the laughter of our children, because no one will try to shoot them or sell them drugs anymore. Everyone who can work, will work, with today's permanent under class part of tomorrow's growing middle class. New miracles of medicine at last will reach not only those who can claim care now, but the children and hard-working families too long denied.

We will stand mighty for peace and freedom and maintain a strong defense against terror And destruction. Our children will sleep free from the threat of nuclear, chemical, or biological weapons. Ports and airports, farms and factories will thrive with trade and innovation and ideas. And the world's greatest democracy will lead a whole world of democracies.

Our land of new promise will be a nation that meets its obligations, a nation that balances its budget, but never loses the balance of its values, A nation where our grandparents have secure retirement and health care, and their grandchildren know we have made the reforms necessary to sustain those benefits for their time, a nation that fortifies the world's most productive economy even as it protects the great natural bounty of our water, air, and majestic land. And in this land of new promise, we will have reformed our politics so that the voice of the people will always speak louder than the din of narrow interests, regaining the participation and deserving the trust of all Americans.

Fellow citizens, let us build that America, a nation ever moving forward toward realizing the full potential of all its citizens. Prosperity and power, yes, they are important, and we must maintain them. But let us never forget, the greatest progress we have made and the greatest progress we have yet to make is in the human heart. In the end, all the world's wealth and a thousand armies are no match for the strength and decency of the human spirit.

Thirty-four years ago, the man whose life we celebrate today spoke to us down there, at the other end of this Mall, in words that moved the conscience of a nation. Like a prophet of old, he told of his dream that one day America would rise up and treat all its citizens as equals before the law and in the heart. Martin Luther King's dream was the American dream. His quest is our quest: the ceaseless striving to live out our true creed. Our history has been built on such dreams and labors. And by our dreams and labors, we will redeem the promise of America in the twenty-first century.

To that effort I pledge all my strength and every power of my office. I ask the Members of Congress here to join in that pledge. The American people returned to office a President of one party and a Congress of another. Surely they did not do this to advance the politics of petty bickering and extreme partisanship they plainly deplore. No, they call on us instead to be repairers of the breach, and to move on with America's mission. America demands and deserves big things from us, and nothing big ever came from being small. Let us remember the timeless wisdom of Cardinal Bernardin, when facing the end of his own life. He said, "It is wrong to waste the precious gift of time on acrimony and division."

Fellow citizens, we must not waste the precious gift of this time. For all of us are on that same journey of our lives, and our journey, too, will come to an end. But the journey of our America must go on.

And so, my fellow Americans, we must be strong, for there is much to dare. The demands of our time are great and they are different. Let us meet them with faith and courage, with patience and a grateful and happy heart. Let us shape the hope of this day into the noblest chapter in our history. Yes, let us build our bridge. A bridge wide enough and strong enough for every American to cross over to a blessed land of new promise.

May those generations whose faces we cannot yet see, whose names we may never know, say of us here that we led our beloved land into a new century with the American dream alive for all her children, with the American promise of a more perfect Union a reality for all her people, with America's bright flame of freedom spreading throughout all the world.

From the height of this place and the summit of this century, let us go forth. May God strengthen our hands for the good work ahead, and always, always bless our America.

George W. Bush

Remarks at the National Day of Prayer and Remembrance

(Delivered at the National Cathedral in Washington, D.C., September 14, 2001)

We are here in the middle hour of our grief. So many have suffered so great a loss, and today we express our Nation's sorrow. We come before God to pray for the missing and the dead and for those who love them.

On Tuesday our country was attacked with deliberate and massive cruelty. We have seen the images of fire and ashes and bent steel. Now come the names, the list of casualties we are only beginning to read.

They are the names of men and women who began their day at a desk or in an airport, busy with life. They are the names of people who faced death and in their last moments called home to say, "Be brave," and "I love you." They are the names of passengers who defied their murderers and prevented the murder of others on the ground. They are the names of men and women who wore the uniform of the United States and died at their posts. They are the names of rescuers, the ones whom death found running up the stairs and into the fires to help others. We will read all these names. We will linger over them and learn their stories, and many Americans will weep.

To the children and parents and spouses and families and friends of the lost, we offer the deepest sympathy of the Nation. And I assure you, you are not alone.

Just three days removed from these events, Americans do not yet have the distance of history. But our responsibility to history is already clear: To answer these attacks and rid the world of evil.

War has been waged against us by stealth and deceit and murder. This Nation is peaceful, but fierce when stirred to anger. This conflict was begun on the timing and terms of others. It will end in a way and at an hour of our choosing.

Our purpose as a nation is firm. Yet, our wounds as a people are recent and unhealed and lead us to pray. In many of our prayers this week, there is a searching and an honesty. At St. Patrick's Cathedral in New York on Tuesday, a woman said,

"I prayed to God to give us a sign that He is still here." Others have prayed for the same, searching hospital to hospital, carrying pictures of those still missing.

God's signs are not always the ones we look for. We learn in tragedy that his purposes are not always our own. Yet, the prayers of private suffering, whether in our homes or in this great cathedral, are known and heard and understood.

There are prayers that help us last through the day or endure the night. There are prayers of friends and strangers that give us strength for the journey. And there are prayers that yield our will to a will greater than our own.

This world He created is of moral design. Grief and tragedy and hatred are only for a time. Goodness, remembrance, and love have no end. And the Lord of life holds all who die and all who mourn.

It is said that adversity introduces us to ourselves. This is true of a nation as well. In this trial, we have been reminded, and the world has seen, that our fellow Americans are generous and kind, resourceful and brave. We see our national character in rescuers working past exhaustion, in long lines of blood donors, in thousands of citizens who have asked to work and serve in any way possible.

And we have seen our national character in eloquent acts of sacrifice. Inside the World Trade Center, one man, who could have saved himself, stayed until the end at the side of his quadriplegic friend. A beloved priest died giving the last rites to a firefighter. Two office workers, finding a disabled stranger, carried her down sixty-eight floors to safety. A group of men drove through the night from Dallas to Washington to bring skin grafts for burn victims.

In these acts, and in many others, Americans showed a deep commitment to one another and an abiding love for our country. Today we feel what Franklin Roosevelt called the warm courage of national unity. This is a unity of every faith and every background. It has joined together political parties in both Houses of Congress. It is evident in services of prayer and candlelight vigils and American flags, which are displayed in pride and wave in defiance.

Our unity is a kinship of grief and a steadfast resolve to prevail against our enemies. And this unity against terror is now extending across the world.

America is a nation full of good fortune, with so much to be grateful for. But we are not spared from suffering. In every generation, the world has produced enemies of human freedom. They have attacked America, because we are freedom's home and defender. And the commitment of our fathers is now the calling of our time.

On this National Day of Prayer and Remembrance, we ask Almighty God to watch over our Nation, and grant us patience and resolve in all that is to come.

We pray that He will comfort and console those who now walk in sorrow. We thank Him for each life we now must mourn and the promise of a life to come.

As we have been assured, neither death nor life, nor angels nor principalities nor powers, nor things present nor things to come, nor height nor depth, can separate us from God's love. May He bless the souls of the departed. May He comfort our own, and may He always guide our country.

God bless America.

Barack Obama

First Inaugural Address

(Delivered in Washington, D.C., January 20, 2009)

I stand here today humbled by the task before us, grateful for the trust you have bestowed, mindful of the sacrifices borne by our ancestors.

I thank President Bush for his service to our nation [applause] as well as the generosity and cooperation he has shown throughout this transition.

Forty-four Americans have now taken the presidential oath.

The words have been spoken during rising tides of prosperity and the still waters of peace. Yet, every so often the oath is taken amidst gathering clouds and raging storms. At these moments, America has carried on not simply because of the skill or vision of those in high office, but because We the People have remained faithful to the ideals of our forebears, and true to our founding documents.

So it has been. So it must be with this generation of Americans.

That we are in the midst of crisis is now well understood. Our nation is at war, against a far-reaching network of violence and hatred. Our economy is badly weakened, a consequence of greed and irresponsibility on the part of some, but also our collective failure to make hard choices and prepare the nation for a new age.

Homes have been lost, jobs shed, businesses shuttered. Our health care is too costly, our schools fail too many, and each day brings further evidence that the ways we use energy strengthen our adversaries and threaten our planet.

These are the indicators of crisis, subject to data and statistics. Less measurable, but no less profound, is a sapping of confidence across our land; a nagging fear that America's decline is inevitable, and that the next generation must lower its sights.

Today I say to you that the challenges we face are real: they are serious and they are many. They will not be met easily or in a short span of time. But know this, America: They will be met. [Applause]

On this day, we gather because we have chosen hope over fear, unity of purpose over conflict and discord.

On this day, we come to proclaim an end to the petty grievances and false promises, the recriminations and worn out dogmas that for far too long have strangled our politics.

We remain a young nation, but in the words of Scripture, the time has come to set aside childish things. The time has come to reaffirm our enduring spirit; to choose our better history; to carry forward that precious gift, that noble idea, passed on from generation to generation: the God-given promise that all are equal, all are free, and all deserve a chance to pursue their full measure of happiness. [Applause]

In reaffirming the greatness of our nation, we understand that greatness is never a given. It must be earned. Our journey has never been one of shortcuts or settling for less.

It has not been the path for the faint-hearted, for those who prefer leisure over work, or seek only the pleasures of riches and fame.

Rather, it has been the risk-takers, the doers, the makers of things—some celebrated, but more often men and women obscure in their labor—who have carried us up the long, rugged path towards prosperity and freedom.

For us, they packed up their few worldly possessions and traveled across oceans in search of a new life. For us, they toiled in sweatshops and settled the West, endured the lash of the whip and plowed the hard earth.

For us, they fought and died in places like Concord and Gettysburg; Normandy and Khe Sahn.

Time and again these men and women struggled and sacrificed and worked till their hands were raw so that we might live a better life. They saw America as bigger than the sum of our individual ambitions; greater than all the differences of birth or wealth or faction.

This is the journey we continue today. We remain the most prosperous, powerful nation on Earth. Our workers are no less productive than when this crisis began. Our minds are no less inventive, our goods and services no less needed than they were last week or last month or last year. Our capacity remains undiminished. But our time of standing pat, of protecting narrow interests and putting off unpleasant decisions—that time has surely passed.

Starting today, we must pick ourselves up, dust ourselves off, and begin again the work of remaking America. [Applause]

For everywhere we look, there is work to be done.

The state of the economy calls for action: bold and swift. And we will act—not only to create new jobs but to lay a new foundation for growth.

We will build the roads and bridges, the electric grids and digital lines that feed our commerce and bind us together.

We will restore science to its rightful place and wield technology's wonders to raise health care's quality [applause] and lower its costs.

We will harness the sun and the winds and the soil to fuel our cars and run our factories. And we will transform our schools and colleges and universities to meet the demands of a new age.

All this we can do. And all this we will do.

Now, there are some who question the scale of our ambitions, who suggest that our system cannot tolerate too many big plans. Their memories are short, for they have forgotten what this country has already done, what free men and women can achieve when imagination is joined to common purpose and necessity to courage.

What the cynics fail to understand is that the ground has shifted beneath them, that the stale political arguments that have consumed us for so long no longer apply.

The question we ask today is not whether our government is too big or too small, but whether it works, whether it helps families find jobs at a decent wage, care they can afford, a retirement that is dignified.

Where the answer is yes, we intend to move forward. Where the answer is no, programs will end.

And those of us who manage the public's dollars will be held to account, to spend wisely, reform bad habits, and do our business in the light of day, because only then can we restore the vital trust between a people and their government.

Nor is the question before us whether the market is a force for good or ill. Its power to generate wealth and expand freedom is unmatched.

But this crisis has reminded us that without a watchful eye, the market can spin out of control. The nation cannot prosper long when it favors only the prosperous.

The success of our economy has always depended not just on the size of our gross domestic product, but on the reach of our prosperity; on our ability to extend opportunity to every willing heart—not out of charity, but because it is the surest route to our common good. [Applause]

As for our common defense, we reject as false the choice between our safety and our ideals.

Our founding fathers faced with perils we can scarcely imagine, drafted a charter to assure the rule of law and the rights of man, a charter expanded by the blood of generations.

Those ideals still light the world, and we will not give them up for expedience's sake.

And so, to all other peoples and governments who are watching today, from the grandest capitals to the small village where my father was born: know that

America is a friend of each nation and every man, woman, and child who seeks a future of peace and dignity, and that we are ready to lead once more. [Applause]

Recall that earlier generations faced down fascism and communism not just with missiles and tanks, but with sturdy alliances and enduring convictions.

They understood that our power alone cannot protect us, nor does it entitle us to do as we please. Instead, they knew that our power grows through its prudent use. Our security emanates from the justness of our cause, the force of our example; the tempering qualities of humility and restraint.

We are the keepers of this legacy, guided by these principles once more, we can meet those new threats that demand even greater effort, even greater cooperation and understanding between nations. We will begin to responsibly leave Iraq to its people and forge a hard-earned peace in Afghanistan.

With old friends and former foes, we'll work tirelessly to lessen the nuclear threat and roll back the specter of a warming planet.

We will not apologize for our way of life, nor will we waver in its defense.

And for those who seek to advance their aims by inducing terror and slaughtering innocents, we say to you now that, "Our spirit is stronger and cannot be broken. You cannot outlast us, and we will defeat you." [Applause]

For we know that our patchwork heritage is a strength, not a weakness.

We are a nation of Christians and Muslims, Jews and Hindus, and nonbelievers. We are shaped by every language and culture, drawn from every end of this Earth.

And because we have tasted the bitter swill of civil war and segregation and emerged from that dark chapter stronger and more united, we cannot help but believe that the old hatreds shall someday pass; that the lines of tribe shall soon dissolve; that as the world grows smaller, our common humanity shall reveal itself; and that America must play its role in ushering in a new era of peace.

To the Muslim world, we seek a new way forward, based on mutual interest and mutual respect.

To those leaders around the globe who seek to sow conflict or blame their society's ills on the West, know that your people will judge you on what you can build, not what you destroy.

To those [applause] who cling to power through corruption and deceit and the silencing of dissent, know that you are on the wrong side of history, but that we will extend a hand if you are willing to unclench your fist. [Applause]

To the people of poor nations, we pledge to work alongside you to make your farms flourish and let clean waters flow; to nourish starved bodies and feed hungry minds.

And to those nations like ours that enjoy relative plenty, we say we can no longer afford indifference to suffering outside our borders, nor can we consume the world's resources without regard to effect. For the world has changed, and we must change with it.

As we consider the road that unfolds before us, we remember with humble gratitude those brave Americans who, at this very hour, patrol far-off deserts and distant mountains. They have something to tell us today, just as the fallen heroes who lie in Arlington whisper through the ages.

We honor them not only because they are guardians of our liberty, but because they embody the spirit of service, a willingness to find meaning in something greater than themselves. And yet, at this moment, a moment that will define a generation, it is precisely this spirit that must inhabit us all.

For as much as government can do and must do, it is ultimately the faith and determination of the American people upon which this nation relies.

It is the kindness to take in a stranger when the levees break; the selflessness of workers who would rather cut their hours than see a friend lose their job which sees us through our darkest hours.

It is the firefighter's courage to storm a stairway filled with smoke, but also a parent's willingness to nurture a child, that finally decides our fate.

Our challenges may be new, the instruments with which we meet them may be new, but those values upon which our success depends, honesty and hard work and honesty, courage and fair play, tolerance and curiosity, loyalty and patriotism—these things are old.

These things are true. They have been the quiet force of progress throughout our history.

What is demanded then is a return to these truths. What is required of us now is a new era of responsibility—a recognition, on the part of every American, that we have duties to ourselves, our nation and the world, duties that we do not grudgingly accept but rather seize gladly, firm in the knowledge that there is nothing so satisfying to the spirit, so defining of our character than giving our all to a difficult task.

This is the price and the promise of citizenship.

This is the source of our confidence: the knowledge that God calls on us to shape an uncertain destiny.

This is the meaning of our liberty and our creed: why men and women and children of every race and every faith can join in celebration across this magnificent mall. And why a man whose father less than sixty years ago might not have been served at a local restaurant can now stand before you to take a most sacred oath. [Applause]

So let us mark this day with remembrance of who we are and how far we have traveled.

In the year of America's birth, in the coldest of months, a small band of patriots huddled by dying campfires on the shores of an icy river.

The capital was abandoned. The enemy was advancing. The snow was stained with blood.

At a moment when the outcome of our revolution was most in doubt, the father of our nation ordered these words be read to the people:

"Let it be told to the future world that in the depth of winter, when nothing but hope and virtue could survive, that the city and the country, alarmed at one common danger, came forth to meet it."

America, in the face of our common dangers, in this winter of our hardship, let us remember these timeless words; with hope and virtue, let us brave once more the icy currents, and endure what storms may come; let it be said by our children's children that when we were tested we refused to let this journey end, that we did not turn back nor did we falter; and with eyes fixed on the horizon and God's grace upon us, we carried forth that great gift of freedom and delivered it safely to future generations.

Thank you. God bless you. [Applause]

And God bless the United States of America. [Applause]

Biographical Notes

JOHN QUINCY ADAMS (1767–1848) was the son of President John Adams, and himself served one term as the sixth president of the United States of America between 1825 and 1829. He delivered his oration "On American Independence" at the request of the citizens of Boston, Massachusetts, on the seventeenth anniversary of American independence.

SAMUEL ADAMS (1722–1803) was an American statesman who was one of the signers of Declaration of Independence and who later helped to draft the Articles of Confederation. He delivered his speech "American Independence" in the Philadelphia State House less than a month after the Continental Congress adopted the Declaration of Independence on July 4, 1776.

SUSAN B. ANTHONY (1820–1906) was a leading advocate for women's suffrage, a co-founder of the Women's Temperance Movement, and an editor of *The Revolution*, the official magazine of the National Woman Suffrage Movement. She delivered her "Constitutional Argument" speech after her arrest on November 5, 1872, for voting in the presidential election.

WILLIAM JENNINGS BRYAN (1860–1925) represented Nebraska in the United States House of Representatives and served as secretary of state under President Woodrow Wilson. A critic of America's reliance on the gold standard, Bryan delivered his "Cross of Gold" Speech, advocating the use gold and silver as legal tender, at the close of the Democratic National Convention of 1896. The speech helped to earn Bryan his party's nomination for the presidency.

GEORGE W. BUSH (1946–) served as forty-third president of the United States of America between 2001 and 2009. He delivered his "Remarks at the National Day of Prayer and Remembrance" three days after the terrorist attacks on September 11, 2001, claimed more than 3,000 lives on American soil. His term in office is associated with the retaliatory invasion of Afghanistan and the Second Iraq War.

JIMMY CARTER (1924–) served as the thirty-ninth president of the United States of America between 1977 and 1981. His term of office is associated with the creation of the Department of Energy and the Department of Education, and the Camp David Accords that earned a shared Nobel Peace Prize for Israeli Prime Minister Menachem Begin and Egyptian President Anwar El Sadat. The end of his term in office coincided with the end of the 444-day-long Iran Hostage Crisis.

WILLIAM CLINTON (1946–) served as the forty-second president of the United States of America between 1993 and 2001. His term in office was marked by America's longest period of peacetime economic expansion, as well as increasing conflict with the militant Islamist organization Al-Qaeda.

EUGENE V. DEBS (1855–1926) was a founding member of the Industrial Workers of the World and the American Railway Union and several times was the Socialist Party of America candidate for the presidency. A distinguished orator, he delivered his address "Liberty" after serving a six-month sentence for his involvement in the nationwide Pullman Strike of 1894.

FREDERICK DOUGLASS (1818–1895) escaped from slavery in Maryland in 1838 and became a leader of the abolitionist movement. "What to the Slave Is the 4th of July?" is one of many orations in which he denounced the institution of slavery. Douglass chronicled his life as a slave and his escape to freedom in his autobiography *Narrative of the Life of Frederick Douglass, an American Slave*.

W. E. B. DU BOIS (1868–1963) was a civil rights activist and co-founder of the National Association for the Advancement of Colored People (NAACP). As a leader of the Niagara Movement, Du Bois encouraged African Americans to fight for equal rights, a more aggressive political philosophy at odds with that of his one-time ally Booker T. Washington. Du Bois expressed his political and philosophical beliefs in his essay collection *The Souls of Black Folk*, published in 1903.

DWIGHT D. EISENHOWER (1890–1969) served as the thirty-fourth president of the United States of America between 1953 and 1961, after a distinguished military career that included serving as Supreme Commander of Allied Forces in Europe during World War II. His administration is closely identified with cold war policies to counter the spread of communism and the start of the space age. His Farewell Address is memorable for its call for oversight of the military-industrial complex.

RALPH WALDO EMERSON (1803–1882) was an essayist and lecturer and a leading figure in America's Transcendentalist movement. His speech "Man the Reformer" expresses his belief in the importance of self-help and self-reliance, a theme that runs through much of his writing.

EDWARD EVERETT (1794–1865) served as governor of Massachusetts and as secretary of state under President Millard Fillmore. He was also an editor of the *North*

American Review and was regarded as one of the greatest American orators of the antebellum and Civil War eras.

BENJAMIN FRANKLIN (1706–1790) was an American statesman and diplomat and a signer of the Declaration of Independence. He was also renowned for his scientific discoveries and inventions and the publication of such works as *Poor Richard's Almanack*. His "Speech in the Constitutional Convention, at the Conclusion of Its Deliberations" expressed the ambivalence many of the Founding Fathers felt toward the Constitution as an imperfect blueprint for American government that was nonetheless crucial for the newborn nation to adopt.

ALEXANDER HAMILTON (1755–1804) was an American statesmen who was one of the major architects of the Constitution of the United States of America and who, with James Madison and John Jay, wrote the eighty-five essays known as the *Federalist Papers* that strongly influenced the ratification of the Constitution. He delivered his speech "On the Expediency of Adopting the Federal Constitution" in the New York Constitutional Convention.

JOHN HANCOCK (1737–1793) was one of the original signers of the Declaration of Independence and served as president of the Second Continental Congress and governor of the Commonwealth of Massachusetts. He delivered his speech "On the Boston Massacre" on the fourth anniversary of the incident, in which British troops, garrisoned in Boston to suppress colonist unrest, fired upon a crowd of civilians, killing five and injuring six. The incident, which occurred on March 5, 1770, significantly foreshadowed the outbreak of the American War for Independence five years later.

PATRICK HENRY (1736–1799) was an American statesman who served as governor of Virginia. One of the most renowned orators of America's Revolutionary War era, he delivered his call to arms in the Convention of Delegates of Virginia on the eve of the outbreak of the American War for Independence. He participated in the Virginia Convention for the ratification of the Constitution and, although he opposed the Constitution, he played a key role in the adoption of the Bill of Rights.

OLIVER WENDELL HOLMES, JR. (1841–1935) served as an associate justice of the Supreme Court of the United States of America from 1902 to 1932. He was one of the most influential American common law judges and is the third-most-cited American legal scholar of the twentieth century.

THOMAS JEFFERSON (1743–1846), the principal author of the Declaration of Independence, served as secretary of state under George Washington and as vice president under John Adams. He served two terms as the third president of the United States of America between 1801 and 1809.

LYNDON B. JOHNSON (1908–1973) served as the thirty-sixth president of the United States of America between 1963 and 1969. His term of office is associated with the escalation of the war in Vietnam and consequent antiwar movement, and with what he termed "The Great Society"—a series of domestic programs that included the War on Poverty, healthcare reform, and civil rights legislation includ- ing the Civil Rights Act of 1964 and the Voting Rights Act.

JOHN F. KENNEDY (1917–1963) served as the thirty-fifth president of the United States of America between 1961 and 1963, and was the only president to win a Pulitzer Prize (for his book *Profiles in Courage*). His term in office is identified with Cold War events that included the Cuban Missile Crisis and the construction of the Berlin Wall, as well as the founding of the Peace Corps, America's civil rights movement, and the increasing American presence in Vietnam.

HENRY LEE (1756–1818)—who was known as "Light-Horse Harry Lee" during his service in the Continental Army—served as a delegate to the Continental Congress and as a governor of Virginia. A personal friend of George Washington, he delivered his famous eulogy on Washington's death to a joint session of Congress.

ABRAHAM LINCOLN (1809–1865) served as the sixteenth president of the United States of America and was elected to two terms that encompassed the years of the American Civil War. A gifted orator who famously debated Stephen A. Douglas in 1858 in their campaigns for the Senate, Lincoln opposed the Kansas-Nebraska Act which overturned the Missouri Compromise engineered by his mentor, Henry Clay, and spoke out frequently on the threat to the American Union posed by the nation's divided attitudes regarding slavery. His "Gettysburg Address" is considered one of the greatest speeches in American history.

RICHARD M. NIXON (1913–1994) served as the thirty-seventh president of the United States of America between 1969 and 1974. His administration is associ- ated with the end of American involvement in Vietnam in 1973, the opening of diplomatic relations with China, and the first lunar landings. Nixon was the only American president to resign from office, following his involvement in the Watergate scandal.

BARACK OBAMA (1961–) served as forty-fourth president of the United States of America, starting in 2009. He is the first African American to serve in that capacity. His term in office is associated with the end of the Second Iraq War and the reform of America's healthcare system.

WENDELL PHILLIPS (1811–1884) was a well-known orator who gave up his law practice to dedicate himself to the abolitionist movement. "The Burial of John Brown" is considered one of the most eloquent eulogies delivered for fellow-abolitionist John Brown, after his execution for a failed raid on the federal armory at Harper's Ferry, West Virginia.

RONALD REAGAN (1911–2004) served as fortieth president of United States of America between 1981 and 1989. His term in office is associated with nuclear de-escalation in the United States and the Soviet Union under the INF Treaty, the end of the cold war, and the tearing down of the Berlin Wall.

FRANKLIN D. ROOSEVELT (1882–1945) served as the thirty-second president of the United States between 1932 and 1945. Through his New Deal program, he instituted sweeping reforms designed to bring economic relief at the height of the Great Depression. Although his administration maintained American neutrality at the outbreak of World War II in 1939, he called on Congress to declare war on Japan in his now famous Joint Address in Congress Leading to a Declaration of War Against Japan following the attack on Pearl Harbor on December 7, 1941. Roosevelt communicated many of his policies to the American people through a series of thirty "Fireside Chats" broadcast over the radio between 1933 and 1944.

THEODORE ROOSEVELT (1858–1919) served as the twenty-sixth president of the United States of America, after earning renown as the leader of the volunteer cavalry unit, the Rough Riders, during the Spanish-American War in 1898. His speeches "The Strenuous Life" and "National Duties"—the latter remembered for the famous line "Speak softly and carry a big stick"—both expressed his belief that America needed to have a formidable presence in world politics.

CARL SCHURZ (1829–1906) was a general in the Union Army and served as secretary of the interior under President Rutherford B. Hayes. His famous speech, "True Americanism," was a rebuke to the then-popular Know-Nothing movement and its call for a proscription of voting rights for two years for any newly made United States citizens.

ELIZABETH CADY STANTON (1815–1902) was a social activist credited with inaugurating the women's suffrage movement through the "Declaration of Sentiments" that she delivered to the Seneca Falls Convention of 1848. Her "Address to the Legislature of the State of New York" helped to lay the foundations of the women's rights movement.

TECUMSEH (1768–1813) was a leader of the Shawanee tribe who spent his final years trying to forge alliances between his and other tribes to form an independent Native American nation. He delivered his "Speech at Vincennes" to William Henry Harrison, then governor of the Indiana Territory, to express his dissatisfaction with Harrison's purchase of Native American lands along the Wabash River.

HARRY S. TRUMAN (1884–1972) served as the thirty-third president of the United States of America between 1945 and 1953. In addition to instituting the Truman Doctrine to help contain communism and passing the Marshall Plan to assist in the rebuilding of Europe following World War II, he helped to found the United Nations. His address to America following the dropping of an atomic bomb on Hiroshima marks the dawn of the nuclear age.

BOOKER T. WASHINGTON (1856–1915) was born into slavery and, after completing his college education following the emancipation, was appointed head of the Tuskegee Institute, a state school for blacks in Alabama. He was recognized as the pre-eminent representative of the African-American community in the late nineteenth and early twentieth centuries. In his address at the Atlanta Cotton States and International Exposition, he advocated the advancement of blacks through education and entrepreneurship, rather than through direct challenges to the prevailing Jim Crow laws. Washington expressed many of his political views in his 1901 autobiography *Up from Slavery*.

GEORGE WASHINGTON (1732–1799) was commander-in-chief of the Continental Army during the American War of Independence, and served two terms as the first president of the United States of America between 1789 and 1797. He delivered his first inaugural address after being elected unanimously by the Electoral College. He issued his "Farewell Address to the People of the United States" as a public letter, after declining the offer to serve a third presidential term.

DANIEL WEBSTER (1782–1852) represented the state of New Hampshire in the House of Representatives, served as senator of Massachusetts, and served as secretary of state under three presidents. He was an ardent Unionist and, with Henry Clay and John C. Calhoun, a major architect of the Missouri Compromise of 1820.

WOODROW WILSON (1856–1924) served as the twenty-eighth president of the United States of America between 1913 and 1921. Although he advocated neutrality for the United States at the outbreak of World War I, he eventually asked Congress to declare war on Germany in 1917. Wilson's plans to create the League of Nations after the armistice of 1918 earned him the Nobel Peace Prize in 1919, but they met with bitter opposition in the Republican-controlled Senate and were never realized.